ČS. ZBROJOVKA, A.S.
BRNO.

MODERN
SMALL
ARMS

An Illustrated Encyclopedia of Famous Military Firearms from 1873 to the present day

MODERN SMALL ARMS

An Illustrated Encyclopedia of Famous Military Firearms from 1873 to the present day
Major Frederick Myatt M.C.

a Salamander book

Published by Salamander Books Limited
LONDON

A Salamander Book

Published 1978 by
Salamander Books Ltd,
Salamander House,
27 Old Gloucester Street,
London WC1N 3AF,
United Kingdom

© Salamander Books Ltd 1978

ISBN 0 86101 024 8

Distributed in Australia/
New Zealand by Summit Books,
a division of Paul Hamlyn Pty Ltd,
Sydney, Australia

Editor:
Philip de Ste Croix
Editorial Consultant:
John Weeks
Designers:
Barry Savage, Chris Steer
Colour cutaway drawings:
Terry Hadler
© Salamander Books Ltd
Line diagrams:
Paul Morris
© Salamander Books Ltd
Photography of weapons:
Bruce Scott
© Salamander Books Ltd
Filmset:
Modern Text Ltd, England
Colour reproduction:
Positive Colour Ltd,
Culver Graphics Ltd and
Paramount Litho Company,
England
Printed by:
Henri Proost et Cie,
Turnhout, Belgium

The Author

Frederick Myatt is a retired
officer of the Royal Berkshire
Regiment into which he was
commissioned in 1940. He
was seconded to the Royal
West African Frontier Force
for most of World War II and
won the Military Cross in
Burma. He retired in 1969
and immediately took up his
present position as Curator of
the Weapons Museum and
Librarian at the School of
Infantry, Warminster,
Wiltshire. He is a regular
contributor to such well-
known journals as *American
Rifleman, Guns Review* and
the *British Army Review,* and
his previous publications
include *The Golden Stool,
The Royal Berkshire
Regiment, The March to
Magdala, A Short History of
the Small Arms School Corps*
and *The Soldier's Trade.*

The Consultant

Colonel John Weeks was
commissioned into the
Staffordshire Regiment in
1948, later transferred to the
Parachute Regiment, and has
served with the British Army
throughout the world. He was
a lecturer in infantry weapons
at the Royal Military College of
Science, Shrivenham and
subsequently Project
Manager, Infantry Weapons,
British Ministry of Defence.
He retired from this post in
May 1978 to devote himself to
full-time writing. He is a
military adviser to the

Contents

authoritative publications,
*Jane's Weapon Systems,
Jane's Infantry Weapons* and
Brassey's Infantry Weapons,
and has written several books
himself, including *Men
Against Tanks, Airborne
Equipment, Infantry Weapons
of World War II* and *Military
Small Arms of the Twentieth
Century* (with Ian Hogg). He
has also contributed
numerous articles on military
equipment to such respected
journals as *Ordnance,
American Rifleman, British
Army Review, War Monthly*
and *Guns Review.*

Author's Foreword

Although a great many people are interested in firearms, the modern necessity for security prevents most of them from ever getting a chance to inspect actual specimens. This book therefore sets out to provide the next best thing, a large number of excellent close-up colour photographs supplemented by a mixture of technical details and historical background. Some information is of course common to several weapons and in this case it seemed better to accept a little duplication rather than have to refer the reader to other descriptions.

As far as possible the appropriate cartridge for each gun has been included in the photograph together with a British ·303″ round for scale comparison. This is reproduced at its actual size on the facing page. It will be understood that some weapons, particularly early revolvers, were designed to accept a variety of cartridges, and when this is the case a representative round only has been included. The weapons are arranged chronologically within each national entry. Nations are listed alphabetically, but we have had to 'cheat' occasionally to ensure that certain countries get the coverage that their weapons deserve. The machine gun section is split into two halves—heavy and medium machine guns, and light machine guns respectively. The

revolvers and pistols section is rounded off by a brief survey of stocked weapons.

The term 'modern' has been taken, broadly speaking to mean 20th century but this has not been rigidly applied; all the arms illustrated are breech-loaders. It is not of course possible to give complete coverage with photographs of this size, but the illustrations have been carefully selected to cover the subject in detail.

It may be as well to include a note here on data. Dimensions do vary slightly, as does the method of taking them, so that few authorities are ever in total agreement except for calibre, magazine capacity, and similar absolutely standard detail. In cases where no reliable data exist, or where there are wide differences of opinion, actual specimens have been weighed and measured in order to reach our version, although such things as muzzle velocity and rate of fire have to be to some extent taken on trust from existing authorities.

Virtually all the weapons were photographed in the Weapons Museum at the British School of Infantry, Warminster, England, which houses a comprehensive collection of British Infantry firearms, dating from the 17th century to the present day and ranging from pocket pistols to wheeled anti-tank guns, together with

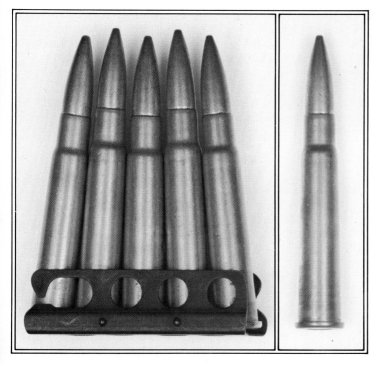

representative displays from other major countries. The collection was set up in 1853 when the School of Musketry was formed at Hythe, on the Kent Coast, and is now the official museum of the Small Arms School Corps. I have the good fortune to be the curator of this collection and I am most grateful to the School Commandant, Brigadier David Anderson, CBE, for his great help and encouragement with the preparation of this book. I must also thank Major-General M. E. Tickell, CBE, MC, Commandant of the Royal Military College of Science at Shrivenham, for allowing me to photograph eight items from the College collection.

Mr F. Davie, who is assistant curator and technician has, as always, been of the greatest help. There are few people who can match his knowledge of modern military firearms and I should have found it difficult to produce this book without his advice and assistance.

Colonel John Weeks, an old friend, is too well known in the field of firearms to need any introduction from me and I am delighted that he has found time to act as technical consultant and to write the introduction.

Lastly I must thank Mrs P. Kedge who typed the whole thing with great confidence often from manuscripts which I, the writer, found hard to read back.

F.M.
Warminster, Wiltshire
1978

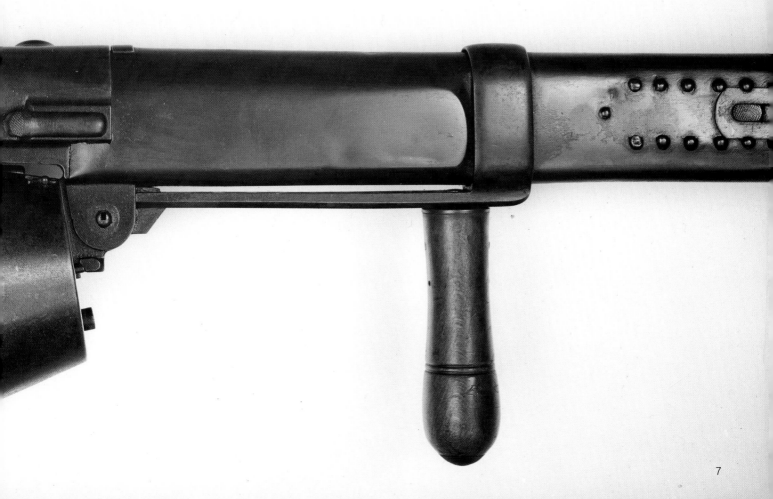

Introduction

"Without infantry you can do nothing, absolutely nothing."
Field Marshal The Lord Montgomery

There is a popular myth, well supported by the Press and certain military observers who should know better, that wars are won by weapons alone, by nuclear missiles, by ships, by artillery, by tanks, by aircraft and by bigger and better electronics equipment. It just is not true; all these things help to win a war, and without them you can lose a war very quickly these days, but wars are actually won by men on their feet, just as they always have been. The scientists, the engineers, the radar designers and the manufacturers do not like to hear this; after all why should they when it makes a nonsense of their elaborate claims? But it is fact none the less. It was all summed up by an American general just after World War II who said, "You can keep your atom bombs, your tanks, and your airplanes; you'll still have to have some little guy with a rifle and bayonet who winkles the other bastard out of his foxhole and gets him to sign the Peace Treaty."

This then is a book about that little guy and the tools of his trade.

The whole story of infantry weapons and small arms is far too long to tell in one volume and in this book Major Myatt has taken selected highlights and discussed them in detail. He starts, wisely, in the late 19th century when the whole civilised world was galloping ahead with the newly learned methods of manufacture by machine, and with this came an explosion of inventions from every direction. In small arms this was particularly true; some were good and we are still using them today. Some were wildly optimistic and never got beyond the prototype stage, some suffered from economic pressures and were never given a proper chance, while some, an intriguing selection as it happens, stayed as drawings and patent descriptions of quite incredible improbability and mechanical naivety. The last three

decades of the century were the time of the great colonial land grab and all the European nations were involved to some extent. They tended to equip their armies largely for wars against primitive savages, though none so thoroughly as the British, and the lessons of the Franco-Prussian war of 1870 — which was one more grisly foretaste of what was to come in 1914 — were cheerfully put aside.

Things scarcely improved in the early 20th century. Britain was mesmerized by the Boer War and only Japan and Germany had the sense to see that the machine gun was the coming weapon of the battlefield. All countries were experimenting more or less seriously with automatic weapons of one kind or another, and this was the time when the first hesitant steps were taken to make a self-loading rifle, surely the greatest advance in small arms since the breech-loader. At the same period smokeless propellant was introduced, and with that came the high powered long-range round and the rifles to fire it. Germany built the Mauser bolt-action series and in the last sixty years more than twenty million of them have been made. Britain evolved, not without opposition, the Lee-Enfield models that were to last her through two World Wars and the Russians modified a Belgian design to suit their needs. It was a time of trial and development, with some very wrong ideas predominating.

Within a few years the whole thing was put to the test in the trenches, and much was found wanting. The neglected machine gun became the ruler of No Man's Land and factories worked day and night turning them out in thousands. The light machine gun was found to have a definite place in warfare and was brought in to supplement the heavy water-cooled Maxims that all except the French were using. Bayonet charges and similar Victorian tactics proved useless against the

firepower of modern weapons, which the American Civil War had shown clearly, and a round that could travel a mile was of little value when the enemy was only a hundred yards away in a shell hole.

After World War I there was a good deal of hard thinking, but few countries could hope for a change in their equipment or weapons since so much investment was tied up in the current models. The British wanted to change to a smaller calibre of rifle, but there was no money. The French just managed to improve their elderly ammunition, but only very slowly, and it was in USA that one of the great advances was made with the adoption of the Garand self-loading rifle. Even so, the design had to be modified to accept the 30-06 round, and so there came about the curious eight-cartridge clip. In Germany there was plenty of time for designing, and little chance of practising due to the Versailles Treaty. In retrospect that Treaty probably did more good for the German military than anything else, since it allowed them to start with a clean slate and to re-think not only the tactics of modern war, but the weapons to go with them. Two ideas they produced in that time were the medium-powered cartridge and the general purpose machine gun, both used universally now.

World War II was the apogee of small arms development in this century; never before or since has there been so much activity and variety. Among the innovations were the sub-machine gun (though it had made a bow in World War I), the medium-powered cartridge, the self-loading rifle and its derivative, the assault rifle, and that wonderful abberation of the 1930s — the anti-tank rifle. At the same time the war finally killed off the Maxim machine guns and reduced the bayonet and pistol to their rightful place as minor

weapons. Nothing was too unlikely to be tried, and in Germany there was so much emphasis on experiment that at times it seriously interfered with the making of ordinary weapons.

Perhaps the greatest innovation was the use of modern factory methods to make guns. The Germans were once again the leaders in this and they used the experience of men who had been in the automobile industry to advise the small arms designers. The result was the use of steel pressings and stampings, welding and pinning, plastics and plywood instead of fine machining, careful fitting and polished walnut. Major Myatt weeps for the loss, but it made economic sense and it still does. Most of the weapons of World War II would never get a prize in a beauty contest, but they work and that is what the soldier asks for.

In the post-war years the same trend has continued. Weapons have become simpler and cheaper and we have seen the incredible spread of small arms throughout the world as nationalism and terrorism grow around us. The two dominant infantry weapons now are the Soviet Kalashnikov, firing a wartime intermediate round of medium calibre, and the American Armalite firing a modern small calibre high-velocity bullet of light weight. God knows how many of both have been made, nor how many people have been killed by them.

This is the canvas on which Major Myatt paints his picture. Little escapes his eye as he takes you through the intricacies of each weapon. He has had a wide and exciting experience of warfare in his own career, and he has a rare ability to explain his meaning with humour and a practical basis. Few know their subject better, for he lives among it every day. Follow him through the fascinating and diverse byways of history and listen as he tells the story of the men who actually win the wars.

John Weeks
Purton Stoke
May 1978

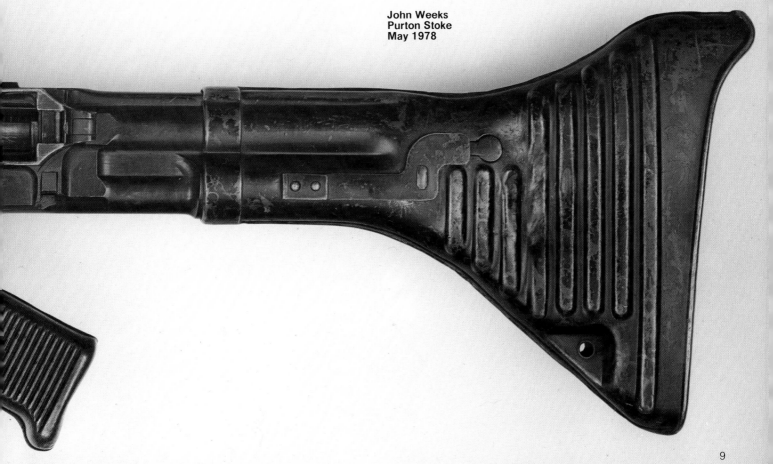

The Machine Gun

No sooner had firearms been developed than men began to try to improve their performance, particularly their accuracy and rate of fire. Some soldiers, realizing the potential of the new arms, dreamed of weapons with which one or two men could do the work of ten times their number of musketeers, but although there was no lack of ingenious ideas little progress was made. The main stumbling block was the lack of an efficient system of ignition, for as long as sparks from the flintlock remained the only means of firing the charge the problems were well nigh insuperable.

It is true that in 1718 one James Puckle patented a repeating gun on the lines of a large-scale revolver, but although he made some extravagant claims for its powers, it is clear that it was far from effective. Its principal interest thus rests on the fact, perhaps a sad fact, that it is the only machine gun ever invented by a Briton.

Most new developments took the form of multi-barrelled volley weapons and it was not until the introduction of the percussion system, and in particular its logical successor the self-contained cartridge fired from a breech-loader, that any real progress was made. One of the first weapons of this type was the United States Gatling gun, which saw some use in the American Civil War, but achieved such legendary fame that its crank operated cluster of revolving barrels needs no further description.

The first major use of a weapon of this type firing proper cartridges came in 1870 when the French produced their ill-fated *mitrailleuse*, a weapon with thirty seven rifle barrels contained in a cylindrical jacket and mounted on an artillery style carriage. The magazine for this weapon consisted of a metal plate with thirty seven holes in it, each the diameter of a cartridge and each corresponding with a barrel. To load the gun the breechblock was drawn back and a plate containing thirty-seven cartridges was placed into position in guide grooves after which the breechblock was screwed forward, thus driving the rounds into the chambers. They were then fired by the rotation of a handle, and given sufficient spare 'magazines' a rate of fire in excess of 300 rounds per minute was said to have been possible.

By the time of the outbreak of war with Prussia the *mitrailleuse* had been modified by reducing the number of barrels to twenty-five. In view of its successful trials the French had great hopes of this new, and as they believed, deadly weapon, which they had taken great pains to keep secret. These hopes were not justified; the gun itself was a formidable enough arm, but the French presumably through lack of time to formulate any tactical doctrine, insisted on regarding it as an artillery weapon. Batteries of them were thus brought into action in neat rows in the open, where not surprisingly they were quickly knocked out by the excellent Prussian field-guns. This was a pity because on the relatively few occasions when they were correctly handled, they inflicted fearful casualties.

EUROPEAN REACTIONS

The lack of success of the new type of weapon in its first real test in European warfare tended to give a very wrong impression of its real potential when properly handled. The Prussians scoffed at it, and as they had by then established themselves as the major military nation in Europe it is perhaps not surprising that most other countries saw little need to bother about them. The principle exception was Russia who quickly adopted her own version of the Gatling gun and made good use of it in her almost continuous campaigns of expansion and pacification along her eastern frontiers. At that time the British were also involved in extensive colonial warfare, and they too soon saw the value of this new weapon. The British Army was rarely strong enough to undertake the numerous tasks allotted it, so that any reasonably reliable means of augmenting its fire-power was welcomed. In the years that followed they too adopted the Gatling and the Gardiner. The Royal Navy experimented with the similar but heavier-calibred Nordenfeld which they used principally as secondary armament on their battleships against fast steam-driven torpedo boats which were becoming a new menace in naval warfare.

Although weapons of this type were useful in an auxiliary role, their reliability was always to some degree suspect. This was due to two main reasons; firstly the danger of black-powder cartridges hanging fire, partiularly under damp conditions, which meant that there was the risk of the cartridge not actually firing until extraction had started, which was liable to be damaging both to the gun and the morale of its firer. Secondly, as most weapons of this type had gravity feed,

1 *The Belgian 7·62mm FN MAG general purpose machine gun—an excellent modern weapon.*
2 *Wheeled and fixed mounts for Maxim guns in the 1890s.*

it was essential that the operator should maintain a nice easy 'barrel-organ' type action; if he turned too fast, which was a very understandable reaction in the face of a mob of charging savages, there was a risk that the cartridge would fail to feel and a jam result.

MAXIM'S INVENTION

These disabilities were soon swept away by the appearance of the first true machine gun. It was invented by Hiram Maxim, a larger-than-life American of Huguenot extraction. He was born in 1840 in Maine, at that time very much in the backwoods, and was a man of huge physical strength which stood him in good stead in his rough and ready environment. More important however was his unusual mental capacity, for although he had had little formal schooling he soon displayed an inventive ability amounting to genius, which together with an apparently unlimited capacity for hard work soon led him to make a name for himself. Starting with rural carpentry, painting, and metal work, he soon proceeded to a self-setting mousetrap followed by an automatic gas machine for domestic illumination, which led him logically enough to the then new force, electricity. He attended the Paris Exhibition in 1881 and it was this visit to Europe which seems to have convinced him that there was money to be made in fire-arms, for which the warring nations of Europe had an almost insatiable demand. At that time, as we have seen, all so-called

machine guns were manually operated, but Maxim had advanced ideas. He knew from much practical experience with firearms in his native Maine that when a cartridge was fired a great deal of the energy generated was dissipated backwards in the form of recoil, a fact well known to anyone who has ever discharged a firearm. It seemed to him that this wasted energy might in fact be harnessed to do the work previously performed by human muscle applied to a handle. A clever conversion of a standard Winchester rifle soon proved him correct and he at once set up a workshop at 57 Covent Garden, London, and started work. In a remarkably short time he had invented, patented, and manufactured a true automatic gun in which the recoil of one cartridge was used to load and fire the next, and this novel arm, which was first demonstrated at the Inventors Exhibition in Kensington in 1884, was an immediate success. Everyone of importance, from the Prince of Wales downward, came to see it fired, and although it cost five pounds a minute to fire it Maxim rightly considered that the vast sums he expended on buying some 200,000 cartridges for these displays were well spent. One of the earliest purchasers was the American explorer, Stanley, perhaps best known for his search for Dr Livingstone, who took one with him on the Emin Pasha relief expedition, a useful additional piece of publicity.

One of his greatest supporters was Sir Garnett Wolseley, then probably

the best, and certainly the best known, British General. His services were in more or less constant demand for conducting a wide variety of warlike expeditions to the more remote parts of the British Empire. Although a somewhat flamboyant character and publicity seeker, he was nevertheless a capable and forward-looking soldier who at once saw the value of Maxim's new gun, particularly perhaps in the type of colonial campaign on which much of his experience was based. In 1884 Maxim went into business with Vickers, the well-known British firm of engineers and shipbuilders, and a company was formed to make his machine guns at the steelworks at Crayford in Kent. As was to be expected the resulting weapons were a success and by 1891 the British Army had purchased them in large numbers, two being allotted to each infantry battalion.

The British Army had fought no major European war since the Crimea but it had unrivalled experience in small-scale colonial operations of all types. Most of these involved the dispatch of often quite small expeditions which were expected as a matter

2

3

1902, the first to be fought by Great Britain against a brave, mobile enemy armed with the most modern magazine rifles, came as something of a shock to British military opinion. After some initial reverses the first, formal, phase was soon successfully dealt with, but the second guerrilla phase was a long-drawn-out affair. The machine gun proved generally disappointing in South Africa, chiefly through lack of intelligent handling. The gun in use at that time was mounted on a relatively high wheeled carriage which made it an obvious target for the well concealed Boer rifleman who soon shot down the crew. As had happened with the *mitrailleuse* thirty years ealier, this lack of success gave rise to serious doubts as to the efficiency of the machine gun in modern war, doubts which the Russo-Japanese war of 1904 failed to dispel. One of the notable features of that war was the success of the Japanese in the attack which gave rise to a renewed faith in the bayonet charge without really considering the supporting fire which alone had made success possible.

The Germans, in spite of their earlier contempt for the *mitrailleuse*, had no hesitation in adopting the modern machine gun. When the Kaiser saw Maxim's weapon demonstrated he announced, 'That is the gun—there is no other', and it was adopted forthwith. By the outbreak of World War I in 1914 ,they are said to have had 12,500 Maxim-type guns actually in service with three times as many again on order.

McMAHON'S INFLUENCE

One of the great British military advocates of the machine gun was Lieutenant-Colonel McMahon, whose name will be met again in connection with the development of the rifle. He became Chief Instructor at the School of Musketry in Hythe in 1905 at a time when events were beginning to show that Great Britain's alliance with France would eventually lead her to war with Germany. He, like a good many other thinking soldiers, saw that an important feature in any future war would be superior firepower. In 1907 he gave a lecture on the subject to the Aldershot Military Society which was considered so important that many of the principles he laid down were subsequently incorporated not only into the British Field Service Regulations, but actually, it is said, into the German equivalent.

McMahon, and many others, pressed for an increase in the scale of machine guns but nothing was done. As late as 1912 the Treasury would not sanction the replacement of the older Maxim guns by a new, lighter and much more efficient version, which in consequence did not go into production until after the outbreak of World War I.

It was this neglect of the machine

of course to disappear into remote areas and deal with hordes of brave but more or less savage enemies. As warriors of this type had few missile weapons, the only way they could fight a battle was by coming to close quarters with sword, spear, or club. The British technique was therefore to provoke attacks of this kind against their close military formations from which they could pour out an almost unending stream of fire. In spite of the occasional disaster these tactics were usually successful, a good deal of this success being due to the new Maxim guns which cut a fearful swathe of death in Matabele-land, the Sudan, Ashanti, and on the North-West frontier of India. When Hilaire Belloc wrote:

'Whatever happens we have got,
The Maxim gun, and they have not'
he was doing no more than propound a military truism.

The South African War of 1899-

gun which led to the huge improvement in the quality of the British military rifle shooting in the years immediately before 1914, an improvement which owed much to the efforts of the Chief Instructor at Hythe. When the war started McMahon was in command of a battalion of the Royal Fusiliers and it is perhaps no coincidence that the first two Victoria Crosses of the war were won by members of his machine gun section. His death in action soon afterwards was a great loss to the British Army.

The almost legendary feats of the British rifleman in 1914 tend to overshadow the vital and gallant part played by the British machine guns in the early months of the war. The whole British Expeditionary Force had less than 150 of these weapons, not even, as we have seen, of the latest type, and their losses were huge. They became obvious targets for the numerous well-handled German artillery and machine guns, with the result that by the end of 1914 trained machine gunners hardly existed in the British Army until a reservist officer, and ex-Hythe instructor, took action. Captain Baker-Carr, not a man to be hampered by red tape or intimidated by superior rank, set up a machine gun school almost entirely on his own initiative and in doing so made a vital contribution to the war. He later transferred his allegiance to the tanks, which were after all little more in those days than mobile machine gun posts, and ended the war as a Brigadier-General.

The need to group machine guns was soon apparent. The German guns were already organized into separate companies, and as soon as the operations settled down into static trench warfare the British adopted the same policy. At first the arrangements were local, and the more enterprising brigadiers simply

1 *The German 7·92mm MG34, seen here in the sustained-fire role on a tripod mount, was the world's first mass-produced GPMG.*
2 *The basic modern US machine gun is the 7.62mm belt-fed M60.*

concentrated their four battalion machine gun sections into extemporized sub-units under the Brigade machine gun officer. These proved successful, but as trench systems became more and more complex it became apparent that an even greater degree of centralization was necessary, and in October, 1915 a new Machine Gun Corps came into existence, and all the Brigade companies were transferred to it. At first this new Corps was short of both trained men and equipment, but the Machine Gun School provided the former and once British industry had been placed on a wartime footing the supply of guns and equipment improved rapidly. By the middle of 1916 the Corps strength had risen to 500 officers and over 80,000 other ranks, a total roughly equivalent to the size of the whole original BEF.

TACTICS OF TRENCH WARFARE

Tactical doctrine was at first elementary, but hard experience, an effective if costly way of learning, soon produced great improvements. In defence, which in the nature of trench warfare tended to be their chief role, guns were sited in depth, mutually supporting, and as far as possible protected from the front, since flanking fire against advancing lines was clearly the most effective way of using them. Low wire entanglements were frequently sited to hold up advancing troops at points where the machine guns had a good field of fire, and later on guns were often protected by reinforced concrete bunkers, proof against anything but the heaviest howitzer shells.

Although, however, the machine gun has come to be regarded as something of a static weapon, its value in the attack was also very great. Both the British and Germans handled them boldly in forward positions, and in the absence of reliable communications a great deal had to be left to the initiative of individuals to ensure their best use. In France, where mud greatly reduced mobility, the machine gun was often the only support weapon which could be got forward, for even when the horses and limbers got bogged down machine guns could still be manhandled, although it was no job for weaklings.

By 1915 the machine guns practically ruled the battlefield and endless ingenuity was employed to increase their effectiveness. Being virtually a

2

new arm, they attracted a certain type of enthusiastic scientist and mathematician-turned-soldier, who developed endless techniques for indirect fire by map and survey instruments and many other improvements.

Given good detachments and adequate supplies they were capable of incredibly long periods of sustained fire. On one famous occasion, during the British attack on High Wood on 22 August, 1916, ten guns fired only 250 short of 1,000,000 rounds in a little over twelve hours with no longer breaks than were necessary to clean, oil, and reload guns, change worn out barrels, and top-up water jackets. Two whole companies of infantry acted as carrying parties and when supplies of water for the water-jackets ran out the contents of every urine tub for a long distance round were requisitioned for the same purpose. The task of the guns was to

neutralize an area behind the enemy front line, the range being 2000 yards (1820m) and although it is probable that few of the individuals actually saw a German in the period the results of their fire were later found to have been devastating.

One of the most valuable roles of the machine gun was to cover withdrawals, for although the artillery were traditionally reluctant to lose guns, machine guns were sacrificed without scruple if the situation warranted it. Large scale operations of this kind were not common on the Western Front until 1918 when the Allied retreat in March, followed a few months later by that of the Germans, gave the machine gunners of both sides endless chances to display their devotion to duty.

By the end of World War I the British Machine Gun Corps consisted of fifty-seven battalions, each of sixty-four

guns, on the Western Front alone, together with similar units of Australian, Canadian and New Zealand forces and a variety of independent squadrons and companies. Many people felt that a new arm, neither infantry nor artillery but somewhere mid-way between them, had come into existence and should be retained. To support this they pointed out that the tank, which having initially come into being as a mobile machine gun post to help the infantry forward, had established itself on a permanent basis. These arguments were however of no avail and in 1922 the Corps was disbanded, the guns themselves reverting to infantry battalions, although on a good deal more generous scale than that of 1914.

The early years of the 20th Century also saw the introduction of a new type of automatic weapon, the light machine gun, a lighter and more portable version of their big brother which was later differentiated from them by the title of 'medium' machine gun.

Although there was naturally a variety of these new weapons, they had strong similarities. Generally speaking they were in the twenty and thirty pound (9-13.6 kg) weight range, usually magazine fed and aircooled, and fired from the shoulder with the assistance of a light bipod. One of the earliest was the Danish Madsen gun which the Russians had first adopted, chiefly as a cavalry weapon, as early as 1904, but the real proliferation began in 1914-15 when World War I settled down to stalemate. Trench warfare called for large volumes of fire, often at close ranges, and by 1915 most armies had adopted a weapon of this type.

The British infantry settled for the American-invented Lewis gun which to some extent filled the gap left by the withdrawal of the Vickers; the scale was originally no more than one per company, but by the end of the war had risen to one per platoon with a further four at Battalion Headquarters, a total per battalion of thirty-six guns. The cavalry adopted the light Hotchkiss gun in 1916.

The French used the St Etienne and the Chauchat while the Germans developed a lighter version of their Medium Maxim gun which was unusual in being water-cooled and using a fifty round belt in a metal container instead of the more usual magazine. A simplified, air-cooled version of this gun was also developed and issued in 1918.

By the end of World War I most of the participants were both physically and financially exhausted. There was little enthusiasm to spend large sums on new armaments when vast stocks of the old were available, so that for the first few years at least changes were relatively few. The British stuck to their well-tried Vickers and Lewis guns, while the main change made by the French was to replace their rather poor Chauchat light machine gun with the new and much more reliable Chatellerault. The United States, whose armies in France in 1918 had had to rely mainly on their Allies for automatic weapons, naturally decided to re-equip themselves with American-made weapons, which were in any case coming off the production lines in large numbers as their war economy got under way, and were soon using the fine Browning M1917 medium gun and the equally good automatic rifle made by the same firm. Some of these latter arms had reached France in time to be used in the final battles and had proved to be excellent weapons; in spite of their official nomenclature they were for all practical purposes light machine guns. The Germans were naturally very strictly limited regarding the quantity

and type of weapons they were allowed to retain and had ceased for the time being to have an effective army, a situation which was to change relatively quickly.

When World War II broke out in 1939 the British had still made few changes. They had indeed begun in the previous year or two to remove their Vickers guns from normal infantry battalions and concentrate them in certain nominated machine gun battalions, but this was really no more than a reversion to the principle of the earlier Machine Gun Corps. One great improvement had been to replace the ageing Lewis gun with the new and much more effective Bren although not all units were in possession of their full quota of this new weapon when war broke out. At this stage British battalions in India were in process of being re-equipped with the Vickers-Berthier light machine gun which the Indian authorities had opted for in place of the Bren. The old Hotchkiss had disappeared with the horsed cavalry

DEVELOPMENT OF THE MG34

The French had made few changes, as had the Americans who were not of course at that stage directly involved in the war. But as to be expected the Germans, starting from scratch, had made great advances. After some experiments they had settled on the MG34, a versatile weapon which could be used either as a medium or light machine gun as required, and was thus the fore-runner of a great variety of 'general purpose' machine guns which

were later to come into almost universal use in the major armies of the world. It was followed during the war by the MG42, an essentially similar weapon but designed for ease of wartime manufacture. Like its predecessor it proved to be an excellent gun with an unusually high rate of fire.

Another major participant was the Soviet Union, who started the war with the Degtyaryev range of light machine guns and a Maxim-type medium machine gun of World War I vintage which was to be replaced in 1943 by the more modern Goryunov. The Japanese armies used the reliable Hotchkiss medium gun progressively developed from a French prototype which they had been making under licence since their war with Russia in 1904; their principal infantry light machine gun was the Type 96, an adequate weapon but of no particular distinction.

After the end of World War II most of the major powers found themselves involved in various wars or warlike operations, but, as in 1919, such huge stocks of arms were available that there seemed to be no great incentive to make immediate changes. Some experimentation did start, but as development is always slower in peacetime, the fruits of this took some time to emerge. It was not really until the end of the war in Korea that new weapons started to get into the hands of the soldiers with the introduction of the General Purpose Machine Gun into the British Army and its counterpart the M60 into that of the United States. The French, whose own armament industry was

1 A technician checks the head space on a Browning 0.5in Heavy Barrel M2, the main US heavy machine gun for 50 years.
2 The M55 trailer, with four 0.5in Browning HB machine guns in a semi-armoured mount with self-contained power unit, provides AA protection.
3 Romanians on night manoeuvres with a 7·62mm PK machine gun — the first true Soviet GPMG.

almost non-existent, had been compelled to use Allied and German weapons (particularly the MG42) in Indo-China, but they too developed their own general purpose gun in the shape of the AAT 52.

Russia, although not officially involved in any major war, was busy consolidating her hold over Eastern Europe while simultaneously providing arms for China and a host of lesser left-wing regimes and various guerrilla organizations. In this period she developed her new RPD light machine gun but continued with an up-dated Goryunov under a new designation, SGM.

When the Germans began to rearm they had no hesitation in re-adopting their well-tried and reliable MG42, which after various relatively minor changes is still in service as the MG3.

This is the situation at the moment and it is difficult to forecast major changes in the future. It is possible that the proliferation of medium machine guns on tanks and other armoured vehicles may eventually make the infantry ground medium machine gun obsolete, but this, if indeed it happens, will not be for some time.

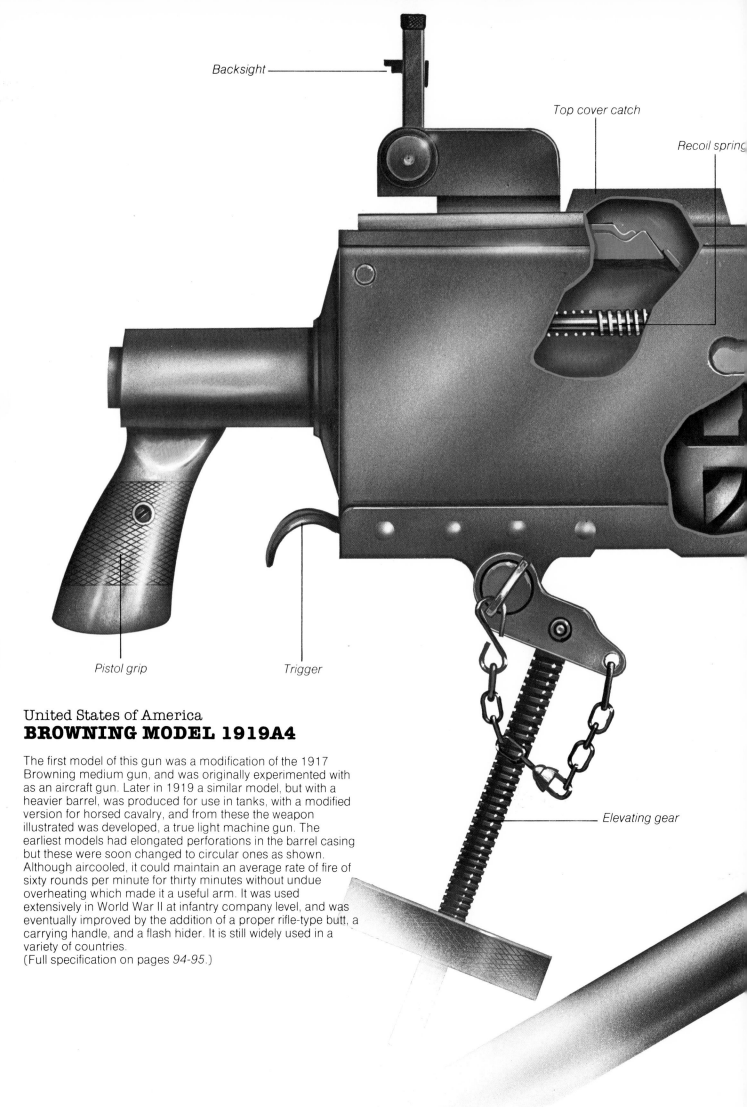

Backsight

Top cover catch

Recoil spring

Pistol grip

Trigger

Elevating gear

United States of America
BROWNING MODEL 1919A4

The first model of this gun was a modification of the 1917
Browning medium gun, and was originally experimented with
as an aircraft gun. Later in 1919 a similar model, but with a
heavier barrel, was produced for use in tanks, with a modified
version for horsed cavalry, and from these the weapon
illustrated was developed, a true light machine gun. The
earliest models had elongated perforations in the barrel casing
but these were soon changed to circular ones as shown.
Although aircooled, it could maintain an average rate of fire of
sixty rounds per minute for thirty minutes without undue
overheating which made it a useful arm. It was used
extensively in World War II at infantry company level, and was
eventually improved by the addition of a proper rifle-type butt, a
carrying handle, and a flash hider. It is still widely used in a
variety of countries.
(Full specification on pages 94-95.)

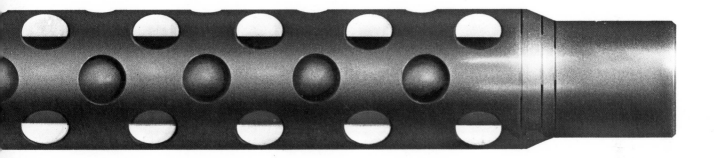

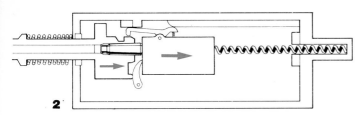

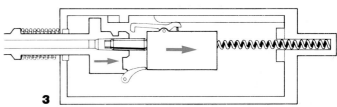

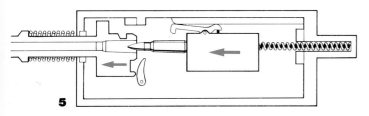

1 The weapon has to be cocked manually for the first shot. When the trigger is pressed the trigger bar is disengaged from the sear block which allows the firing pin to be driven forward by its spring and fire the cartridge.
2 The violent backward thrust of the gases drives the base of the cartridge sharply against the face of the bolt and pushes it backward compressing the driving spring (in British terminology usually known as the return spring) as it does so. The barrel and barrel extension, being at this stage locked to the bolt, both necessarily recoil with it for a distance of about five-eighths of an inch (16mm).
3 For half this distance the residual pressure in the barrel is very high, but it drops rapidly thereafter to the stage where it will not rupture the case, at which time projections on the lock frame force the block downwards and unlock the bolt from the barrel extension.
4 The barrel extension then stops but the bolt continues rearwards, extracting and ejecting the used case, drawing a fresh round from the belt, and compressing the firing pin spring.
5 When the bolt has reached its rearmost position any residual force is absorbed by a buffer so as to reduce undue vibration; the compressed driving spring then forces the parts forward again and the cycle repeats.

Flash hider

Recoil booster

Flash hider retaining bar

Foresight

Germany
MASCHINEN GEWEHR MODEL 42

At the outbreak of World War II the German Army was armed with the MG34. This was an excellent weapon but, having been made between the wars, it was if anything too well finished and did not lend itself to mass-production. The Germans, however, needed effective machine guns in large numbers and were not much worried about finish, and once the basic design of the MG42 was settled it was placed in the hands of one of the greatest German experts on mass-production. In the event it turned out to be a very fine machine gun indeed and like its predecessor it could be used either shoulder-controlled from a bipod or in the sustained fire role on a tripod. It had a very high rate of fire which caused some vibration and loss of accuracy but these were minor defects in an otherwise excellent gun. It is still produced, virtually unchanged, as the MG3.
(Full specification on pages *36-37*.)

Bipod

Locking shoes

rrel casing

Backsight

Barrel

Chamber

1 *This diagram shows the gun in readiness to fire. The action has been cocked manually by means of the cocking handle on the right-hand side of the gun and the bolt is in its rearward position, with a round in front of it.*

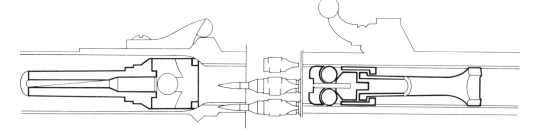

2 *Pressure on the trigger allows the bolt to be driven forward by the coiled return spring. On its way it strips a cartridge from the belt and forces it into the chamber. The rollers at this stage enter cammed slots and begin to move outwards.*

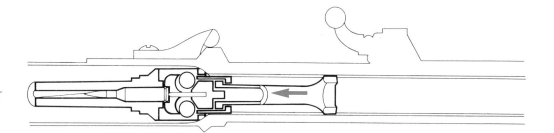

3 *The striker sleeve is shaped in such a way that on its movement forward it assists the outward movement of the rollers. As soon as the bolt and barrel extension are locked together the striker sleeve passes between them and the round if fired.*

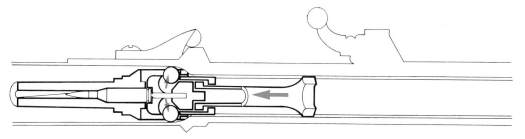

Perforated outer casing

Bore showing rifling

Barrel

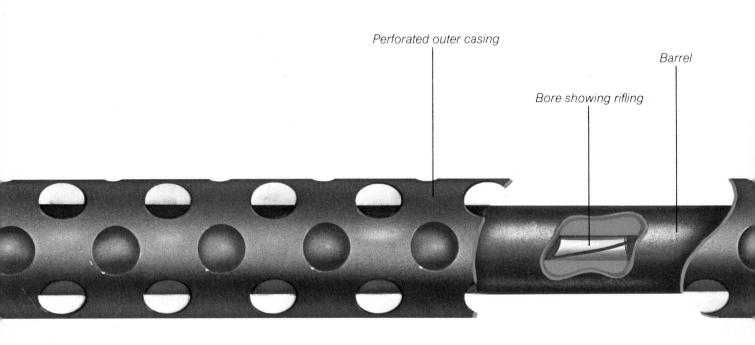

Bottom plate

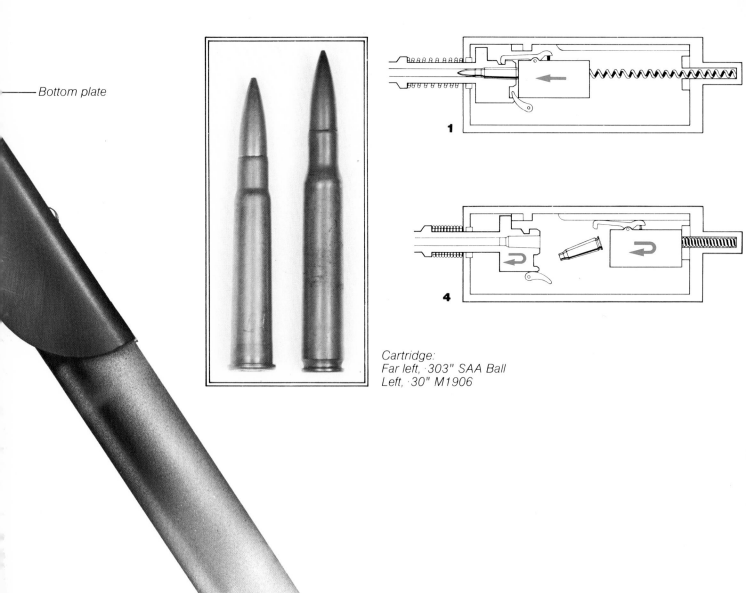

Cartridge:
Far left, ·303" SAA Ball
Left, ·30" M1906

1

4

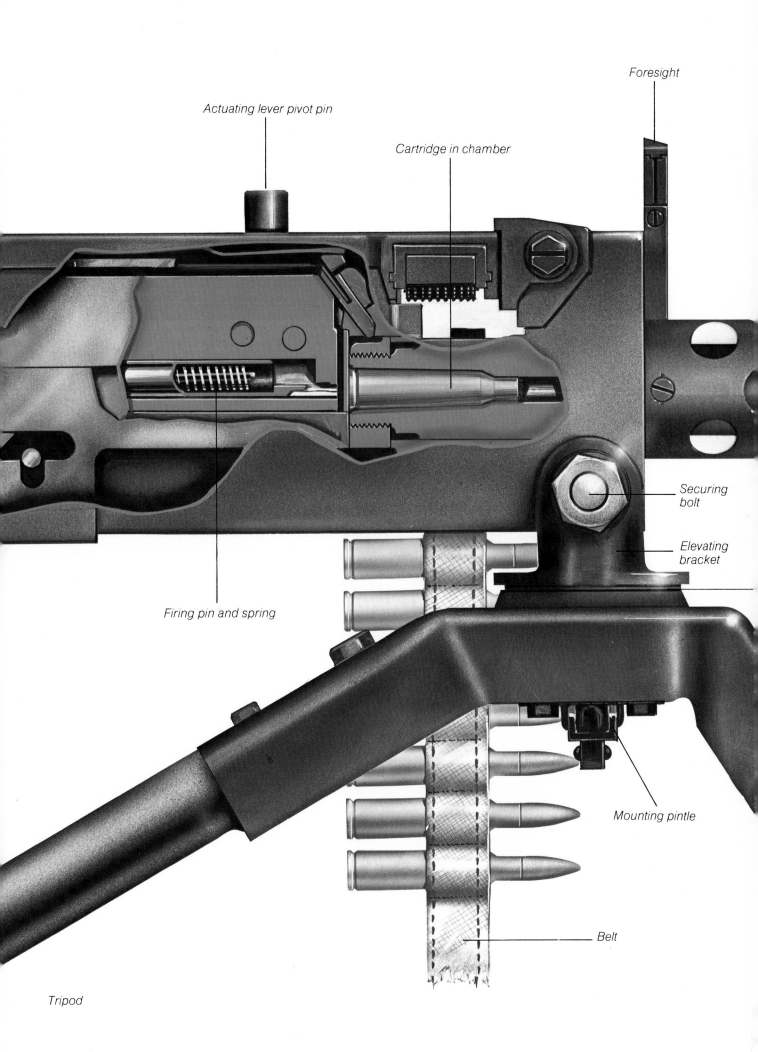

Actuating lever pivot pin

Cartridge in chamber

Foresight

Securing bolt

Elevating bracket

Mounting pintle

Belt

Firing pin and spring

Tripod

19

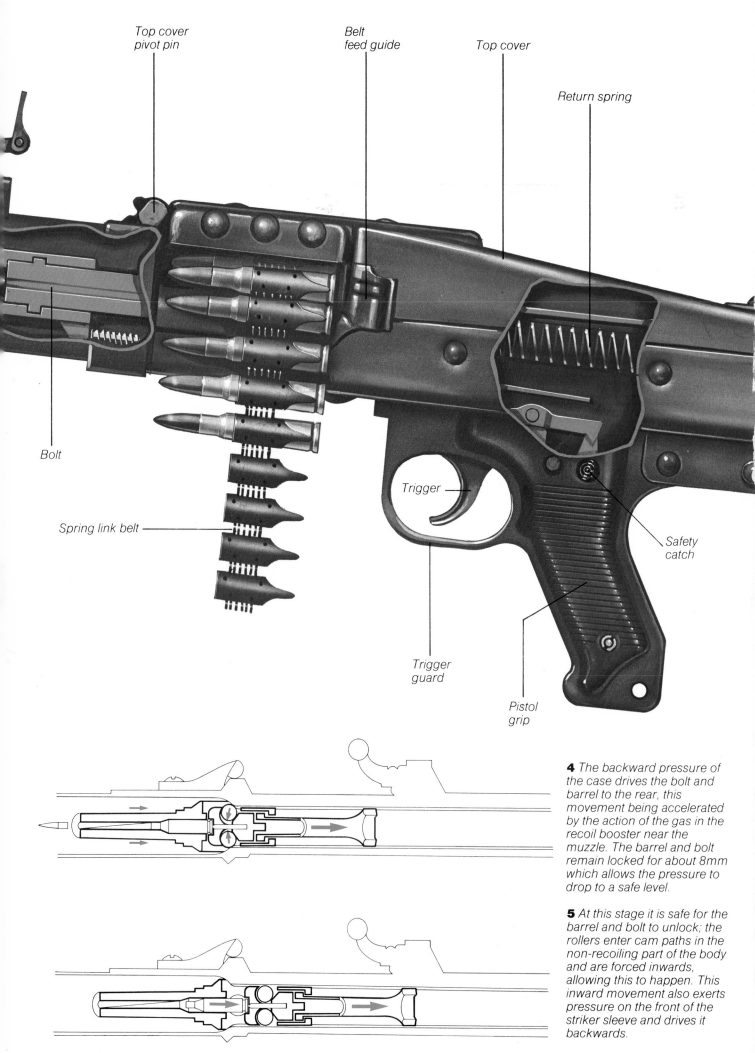

Top cover
pivot pin

Belt
feed guide

Top cover

Return spring

Bolt

Spring link belt

Trigger

Trigger
guard

Pistol
grip

Safety
catch

4 The backward pressure of the case drives the bolt and barrel to the rear, this movement being accelerated by the action of the gas in the recoil booster near the muzzle. The barrel and bolt remain locked for about 8mm which allows the pressure to drop to a safe level.

5 At this stage it is safe for the barrel and bolt to unlock; the rollers enter cam paths in the non-recoiling part of the body and are forced inwards, allowing this to happen. This inward movement also exerts pressure on the front of the striker sleeve and drives it backwards.

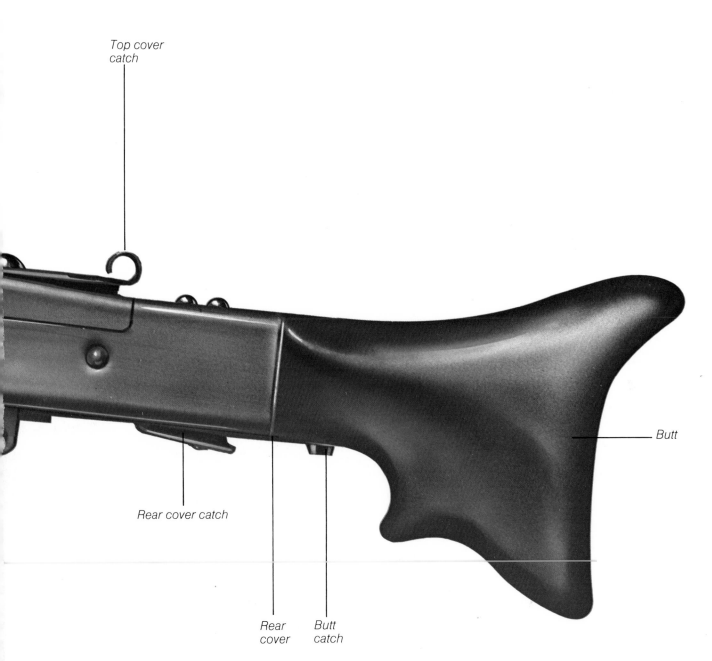

Top cover
catch

Butt

Rear cover catch

Rear
cover

Butt
catch

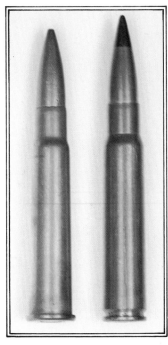

Cartridge:
Far left, ·303" SAA Ball
Left, 7·92mm Patrone 98

Austria-Hungary
SCHWARZLOSE MASCHINENGEWEHR MODELL 05

Length (gun): 42" (1067mm)
Weight (gun): 44lb (20kg)
Weight (tripod): 44lb (20kg)
Barrel: 20·75" (527mm)
Calibre: 8mm
Rifling: 4 groove r/hand
Operation: Blowback
Feed: Belt
Cooling: Water
Cyclic Rate: 400 rpm
Muzzle Velocity:
2000 f/s (610 m/s)
Sights: 3062 yds (2800m)

This gun was invented by a German, Andreas Schwarzlose of Charlottenburg. He did a great deal of work on self-loading pistols in the closing years of the 19th Century, including one unusual weapon in which the breech remained stationary while the barrel blew forward. This preliminary work clearly stood him in good stead when he finally turned his considerable talents to larger weapons which he did soon afterwards—his first machine-gun being originally patented in 1902 although manufacture did not finally start until three years later. His principal object seems to have been to produce a simple weapon with less complex mechanism than those then existing. All machine guns operated either by recoil or by gas and required quite intricate

working parts, and intricate mechanism is out of place on any battlefield if it can be avoided. Schwarzlose finally struck upon the idea, now common in sub-machine guns, of allowing the cartridge case to blow the breechblock to the rear, compressing a spring as it did so in order to provide power for the forward thrust needed to load and fire the next round. The chief problem with this sort of mechanism, when used with a full-sized rifle cartridge, is to control the backward movement of the block in its initial stages. It must be borne in mind that the pressure inside the barrel is very high while the bullet is still travelling down it, so that if the breech is opened prematurely the cartridge case is liable to rupture when it loses the support of the chamber walls and

breechblock. Schwarzlose overcame this difficulty by using a heavy breechblock and an unusually powerful mainspring which, combined with a series of mechanical checks, effectively controlled the rearward movement of the block. The mainspring was also ingeniously adopted to act both as shock absorber and firing pin spring, thus significantly reducing the number of working parts. In spite of these purely mechanical aids it still nevertheless remained vitally necessary to lower the gas pressure as rapidly as possible and this was done by using a short barrel, which naturally meant that the bullet cleared it earlier and allowed the pressure to drop accordingly. Finally it was found that the high pressure inside the case caused it to adhere to the chamber, and

in order to reduce the probability of this the inventor installed an oil pump in the gun which spat a drop of oil on each cartridge case as it was being fed into the chamber, thus lubricating its backward movement after the shot had been fired. These various means necessarily employed to retard the blowback also slowed the action as a whole, so that the Schwarzlose machine had a characteristically slow cyclic rate of fire of about four hundred rounds per minute. The system of lubricating the cartridge case in order to assist its extraction, although quite widely used in those days, was in many ways an undesirable one, since it was always liable to lead to difficulties on service particularly in very dry or dusty countries. After some further work Schwarzlose

finally succeeded in actually eliminating this feature from his machine gun. This he did by increasing the weight of the breechblock and the strength of the spring, and also by increasing the various mechanical disadvantages working against the bolt during the initial stages of its rearward action. These improvements resulted in a second model of his gun which first appeared in 1912. The new Schwarzlose, which like most similar weapons of the period was belt-fed and water-cooled, had proved to be a reliable weapon from the beginning, when two of the early models fired thirty-five thousand rounds each with minimal stoppages and no apparent loss of accuracy. It was also simple to fire and maintain and was soon in service with the Austro-Hungarian Army, where it

was used with considerable success. Part of this at least was probably due to a most liberal provision of training ammunition, and the gun was also supplied with a special bulleted blank for manoeuvres; the bullet, which was made of wood, offered sufficient resistance to the gas to operate the mechanism but disintegrated soon after leaving the muzzle, and provided that no one was immediately in front of the gun, was quite safe and reliable. It was a new idea in those days but widely used since. The Austrians calculated the fire of a single well-handled gun as being equivalent to that of eighty riflemen. The gun was also used as a cavalry support weapon, each regiment having two guns carried on packhorses. The detachment for these consisted of three

officers and forty-five men, all mounted, plus twelve pack horses carrying extra ammunition. The gun was also used by Sweden, the Netherlands, and Czechoslovakia at different times and in different calibres. At the end of World War I Italy received large numbers of them from Austria as part of war reparations and many remained in service in the Italian Army during World War II. A considerable number, many of them the original models with the oil pump, were captured from the Italian Colonial Army in East Africa in 1940-41 and at one time several Home Guards in what were then British colonies in West Africa were armed with them. The weapon is now officially obsolete but there may be a few still in use in remote areas of the globe.

8mm Patrone Modell 1893

·303" SAA Ball (clip)

France
SAINT-ETIENNE MODÈLE 1907

Length (gun):
46·5" (1181mm)
Weight (gun):
56·75lb (25·74kg)
Weight (tripod):
60lb (27·24kg)
Barrel: 28" (711mm)
Calibre: 8mm
Rifling: 4 groove r/hand
Operation: Gas
Feed: Strip
Cooling: Air
Cyclic Rate: 4/500 rpm
Muzzle Velocity:
2300 f/s (700 m/s)
Sights: 2625 yds (2400m)

The prototype of this weapon appeared at a time when machine guns were still in their infancy and the field was thus open to new inventors, of whom there was no lack. The nations of Europe were more or less constantly either at war or in the middle of some crisis threatening war, and even when things were quiet internationally, someone, somewhere was engaged in a colonial campaign. In 1893 a Captain in the Austrian Army, Baron von Odkolek, invented a new type of automatic weapon which utilized part of the gases from one round to load and fire the next, and having no manufacturing facilities of his own he turned to the French gun-making firm of Hotchkiss which had its factory near Paris. The company showed great interest, not in the completed weapon which they rightly decided to be of quite impracticable design, but in one of its components, the system of tapping gases from the barrel to activate a piston. As this aspect of the weapon was naturally covered by the patent they bought the whole thing outright and promptly incorporated the piston into a weapon of their own which they called the Hotchkiss. This gun, which proved very successful, was bought by the French in small numbers, chiefly because its effective air-cooling system made it useful in their various colonial campaigns where water was always in short supply. The French Army was anxious to develop an automatic weapon of its own, and having had the opportunity of testing the Hotchkiss very thoroughly under a variety of conditions they used this information to help them to design a 'perfect' machine gun, still based on the basic system of the gas piston but incorporating all

8mm Cartouche Mle 86
·303" SAA Ball (clip)

28

sorts of improvements. By 1905 all the preliminary designs had been completed and the National Arsenal at Puteaux had produced the first tangible results of all this activity in the form of a machine gun which incorporated a device for varying its rate of automatic fire from eight rounds a minute to something over six hundred, but which otherwise had no claim to distinction. It had a very short active life and soon disappeared into reserve, nor does it seem likely that any French soldier regretted its departure. At this stage in the history of France there was continual agitation for military reform and in particular an immediate demand for a really effective machine gun. The French, like the British, had appreciated the value of the machine gun in colonial warfare where the most gallant and numerous massed charges of both horse and foot could be stopped by the horrifying volume of deadly aimed fire produced by weapons of this type. The Russo-Japanese war had also shown that these same weapons had an important part to play in the more modern forms of warfare. In particular, the French noted with some concern that their ancient enemies, the Germans, were showing a great interest in automatic weapons. There was therefore a great incentive to the French arms factories to produce something out of the hat and this time they produced in 1907 the weapon illustrated. Although basically of Hotchkiss type it worked in reverse, the piston being blown forward instead of backward to activate a mechanism of astonishing complexity, as may be glimpsed in the photograph. For example, the reversed piston operation necessitated the introduction of a rack and pinion mechanism to reverse the motion again. The main-spring, which was coiled on a steel rod, was largely exposed below the massive brass receiver so as to keep it cool and the gun was fed by thirty-round strips of standard Lebel rifle cartridges. The gun shown is mounted on a 1914 pattern tripod; this was interchangeable with the 1907 pattern, the main obvious difference being the very large brass wheel which was essentially used for clamping the elevating gear in the earlier model.

Length (gun):
51·6″ (1311mm)
Weight (gun):
55·7lb (25·26kg)
Weight (tripod):
60lb (27·24kg)
Barrel: 31″ (787mm)
Calibre: 8mm
Rifling: 4 groove l/hand
Operation: Gas
Feed: Strip
Cooling: Air
Cyclic Rate: 500 rpm
Muzzle Velocity:
2325 f/s (709 m/s)
Sights: 2625 yds (2400m)

Benjamin Hotchkiss was an American engineer and designer who, after helping to design Colt revolvers, went to France in 1867 at the age of forty and set himself up as a manufacturer of manually operated guns. He died in 1885 and two years later the shareholders of the company appointed a successor in the person of another American, Laurence Benét. Benét was the son of a United States general, an ex-chief of United States Ordnance who had himself done a great deal of work on earlier guns of the Gatling type, so that there was already a strong family interest and connection with the whole subject. Benét eventually discovered a talented young French engineer named Mercie, and between them they made the Hotchkiss company famous. In the early 1890s the firm succeeded in purchasing the patents for an automatic weapon which had been offered to them by its inventor, Captain Baron von Odkolek, an officer of the Austrian Army. The two partners saw at once that although the gun itself was quite unworkable it had certain features which could be extremely useful for their own developments, notably the system of using the energy of some of the gases tapped off from the bore to drive back a piston. Once they had this patent safely in their hands they set to work and very soon they had produced an automatic weapon of modern type. The principle, which is still extensively used, was a simple one. The piston blew back, taking with it the breechblock and compressing a spring as it did so; once the power of the piston was exhausted the spring drove the mechanism forward, feeding a round from the strip (which was used in preference to the then more common canvas belt) and firing it, and this reciprocating movement continued as long as the trigger was pressed and there were cartridges available in the strip. Although this new gun worked very well there was one serious disadvantage, and that was that it overheated very quickly. In view of the fact that ten high-powered cartridges were fired in the chamber each second this was not surprising but it nevertheless had to be dealt with. Other guns of the period, notably those of Maxim and his imitators, were equipped with waterjackets which were efficient but bulky. As the water had to be constantly replaced they posed something of a military problem when operations were being conducted in desert or semi-desert country where water was difficult enough to procure for men and horses without the additional needs of water-cooled guns. Benét, who dealt with the problem, soon came to the conclusion that

what was required was a mass of metal at the breech end to absorb the heat as close as possible to the point where it was generated, and so shaped that it would present as large a surface as possible to the air into which the surplus heat had to be dispersed. His answer was to encircle the breech end of the barrel with five solid metal discs which, although they added little weight, immediately increased the radiating surface by more than ten times its original area. The general shape of these discs, which were about 3·15" (80mm) in diameter, can be seen from the photograph of the weapon itself. Lieutenant-Colonel George M. Chinn describes them in his well-known book *The Machine Gun* as being 'doughnut shaped fins' and this homely description is probably as good a one as

any. This relatively simple improvement to the gun made it an extremely serviceable weapon. In 1900 a United States Army board tested one at the Springfield Armoury, principally to compare its performance with that of a more orthodox water-cooled gun. The trial was very rigorous, thousands of rounds being fired almost continuously; it was found that after just over four minutes of continuous fire the whole barrel was bright red from the cooling rings to the muzzle. Five minutes later, fire was resumed, and so the gruelling test continued until nearly five thousand rounds had been fired at an intensity unlikely to be encountered in the fiercest battle. The report by the Board (one of whom was Captain J. T. Thompson who later invented the famous sub-machine gun which bears his name) was a very

fair one, for although it considered that water-cooling and belt-feed were in general preferable alternatives to the Hotchkiss system, the latter had nevertheless performed remarkably well. A few years later the two methods were to be compared in the most practical way possible, for in the course of the Russo-Japanese war of 1904-5 the Russians used a water-cooled belt-fed gun of Maxim type while the Japanese used a Hotchkiss. This proved that both systems were quite capable of standing up to the demands of modern warfare. When World War I started in 1914 the French Army found itself in serious difficulties over its relative lack of automatic weapons, which trench warfare quickly showed to be required in vast numbers. Fortunately the reliable Hotchkiss was readily available and manufacture

soon started in huge quantities. The earliest models went to reserve units, the regular Army being then largely equipped with the Saint-Etienne 07, but once the Hotchkiss guns began to appear in large numbers they quickly demonstrated their superiority and the French Army clamoured for more and more of them. In 1916 a section of two Hotchkiss guns engaged in the defence of Verdun remained in almost continuous action for ten days during which they fired away the astonishing total of over one hundred and fifty thousand rounds without anything worse than brief and easily cleared stoppages. When the American Army arrived in France in 1918 it had almost no machine guns of its own, and twelve of its divisions were therefore equipped with the Modèle 1914 Hotchkiss.

8mm Mle 86
·303" SAA Ball (clip)

Germany
MAXIM 1908-15 (MG08)

Length (gun):
46·25" (1175mm)
Weight (gun):
58·5lb (26·54kg)
Weight (tripod):
70·5lb (31·98kg)
Barrel: 28·3" (719mm)
Calibre: 7·92mm
Rifling: 4 groove r/hand
Operation: Recoil
Feed: Belt
Cooling: Water
Cyclic Rate: 3/400 rpm
Muzzle Velocity:
2925 f/s (892 m/s)
Sights: 2188 yds (2000m)

The failure of the French Mitrailleuse (although largely through bad tactical handling) in the war of 1870-71 had given the victorious Germans a low opinion of weapons of this type which was to persist for a surprisingly long time. They had of course, like the British, used machine guns in their various colonial wars, but again like the British the German Army in general had little regard for them as a serious weapon. They might be useful for breaking up the wild and unscientific rushes of hordes of natives, but their role in more orthodox warfare was so ill-defined as to be non-existent. It was apparently the Kaiser who was instrumental in introducing the machine gun into the German Army. He watched a demonstration of one of Hiram Maxim's new guns and according to the inventor at once said 'That is the gun—there is no other'. Maxim was not above a little mild exaggeration, but this seems to have been true enough, for in 1899 a number of Maxim batteries, each of four guns, were tried out for the first time at the Imperial manoeuvres. At that period the inevitable decline of cavalry was well advanced, but the desire to retain it was so great that every effort was made to give it the means to contend on equal terms with infantry, so that the first Maxim guns in German service were told off for this specific purpose. The real breakthrough came after the Russo-Japanese war of 1904-5. This war, with its trenches, barbed wire, heavy artillery concentrations, and extensive use of machine guns, gave a grim foretaste of what war might be like in the future, and as all the major European powers had numerous observers present the conflict was extensively reported by trained military men. German reaction was immediate. The German General Staff, a highly professional body, had been feeling its way cautiously as far as machine guns were concerned but reports of

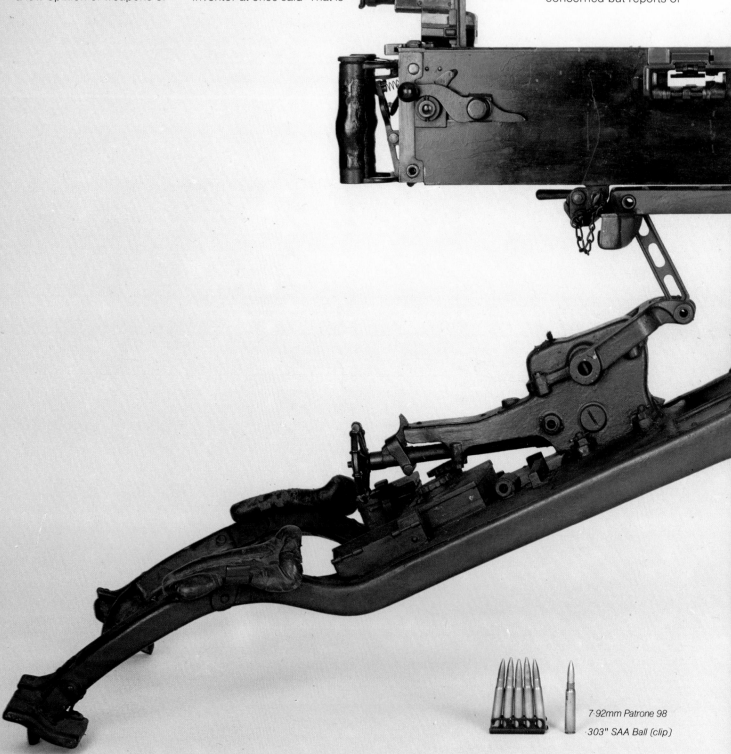

7·92mm Patrone 98

·303" SAA Ball (clip)

32

actual fighting finally convinced them that they would need them in considerable quantities in the event of a major European war. A heavy Maxim gun was therefore developed at the great factory at Spandau and came into service in 1908. The gun itself was of normal Maxim pattern but its mount was distinctly new, for instead of either a wheeled artillery-type carriage or a tripod it had a solid heavy mount based on a sledge. As can be seen from the photograph it was only necessary to elevate the gun and swing the forward legs over it to have it ready to drag along. When the legs were down they could readily be adjusted so that the firers

could sit, kneel, or lie down according to the type of cover available. By the end of 1908 every German regiment of three battalions had its own six-gun battery. The guns were carried on light horse-drawn carts and the detachments, usually of four men each, marched, extra vehicles being of course provided for ammunition. Unlike the British organization which allotted a section of two guns permanently to each battalion, the German battery was under the direct hand of the Regimental Commander. Similar batteries were also provided for the cavalry but these were more mobile, the wagons having four horses instead of two and the

detachments being mounted on horses. A modified sledge mount was also introduced at this time which reduced the total weight significantly and allowed the individual guns to be manhandled if necessary, either by carrying or dragging. By the outbreak of war in 1914 the German Army probably had twelve or thirteen thousand guns in actual service, a few even being mounted on early armoured cars, with three times that number in actual process of manufacture, so that it disposed of a very formidable fire power. In the early months of the war the French armies, trained on a doctrine that battles could only be won by gallant

charges across open ground, suffered terribly. Even the British, trained to a somewhat more realistic approach based on well-trained riflemen, were forced back by superior numbers and firepower although they inflicted heavy casualties on their opponents in the process. As the war progressed, and the armies dug in, the battlefield became more and more dominated by the machine gun, often in a concrete emplacement and designed to fire in enfilade along carefully sited belts of barbed wire. This lasted until the tank, itself no more than a mobile pill box, restored some degree of mobility to the battlefield.

Length (gun): 48" (1220mm)
Weight (gun): 26·7lb (12·1kg)
Weight (tripod):
42·3lb (19·19kg)
Barrel: 24.75" (628mm)
Calibre: 7·92mm
Rifling: 4 groove r/hand
Operation: Short recoil
Feed: Belt or saddle drum
Cooling: Air
Cyclic Rate: 8-900 rpm
Muzzle Velocity:
2480 f/s (756 m/s)
Sights: 2188 yds (2000m)

German manufacture of
military arms, and more
particularly automatic
weapons, was seriously
restricted after 1918 by the
conditions of the Treaty of
Versailles. There were,
however, ways of evading
these conditions to a
considerable degree and
every advantage was taken of
them. Factories which
concentrated on non-
automatic or sporting
weapons continued in
operation and a great deal of
valuable research was
conducted, partly under
cover of these and partly
through German-owned
subsidiary companies
elsewhere in Europe. By
1934 Hitler felt himself to be
in a sufficiently strong position
to defy the rest of Europe and
he therefore began quite
openly to re-arm Germany for
whatever might lie ahead.
One of the basic needs was
for a good, reliable light
machine gun and the task of
producing prototypes was
given to the firm of Mauser.
Mauser was a very long-
established and influential
firm in the sphere of arms
manufacture, having been in

existence since 1871, and in
its time it had armed a large
number of the armies of
Europe and the rest of the
world. The specification for
the new weapon envisaged a
general purpose machine
gun, an expression then new
but one which has since
become almost universal. It
was to be capable of light
work at section level from a
bipod, or in a medium role off
a tripod, with the additional
capacity of feed either by belt
or drum as required, using
the standard rifle cartridge
then in service. The basic

design was produced by
Louis Stange, a well-known
designer who worked for the
firm of Rheinmetall, and
Mauser at once set to work to
produce the first truly modern
machine gun ever to be
placed in the hands of the
German Army. As was to be
expected from such
distinguished antecedents,
the new weapon, which
appeared in 1934 and which
was thus allotted the year of
its appearance in its
designation, was a
remarkable achievement in
many respects. It worked by

the somewhat unusual
combination of recoil and
gas; when the round was
fired the barrel recoiled,
additional thrust being given
to this by some of the gases
which were trapped in a
muzzle cone and deflected
backwards. The actual recoil
of the barrel was short, just
enough in fact for the
bolthead to be rotated
through 90° and unlocked
when the pressure was low
enough for this to happen
safely. This rearward
movement of the bolt
continued after that of the

7·92mm Gewehr Patrone 98
·303" SAA Ball (clip)

barrel had stopped, until the return spring was fully compressed, when the forward action started. This involved the forward movement of the bolt which fed the next cartridge from the belt into the chamber, locked itself, and fired the round. This new gun had many excellent features including a quick means of changing the barrel, easy stripping and the use of high impact plastics, and was unusual in that it had no change lever. There was simply a two-part trigger

which fired single rounds or automatic according to whether the upper or lower part was pressed. The MG 34 would fire either a belt, sometimes coiled inside a drum for transport, or a double saddle drum of the type used on the earlier MG 15. The belts could be joined together if required to give a considerable degree of sustained fire and as long as the barrel was changed after a maximum of two hundred and fifty rounds, a reasonable rate could be continued more or less indefinitely. The MG34

was equipped with a tripod, somewhat complex in design but capable of a wide range of adjustment and light enough to be carried by one man, the pads visible on the forward leg being there to protect the carrier's back when the tripod was slung like a rucksack. The tripod afforded a reasonable traverse and offered a suitable mounting for indirect fire, although like most pieces of equipment of its kind it really required a sandbag at each foot for added stability. In addition to the normal

battlesights a dial-type sight was also fitted for indirect or night fire, and as the trigger was not directly accessible when the gun was on its tripod a remote control trigger of grip type was incorporated into the right hand side of the rear mounting post. If the gun was required in a light role all that was necessary was to take it off the tripod, a very simple process, and unfold the bipod legs. The MG34, although an excellent gun, was by no means perfect, mainly, paradoxically enough, because it was too well made. Between the wars quality was everything and the gun was beautifully machined and finished. Tolerances were thus very fine and although this did not matter under ideal conditions it was liable to lead to functioning difficulties in dry, dusty climates. This, however, was a relatively minor defect for an otherwise well made gun in the hands of experienced troops, and the German Army certainly had no cause to complain of the service it gave them. It was manufactured in a variety of factories in Germany, Austria, and Czechoslovakia and it remained at least partly in service in the German Army until the end of the war. There were some variations in the MG34 for special purposes, but no significant changes to it in its history. After the war it was used at various times by the Czechs, the Israelis, the French and by the Biafrans. A few even turned up in Vietnam, these presumably being some of the ones captured from the French.

Germany
MASCHINENGEWEHR MG42

Length (gun): 48" (1220mm)
Weight (gun):
25 5lb (11·57kg)
Weight (tripod):
42·3lb (19·19kg)
Barrel: 21" (533mm)
Calibre: 7·92mm
Rifling: 4 groove r/hand
Operation: Recoil/gas
Feed: Belt
Cooling: Air
Cyclic Rate: 11/1200 rpm
Muzzle Velocity:
2480 f/s (756 m/s)
Sights: 2188 yds (2000m)

The German Army entered World War II with their MG34. This was an excellent gun of its kind but having been made between the wars it was too highly machined and too carefully finished to lend itself to mass-production. A mass-production gun, regardless of fine finish, was the one thing required by the Germans at that time for they were at war with the combined forces of the United States, Great Britain and the Soviet Union and once these three great countries had completed the rather slow transition from peace to wartime production, their combined output soon began to swamp the Germans. As far as a machine gun was concerned the Germans decided to base their new model as far as possible on the old, but without hesitating to make any improvements based on captured weapons, and certainly without making any sacrifices to ensure fine finish. All they wanted was a gun which would be effective and which could be mass produced without undue strain on their dwindling resources. Once the basic design of the weapon had been established the whole thing was placed in the hands of Dr Grunow, a well-known German industrialist whose particular forte was mass-production by metal stampings, rivetting, spot welding and brazing, and any other method not requiring complicated equipment or specialized techniques which called for the use of skilled manpower. The result, based on long experience, high industrial skills, and a great deal of active service experience was the MG42, possibly one of the finest weapons to come out of World War II. In general appearance it resembled the MG34, to which in many ways it was also mechanically similar. It made use of the same principle of short recoil assisted by gas pressure from a muzzle booster, perhaps its main difference being the way in which the bolt locked. Its predecessor, the MG34, had made use of a rotating bolt with an interrupted thread which locked into the barrel extension, but the new gun used a system originally patented by one Edward Stecke, a Polish citizen. It is said that when the Germans overran Poland in 1939 they found a rough prototype of Stecke's design which immediately impressed them with its strength and simplicity. In this system the bolt head carried two small rollers which were held close to the bolt until it was ready to lock when they were forced outwards into grooves in the barrel extension. The firing

7·92mm Patrone 98

·303" SAA Ball (clip)

pin could not move forward between them until they were fully into their grooves which ensured that the bolt was locked at the moment of firing. Once recoil started the rollers hit a cam path which forced them inwards out of their recesses, thus unlocking the bolt and allowing the cycle to continue. The gun fired fifty-round belts of the standard 7·92mm cartridge using a new and effective feed system which has since been copied by various other makers notably in the FN general purpose machine gun, the Swiss general purpose machine gun and the United States Model 60. The lightness of the MG42, combined with its particular system of operation, led to a very high rate of fire of about twelve hundred rounds a

minute which produced a considerable degree of vibration that had some adverse effect on accuracy. The muzzle brake was ingeniously designed to help stabilize the weapon but the problem was never fully overcome. The gun would not fire single rounds so the only practical answer in the field was to fire short bursts only. It is of course easy to order this but more difficult for the soldier to remember it in the excitement of battle, although German discipline undoubtedly helped. The high rate of fire also led, naturally, to a high rate of ammunition consumption, and to a considerable degree of overheating. Fortunately the system of changing barrels was so simple that this never caused any serious problem.

The vibration also had some effect on the gun when used on its tripod, which was the same as the one for the MG34. The Germans felt that any slight disadvantages caused by the high rate of fire were more than compensated for by the moral effect of the noise, which sounded like the tearing of huge sheets of canvas; it is a feeling with which most Allied infantry men would have probably agreed. The gun itself was strictly functional and even shoddy looking compared with the quality workmanship of its predecessor, but it was highly effective which was the important thing. It is said that the MG42 was first used in action by the Panzergrenadiers of Rommel's Afrika Corps against the British 8th Army in

Tunisia and it is certain that in desert conditions it functioned better than the precision-made MG34. It continued in service until the end of the war, although it never came even near to replacing the old MG34 which lasted to the end. At one stage the Americans decided to copy the MG42 but the experiment was not a success and was eventually abandoned. At the end of the war many MG42s were used to rearm the French and other countries which had been under German occupation. When the West German Army was reformed it adopted a version of the MG42 chambered to take the standard NATO round. It is still in use as the MG3, a weapon which came into service in 1968 and which fires a 7·62mm cartridge.

Great Britain
MAXIM GUN

Length (gun): 46″ (1169mm)
Weight (gun): 26lb (11·8kg)
Weight (tripod): 15lb (6·8kg)
Barrel: 24″ (610mm)
Calibre: ·45″
Rifling: 4 groove r/hand
Operation: Recoil
Feed: Belt
Cooling: Water
Cyclic Rate: 500/600 rpm
Muzzle Velocity:
1600 f/s (488 m/s)
Sights: 1500 yds (1372m)

Hiram Maxim, born in Maine in 1840 and largely self-taught, was a man of natural genius who had an apparently unlimited capacity for inventing things, many of which he made with his own hands. A visit to Europe in 1881 apparently convinced him that the one common need among the nations of Europe was for new and more effective weapons and being not only an inventor but also a sharp businessman he at once set out to gratify this demand. Long years of hunting in the backwoods had given him a great deal of

first-hand experience of guns and he well knew that a considerable part of the force of the explosion of any cartridge was expended against the firer's shoulder. He soon set to work to harness this wasted energy, and having proved his theory practically by converting a Winchester rifle to the self-loading principle, he packed and left for England and rented a small office at 57D Hatton Garden where he began the detailed design of his new project. Very soon he had designed, built (largely it seems with his own hands), tested and patented a true automatic gun in which the recoil of the first manually loaded round was used to fire the next. The principle was that the barrel recoiled a short distance before unlocking the breechblock from it and allowing that to continue backwards under the momentum given to it, extending a strong fuzee spring as it did so, and also drawing a cartridge from the belt. When the bolt had reached its most rearward position the extended fuzee

spring drew it forward again, so that it chambered and fired the cartridge, after which the process was repeated as long as the trigger was pressed and there were cartridges in the belt. The actual cyclic rate of fire was about six hundred rounds per minute, the cartridges being of ·45″ Boxer type loaded with black powder, and the barrel got so hot that it was necessary to surround it with a brass water-jacket. The gun itself was mounted on a rather long tubular metal tripod with a canvas seat for the firer. It was fitted with elevating and traversing gear and was sighted to a thousand yards (914m). In 1884, the gun having proved a huge draw, Maxim went into partnership

with Messrs Vickers and began making the gun in some quantities, most of rifle calibre, but some large enough to fire a three pound (1·36kg) shell of 1·85″ calibre. The British Army used the rifle-calibre gun of the type illustrated (mounted on a light two-wheel artillery type carriage instead of the tripod) in its various colonial wars where it proved

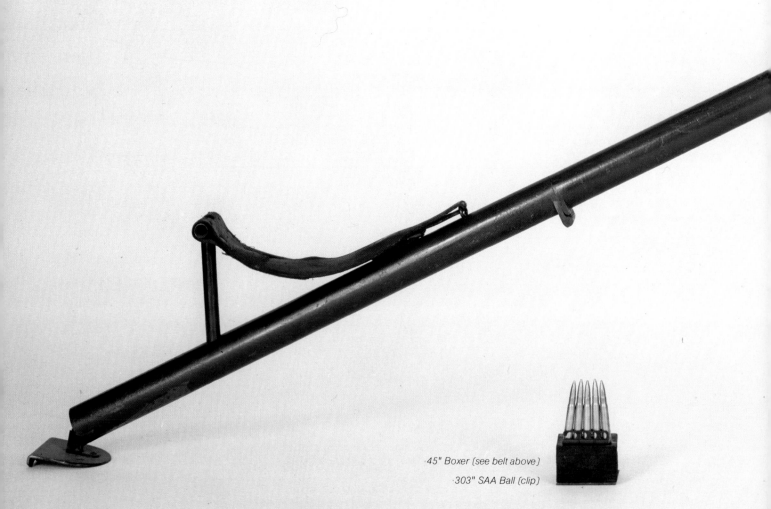

·45″ Boxer (see belt above)

·303″ SAA Ball (clip)

remarkably effective in breaking up mass attacks of Dervishes and the like. It was best sited on a flank and the enormous cloud of grey smoke resulting from its high rate of fire with black powder made it very desirable to position it so as to take advantage of a good breeze to disperse it. In 1891 the British Army adopted a cordite cartridge for its small-bore Lee-Metford rifle and most military machine guns were converted accordingly. This in fact improved the performance of the Vickers-Maxim considerably because the more powerful cartridge gave a much increased recoil and thus improved the basic source of power of the gun. The Maxim did not prove particularly successful in the peculiar circumstances of South Africa but the Russo-Japanese war showed the need for machine guns and many countries adopted weapons either made by, or under licence from, Vickers-Maxim. Maxim was the father of the modern machine gun in a very real sense and there were few weapons of that type for many years afterwards which did not owe something to the influence of his early work. Although an American by birth Maxim became a British citizen and was knighted in 1901. The gun illustrated, a very early model bearing the Hatton Garden address, was presented to the Science Museum by Sir Hiram in 1914, two years before his death, but was transferred to the School of Musketry in 1933 at the request of his widow.

Great Britain
•303″ VICKERS-MAXIM

Length (gun): 42·5″
(1079mm)
Weight (Gun): 60lb (27·21kg)
Length (Mounting): 75″
(1905mm)
Weight (Mounting): 178lb
(80·74kg)
Barrel: 26·5″ (673mm)
Calibre: ·303″
Rifling: 4 groove r/hand
Operation: Recoil
Feed: Belt
Cooling: Water
Cyclic Rate: c550 rpm
Muzzle Velocity: 2440 f/s
(744 m/s)
Sights: 2900 yds (2652m)

The earliest true machine gun was invented by the American Hiram Maxim in the 1880s and is described elsewhere in this book. It worked on the principle of using the recoil of one cartridge to load and fire the next one and its use soon spread throughout Europe where no country trusted its neighbour and everyone was anxious for more and better weapons. The machine gun at first was regarded as being mainly suitable for colonial warfare against more or less savage peoples since its huge firepower was of great assistance to small expeditionary forces faced with hordes of

enemies. Even in the early days of muzzle-loaded small arms it had been possible for mere handfuls of Europeans to beat off a hundred times their number, particularly if they could be concentrated in some reasonable defensive position. A good example of this was the wagon leaguer used by both American settlers and Boers against mass attacks of brave and numerous enemies who were not equipped with enough firearms to inflict long range casualties. Armies also learnt this lesson and as far as possible took up good fire positions in the hope, frequently realised, of provoking the sort of mass attacks which offered easy targets for arms of precision. In 1889 the British Army adopted a small bore bolt action magazine rifle, and its machine guns were gradually altered to conform to this new calibre. These new arms still used a propellant consisting of compressed black powder packed into bottle-shaped cartridges to give sufficient power. The firer therefore suffered from the problem of not being able to see the target after a few rounds because of the vast clouds of dirty-grey smoke. The only hope was to have a good cross wind, but this was

not always easy to arrange. In 1886 the French began to use a new cartridge loaded with a type of smokeless powder developed by a chemist named Vieille in conjunction with Captain Desaleux, and the advantages of this new propellant were obvious. Apart from the extra power, which gave a flatter trajectory and better range, the target was never obscured and the riflemen never gave away their position, so that in a few years virtually all armies had adopted it. The British Army changed over to a similar propellant, cordite, in 1891 and soon found that the greater heat and pressures generated by the force of its thrust necessitated a new type of rifling, so all rifles and machine guns were changed yet again. This change was particularly beneficial to the Vickers-Maxim because, apart from the better range and flatter trajectory, the more powerful propellant naturally increased the recoil and thus the amount of power required to ensure a smooth operation. In black powder days the recoil had been just about sufficient, provided plenty of attention was paid to cleanliness and lubrication, but cordite allowed for an ample working reserve even under the worst

conditions. The new rifle-calibre cordite cartridge gun soon showed its fearful capacity, particularly perhaps in Kitchener's campaign in the Sudan in 1898. At Omdurman the huge Dervish armies, charging with the most reckless bravery across flat, open desert, sustained hideous casualties in their fruitless attempts to reach the British firing line. It proved its worth in jungle and forest too, since when soldiers were advancing in single file in

circumstances which made it difficult to deploy, a single Maxim gun carried by porters close behind the leading section could supply enough almost instant firepower to deal with an ambush until it could be outflanked. It proved somewhat less useful in South Africa but this was principally due to inept handling. The standard gun was mounted on a wheeled artillery-type carriage and was thus very conspicuous, particularly in dry conditions where the muzzle blast tended to kick up sufficient dust to give its exact position away in spite of the cordite cartridge. This did not matter against an enemy armed with sword or spear but the deadly shooting of the modern Mauser rifles in the hands of the Boers, well accustomed to them, made it extremely

vulnerable. Nor was it until the peculiar conditions of the trench warfare of 1914-18 that they were finally recognized as an indispensable arm for modern warfare. The weapon illustrated has been specially selected because of its unusual mounting, which was usually referred to as a parapet mount or carriage. It had originally been invented for the Gardner gun but was readily adapted to both the Hotchkiss and the Vickers-Maxim and was a purely defensive mounting which enabled forts, defended bases, supply dumps and other vulnerable installations to be held by a minimum of men, thus freeing the bulk of a force for mobile operations in the field. The idea was that the two horn-shaped projections at the front could be raised and hooked into the

top of a wall or earth parapet so that the gun, mounted on a sleeve which could be slipped up and down the central pole as required, could be raised to fire over the defences with a reasonably wide arc of traverse. The flat circular plate at the rear of the central pole was simply a foot to give the third point of support to the triangle. It had two holes in it of about one inch (25·4mm) diameter so that it could be held rigidly in place by pegs if necessary. The two small wheels, which were twenty-two inches (559mm) in diameter and on a narrow axle only eighteen inches (457mm) long, were simply intended to facilitate local movement of the gun, perhaps from one point of a perimeter to another, and were in no sense travelling wheels in the normal sense.

The standard carriage, mentioned briefly earlier, was of basic artillery type and its wheels were of 3·5ft (1·06m) diameter which made them large enough to be drawn by a horse. The gun itself is of standard Maxim type, the particular specimen illustrated being marked ENFIELD 1899. A new version was introduced in 1912 in which mechanical improvements made it possible to reduce the depth of the body of the gun, a difference which can be seen clearly if compared with the photograph of the Vickers gun. The waterjacket was made of brass partly because it was a relatively cheap and easily worked metal and partly because of its good conductivity of heat. On service of course it was usually painted to make it less conspicuous.

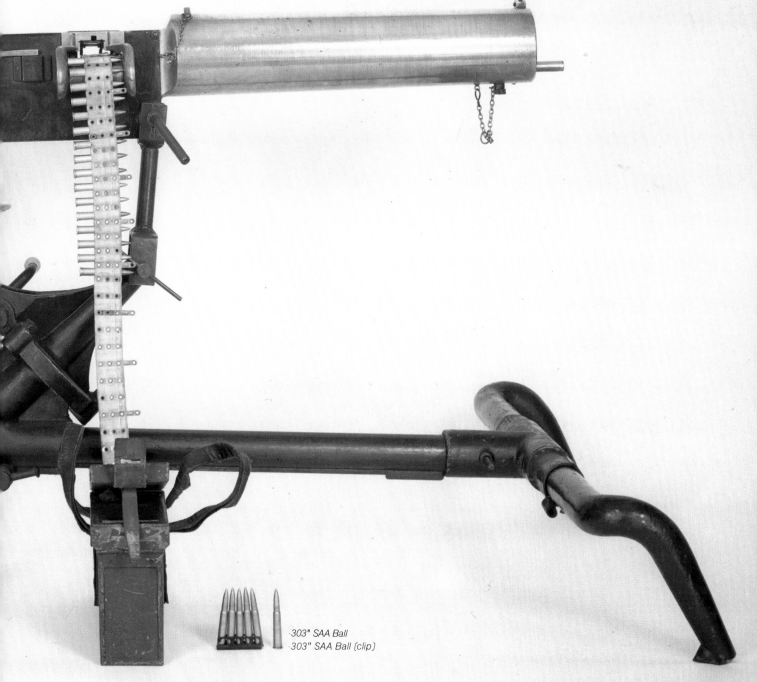

·303" SAA Ball
·303" SAA Ball (clip)

Great Britain
VICKERS ·303″ MACHINE GUN

Length (gun): 43″ (1092mm)
Weight (gun): 33lb (14·97kg)
Weight (tripod): 50lb (22·7kg)
Barrel: 28·4″ (722mm)
Calibre: ·303″
Rifling: 4 groove r/hand
Operation: Recoil
Feed: Belt
Cooling: Water
Cyclic Rate: 500 rpm
Muzzle Velocity:
2440 f/s (744 m/s)
Sights: 3800 yds (3475m)

The British Army had used the original Maxim gun with great success, and before the end of the 19th century every British battalion had a section of two under an officer. Their poor performance in the South African war caused them to fall into some degree of disrepute as weapons for regular warfare, however well they may have slaughtered charging tribesmen. The Russo-Japanese war led to a renewed interest in weapons of this type. One of the problems of the Boer War had been the high wheeled carriage, difficult to conceal on the open veldt, but in 1908 this carriage was changed for a tripod which greatly assisted the handling of the gun. Events in Europe seemed to indicate the possibility of a major war and at least a few enlightened soldiers, among them Lieutenant-Colonel McMahon who has already been mentioned in the introduction to this section, did a great deal to stimulate military interest, in spite of a fixed determination on the part of the Treasury to spend no more money than the absolute minimum necessary. In 1912 a considerably improved version of the gun appeared. Previous models had been made progressively lighter by the use of better metals, but

the 1912 gun incorporated a major change in the lock which improved the mechanical efficiency of the gun very considerably.

Unfortunately no one in the Government would sanction the immediate abandonment of the old guns in place of this new model (which was known for the first time as the Vickers gun) with the result that the British Expeditionary Force went to France with the pre-1912 model. These in fact did very well and in conjunction with the

impressive rifle fire which was a speciality of the British infantry they inflicted heavy casualties on the Germans before finally bringing them to a halt on the Marne, a preliminary to four years of static warfare. Mechanically the Vickers was similar to the earlier Maxim, the rear impulse being produced by recoil supplemented by the action of a muzzle attachment which deflected some of the gas. This thrust the lock backwards taking with it a round from the belt and

·303″ SAA Ball
·303″ SAA Ball (clip)

extending the fuzee spring which was situated in an elongated box on the left-hand side of the gun. The fuzee spring then took over and forced the bolt forward and so the cycle was repeated. The gun had a remarkable capacity for sustained fire but this led to obvious problems of wear. A barrel would last for about ten thousand rounds at two hundred rounds a minute, after which the rifling would have been worn away to the stage where the bullet ceased to be spun effectively by it and so lost accuracy very quickly. The barrel could be changed very quickly and as spares were carried this was not a serious problem. The gun was, of course, water-cooled with a jacket capacity of about seven pints. This began to boil after 3,000 rounds of steady fire, about two hundred a minute, and thereafter evaporated steadily at the rate of one or two pints for each thousand rounds fired depending on the rate of fire and the climatic conditions at the time. The gun was fitted with a condenser tube leading into an old-fashioned one-gallon petrol can, and if some water was put into the can first and the steam passed through it, a considerable amount of the water lost could be used again, which was an important factor in desert conditions where water was scarce. In both World Wars it was not unknown for a few belts to be fired in order to enable the detachment to make a brew of tea, unofficial but very convenient. There were various models of Vickers gun, none very different from the rest. Some water jackets are fluted and some plain, but this does not necessarily indicate a different mark of gun. In the first few years of the 20th century the United States neglected its Army a good deal on the basis that it had no aggressive intentions towards anyone and that in any case its Navy would keep it safe. By 1913 these beliefs seemed somewhat unrealistic in the light of world events and in that year the United States Army Board tested a variety of guns including the Vickers-Maxim made by the famous Colt factory. The Vickers was reported as being an excellent weapon, and far superior to the others submitted. Eventually four thousand of these were ordered, but deliveries were slow and by the end of the war only some twelve thousand had been made and very few ever saw action. These guns, which were known as the US Machine Gun Model 15, were made in ·30" calibre to take the standard rifle round, but soon after the war they were withdrawn in favour of the excellent 1917 Browning on the very understandable grounds that a nation the size of the United States should use home-produced arms. Some of these American-made guns found their way to England in 1940 where they were allotted to the Home Guard, a good deal of red paint being put on them in various vital places to ensure that no enthusiast tried to fire the standard British ·303" cartridge from them. The Vickers gun was used extensively by the British Army in World War II, and remained in service for some years afterwards until replaced by the General Purpose Machine Gun.

BESA MARKS 1-3

Length (gun):
43·5" (1105mm)
Weight (gun):
41·8lb (18·97kg)
Weight (tripod):
38·5lb (16·11kg)
Barrel: 26·7" (679mm)
Calibre: 7·92mm
Rifling: 4 groove r/hand
Operation: Gas
Feed: Belt
Cooling: Air
Cyclic Rate: 500 or 700 rpm
Muzzle Velocity:
2600 f/s (793 m/s)
Sights: 2500 yds (2287m)

This gun was originally produced by a Czechoslovakian firm in Brno, which in order to overcome the difficulties of pronunciation was usually known abroad as ZB. The factory originally started production in 1922 and at first manufactured a variety of small arms including the French Hotchkiss under licence. In 1924 the leading designer, Vaclac Holek, developed a prototype light machine gun based on the best features of the various guns used in World War I and it is for this gun, which subsequently became the famous Bren gun, that he is probably best remembered.

Until the late 1920s the factory concentrated on a variety of gas-operated guns including one for the Japanese which subsequently formed the basis for all their future light automatics, and as their reputation in this field stood high they decided in about 1930 to experiment with a medium machine gun. Like the designers and producers of most other medium machine guns they initially settled for a weapon based on recoil rather than gas on the usual basis that it was both reliable and clean. The latter characteristic was an important one in any weapon designed for sustained fire, where the fouling inseparable from a gas-operated mechanism could have serious effects on the working of the weapon in circumstances which demanded the production of considerable volumes of fire over more or less considerable periods. This gun was a success but it was somewhat overshadowed by the reputation of the Bren which led the firm to develop another medium machine gun, but this time one which reverted, somewhat surprisingly, to a system of gas action. This gun, which was given the designation ZB

53, greatly impressed the British, who were then principally concerned with finding a good medium machine gun as armament for tanks. They began tests and experiments with it even before it officially appeared in 1937, since the proceedings of the Small Arms Committee for 1936 indicate the purchase of several of these early prototype guns at a cost of about £310 per weapon, together with fifteen thousand rounds of ammunition for them. Although the gun was, strictly speaking, gas operated, the barrel also moved back under the force of the recoil, the timing being so arranged that the cartridge was fed into the chamber and fired as the barrel went forward. This, of course, meant that the backward force of the recoil had first to arrest, and then reverse, the forward movement, which had the effect not only of diminishing the next recoil considerably but also reducing various stresses and strains on the weapon generally. The guns had very heavy barrels, some finned, which allowed for sustained fire, and the earlier models also had the means to vary their cyclic rate of fire from four hundred and fifty to eight hundred and fifty rounds per minute. All reports

indicated that the gun was a success. It worked well as a tank gun, although the need to raise the top cover to put a belt in meant that a minimum of eight inches head room was needed, not always an easy thing to achieve in the cramped conditions of a tank, and it was also found that the considerable quantity of carbon monoxide produced by it made it necessary to fit auxiliary extractor fans to clear them. These, however, were minor defects, and the gun was otherwise found to be so reliable that in 1937 there was a possibility that it would replace the Vickers gun in the ground role. The reason it did not do so was due to the fact that it fired the

7·92mm SAA Ball
·303" SAA Ball (clip)

7·92mm rimless round and could not be modified to handle the rimmed ·303" British cartridge. The British have always insisted, very sensibly, that their service small arms, rifle, light machine gun and medium machine guns, should use the same round and were not prepared to depart from it as far as infantry weapons were concerned. Tank guns were in a somewhat different category, since there were relatively few of them and it was possible to keep them supplied without risk of confusion in the Ordnance department. The actual manufacture of the ammunition caused no problems once a factory had

been tooled up for the task. The weapon illustrated is something of a mystery, since although it is an obvious ZB 53 it bears no markings of any kind. It seems probable that it is one of the early prototypes sent from Czechoslovakia to England for testing at the Small Arms School at Hythe. It is mounted on the standard Czech Model 45 tripod, which offers a rigid platform. Its considerable size is due to the fact that it is designed for the anti-aircraft role if necessary. The gun having been dismounted, the two fore legs are unclamped and swung forward in direct prolongation of the main frame. The rear leg consists of two parts, a long and a short

one, side by side. The long one is unclamped and turned under to complete the high tripod leaving the shorter one rising vertically from it. It is this shorter one which takes the gun. In 1936 the Birmingham Small Arms Company came to an arrangement with ZB under which they were allowed to manufacture the No 53 gun, and work started soon afterwards. These guns were given the name Besa from the intial letters of Brno and Enfield and the last two of BSA. A number of changes were made in the weapon but these were only to simplify the problems of large-scale production and did not involve any alterations in design. All the guns made by

BSA were for tanks and had pistol grips, but although there were a number of variations, chiefly to facilitate production as World War II progressed, the guns remained in general remarkably similar. The main change came with the Mark 3, which finally abandoned the selective fire device, being geared for the higher rate of fire only. It was in its various forms an excellent gun, very reliable and unusually accurate, this factor being largely due to the combined use of recoil and gas which made the gun very smooth and easy in action. There was a larger version, also for tanks, which was produced in 15mm calibre.

Great Britain/Belgium
GPMG L7A1

Length (gun):
49·75" (1264mm)
Weight (gun): 24lb (10·89kg)
Weight (tripod): 29lb (13·2kg)
Barrel: 24.75" (629mm)
Calibre: 7·62mm
Rifling: 4 groove r/hand
Operation: Gas
Feed: Belt
Cooling: Air
Cyclic Rate: 8/900 rpm
Muzzle Velocity:
2800 f/s (855 m/s)
Sights: 1800 yds (1646m)

Since 1914 the British Army had relied on two types of machine gun, a medium gun (which had been the Vickers throughout) and a light gun (which had originally been the Lewis and later the Bren). The success of the Germans with their MG34 and in particular its successor the MG42, however, seemed to indicate that the proper answer was to replace the two types by a single general purpose machine gun, and the adoption by NATO of a standard calibre of small arms ammunition seemed to offer a suitable opportunity to make the change. By 1957 a possible successor had already been developed and produced in small numbers; it was based fairly closely on the earlier Bren gun but with a heavier barrel and a system of belt feed so as to give it a good deal greater capacity for sustained fire than had ever been possible with the earlier, lighter gun. Although very accurate this gun had certain defects, notably in the fact that the system of belt feed lacked power; it worked well enough under normal circumstances but when the gun was elevated much above ground level, which of course increased the length and weight of loaded belt it had to lift, the gun tended to

7·62mm NATO
·303" SAA Ball (clip)

slow down due to friction. It was also expensive to make since the body was machined from a solid block. In 1958 this prototype, which was provisionally known as the XII E4 Machine Gun, was extensively tested against a number of similar weapons including the American M60. As a result of these trials there seemed no doubt that the Belgian FN MAG, these latter initials standing for Mitrailleur à Gaz, was the best available. Like the other Fabrique Nationale products, this machine gun was well made, robust and reliable, and has since been adopted by several NATO countries. The first guns used by the British Army were made in Belgium, but later they were made at the Royal Small Arms Factory at Enfield. This involved certain modifications to conform with British manufacturing processes but there were no fundamental changes made to the gun, which remained substantially as it had been in its original state. The British-made gun is designated the L7A1, but is generally referred to as the GPMG. The new gun, like many original FN products, owes a great deal to the patents of John Browning, an American and one of the most prolific and most successful designers in the field of firearms that the world has ever seen. It is gas-operated with a bolt locking system similar to the original Browning Automatic Rifle of 1917, its feed mechanism being virtually identical with that of the German MG42, as is its trigger. The original idea was to have two different barrels for the gun, a plain steel one for the light role and a heavy barrel with a special liner for the sustained fire role. The liner was to be made of Stellite, a non-ferrous alloy of extreme hardness and very difficult to machine, but with the great advantage of retaining its intrinsic strength at high temperatures. Unfortunately, in the event it proved impossible to manufacture these liners to the very close dimensions needed. It was found on trials that sustained fire tended to move them, and as a result they had to be abandoned. The original concept had been to fire bursts of twenty rounds through the special barrel but this had to be reduced to ten, and even then it was desirable to change barrels after four belts, each of two hundred rounds, had been fired. Four tripods are held by each rifle company in the British Infantry, together with extra barrels and dial sights so that a proportion of the guns in the company can be converted to sustained fire if required. When the gun is used in this role the butt is normally removed and bipod legs folded back. The gun illustrated is an early model and lacks the dovetail necessary for the dial sight. It is also mounted on an experimental tripod. Other accessories include special barrels for blank firing and a belt box which can be clipped on to the side of the gun when it is required to be mobile in the light role. This item is not extensively used. A version of this gun, the L8A1, has been developed for use as a co-axial gun for tanks. It is fitted with a heavy steel barrel and a device for ensuring that the gases arising from firing are led outside the vehicle. There is also a L37A1, basically for use in other armoured vehicles but so designed that it can be quickly dismounted and used in the ground role. Yet another variation, the L20A1, is for use in helicopters. Although the gun is efficient, it is arguable that the concept of a general purpose machine gun has not proved altogether satisfactory. Compromise weapons, designed to fulfill tasks originally carried out by two separate weapons are rarely quite as effective in either role as the two originals, and the GPMG is no exception, being somewhat too heavy and cumbersome for the light role and obviously lacking the true sustained fire capacity of the original water-cooled Vickers. It does, however, reduce the problems of training very considerably, an important factor in a modern army with complex equipment.

Belt box

Removable butt

Barrel for blank firing

Italy
BREDA MODELLO 37

Length (gun): 50" (1270mm)
Weight (gun):
42·8lb (19·28kg)
Weight (tripod):
41·5lb (18·8kg)
Barrel: 25" (635mm)
Calibre: 8mm
Rifling: 4 groove r/hand
Operation: Gas
Feed: Strip
Cooling: Air
Cyclic Rate: 450 rpm
Muzzle Velocity:
2600 f/s (793 m/s)
Sights: 3280 yds (3000m)

The Società Italiana Ernesto Breda is located in Brescia, a town in Northern Italy famous for its iron works of various types and in particular for the quality of the firearms made there. The firm started as a locomotive works but in 1915 Italy declared war on Austria and this was followed by a further declaration of war against Germany in 1916, by which time the whole country had been placed on a war footing and much of its then rather limited manufacturing capacity turned to the production of war *matériel.* In the course of this change-over Breda started making Revelli machine guns, almost as a subsidiary of Fiat which held the original patents for these weapons. By the time of the Armistice in 1918 the company had established a high reputation and in spite of the natural drop in the requirement for firearms it managed to continue making machine guns, although on a very limited scale. During the war Italy had relied on other countries to a considerable extent for her automatic weapons, but in the early 1920s she decided to investigate the possibilities of a reliable light machine gun for use on the ground or in the air as required. The Italian Government therefore invited its various factories to design something on these lines and by 1924 Breda had produced a light machine gun which after some modification went into production in 1928. The Government then showed interest in a heavy machine gun for use in (and against) tanks and aircraft, and in 1931 Breda produced a gun of 13·2mm calibre. This proved to be of basically very sound design and the firm at once set out to scale it down to a medium machine gun to fire the 8mm Modello 35 cartridge. The work progressed remarkably well and in 1937 the firm produced the machine gun, a specimen of which is illustrated. The mechanism was orthodox and basically simple, being worked in the normal way by a piston worked by gases tapped off the bore. The piston also activated the breechblock which was locked in the firing position by the action of a ramp on the piston which lifted the end of the block into a recess on the top of the body. The gun fired automatic only and it was possible to control its cyclic rate by the use of a gas

8mm Modello 35
·303" SAA Ball (clip)

regulator through which the gases passed on their way to the piston head, which was interchangeable. The need to keep the gas port in its proper place in relation to the gas regulator made it impossible to increase or decrease the headspace, which was therefore somewhat larger than necessary. This naturally gave rise to the risk of ruptured cases, due to the direct lack of support by the breechblock, but Breda overcame this by the familiar method of oiling each case as it entered the chamber by means of a pump. This allowed the case to 'float' in the chamber and set back firmly against the block before the pressure got too high. This system of lubricating cartridges was widely used and it is possible

that Breda got the idea from the Schwarzlose which they had received in large numbers from the Austrians after the end of World War I. It is not, however, altogether satisfactory and can sometimes cause trouble in hot and dusty climates, although the Italians do not seem to have suffered unduly from this defect in their African campaigns. The gun was air-cooled, and its heavy barrel of 9·7lb (4·4kg) allowed a satisfactory degree of sustained fire without over-heating. The gun was fed by a type of strip, more correctly described as a tray, and without any doubt the most unusual aspect of this system was the fact that the empty cases were replaced tidily in the tray after they had

been fired. The object of this very remarkable device is by no means clear, since it used a good deal of power and also meant that if the trays had to be reloaded quickly the empties had first to be removed. The Breda was modified in 1938 for use in tanks, the main difference being the substitution of a box magazine for the peculiar tray device and the addition of a pistol grip in place of the spade grips previously used. The Modello 1937 was mounted on a simple, robust tripod, based very closely on the one used for the Austrian Schwarzlose. The main difference between the two, which can be seen by reference to the photo-graphs, is that the traversing arc of the Austrian gun was clamped to the rear leg of the

tripod whereas that of the Breda is fixed to a horizontal plate fastened to the forward-most point of the tripod. The Breda served the Italian Army well enough during the war and emerged from it with a considerable reputation for reliability, in spite of the fact that most of the cam-paigns undertaken by the Italian Army took place in North and East Africa where the constant presence of dust and windblown sand might have been expected to have had seriously adverse effects on the efficiency of a weapon relying on lubricated cartridge cases. The Italians now use what is essentially a version of the original German MG42, made under licence, and known in Italy as the Mitragliatrice Leggere 42/59.

Japan
TAISHO 14

Length (gun):
45·5" (1155mm)
Weight (gun): 62lb (28·1kg)
Weight (tripod):
60lb (27·25kg)
Barrel: 29" (737mm)
Calibre: 6·5mm
Rifling: 4 groove l/hand
Operation: Gas
Feed: 30-round strip
Cooling: Air
Cyclic Rate: 450 rpm
Muzzle Velocity:
2400 f/s (732 m/s)
Sights: 2406 yds (2200m)

By the end of the 19th century Japan had emerged from many centuries of seclusion and was well on the way to becoming a modern industrialised state. Her armed forces, like the rest of her institutions, had been properly organized, with a good deal of European advice and assistance, and she had a potentially large capacity to produce rifles. Even in her war with China in 1894 she had used a domestically produced rifle, and on the basis of her experience in that war she had improved this early version considerably. Understandably, however, there was a limit to what even the industrious Japanese could achieve in a few years and one of the weapons she was lacking was any form of machine gun. The machine gun was not then universally regarded as a vital weapon in modern warfare, even by many European soldiers, but the Japanese, having no pre-conceived ideas, realized the potential of the new weapon very early on, and soon after 1900 they had begun to manufacture the French Hotchkiss gun Model 1897 under licence. Most of their military advisers were Germans so it is not clear why they settled for a French gun. It may be that the Germans were not then convinced as to the utility of the machine gun; it may be that the French were better salesmen. What is most likely is that the Japanese settled for an air-cooled weapon and decided that the Hotchkiss was the best available. A number of the machine gun captions in this book make passing reference to the Russo-Japanese war of 1904-5, for the good reason that this was the first 'modern', as opposed to 'colonial', war in which machine guns were extensively used. Much of the war was concerned with the defence of Port Arthur (now better known as Lu-Shun) in Manchuria by the Russians. The Russian Far Eastern Fleet was blockaded in the harbour there and the whole of the land side had been heavily fortified against attack by the Japanese, who had three divisions deployed against it. Each of these divisions had up to twenty-five Hotchkiss guns allotted to it and the Japanese handled them with great skill and boldness. There had previously been a theory widely held by European

6·5mm Meiji 30
·303" SAA Ball (clip)

soldiers that the machine gun was fundamentally a defensive arm, designed to break up mass attacks, but the Japanese quickly decided that it was also an ideal support weapon for offensive operations. The critical problem in the days of the small bore magazine rifle was how to get an attacking force through a firezone sufficiently unscathed to attack successfully on the other side of it. The Japanese solved it by massing their machine guns and concentrating their huge firepower onto the enemy's defences, which though strong were often clearly visible. Ideally this sort of fire should be delivered in enfilade, that is from a flank, but the Japanese had no hesitation in using overhead

fire. Assuming the guns to be sited some 2000 yards (1829m) behind the objective this was of course perfectly safe, and when the ground allowed it they continued this fire to within very narrow limits of safety. It is indeed certain that their own forward infantry suffered some casualties from this fire but if a few casualties from one's own fire prevent many more from that of the enemy then they are obviously justified. The gun illustrated is of Japanese design but is based very closely on the Hotchkiss model of 1914 and appeared in the same year. The original French guns used by the Japanese against the Russians had, of course, been of 8mm calibre, but the 1914

version was designed to fire their normal 6·5mm rifle cartridge. This was a poor round, of only moderate power, and not well adapted to machine guns because the relative lack of taper of its case caused problems of extraction. The Japanese also had difficulties in adjusting their head space, that is the distance between the base of the round and the face of the bolt. This is very important because if it is too small the breech will not always close, whereas if it is too great the cartridge blows back unsupported and is liable to rupture. The Japanese solved the problem by oiling each round as it was fed into the chamber. This allowed the round to slip back easily and be supported

by the face of the bolt before the pressure reached its maximum. In view of the propensity of the earlier Hotchkiss to overheat, the Japanese increased the number of cooling rings so that they extended along the full length of the barrel. As mobility was an important feature in Japanese machine gun tactics, the tripod legs had sockets on them into which carrying handles could be inserted so that if necessary three men could transport the gun. In 1932 the gun was modified to take the more powerful 7·7mm cartridge, but apart from the barrel and the breech it is almost identical with the Type 3, the chief difference being the abolition of the old spade-

grips in favour of a double pistol type. Strangely enough the new version still incorporated a cartridge oiler; this was an undesirable device, particularly in dry, dusty conditions and it is surprising that the Japanese did not take the opportunity of doing away with it when the gun was remodelled for the new round. This new gun, known as the Type 92, proved itself in the long wars against China in the 1930s and was the standard medium machine gun of World War II. It fired a rather heavy thirty-round strip, and due presumably to the inertia of this dead weight the gun fired its first few rounds rather hesitantly before picking up speed. It was a characteristic sound which made the presence of the gun very easily identified in action.

Soviet Union
SGM (GORYUNOV)

Length (gun): 44·1"
(1120mm)
Weight (gun): 29·76lb (13·5kg)
Weight (mount): 50·9lb
(23·1kg)
Barrel: 28·3" (719mm)
Calibre: 7·72mm
Rifling: 4 groove r/hand
Operation: Gas
Feed: Belt
Cooling: Air
Cyclic Rate; c650 rpm
Muzzle Velocity: 2700 f/s
(823 m/s)
Sights: 2187 yds (2000m)

The first medium machine gun adopted by Russia was a type of water-cooled Maxim which went into service in 1910. This gun was still in service at the outbreak of World War II, but it was a complex and expensive weapon to manufacture and by 1942 it was clear that the huge Soviet armies could only be equipped (and their earlier losses made good) with arms which could be quickly and cheaply produced by modern mass-production methods. The new gun, which was designed by Goryunov, was belt fed and gas-operated, and of simple, robust construction. When the first round was fired a part of the gases passed through a gas port in the barrel and struck the piston which was forced to the rear, taking the slide with it. The first brief movement of the slide unlocked the bolt and allowed the whole to go to the rear, compressing the return spring as it did so. In the course of this

rearward action a pair of claws drew the next cartridge from the belt whence it was forced into a cartridge guide in readiness for the bolt to feed it into the chamber on its forward travel. This somewhat complex arrangement was made necessary by the fact that the gun fired a rimmed cartridge which could not therefore be thrust straight forward from the belt, but this action appeared to be efficient. As the bolt approached its forward position, a cam forced it slightly to the right, where it engaged in a recess in the body and was thus locked before the round was fired. This was effective but meant that the face of the bolt had to be recessed at an angle so that it gave proper support to the base of the cartridge. Cooling was achieved by the use of a very heavy barrel with a chromed bore. This barrel could be changed very quickly and therefore allowed the gun to fire almost continuously for

long periods without undue overheating. Although a number had been made by 1945 the old Maxim remained in service until the end of the war. The gun illustrated is the modernized version of the Goryunov and has some mechanical improvements. It is, however, fundamentally the same gun, its chief distinguishing feature being the distinctive longitudinal flanging of the barrel to assist cooling. The gun was originally provided with a mount very similar in essence to the characteristic small wheeled Sokolov mount used with the original Maxim gun. The main trail of this mount is a single solid bar with a hinged end and it has a detachable shield. This is the mount shown in the illustration, but there is a later one with a U-shaped tubular metal trail and also a tripod. All guns will fit all mounts. The mounts are all designed to be convertible for anti-aircraft use.

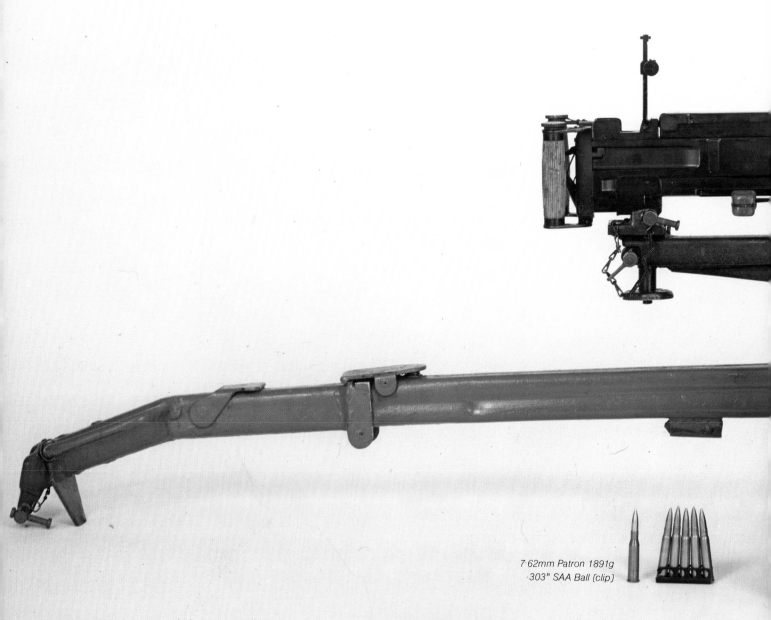

7·62mm Patron 1891g
·303" SAA Ball (clip)

In the one illustrated the gun is removed and the mount tilted forward until the top edge of the shield is firm on the ground. The gun is then remounted on the end of the trail. It can also be used as a vehicle weapon—in this role it is fitted into a special frame with a tray to hold the belt box, a bag for empty cases, and a retractable shoulder stock. The Goryunov has proved to be a reliable weapon and is still in extensive use in almost all Communist countries all over the world. It has been made and employed in large numbers by the Chinese and many were used against United States forces in Vietnam, and it is in production in Poland, Czechoslovakia and Hungary. Although still in service in the Soviet Union it is being replaced by the new PK general purpose machine gun. This is the first GPMG to enter Soviet service although it still fires the 1891 cartridge.

COLT-BROWNING MODEL 1895

Length (gun):
40·75" (1035mm)
Weight (gun):
35lb (15·87kg)
Weight (tripod):
61·25lb (27·8kg)
Barrel: 28" (712mm)
Calibre: ·30"
Rifling: 4 groove r/hand
Operation: Gas
Feed: Belt
Cooling: Air
Cyclic Rate: 480 rpm
Muzzle Velocity:
2800 f/s (855 m/s)
Sights: 2000 yds (1829m)

The Colt machine gun, like many other developments and inventions in the field of firearms, had its origins in an idea of John M. Browning, the most famous of designers in America and very probably in the whole world. It is said that while firing a rifle in long grass he noticed the effect the muzzle blast had on it and decided that with a little in-genuity a vast amount of power could be made available. This was a discovery comparable to that of Maxim regarding the harnessing of recoil, and like Maxim, Browning conducted his first experiments on a rifle. By tapping gases near the muzzle he was able to harness their power by using a piston connected to a bolt, and having established the feasibility of the concept he settled down to a great deal of work and experiment which in 1890 resulted in a prototype automatic gun. This gun he offered to the famous firm of Colt who were glad to accept it. By 1893 it had reached a stage where it had been successfully tested by the United States Navy, which like others at that period was anxious to get away from its somewhat clumsy manually operated guns. Fifty Colt guns, it having proved superior to all its competitors, were at once ordered, these being the first true automatic guns ever taken into use by the United States Armed Forces. A further one hundred and fifty were soon completed and by 1898 the whole US Navy was equipped with them. The general style of the Colt gun is clear from the photograph. It worked by gas but in a somewhat unusual way in that the piston, which was below the barrel, was hinged at the rear. The gas port was situated in the bottom of the bore and when the gas passed through it struck the front end of the piston and blew it downwards through 90°. A lever from this piston then activated the working parts. The gun was belt fed and had a single handle of Colt revolver type. It was mounted on an adjustable tripod which gave it a very stable platform from which to operate. It had no cooling system beyond a heavy barrel, which limited the number of rounds it could fire without over-heating. The Navy used the Colt gun with some success in the Spanish-American war at a time when the Army still had manually

operated Gatlings and this led the Army to investigate the possibility of adopting them. They were, however, of 6·5mm calibre, the same as the Lee straight-pull rifle, which led to delays until the question of a standardized inter-service round had been settled. The Colt machine gun was retested by the Army, but it was finally decided that it was too complex for land service and no further action was taken in the matter. In the meanwhile some modifications were made, and the eventual result, the Model 1904, was bought by a number of other countries. It so happened that when the United States entered World War I in 1917 its Army had no modern machine guns.

Therefore, although the Colt was obsolete, the factory was still equipped to make it and a new model, the 1917 (Army) was ordered in considerable quantities, about fifteen hundred being supplied before the end of the war. By this time the American Army had reached France where it had been almost entirely re-equipped with Allied automatic weapons, mainly either the British Vickers or the French Model 1914 Hotchkiss, both well-tried guns with consider-able reputations for reliability. A modern Browning water-cooled machine gun was also in limited production at this stage so that it is improbable that the United States Army ever used their Colt guns in action. In the circumstances then prevailing in France in 1918 this was probably just as well since the Colt, although mechanically reliable,

was prone to over-heating and would certainly have never stood up to the enormous demands likely to have been made on it in the intense fighting of the last year of the war. The sales literature provided for the gun suggested that in fact the forward action of the mechanism acted like a pump and forced cold air into the chamber but this claim does not seem to have been borne out in practice. Another serious defect was that it could not be used in the prone position because the 10" (254mm) piston used to hit the ground if the gun was too low. This tendency inevit-ably led the United States infantrymen to nickname it the 'potato digger', a name by which it is often recognized by people otherwise quite

ignorant of its official designa-tion. Apart from limited use by naval landing parties, who found it convenient and easy to handle in Cuba, the gun can at least claim to have seen service on the mainland of China. When the Legations at Peking were besieged by the so-called Boxer insurgents they were defended by the Marine Guards of the various countries involved, that of the United States Marines being equipped with a small number of Colt guns. The Canadian Army also took some with them to Europe in 1914 but there is no record of them ever having used the guns except for training. In the early days of World War I the British and French both experimented with this gun on their aircraft but they eventually abandoned it.

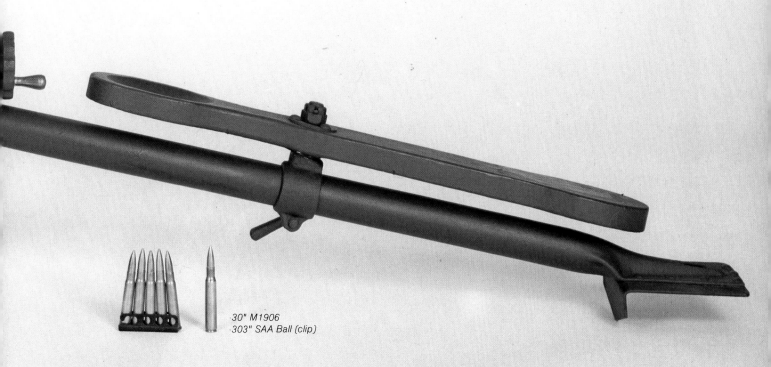

·30" M1906
·303" SAA Ball (clip)

United States of America
BROWNING MODEL 1917

Length (gun): 38·5" (978mm)
Weight (gun):
32·6lb (14·97kg)
Weight (tripod): 53lb (24kg)
Barrel: 24" (610mm)
Calibre: ·30"
Rifling: 4 groove r/hand
Operation: Recoil
Feed: Belt
Cooling: Water
Cyclic Rate: 5/600 rpm
Muzzle Velocity:
2800 f/s (855 m/s)
Sights: 2800 yds (2560m)

Although John M. Browning was one of the pioneers in utilizing gases from the barrel to provide the motive power in automatic weapons, he seems to have come to the conclusion fairly quickly that as far as medium machine guns (that is rifle calibred weapons fired from a tripod) were concerned, the best form of power to use was recoil. Given modern smokeless cartridges the force produced by firing the cartridge was ample for the purpose, and perhaps more important, was clean. Gas-operated guns necessarily get very foul, and although this is acceptable in a light machine gun which is not intended for sustained fire it is very liable to cause some problems in a weapon intended to fire possibly hundreds of rounds without intermission. As early as 1901, therefore, Browning

filed a patent for an orthodox medium gun, water-cooled and worked by short recoil and by 1910 he had produced an excellent weapon. His trouble, however, was to find someone who wanted to buy it. At the beginning of the 20th century the United States were somewhat more remote from Europe in practical terms than they are now, and they still tended to look westward. The American Army, Browning's only prospective customer, was small and chronically short of funds and although it had been interested in a modern gun, as opposed to the reliable but manually operated Gatling, it either would not or could not do anything about it. Perhaps fortunately there was an almost unlimited civilian market for pistols and sporting firearms of all kinds, and as Browning's reputation stood high he was able to subsist very comfortably on this end of the business. He was, nevertheless, extremely interested in military automatic weapons and continued to add various refinements to his already excellent prototype until he was satisfied that he had achieved near perfection in design, functioning, and general reliability. The United States, like the other great democracies in the early 20th century, was ill prepared for modern war and when she declared war on Germany in April 1917 her capacity to

fight battles on land was extremely limited. She had a small professional army, well enough trained in a somewhat old-fashioned way, and her infantry was armed almost entirely with rifles. The total availability of machine guns in the United States was a little over one thousand and many of these were already almost museum pieces. Browning wasted no time in offering his gun to the American Government and in May 1917 it was rigorously tested, and accepted by the authorities. The main trouble was, of course, that although an excellent gun there were only two of them in existence at the time, and even in a highly industrialized country like the United States it took time to turn industry over to a war footing. In the event America did well and by the end of the war had produced something in the order of forty-three thousand of these guns. This figure, though impressive, should not conceal the fact that the American Army which actually fought in France in the last few months of the war relied almost entirely on its Allies for medium machine guns, and few, if any, of the 1917 model were ever used in action. The outstanding feature of the Browning was its mechanical simplicity which not only helped mass-production but also made it relatively easy to teach to the hastily raised American

troops. When the trigger was pressed (the first round having been loaded manually by means of a cocking handle which duplicated the action of the recoil) and the round fired, the barrel and breech-block recoiled together, for just over half an inch until

pressure had dropped to a safe level and the barrel and breechblock unlocked, the barrel stopping while the block continued backwards under its initial impetus. During this time the empty case was extracted from the breech and ejected from the gun, and a fresh cartridge drawn from the belt. When this backward phase was complete the return spring drove the working parts forward again, chambering the cartridge, locking the block to the barrel, and firing the round, and this cycle could continue as long as the trigger was pressed and there were rounds in the belt. The Browning gun was made in considerable variety, including air-cooled models for use in tanks and aircraft for which water-cooled weapons were clearly unsuitable, but there were no fundamental changes made mechanically. The final modification before the outbreak of World War II resulted in the Model 1917A1 which was introduced in 1936. When the Japanese struck at Pearl Harbor in December 1941 the United States Army was almost as little prepared for large scale war as it had been in 1917, but at least it had no trouble in deciding on a medium machine gun for the well-tried Browning was available, and under modern industrial conditions it soon became possible to produce it in the huge numbers required for global war. This was to be the first real combat test of the Browning gun since its introduction and, as was to be expected, it turned out to be an excellent weapon. It also saw much service in Korea, and was not replaced until the early 1960s when the new M60 came into service.

·30" M1906

·303" SAA Ball (clip)

United States of America
BROWNING .50″ CALIBRE M2(HB)

Length (gun): 65″ (1651mm)
Weight (gun): 84lb (38·11kg)
Weight (tripod);
44lb (19·86kg)
Barrel: 45″ (1143mm)
Calibre: ·50″
Rifling: 8 groove r/hand
Operation: Recoil
Feed: Belt
Cooling: Air
Cyclic Rate: 500 rpm
Muzzle Velocity:
2930 f/s (894 m/s)
Sights: 2600 yds (2378m)

When the United States Expeditionary Force arrived in France in 1917 it was almost entirely dependent for automatic weapons on its allies. At that time the British and French were both conducting fairly extensive experiments with heavy machine guns, that is machine guns firing a good deal larger cartridge than the standard rifle round which until that time had been universally used. These guns were intended principally to counter the few enemy tanks, some of which were captured ones that had been refurbished, which were just beginning to appear but were of value against normal defences which were getting progressively stronger as the war progressed. These included steel loophole plates and even rudimentary body armour, which were of course designed to be proof against the normal rifle cartridge. There was also a further role envisaged, that of shooting down enemy observation balloons since the heavy bullets were not only accurate but also had the capacity to carry more incendiary compound than could be incorporated into a normal bullet. The United States Army in France was naturally very interested in these experiments and at one stage its Ordnance experts on the spot made various local attempts to convert some of their few ·30″ Brownings to take the 11mm cartridge with which the French had been experimenting. These met only with limited success because any machine gun is a carefully designed weapon intended for a specific cartridge and any significant increase in the power of the round naturally places a considerable strain on the working parts. To crown everything it was then found that the French cartridge lacked the necessary penetrative power, so local experiments ceased and it was left to the indispensible John Browning to do what he could to restore the situation. He had in fact made good progress with a new ·50″ water-cooled gun which was in effect a larger scale version of his original medium model, but although this worked perfectly well the cartridge still remained a problem. At this critical stage the Americans very fortunately captured some of the new German Mauser anti-tank rifles together with a quantity of ammunition, and when tests on these rounds were made it was found that they had a muzzle velocity in excess of two thousand eight hundred f/s (853 m/s). A new United States cartridge was quickly developed along the same lines and the problem was solved; but like many American enterprises in 1918 the solution came too late, for by that time the war was over and economy was again the order of the day. Some limited experiments continued, chiefly with a view to the possibility of using heavy machine guns as light anti-aircraft weapons, since their flat trajectory and greater capacity for armour piercing, tracer, and incendiary purposes appeared to make them well suited to this role. Some useful work was also done in standardizing parts, particularly the development of a basic receiver which could be used in a wide variety of guns, an innovation which greatly speeded wartime mass production a few years later on. In 1933 an air-cooled version of the basic gun was developed. It was

·50″ Browning
·303″ SAA Ball (clip)

intended principally for use on multiple anti-aircraft mounts but there was a version for use as a tank turret gun and yet another for use on a ground mount. This gun was called the M2, and it worked on the usual Browning system of short recoil. When the cartridge was fired the barrel and breechblock, securely locked together, recoiled for just under an inch when the barrel was stopped by means of an oil buffer. At this stage the pressure had dropped sufficiently for the breechblock to unlock and continue to the rear under the initial impetus given to it by the barrel, extracting and ejecting the empty case and extracting the next live round from the belt. Once the rearward action had stopped the compressed return spring then took over and drove the working parts sharply forward, chambering the round, locking the breechblock, and firing the cartridge, after which the

cycle continued as long as the trigger was pressed and there were rounds in the belt. The gun would fire automatic only, although some were equipped with bolt latches to allow single rounds to be fired if necessary. The adjustment of the headspace of the M2 was very important as even a few thousandths of an inch could be vital. If the distance was too great the cartridge might be blown back against the breechblock and cause damage; if it was too small the mechanism would not close fully which could be even more serious since there was then a risk of the cartridge firing with the breech unlocked which could endanger the crew. Headspace was easy to adjust with a gauge, or it could be done simply by screwing or unscrewing the barrel manually against the breechblock, and it was generally considered desirable to check it whenever the gun was being prepared for firing. When the

gun was being mounted in some relatively inaccessible place in a vehicle, or on a double mount, it was possible to change the feed from one side of the gun to the other, without difficulty. Although this gun functioned well enough mechanically it showed an unfortunate tendency to overheat, so that seventy or eighty rounds was about the maximum which could be fired continuously without a considerable pause for allowing the barrel to cool. This was of course quite unacceptable so a heavy barreled version (usually abbreviated to HB) was adopted, the weapon illustrated being one of these. The extra metal in the barrel made a considerable difference and this new gun was most effective, being extensively used by the United States and many other countries in the course of World War II and in Korea. After the war it was adopted by the British Army as an infantry battalion weapon, its

role being chiefly the protection of troops and troop convoys for whom no other anti-aircraft defence could be provided. A vehicle mounting stand was provided above the passenger seat of three-ton and similar vehicles, access from the inside being through a circular hatch in the roof of the cab; this stand could also be adapted for ground use, powerful balancing springs being used in both cases to help control the movement of the gun. The ground mount, as illustrated, was also provided, so that the gun could be used against armoured vehicles if necessary. The M2 in one form or another is still used in most United States armoured fighting vehicles and is also employed as the ranging machine gun on the British Chieftain tank. It is still also in use in several other countries including a number of the Arab Gulf States where it is often mounted on a vehicle and used for long-range fire against relatively distant targets.

The Light Machine Gun section starts on page 60

Czechoslovakia
LEHKY-KULOMET ZGB VZ33

Length: 45·25" (1150mm)
Weight: 22·5lb (10·2kg)
Barrel: 25" (635mm)
Calibre: ·303"
Rifling: 6 groove r/hand
Operation: Gas
Feed: 30-round box
Cooling: Air
Cyclic Rate: 500 rpm
Muzzle Velocity:
2440 f/s (744 m/s)
Sights: 1200 yds (1098m)

World War I had proved conclusively that the principal need for the infantry was firepower, preferably accurate, sustained and portable. The bayonet, it is true, had seen some use in trench fighting, raiding and similar operations which were necessarily fought at close quarters, but even there the quick snapshot with a rifle, a burst with an automatic, or a well-flung grenade usually did the job. The bayonet had been a vital item of the soldier's armament when all fighting was at close quarters, and it took up to half-a-minute to reload the single-shot muzzle-loaded rifle or musket then in service. However, under modern conditions very few soldiers would use the bayonet if they had a round left in their magazine. The fact which had really been demonstrated was the offensive value of light automatic weapons; four years of trench warfare had tended to make people regard the machine gun as essentially a defensive

weapon, well protected by earth or even concrete emplacements and scientifically positioned to decimate attacking troops brought to a halt by well placed obstacles of barbed wire. In 1918, however, it came as something of a revelation to see the offensive value of light automatic guns, first in the Germans' March offensive and later in the great Allied advances which finally brought the war to an end. Once it was over there were some soldiers who wished to put the clock back to the period before 1914 but there was no possibility of this. The new system had come to stay. The British Army ended the war with the Lewis gun as its light automatic. Each platoon of four sections had two of them, giving a total of thirty-two for the four rifle companies with a further four at battalion headquarters for light anti-aircraft work. This organization remained substantially unchanged in the British Army until 1938. The Lewis gun, however,

although it had given excellent service, was a somewhat complex weapon and needed much time to train the soldier to use it, and in the late 1920s the British Army began to seriously consider whether it should not be abandoned in favour of something lighter, less complex, and generally more modern. In 1932 extensive trials were held to decide which of the contestants, if any, might make an acceptable successor, the two most likely weapons tested being the Madsen and the Vickers-Berthier, which, being already in service in the Indian Army, was regarded as a clear favourite. Then at the critical moment a dark horse appeared. A Military Attaché wrote in glowing terms of a demonstration he had recently attended in which a Czechoslovakian gun had performed remarkably well and the British authorities agreed, perhaps surprisingly, to include it in their tests, thus ensuring in somewhat accidental fashion,

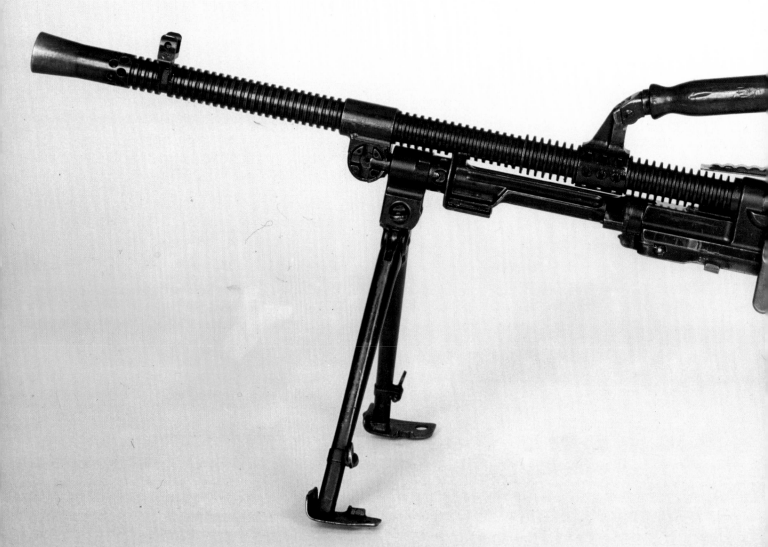

that the British Army would enter World War II with one of the finest machine guns in the world. The Czechoslovakian factory was located at Brno, and in view of its somewhat unpronounceable name it had very sensibly adopted the initials ZB for its international dealings. It had come into existence in 1923 and within a year had begun experiments with a prototype automatic later to be known as the ZB 26. The individual principally responsible for this gun, which incorporated the best features of a variety of early weapons, was Vaclac Holek, a designer of genius. Having started in the ZB works as an ordinary workman he had risen rapidly, and the Czechoslovakian Army's request for a new light automatic gave him his chance; his team included his brother Emmanuel and two expatriate Poles, Marek and Podrabsky. The gun produced was gas operated, with a piston working to a tilting breechblock, an easily

removed barrel, and a vertical box magazine, and was chambered for the rimless 7·92mm German round. After exhaustive tests it was very clear to the British that they had found a potential winner. Some modifications were of course necessary, principally to enable the gun to fire the ·303″ rimmed round which the British insisted on retaining; the barrel finning was also dispensed with, but otherwise there were no fundamental changes. The weapon illustrated is one of the final modified models made in Czechoslovakia. Once accepted the Government decided that it should be made at Enfield which inevitably involved an enormous amount of preliminary planning, and the installation of a large number of machine tools. By January 1935 the most important aspect, a set of drawings dimensioned in inches, had been received and work then started almost immediately. The body of the new gun,

which was cut from solid metal, required two hundred and seventy operations to complete it, involving five hundred and fifty gauges accurate to one two-thousandth of an inch, which gives some idea of the complexity of the undertaking. By September 1937 the first gun was complete. Captain B. H. Liddell-Hart, a famous British military expert, noted in an article for the *Daily Telegraph* in early 1934 that a start was to be made in re-equipping the British Army with a new light machine gun. The first recipients were to be the British cavalry (which was then almost completely horsed), who were to receive it in place of their ancient Hotchkiss, and it is believed that a few of the original prototypes were in the hands of a cavalry regiment in the course of summer manoeuvres in 1935. The new gun clearly needed a name, since the system of using a combination of initials and figures was not then

popular, and eventually the first two letters of Brno, its place of origin, were linked with the first two letters of Enfield, the location of the Royal Small Arms Factory, to produce the composite Bren, one of the famous names in the history of the British Army. Once started, manufacture went smoothly, and by July 1938 the rate of production had reached three hundred a week. In view of what the next fourteen months were to bring this was probably just as well. A few, a very few, actually began to reach home-based infantry battalions in the early spring of 1938, and the writer remembers from his own experience the arrival of the first Bren gun in the company in which he was then serving. Nobody thought of firing it and only senior non-commissioned officers were actually allowed to touch it, but still it came as a ray of hope at a time when war was beginning to seem certain. The decision to adopt it soon proved an excellent one.

·303″ SAA Ball
·303″ SAA Ball (clip)

Denmark
MADSEN 1902

Length: 46" (1169mm)
Weight: 22lb (9·98kg)
Barrel: 19" (483mm)
Calibre: 8mm
Rifling: 4 groove r/hand
Operation: Long recoil
Feed: 30-round box
Cooling: Air
Cyclic Rate: 400 rpm
Muzzle Velocity:
2700 f/s (824 m/s)
Sights: 2188 yds (2000m)

The early history of this weapon is obscured considerably by a remarkable variety in its nomenclature. Patents which applied unmistakably to this weapon were taken out as early as 1899 by J. Rasmussen, a director of the Royal Military Arms Factory at Copenhagen, who later assigned them to the Dansk Rekyl-Riffel Syndikat (usually abbreviated to DRRS). Then in 1902 a Danish officer, Lieutenant Schouboe, a director of DRRS, took out apparently identical patents. The gun was often known as the Madsen after the Danish Minister of War while the British called it the Rexer. The weapon was in many ways an unusual one, its mechanism being virtually unique as far as automatic arms were concerned. The basic breech mechanism consisted of a rectangular steel frame sliding on ribs in the main body of the gun. Inside this steel frame there was a breech-block, pivoted at the rear so that it could only work in a vertical plane. It was similar in principle to the block on the Peabody Martini, but with the important difference that whereas the Martini block only had two positions, locked or dropped, the Madsen had three locked, dropped or raised, its vertical movement being controlled by a curved feed arm attached to the left hand side of the box. The gun was of the long recoil type in which barrel and breech both recoiled sufficiently far for the next cartridge to be stripped from the magazine and fed into the chamber. When the first round, which had of course to be loaded manually by a lever, was fired, the barrel and breech mechanism recoiled together.
In the course of this movement the feed arm caused the front of the breechblock to rise, allowing the empty case to be extracted and ejected

underneath it. When the rearward action was complete a return spring took over, forcing the mechanism forward; during this stage the next round was stripped from the magazine and carried forward on top of the breechblock which acted as a feed tray. At the proper time the feed arm depressed the front of the block so that the chamber was exposed and forced the cartridge in, after which the block rose to the locked position and the round was fired. The weapon was tested in 1903 by the United States Army authorities, who were not particularly impressed with it, partly because the bases of a number of cartridges were ruptured on ejection and partly because the returnspring did not always drive the mechanism fully home. In view of its later reputation for reliability it seems likely that poor ammunition was at least a contributory factor. The Russians used the Madsen

with some success as a cavalry light machine gun in the Russo-Japanese war, but discarded it soon afterwards which does not indicate that they were completely satisfied with it. Some were made under licence by the Rexer Company in London, hence its English name, and the weapon was demonstrated at the Bisley rifle meeting in 1904. Nothing more happened in England although a number were purchased by Natal and used to suppress a Zulu rising in 1906. Once World War I had started, however, there was an almost immediate demand for light automatic weapons, and both the Germans and the British considered the Madsen. The Germans rejected it out of hand, but the British, perhaps more desperate, ordered two hundred from Denmark. At this stage the famous motor firm of Rolls-Royce also turned its attention to firearms and undertook to

manufacture the Madsen in their factories in conjunction with DRRS. However, things went seriously wrong. The drawings and other technical details were badly delayed, and even when they arrived they were too inaccurate to work from, upon which the Army Council sensibly announced in January 1916 that the whole project had been abandoned. New trials were started in 1917, principally to decide whether the Madsen might be suitable as a gun for tanks and aircraft. First reports were favourable, the gun it was said being in many respects superior to the Lewis gun, but as it would not fire upsidedown it was clearly unsuitable for aircraft use. At one stage there had been a suggestion that the DRRS should move its whole factory to England, but this bold proposal was never implemented and the Madsen gun passed from British history. It is probable that the gun's failure in Great Britain

was also due to the British insistence on a rimmed cartridge, which always tends to be a stumbling block in almost any automatic weapon. It is nevertheless clear that it needed robust cartridges since the rising action of the breechblock tended to catch the cartridge on its way into the chamber and distort it, which then led to difficulties over ejection. Its other fault, inherent in long recoil arms, is that the mechanism does not work very fast and the rate of fire is therefore slow. Some later models of the Madsen had a muzzle booster to trap part of the gases and speed the action but this led to an increase in ruptured cases unless the rounds were lubricated, never a desirable feature in an automatic weapon. It was made in a variety of calibres and the later models were equipped with tripods which gave it some of the characteristics of a GPMG.

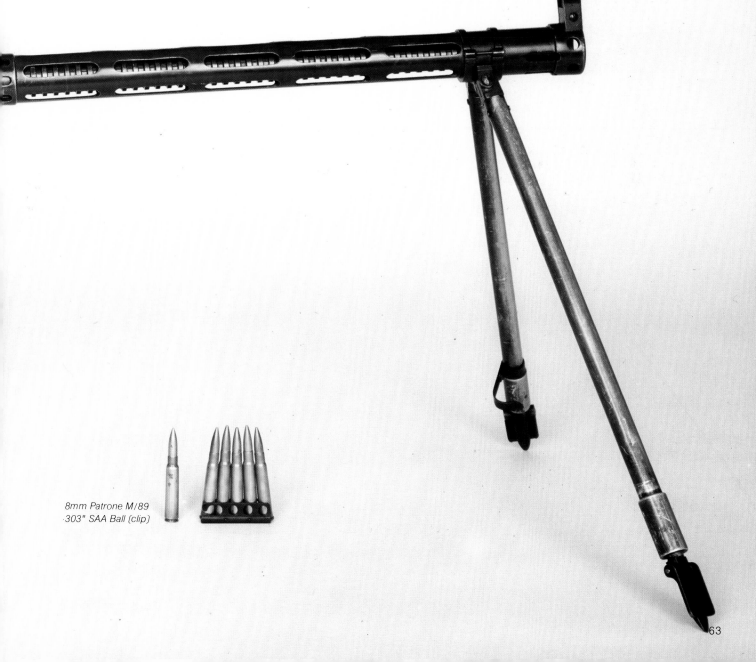

8mm Patrone M/89
·303" SAA Ball (clip)

CHAUCHAT MODÈLE 1915 (CSRG)

Length: 45″ (1143mm)
Weight: 19lb (8·62kg)
Barrel: 18·5″ (470mm)
Calibre: 8mm
Rifling: 4 groove r/hand
Operation: Long recoil
Feed: 20-round box
Cooling: Air
Cyclic Rate: 250 rpm
Muzzle Velocity:
2300 f/s (700 m/s)
Sights: 2188 yds (2000m)

In the early years of the 20th century, the French began to consider the possibility of introducing a very much lighter automatic weapon of the type which later came to be known as an automatic rifle. They therefore appointed a commission of four men to investigate and report on the idea, the individuals concerned being Colonel Chauchat and Messieurs Suterre, Ribeyrolle and Gladiator. After long deliberation this quartet came to the conclusion that the best answer lay in a weapon designed by a Hungarian engineer, Rudolf Frommer, who was an acknowledged expert in long recoil weapons, that is weapons in which the barrel and breechblock remained locked for virtually the whole of the backward action. The choice of this system was a peculiar one since the French were great exponents of the use of gas action to work an automatic weapon and had never previously seriously considered a recoil operated gun, with a long or short pattern. A few of these guns having been made at a French Government Arsenal, the model was accepted without any demur and there the matter rested. When trench warfare started in the autumn of 1914 it soon became apparent to all concerned that the key to the business was to be firepower, and the more the better, and various steps were taken to improve the situation in this respect. The problem was that the old concept of long fields of fire had gone. The opposing trenches were often a hundred yards (91·4m) or less apart and in the initial absence of obstacles (barbed wire being at first in short supply) a rush could some-

times cross this sort of ground, perhaps at first light, before the defenders could line their parapets. The need, therefore, was for light automatics which could be brought into action as easily as a rifle and yet develop fifteen or twenty times its firepower. As we shall see the the British adopted the Lewis, the Germans their light Maxim and the French settled for the Chauchat since it was in theory fully developed and easy to make, which would save a good deal of time. It was a bad decision and resulted in the French Army, and later the American Army, being equipped with what was undoubtedly quite the worst firearm to appear on either side in the whole course of a war which produced an amazing variety of new or newly resuscitated arms, good, bad, or indifferent. In the first place it was extremely badly made, even allowing for the exigencies and short cuts unavoidable in wartime when speed and ease of manufacture are important considerations. Much of it was constructed of ordinary commercial tubing never intended for the strains

inherent in an automatic weapon firing a full-sized rifle cartridge, and even really vital parts, locking lugs and similar essentials were stamped and pressed and screwed and generally botched together. As can be seen from the photograph the pistol grip was rough wood and the forehand grip no more than a crudely shaped tool handle. Lastly, as the components were made by a wide variety of sub-contractors, who had neither the time nor the skill to work to fine limits, and then assembled centrally, there was no real interchangeability. Presumably when a gun was assembled, various bits were roughly filed as necessary to make it work and that was sufficient. When the gun was fired (assuming that it did fire which was by no means always the case) the barrel and bolt recoiled together, the bolt being locked to the barrel by locking lugs. This action continued for the whole of the backward phase when the bolt was turned and unlocked allowing the barrel to go forward. The bolt then followed it, taking a round with it, chambering it, and

firing it. The long recoil necessarily caused a great deal of vibration, and bearing in mind that the gun, including its bipod, only weighed nineteen pounds (8·62kg) this made it virtually impossible to hold it steady on a target when firing automatic. One of the oddest features about the Chauchat was its semi-circular magazine. This was made necessary by the fact that the standard 8mm Lebel rifle cartridge, for which it was designed, had a very wide base. The front end of the magazine was engaged first and then the rear end pulled upwards until it was engaged and held by the magazine catch. The first round then, of course, had to be loaded manually by means of the cocking handle. When the Unites States Army arrived in France in 1918 its infantry was armed almost entirely with rifles, and it had to depend on its allies for automatic weapons of all kinds. The United States therefore contracted with the French to provide sufficient Chauchat guns to equip no less than nine divisions without further inspection or testing of them. If this sounds like bad

business practice, it must be remembered that there was a considerable degree of urgency in the matter which left the unfortunate Americans little choice but to accept what must be regarded as a pretty sharp bargain on the part of the French. After about sixteen thousand of them had been purchased in 8mm Lebel calibre the Americans very sensibly came to the conclusion that the need for two calibres of rifle ammunition was ridiculous and led to serious supply problems, and in August 1918 therefore arrangements were made to convert up to twenty-five thousand Chauchats to fire the standard ·30″ American rifle cartridge. The work was to be carried out by the original suppliers of the weapon, and in the event little more was done than rechamber them and incorporate a more normal box type magazine to suit the better shaped United States cart-cartridge. The resulting conversion, which was officially known as the ·30″ Model 1918, was, incredibly enough an even worse weapon than its predecessor, chiefly

because in addition to inheriting all its original faults it also developed some new ones of its own. In particular the narrower case of the American ·30″ cartridge stuck rather badly in the chamber when the gun became heated after a few rounds had been fired. It is ironical that at a time when the United States press was full of glowing accounts of the new range of Browning Automatic Rifles, the United States Army should be fighting the greatest war in its history with the most defective weapon to be found on either side. The American Infantry, who with true Anglo-Saxon disregard for the niceties of foreign pronunciation called the weapon the Shosho, cursed it interminably and threw it away in fury, so many being discarded in this manner that the original orders had to be increased considerably. To add insult to injury, when the United States Marine divisions arrived in France actually equipped with the excellent and well-tried Lewis gun, which the Savage Arms Company had been producing for some time in ·30″ calibre, they were at

once ordered to hand them in to be replaced by Chauchats. It is not clear whether this was in accordance with the French contract or due to the almost pathological dislike in the American Army's higher echelons of the Lewis gun. Whichever the case, it must have had a seriously adverse effect on these high quality troops. It is difficult after so long to decide quite why the French ever adopted the Chauchat and possibly just as well not to probe too deeply. Weapons developed by Commissions do tend to be unsatisfactory. There is an old story that the camel is the result of an early Commission to design a horse, which perhaps illustrates the case, but even so the Chauchat was exceptionally bad. Some of this no doubt was due to wartime manufacture and in this respect it has been compared to the British Sten gun of 1941, but the Sten, cheap though it may have been, did at least work. Surprisingly enough both the Belgians and the Greeks used the gun after the war, the Greeks calling their version the Gladiator.

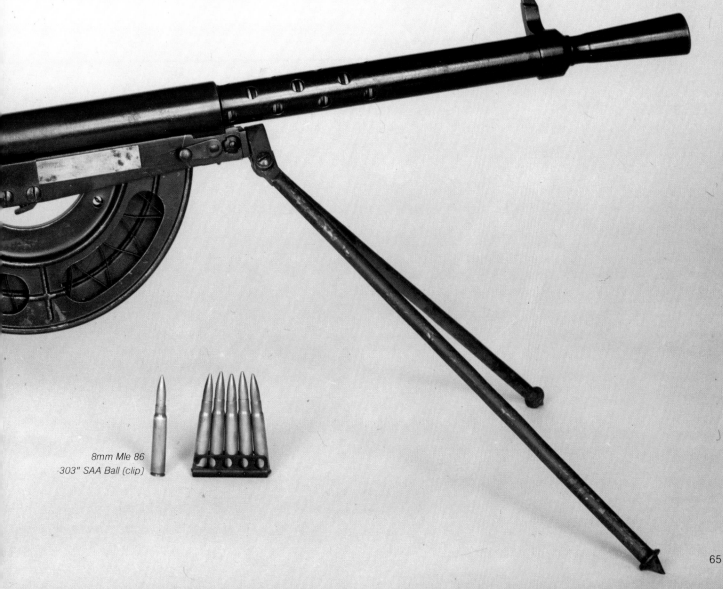

8mm Mle 86
·303″ SAA Ball (clip)

France
CHATELLERAULT MODÈLE 1924-9

Length: 42·5" (1080mm)
Weight: 20·25lb (9·12kg)
Barrel: 19·7" (500mm)
Calibre: 7·5mm
Rifling: 4 groove r/hand
Operation: Gas
Feed: 25-round box
Cooling: Air
Cyclic Rate: 550 rpm
Muzzle Velocity:
2590 f/s (790 m/s)
Sights: 2188 yds (2000m)

Although the main French medium machine gun, the Hotchkiss 1914, had served them well during World War I, they had suffered from start to finish from the lack of a reliable light machine gun, having had nothing better than the notorious Chauchat. At the very end of the war they had indeed ordered fifteen thousand of the new Browning Automatic Rifles from the United States but the war ended before these became available. Once the war had finished the French set to work seriously to remedy this grave deficiency by producing a thoroughly good and reliable light machine gun, and by 1921 prototypes had made their appearance, all having been made at Châtellerault, one of the great national arsenals. Like most nations, the French, impoverished by the war and reluctant to spend more than was essential on armaments when there was so much war damage to make good, had very little money available and it was therefore highly desirable that they should if possible produce a weapon which other countries would be anxious to buy. The first foreign state to show interest was Yugoslavia which was in the market for a new light machine gun. At first the Yugoslav Mission, which had toured much of Europe in their search, decided that the Hotchkiss would do them, but then they were offered the new French experimental gun at such a low price that they could not resist. Unfortunately manufacturing delays prevented this deal being carried through, so the French next turned to the Romanians who were also in the market. They were very interested indeed but unfortunately in the course of the trial an explosion occurred in the gun which injured several of the purchasing commission and caused the project to be abandoned. At first it was suspected that a defective cartridge had jammed a bullet in the bore and so caused the explosion when the next full charge bullet struck it, but this turned out to be false. The French, still confident, adopted the gun themselves in 1926 but before long had a series of similar explosions which naturally shook the morale of the soldiers whose business it was to fire it. This led to embarrassing demands for the replacement of the gun by something more reliable which was upsetting to the individuals who had worked so hard on it. Tests continued and it was eventually found that there was absolutely nothing wrong with the gun itself, the fault being due to poor metal and incorrect heat treatment, both the direct results of the over-riding need for economy. As soon as this was clear manufacture went ahead and there was no further trouble. The 1924 Model Châtellerault light machine gun was of orthodox appearance and action, being a gas and piston operated arm with a mechanism very similar to that of the Browning Automatic Rifle. It had two triggers, the forward one for single shots and the rear one for automatic fire, together with a selector which had to be previously set for the type of fire required. It was fitted with a gas regulator which could be used in conjunction with an

adjustable buffer to allow the firer to vary his cyclic rate, but perhaps most important of all it was designed to fire a new cartridge. The old Lebel 8mm round, which had been in service for many years, was badly shaped for use in automatic guns because of its disproportionately wide base which meant that any box magazine had to be excessively curved, the one on the Chauchat being a case in point. The French therefore designed a new 7·5mm rimless round, similar in type and general performance to the German 7·92mm cartridge, which assisted the proper functioning of the gun. There was a further modification in 1928 when the round was shortened slightly, after which the gun functioned with great efficiency. It was also simple to use and teach, an important matter for a country which relied on fairly short-term conscription for the great bulk of its armed forces. The

French, who had lost horrifying numbers of men in World War I, were naturally apprehensive of some further offensive activity in the future on the part of their German neighbours, and in the period 1929-1934 they worked hard on the Maginot Line, which was designed to place an impregnable barrier between them. In order to increase the firepower of the infantry garrisons the French made certain modifications to their Modèle 1924-29 which resulted in the Modèle 31. This was fundamentally the same weapon, but instead of the usual box magazine it was fitted with a huge side-mounted drum, similar to that of the Lewis gun in general principle but designed to hold no less than one hundred and fifty cartridges. This gun had a pistol grip only and was designed to fire from a loop-hole on a swivel mounting, and in order to allow a long burst without overheating the

French devised a system under which a small jet of cold water was squirted into the barrel between the extraction of the empty case and the loading of the next round into the chamber. The French kept this device secret and their claims regarding its effectiveness have never been finally verified. The gun was known as the Modèle 1931 and it was sufficiently successful for the French Air Force to take an interest in it. Further improvements resulted in two new versions, one belt-fed and the other fitted with a very large drum designed to hold five hundred cartridges; it was sixteen inches deep, and so heavy that it required special gears to drive it. The Châtellerault remained the main light machine gun of the French forces at the beginning of World War II, and after the fall of France the Germans made use of many captured ones to help arm their so-called Atlantic Wall which they

very soon began building, largely with workers from territories which they had over-run in central Europe, against an anticipated invasion by the Western Democracies. When the French Army was re-formed after the end of World War II it had to rely initially on a variety of weapons, British, American, and captured German, but very large numbers of serviceable Châtellerault light machine guns were recovered from varous sources and put to good use, being used extensively in French Indo-China and Algeria in the various colonial campaigns fought there. Although numbers are probably still in service in the ex-French colonies in Africa and elsewhere it is now obsolete in the French Army, which like most of the major military nations of the world now uses a general purpose machine gun, the MAS 52, or Arme Automatique Transformable Modèle 52.

7·5mm Mle 24 and Mle 29
·303" SAA Ball (clip)

Germany
LIGHT MAXIM MG08/15

Length: 55" (1398mm)
Weight: 39lb (17·7kg)
Barrel: 24" (610mm)
Calibre: 7·92mm
Rifling: 4 groove r/hand
Operation: Recoil
Feed: 250-round belt
Cooling: Water
Cyclic Rate: 400 rpm
Muzzle Velocity:
2900 f/s (885 m/s)
Sights: 2188 yds (2000m)

By the end of the first year of World War I the Allies had made good progress in turning over their industries to war production and were in addition greatly helped by the manufacturing capacity of the United States. Thus when the British Vickers guns were withdrawn from battalions the British were in a position to issue Lewis light machine guns to compensate for their loss, only a few to begin with although the scale increased considerably as the war progressed. The Germans naturally had the same idea. The Lewis came as something of a surprise to them but they soon had an answer to it in the shape of a light Maxim gun. Mechanically this new gun was very similar to the standard 08 Maxim, and as it first came into service in 1915 it was designated the Maschinengewehr 08/15, although it is now more generally known as the light Maxim. The new gun was water-cooled like its larger counterpart, but whereas the 08 Maxim had a pump which actually kept the water moving, and so helped it to dissipate its heat, the light Model had a plain but quite effective water jacket, bearing in mind that it was a light machine gun and not therefore intended for long bursts of continuous fire. It fired a fifty-round belt, an unusual system for a light machine gun but one which avoided any major redesign of the original mechanism, and was equipped with a belt box which fitted onto the right-hand side of the gun and allowed it to be moved rapidly without getting the belt twisted or dragging it in the mud, which was a common feature of trench warfare for most of the year. As this gun was so similar to the 08 Model it posed few manufacturing problems and thus the Germans were able to produce it in large numbers in a very short period. It was an effective weapon and soon became as popular with the German infantry as the Lewis gun was with those on the British side. The true value of the light machine gun, however, really became obvious in the early months of 1918. By this time the Russian Revolution had largely solved Germany's problem of fighting on two fronts and she was able to concentrate a higher proportion of her Armies on the Western Front than had previously been the case. The British and the French, who had done most of the attacking in the war until then, were both impatiently waiting the arrival of the new American Armies, which although largely untrained and completely inexperienced, would enable them finally to break the German line by a series of widely spaced blows which their reserves would be inadequate to meet. The Germans therefore decided to strike first, not because they could then hope to utterly defeat the Allies, but principally in the hope that a major success would finally obtain them peace on reasonable terms. The attack fell on the British, who were still weak and exhausted from the terrible wearing battle of Ypres the year before. They were holding a series of redoubts arranged in depth rather than a continuous line, these positions being mutually supporting with machine guns and covered by artillery fire. The German plan was to make a mass attack preceded by specially trained storm troops, and it so happened that on the morning it was launched there was heavy fog which largely neutralized the British machine guns and artillery whilst offering ideal opportunities for infiltration by the storm troops. It was here that the light Maxim really came into its own, since the infiltrators could use it to knock out machine guns from the flank or rear and generally to cause confusion. The bigger Maxims were, of course, far too heavy for this role, but the light one, used in conjunction with some of the new sub-machine guns which were just beginning to

7·92mm Gewehr Patrone 98
·303" SAA Ball (clip)

reach the Germans, was an ideal weapon and indicated clearly the true future role of weapons of this type. In the event the German attack failed, and when the Allied counter-offensive started a few months later the British Lewis guns were handled in the same bold way. Apart from their ground role the Light Maxims were also used in the novel role of arming German Zeppelins against Allied aircraft. Many of the early raids on the United Kingdom were delivered by lighter-than-air aircraft of this description, and as a matter of morale it became necessary for the British to destroy them. The Germans mounted them both along the top of the en- velope and in the cupolas themselves, and as the airships were extremely stable under reasonable weather conditions it was hoped that a sufficient volume of accurate fire could be produced to fend off attack- ing aircraft. In the early days, before the advent of machine guns synchronized to fire through the propellor, it was quite difficult for the pilot of a single-seater aircraft to shoot with any great accuracy, so that the Germans were probably not too optimistic in their assessment of the situa- tion. In a sense there is a close parallel between it and the practice of placing large numbers of machine guns on the American B-17 Flying Fortresses of World War II. As it happened the Zeppelins were finally and conclusively defeated by the invention by the British of the incendiary bullet. The airships were filled with hydrogen, which although very light and thus having good lifting qualities, was also highly inflammable and as they offered huge and relatively slow-moving targets they were shot down in such considerable numbers that the Germans soon ceased to use them for their bombing raids. There was yet another development of the Light Maxim in the shape of an air- cooled model in which the bulky and heavy water jacket was replaced by a simple ventilated casing, it having been found from experience that the movement of airships through the air was in itself a sufficient means of cooling for automatic guns. After the airships had been discontinued a version of this air-cooled Maxim was issued to the German Army under the designation 08/18. It was not a success and was presumably only used because by 1918, the year of its issue, the Germans were so short of *matériel* of all kinds that they could not afford to waste anything. When used on the ground this air-cooled version, which does not appear to have been fitted even with a bipod, overheated so rapidly that it was of very limited use. It is said that the guns had to be grouped into ad hoc batteries so that they could fire one at a time while the others cooled, which can hardly have been a very satisfactory arrangement for the hard pressed German infantry. Apart from its intrinsic interest the Light Maxim is in a sense unique in being the only true light machine gun used in war by the Germans, who in World War II were equipped with general purpose guns in the shape of the MG34 and the MG42.

The air-cooled Maxim

Great Britain
LEWIS MACHINE GUN

Length: 50·5" (1282mm)
Weight: 27lb (12·25kg)
Barrel: 26" (660mm)
Calibre: ·303"
Rifling: 4 groove l/hand
Operation: Gas
Feed: 47-round Drum
Cooling: Air
Cyclic Rate: 550 rpm
Muzzle Velocity:
2440 f/s (744 m/s)
Sights: 1900 yds (1738m)

The opening years of the 20th century saw an awakening interest in light automatic weapons, one of the people involved being Colonel Isaac Newton Lewis of the United States Coast Artillery. His initial interest was naturally in artillery, which he had studied in Europe and in the early years of the 20th century he invented a number of range-finders and other instruments for artillery use. This naturally built his reputation in the world of firearms so it is not altogether surprising that he should have been approached in 1910 by an arms company which offered him a considerable inducement to develop a machine gun, based on patents which they had previously acquired from an inventor named Samuel McClean. The weapon was far too heavy and clumsy but Lewis saw that it had potential and reworked the whole design so extensively that he may be for practical purposes regarded as its inventor. By 1912 Lewis had four guns available, largely hand-made prototypes, and with these he gave some impressive demonstrations to various high-ranking Army officers many of whom were extremely impressed, but

who took no further action. Lewis then carried out an experiment which showed him to be a very forward looking individual. He arranged privately for one of his guns to be fired from an aeroplane, his contact being a Captain Chandler, who successfully fired a magazine at a target on the ground. Considering the primitive nature of the aircraft used the idea was remarkable and the fact that it was not at once followed up does not detract from its value. After this Colonel Lewis formally offered his gun to the United States but it was rejected. The reason for this is by no means clear although it is possible that there was a serious clash of personality between the Army Chief of Staff and Colonel Lewis, who appears to have been an outspoken individual and no respecter of rank. Whatever the cause Lewis went off to Belgium with his guns in 1913 and eventually a company was set up in Liege to manufacture them on a commercial basis. A few were taken into service by the Belgian Army, but when the Germans overran the country in 1914 the whole business was handed over to the large British firm, the Birmingham Small Arms

Company. As the opposing armies settled down to trench warfare it became clear that by far the most important infantry weapon was to be the machine gun. The British Vickers had originally been issued on a basis of two per battalion but the need for flexibility made it clear that they should be grouped. In 1915 therefore they were centralized into a Machine Gun Corps, and in order partially to fill the gap four Lewis guns were issued to each battalion. The principle on which the gun worked was simple. Gases were tapped off from the barrel to drive back a piston, which took the bolt with it, extracting and ejecting the empty case. A stud on top of the bolt also activated a feed arm which took the next round from the double-layer, circular magazine on top of the gun, the mechanism being equipped with two stop pawls which ensured that the magazine rotated the correct amount only. During this backward movement a rack on the underside of the piston engaged a pinion which wound a clock-type spring which took over, driving the working parts forward and chambering and firing the round. The bolt was of the

turning variety with lugs which locked into recesses in the barrel extension. In order to keep the barrel cool it was surrounded by radial fins, the ends of which are visible in the illustration, these being surrounded in turn by a light outer casing to keep the whole thing clean. The gun was designed to fire automatic only, but a good gunner with a sensitive trigger finger could often fire single rounds, while 'double tapping', that is firing two rounds at a time, was very simple. The British Army, being essentially conservative in its outlook, at first regarded the Lewis gun with some suspicion, feeling that it was no more than a cheap second-rate substitute for their well-tried Vickers guns, but they very soon adopted it with enthusiasm. It was of course a light machine gun, the first the British Army every used, with a light machine gun's limitations when compared to a medium type weapon. But it afforded a great volume of aimed fire at the ranges required, usually below two hundred yards (183m). In defence it was considered desirable to place it on a flank so as to take a charging line in enfilade, preferably when it was held

up by wire which gave the gunner a stationary target. In the attack (and it must be borne in mind that in World War I most attacks were over a few hundred yards only) it was regarded as an ideal opportunity weapon for engaging enemy medium machine guns, since owing to its relative lightness it was possible for one or two men to stalk such targets with some degree of success. As manufacture increased, both in England and the United States, the scale of issue of the Lewis gun in the British Army became progressively higher. There were sixteen platoons in a British battalion of four companies and by 1918 each platoon had two Lewis guns, a further four being held centrally at Battalion Headquarters principally for use against low-flying aircraft. Apart from their great value as ground weapons, they were also extensively used to arm aircraft. When the war started in 1914 the early aircraft then available were considered invaluable for reconnaissance, as indeed they were, but were not considered as weapons. It soon came about, however, that pilots and observers began taking up with them

pistols and rifles with which to engage enemy airmen who approached them too closely, and very soon the fighter aircraft had come into existence. Owing to the ease with which the magazine could be changed, the Lewis became popular as an observer's gun. When used in this role the finned cooling device was dispensed with, since the passage of the gun through the air at relatively high speed cooled it effectively. The Lewis gun remained in service with the British Army until almost the outbreak of World War II, when it was replaced with the Bren. Apart from its basic ground role it could also be used as a light weapon against aircraft, being mounted on a rather flimsy contraption like a music stand and fitted with a special type of sight which allowed the firer to make some attempt to estimate lead. Having regard to the relatively slow speed of the aircraft then in service this was reasonably effective, especially when it was possible to use tracer ammunition with the gun. The Lewis was in its day quote 'a good gun of its kind', although its complex construction made it susceptible to a bewildering number of

stoppages. British Small Arms Training, 1931, Volume II lists six 'immediate action' stoppages, and seven possible stoppages, the detailing and explanation of which add up to thirty-one pages of small print, and although these could be taught to the long term regular soldier they were a considerable stumbling block as far as wartime training was concerned. In really expert hands the Lewis gun was capable of quite excellent shooting. In 1932 Quarter Master Sergeant Instructor P.G. Cyster of the British Small Arms School Corps, a veteran of World War I who had won the Distinguished Conduct Medal for gallantry, fired two hundred and nineteen rounds at a target four feet (1·2m) in diameter at 300 yards (274m) range and only missed it three times, the great bulk of his shots being in a central circle two feet (·6m) in diameter. Although the Lewis gun had ceased to be the official light machine gun of the British Infantry before 1939, thousands were still held in store when the war started and in view of the desperate shortage of arms of all sorts these were quickly re-issued, mainly for use as light anti-aircraft weapons.

The Lewis anti-aircraft sight

·303" SAA Ball
·303" SAA Ball (clip)

HOTCHKISS MARK 1

Length: 46·75" (1187mm)
Weight: 27lb (12·25kg)
Barrel: 23·5" (597mm)
Calibre: ·303"
Rifling: 4 groove r/hand
Operation: Gas
Feed: 30-round strip
Cooling: Air
Cyclic Rate: 500 rpm
Muzzle Velocity:
2440 f/s (744 m/s)
Sights: 2000 yds (1829m)

It is difficult to discuss any aspects of automatic weapons without sooner or later introducing the name Hotchkiss, a famous French company which has been closely concerned with the development of such weapons ever since they were first invented. In 1885 Mr B. B. Hotchkiss, founder of the firm, died and in 1887 a young American, Laurence V. Benét, was appointed manager. He had spent many years in the arms business and his father, himself a retired general and a famous name in the United States Ordnance world, had advised him to go to Europe where the demand for military firearms greatly exceeded that of the United States.

Benét very soon saw that the small arms of the future would be automatic weapons, and quickly turned his mind to the problems of producing a series of efficient ones; in this task he was greatly helped by his assistant Henry Mercié. Their joint work on the production of medium machine guns has been described elsewhere in this section and there is therefore no need to cover the same ground here; what is important is that in 1909 the two produced a light machine gun, which they then described as an automatic rifle. It was generally known on the continent as the Hotchkiss Portative, but Great Britain and the United States tended to refer to it as the Benét-Mercié Machine Rifle Model 1909. The French Army adopted this weapon but nothing much happened about it, and like other potentially good arms it had rather disappeared from view by 1914, leaving the field open to the inferior Chauchat. The American Army also adopted it and used it in some of its local border campaigns. Colonel Chinn states in his book *The Machine Gun* that when the famous Mexican bandit Villa raided the town of

Columbus New Mexico, one night, the Benét-Mercié guns failed to open fire because their detachments claimed that they could not use their weapons after dark because the mechanism was too complex. The United States' press ran the story for all it was worth, calling the Benét-Mercié the daylight gun and suggesting unkindly that the rules of warfare should be amended to allow fighting to take place in daylight only, so that the Army could use its machine guns. This sort of derisive treatment finally undermined the confidence of the United States Army in the gun and it was abandoned in 1917, ironically enough at the very period in their history when the United States would require every automatic gun it could lay its hands on. Soon after the outbreak of World War I the British Army adopted the Lewis gun as its infantry light machine gun and soon afterwards there arose the question of a similar weapon for the British cavalry. The role of horsed cavalry in modern war had been shrinking steadily for many years, principally because the rapid improvements in small arms in the second half of the

19th Century meant that mounted troops could not defeat infantry except under the most advantageous circumstances. In the early days both sides had used cavalry for reconnaissance and screening duties and there had even been one or two cavalry versus cavalry actions with sword or lance, but trench warfare had put an end to all this. In the early desperate battles of 1914 and 1915 the British cavalry, well trained as riflemen, had done a great deal of good work by plugging gaps in the over-extended infantry lines, but once the fronts were stabilized they tended to be held in reserve for the great breakthrough which was confidently expected. Their role would then be the exploitation of success and the harassing of enemy rearguards, and for this they would naturally require light automatic weapons to supplement their rifle fire. The Lewis was tried experimentally but found too bulky. The cavalry needed something light which could be carried in a saddle bucket by one man if possible, and their choice fell on the Benét-Mercié. Great Britain purchased the rights to

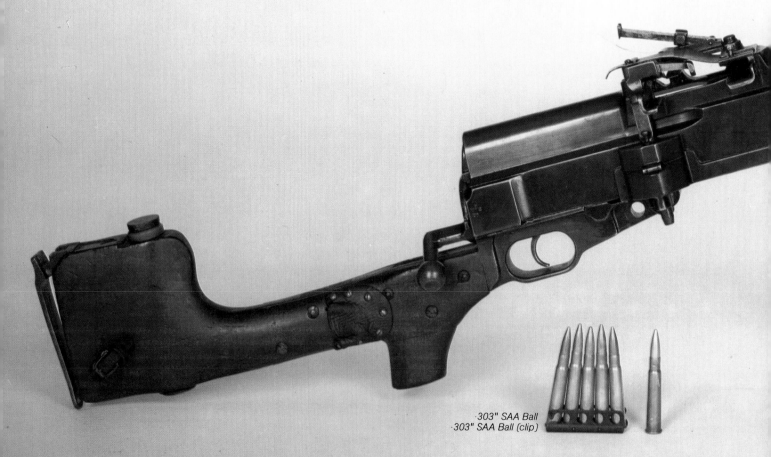

·303" SAA Ball
·303" SAA Ball (clip)

manufacture the gun and it was officially adopted in 1916, when it became known as the Hotchkiss Machine Gun Mark 1. It was of course manufactured to take the British ·303" cartridge. The gun illustrated, which is the Mark 1, operated in the usual way by the action of gas tapped off from the bore and striking a piston to which the breechblock was attached. The forward action of the mechanism under the impulse of the return spring caused the bolt to turn and lock into a fitting, forming part of the barrel extension and known by its French term of fermeture nut. The cocking handle was a long rod, and its rear end, which was basically similar in appearance to a rifle bolt, can be seen just above the pistol grip in the photograph. It was pulled back to its full extent (almost six inches, 152mm) to cock and then forced forward

again. When it was fully home it could then be turned to the right until a line on it coincided with either A, R, or S on the receiver which gave automatic fire, rounds only, or safe as required. It was considered best to use both hands to cock the gun. The great breakthrough on the Western Front, which had been confidently predicted before the battle of Loos in September 1915, finally came three years later, but by that time the tank had come onto the military scene so that the cavalry dreams of hunting a broken German Army back to the Rhine were not realized. The Hotchkiss gun was also a tank weapon, if only a secondary one, and played its part in the last great phase. Many soldiers believed that once World War I was over the cavalry would virtually disappear, to be replaced by the tank and the armoured car, and it would in

fact have been a very sensible, if revolutionary, re-organization. Cavalry influence was, however, too strong. The last war, it was implied, had been a fearful mistake, and in any future conflict better sense would prevail and the cavalry would have a chance to fulfil its traditional role. Allenby's brilliant campaign in Palestine was always quoted in justification, although the circumstances there had been so different that it was dangerous if not downright dishonest to attempt to draw any lessons from it. In the meantime the cavalry survived, if somewhat reduced in size, and with it survived the Hotchkiss gun, bumping along on its packhorse on the flank of the troop. It was a remarkable anachronism at a time when in Germany, the outlines at least of the new Panzer divisions were beginning to

take shape. A few guns even remained in the infantry as armament for the funny little Carden-Loyd carriers which were just beginning to offer a glimpse of what the future would be like. By the time World War II had started in 1939 the British horsed cavalry had virtually gone. A few units remained, mostly in the Middle East and India, but the bulk had become Armoured Corps. The Hotchkiss gun was still in limited service, for when the Mobilized Yeomanry Regiments went to the Middle East in 1940 they went, almost incredibly, on a horsed basis, almost exactly as their predecessors had gone there to fight under Allenby a quarter of a century before, each troop having a section of Hotchkiss guns on led packhorses. Even after they had relinquished it, it remained in reserve and was only finally discarded in 1946.

BEARDMORE-FARQUHAR EXPERIMENTAL

Length: 49·5" (1258mm)
Weight: 19lb (8·62kg)
Barrel: 26·5" (673mm)
Calibre: ·303"
Rifling: 4 groove r/hand
Operation: Gas
Feed: 81-round drum
Cooling: Air
Cyclic Rate: c500 rpm
Muzzle Velocity:
2440 f/s (744 m/s)
Sights: 1800 yds (1646m)

This gun got its name from the well-known Birmingham arms factory of Beardmore, and M. G. Farquhar its inventor. Although best known as a persistent if largely unsuccessful inventor of automatic weapons, Colonel Farquhar had also had a good deal of practical experience of war, having won the Distinguished Service Order in the South African war of 1899-1902. His first recorded venture in the field of automatic weapons was when he produced an automatic rifle which he had jointly invented with a Mr Hill, for trial by the Automatic Rifle Committee set up by the British Army to test weapons of that type. This gun, although well made by the Beardmore company of Birmingham, was extremely complex and was therefore rejected as being unsuitable for service. In 1917 a modified and somewhat improved version was again submitted to the Small Arms

Committee but was again rejected, largely because after about four hundred rounds had been fired the gun fouled badly and the feed was affected. This rifle, it should be said, still had a conical magazine of the type illustrated in the rifles section of this book (see pages 172-173). In 1919 Colonel Farquhar produced what was virtually a new gun, worked by a new system and fed by a horizontal double-layered drum magazine, holding eighty-one rounds and driven by clockwork. The last round in this drum was a fixed dummy which caused the mechanism to stop in the rear position, thus calling attention to the fact that a fresh magazine was required. The inventor was officially informed that there was at that time absolutely no prospect of the British Army being in the market for a new light automatic weapon since it had more than ample supplies of its well-tried Lewis and Hotchkiss guns which had given excellent service during the previous four years, and reasons of economy alone demanded that they should be kept in service. Colonel Farquhar, however, said that he would still like to demonstrate the gun and this was agreed to. The tests were neither complete nor severe, but from its limited observations the committee seemed to be favourably disposed, and although they themselves could hold out no hope of an

order they suggested that the newly-formed Royal Air Force might be interested. It was a new service, still in the process of development and possibly even with funds to spare. The Royal Air Force duly tested the gun with a view to using it in aircraft and their report was favourable. It was light, always a good point for an airman, and it was efficient, having been thoroughly tested at all angles at 18,000 feet. Nevertheless it was not wanted. The war was over, retrenchment and economy were the twin orders of the day so the gun was rejected. Three years later, in 1922, the Beardmore-Farquhar combination, not apparently discouraged, tried something new, this time a belt-fed ·5" calibre heavy machine gun principally for anti-aircraft use, which again was not accepted. In the same year they produced another, updated version of the light model. This new model was of orthodox appearance, bearing in fact a fairly strong resemblance to

the later Russian Degtyaryev, but its main point of interest was its unique mechanism, which was based on a most unusual mixture of gas and spring operation. Virtually all orthodox gas-operated light machine guns have a piston which is driven back by the pressure of gas tapped off the bore near the muzzle, taking the breechblock with it, and which is then driven forward by the energy stored in the return spring which it has compressed on its rearward travel. The Beardmore was unusual in that the piston was not directly connected to the bolt. Instead of an operating rod, there was a coil spring and when the piston moved back it compressed this spring. The other end bore against the bolt and this bolt was so designed that the pressure of the gas helped to keep it locked. When the pressure had dropped to a safe level the piston spring overcame the bolt locking and the usual reciprocating motion began. When the bolt reached the

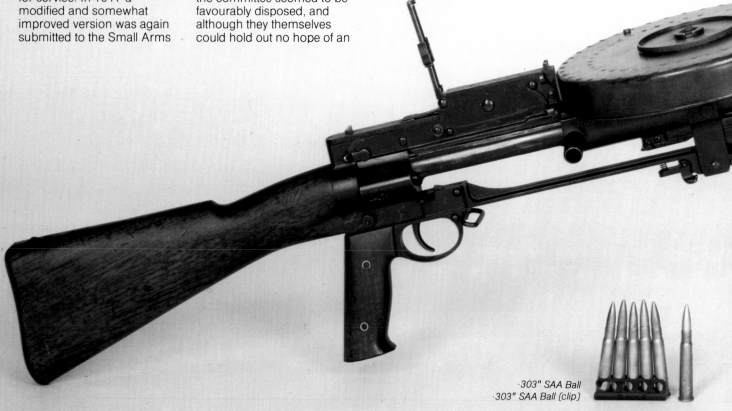

·303" SAA Ball
·303" SAA Ball (clip)

buffer it tripped the piston sear and the return spring could then force bolt and piston forward again to repeat the cycle. The usual feed action took place on the forward stroke, but another peculiarity was that the return spring was stretched, and not compressed as on all other guns. One consequence of this was a smooth action with much less likelihood of stoppages and extraction problems. But it also had a much slower rate of fire than its rivals. The use of an intermediate spring had certain advantages. In the first place it meant that the slight but inevitable difference in the pressure developed by rounds made no difference to the functioning of the gun. Also, and perhaps more important, it did away with a great deal of the jolting inevitable from the rapid backward and forward action of an orthodox piston. This allowed the gun to be made very light in weight without its accuracy being affected by undue vibration. The Hythe

tests, which were comparative ones on a number of light machine guns, were carried out in October 1922, and the Beardmore-Farquhar did not shine. The main complaint, surprising in a Beardmore arm, was of generally poor quality materials which covered a number of defects. Extraction was weak and the gun had a potentially dangerous tendency to stop with the working parts forward and a live round in the chamber, due presumably to the extractor not riding over the cartridge rim and the striker not reaching the cap in consequence. The feed arrangements were reported as being faulty and the accuracy of the gun dropped off badly after the barrel had become hot. Finally, in an endurance test, the gun was said to have blown up after eleven thousand rounds. The reason for this was not stated but it clearly marked the evident demise of this interesting but ill-fated weapon.

Great Britain
VICKERS-BERTHIER MACHINE GUN

Length: 46·5" (1181mm)
Weight: 20·8lb (9·43kg)
Barrel: 23·9" (607mm)
Calibre: ·303"
Rifling: 5 groove r/hand
Operation: Gas
Feed: 30-round box
Cooling: Air
Cyclic Rate: 500 rpm
Muzzle Velocity:
2440 f/s (744 m/s)
Sights: 1600 yds (1464m)

The Vickers-Berthier light machine gun was almost entirely French by origin. By the beginning of the 20th Century the thoughts of many soldiers and designers of military arms were turning to the idea of what could then perhaps best be described as an automatic rifle, a weapon with which one soldier could produce a considerable volume of fire without his mobility being any more restricted than it would have been by a normal rifle. The French were very active in this field and gave a good deal of encouragement to any designer working on such weapons. In particular they encouraged any technically minded officers to try their hand at producing a weapon of this kind; or if not a weapon itself, at least an idea for one and one of the most successful of them was a Lieutenant André Berthier. As early as 1905 he produced a

workable weapon, based on a straight pull rifle with an added piston, and similar in principle to Captain Cei-Rigotti's rifle on which it may have been based. This weapon, which he patented in Belgium, earned him an honorary title from the Sultan of Turkey but achieved little else, principally because it was not considered to be sufficiently robust for service use, but the young officer continued with his experiments and by 1908 had produced another and somewhat more substantial weapon. This worked well, being mechanically similar to the Browning Automatic Rifle, and was particularly remarkable for its cooling system. The barrel had an outer jacket, at each end of which was a length of rubber piping connected to a rubber bulb, something like that of an old-fashioned motor-horn, and filled with water. As the barrel got hot the gunner or his assistant, simply squeezed one bulb thus driving the water through the space between the barrel and the jacket and into the bulb at the other end, whence it could be squeezed back again as required. This odd system was supplemented by a more modern one of using a second barrel which could be changed quickly as often as

was necessary. In spite of its undeniable efficiency nothing more was done about the gun, and even when World War I made clear the need for a weapon of this type the French opted for the crude and inefficient Chauchat, thus missing the chance of arming their soldiers with one of the most advanced light automatic weapons then in existence. Not surprisingly the enterprising inventor became a General, and in 1916 went to America with a view to investigating the possibilities of selling, or at least producing it there. Both the Unites States Army and the Marines liked the weapon and recommended its adoption, and considerable orders were actually placed, but the firm concerned ran into financial trouble, and by the time things were sorted out the **war was over and the project had to be shelved in the early** 1920s the British firm of Vickers bought the manufacturing rights for Berthier guns and began to

make a modified version of the 1908 model. The post-war period was not a good time to sell arms, but a few small countries purchased the gun which just about allowed Vickers to keep their factory going. The British Government was at that time considering the adoption of a new machine gun and in 1924 Vickers, understandably anxious to be considered for such a lucrative contract, wrote to them that they had a new and improved model available. This gun was demonstrated to the Small Arms Committee in January 1925 and apart from some minor points, which could easily be put right, it was reported as being efficient. The first report referred to it as being a serious rival to the Browning Automatic Rifle, which was also being considered, although somewhat heavier and probably more expensive to produce. The chief problem was that the magazine spring jammed occasionally when

·303" SAA Ball
·303" SAA Ball (clip)

the full thirty rounds were put in but performed well with twenty-eight, an odd anticipation of a similar defect in the Bren gun. It was considered that the magazine might perhaps interfere with the use of the gun in the anti-aircraft role, but this was not believed to be serious. The tests proceeded. Two more guns, complete with spare barrels and accessories were bought for some £240, and at the end of this series the Vickers-Berthier came out best. A new entry, the ZB, was second, with the Madsen third and the Browning trailing somewhat in fourth place. Next year there were further tests, this time with a light outer aluminium jacket for cooling purposes, this presumably because the belated General Staff specification made it clear that the need was for a general purpose gun to replace both the Vickers and the Lewis. The stated need was for a gun which could fire fifteen hundred rounds in

fifteen minutes and five thousand in thirty, and the general opinion was that the Vickers-Berthier could be improved to this standard although the report suggested that the sustained fire barrel might have to weigh as much as twenty pounds (9·1kg). Heavier barrels were then produced by Messrs Vickers, the weight not being stated, and the stage was then set for the final trials. Things understandably moved slowly in peacetime, particularly when economy was of paramount importance, and in 1933 the Indian Army became impatient and settled unilaterally on the Vickers-Berthier Mark 3 as a replacement for the Lewis gun, although they did not apparently regard it as being in any sense a general purpose gun and were careful to retain the well-tried Vickers medium gun to fulfil this role. The British Army were somewhat more cautious and decided to go

on with their methodical testing. At that stage the field had been reduced to two, the Vickers-Berthier and the Czechoslovakian ZB26, and the general line of the reports seemed to favour the Vickers. In 1934 the final endurance trials were held at Hythe under the detailed supervision of the War Office Experimental Small Arms Wing, and in the course of these the Czech gun began to demonstrate its unmistakeable superiority. Even with its new heavy barrel the Vickers-Berthier began to overheat very badly until the whole thing jammed with a live round locked in the breech. This round exploded when the breech was opened, blowing off the extractor and generally causing consternation. It was found with the ZB that the fouling was mostly confined to the gas cylinder, and that the ability to rotate the body of the gun inside the bipod sleeve did a great deal to clear it away. The gun fired ninety rounds each minute for

five consecutive minutes whereas the Vickers-Berthier could only maintain that rate for three. The report described it as definitely inferior to its rival, which clinched the matter in favour of the weapon that was shortly to become a good deal better known as the Bren. In spite of its rejection the Vickers-Berthier, which was a perfectly adequate gun, remained in service with the Indian Army for some time, considerable numbers being made at the well-known Indian rifle factory at Ishapore. Once World War II had started the constant interchange between the British and Indian Army formations and units caused complications over spare parts and training so that the Vickers-Berthier was gradually phased out in favour of the Bren gun. Had it not been for the sudden appearance of the ZB gun, the Vickers-Berthier might well have been adopted as the standard British gun.

Great Britain
BREN LIGHT MACHINE GUN

Length (gun):
45·5" (1156mm)
Weight (gun): 22·5lb (10·2kg)
Weight (tripod):
26·5lb (12kg)
Barrel: 25" (635mm)
Calibre: ·303"
Rifling: 6 groove r/hand
Operation: Gas
Feed: 30-round box
Cooling: Air
Cyclic Rate: 500 rpm
Muzzle Velocity:
2440 f/s (744 m/s)
Sights: 2000 yds (1829m)

The Bren gun was developed from the Czechoslovakian ZB 26 in the mid-1930s and began to reach the British infantry in 1938 in place of the older Lewis gun. Its arrival coincided with a reorganization of the infantry under which the Vickers guns were removed from battalions and grouped into special units, leaving battalions with light machine guns only. The new rifle company had three platoons, each of three sections of ten or eleven men, and each section had a Bren gun, extra guns being provided for anti-aircraft defence and as armament for the new light tracked carriers which were just becoming available. The basic mechanism of the new gun was similar to that of its Czech prototype and has been described elsewhere in this book. It was designed for either single rounds or bursts, this being controlled by a change lever, the trigger pull being noticeably longer for single rounds than for automatic fire. The earliest guns had a butt strap so that the firer could keep it in the shoulder without holding it, and a handle below the butt for the left hand grip whilst firing. They also had a rather elaborate backsight with a drum and a pivoted lever carrying the aperture, and in view of the top mounted magazine the sights were offset to the left. Each gun had a spare-parts wallet containing a combination tool and small replacement parts, and a holdall containing cleaning kit and the second barrel which could be put on to the gun in two or three seconds. These items were carried by the firer (No 1) and his assistant (No 2) respectively and were sufficient to keep the gun in action under all battle conditions. Twenty-five magazines were issued for each gun, two steel boxes of twelve each with the other in the gun chest, which led to the issue of the 1937 pattern equipment in which the older multiple pouch pattern was replaced by the familiar box pouches designed to carry Bren magazines. Although the magazine capacity was nominally thirty it was soon found that this was too many, and the total was reduced to twenty-eight. In view of the use of rimmed cartridges magazines had to be loaded carefully and the commonest stoppage on the gun, fortunately easy to clear,

No. 2 barrel

was caused by neglect in this respect. A number of tripods were carried so that the Bren could if necessary be laid on fixed lines so as to be able to cover likely approaches at night or in smoke or fog. The two main members of the frame each contained an extra half-leg and by the use of these a high tripod could be made for anti-aircraft purposes. Brens permanently allocated for air defence were usually mounted in pairs on Motley mountings and had special attachments which allowed them to take hundred-round drum magazines instead of the standard box. The Bren proved to be a most reliable and efficient gun and all who used it, British, Commonwealth, and the Free Forces of a number of occupied countries, had great confidence in it and came to regard it with affection. In defence it formed the basic framework of interlocking fire power, and in the attack it was sufficiently light to be carried and used from the hip like a sub-machine gun. It was in fact possible for a reasonably strong man to fire it from the shoulder in the standing position and this was often done at close quarters. It had a relatively slow rate of fire compared with the German MG 42 and the various Japanese light machine guns which made it easy to identify in battle, but it had a remarkable capacity for sustained fire so that even when very foul an increase in the flow of gas would keep it firing. Regular barrel changing was desirable but even then there were occasions when barrels began to glow with heat. As the Bren fired from an open bolt, that is breechblock and cartridge were to the rear until the trigger was actually pressed, there was no risk of a round cooking-off prematurely in an over-heated chamber. It is said that on occasions the Australians, always enterprising, increased the rate of fire significantly by putting the striker spring from a No 36 grenade on to the return spring rod. The Bren gun inevitably went through a number of modifications during the war. These were entirely concerned with simplifying manufacturing processes by either dispensing with non-essential items or at least making them less complex. Among other items to go were the butt strap and the under-butt handle, while the tripod legs were made non-adjustable and the backsight simplified. In spite of this the gun remained substantially unchanged. As the war progressed the fixed line tripod tended to fall into disuse and was rarely used for anti-aircraft purposes, it having been found that provided tracer ammunition was used, the gun could be fired from the hip against aircraft by the so-called hosepipe method. Initially all Brens were made at Enfield, but by the end of the war over half of them were of Canadian manufacture. The Bren continued to be the standard British and Commonwealth light machine gun for some years after the war and saw a great deal of active service round the world in a series of post-war minor campaigns. When Great Britain went over to the standard 7·62mm NATO round a number of the later marks of Bren were converted to fire it and many weapons of this type are still in use in non-infantry units. These converted guns, which in modern fashion are denominated L4A1 to L4A6, are readily recognizable by the absence of the familiar cone-shaped flash hider and the straight magazine, the latter being made necessary by the different shape of the rimless NATO round.

·303" SAA Ball
·303" SAA Ball (clip)

BREN LIGHT MACHINE GUN (CUTAWAY)

The Bren gun will fire automatic if the change lever is forward, or single shots if it is back. When the cartridge is fired at automatic, some of the gases pass through the gas regulator and into the gas cylinder where they strike the piston and force it back. When the piston has moved about half an inch (13mm) the tail of the breechblock drops down from its locking recess, and block and piston continue back together. During this phase the empty case is extracted and ejected and the return spring is compressed by the action of its rod. When the force of the gas is expended, the backward action stops and the return spring forces the working parts forward. Feed-pieces on the breechblock strip the bottom round from the magazine and push it into the chamber. The piston continues briefly, lifting the tail of the breechblock into its recess; the piston post then hits the striker and fires the round. When single shots are required the initial action is the same, but when the mechanism reaches its rearward position it is held there by the sear, a metal stud connected to the trigger. When the trigger is pressed the sear drops and the working parts go forward.

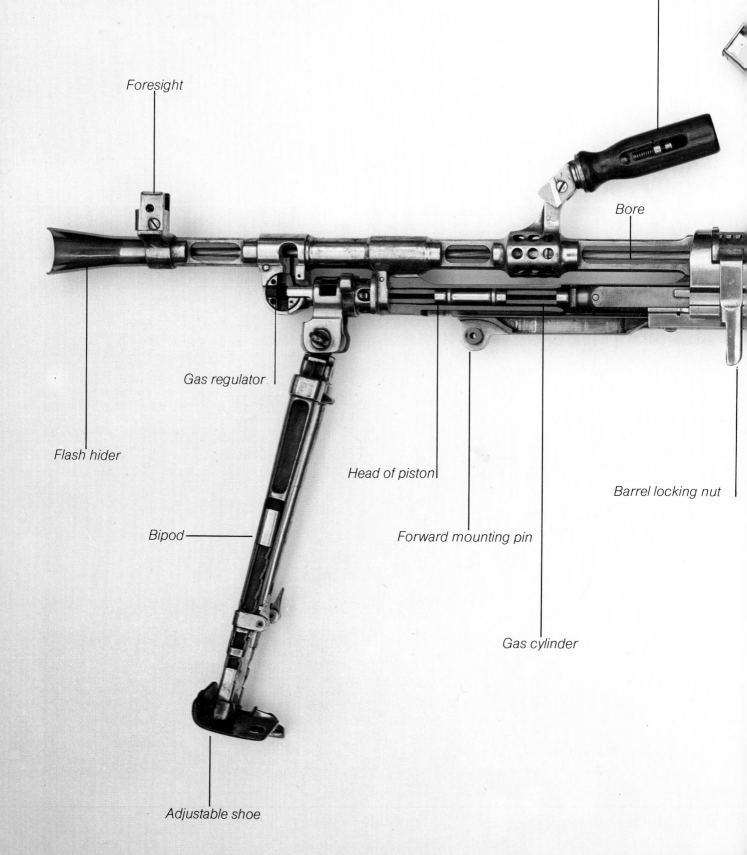

Carrying handle

Foresight

Bore

Gas regulator

Flash hider

Head of piston

Barrel locking nut

Bipod

Forward mounting pin

Gas cylinder

Adjustable shoe

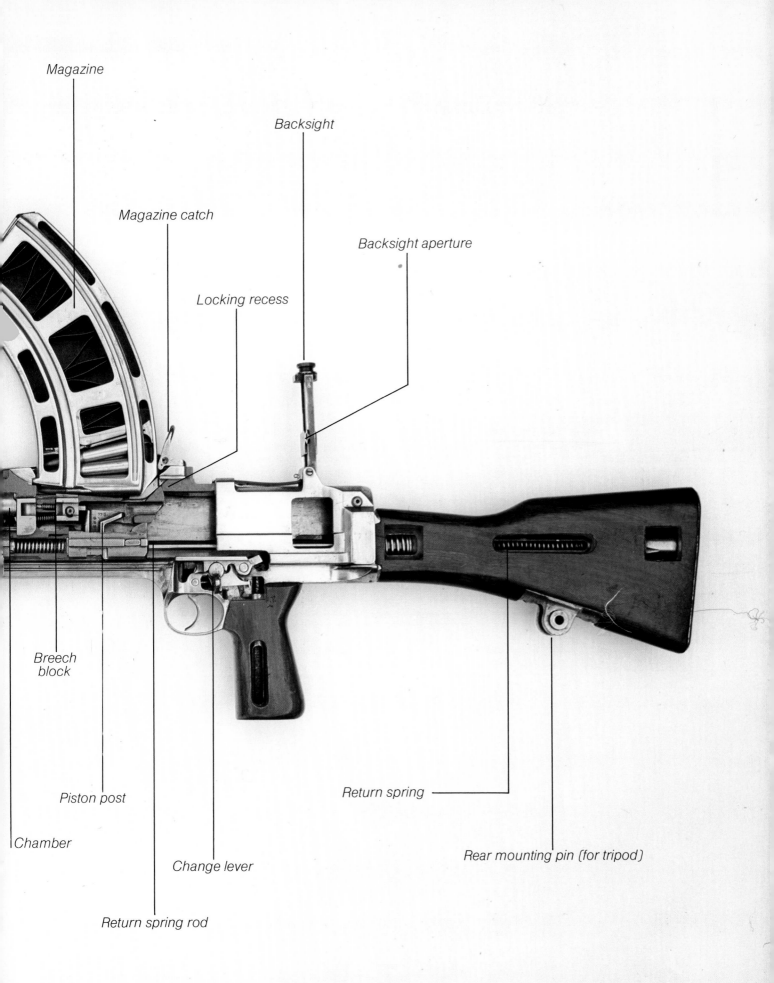

Magazine

Magazine catch

Backsight

Backsight aperture

Locking recess

Breech
block

Piston post

Chamber

Change lever

Return spring rod

Return spring

Rear mounting pin (for tripod)

·303" SAA Ball

·303" SAA Ball

Great Britain
BESAL MK 2

Length: 46·63" (1185mm)
Weight: 21·5lb (9·75kg)
Barrel: 22" (559mm)
Calibre: ·303"
Rifling: 4 groove r/hand
Operation: Gas
Feed: 30-round box
Cooling: Air
Cyclic Rate: 600 rpm
Muzzle Velocity:
2440 f/s (744 m/s)
Sights: 300 yds (274m)

Once the decision had been taken to adopt the Bren gun arrangements to make it went ahead as quickly as possible, which in view of the steady deterioration of the international situation was just as well. The final drawings, with dimensions in inches instead of centimetres, arrived in January 1935 and in September 1937 the first gun came off the line. By July 1938, almost at the time of the Munich Agreement, production had risen to three hundred a week and by the time of the outbreak of war in September 1939 this had reached four hundred. The eight months of the phoney war allowed uninterrupted manufacture to continue but the demand was naturally huge as Great Britain, her Dominions and Colonies were all raising troops as fast as they could. The campaign in France and Flanders in 1940, culminating in the evacuation at Dunkirk, came as a fearful set-back to the British war effort for although a surprisingly large proportion of the British Expeditionary Force were saved, its losses in *matériel* were huge. Although many units brought back at least their small arms, the Bren losses were nevertheless considerable at a time when they could ill be spared. At this stage of the war the entire output of Bren guns was being produced at a single establishment, the Royal Small Arms Factory at Enfield, Middlesex, only a few miles from the centre of London, and when the Blitz of Britain started in the summer of 1940 it immediately became an extremely attractive target for the German bombers. Enemy intelligence was good and as the factory had been in existence in the same location for very many years, neither its presence nor its function could be concealed. Some alternative source of production was obviously desirable, but in the circumstances the problems of setting up, fitting out, and staffing a complete new factory to produce such a relatively complicated item as a Bren gun were so great as to render such an ambitious project completely out of the question. There were of course a number of non-Government armament factories in the country but these were all fully extended in producing a wide variety of weapons, all of which were, in their way, as vital as the Bren gun, so that there again there was no prospect of assistance. Although the number of armaments manufacturers was limited, Great Britain was a highly industrialized country, full of factories and even small workshops capable of turning out a huge variety of competently executed metal work, and among this vast reservoir some at least were capable of turning their hands to weapons as many had already done to other military items. The Bren gun was of course a precision instrument requiring a high degree of engineering skill for its production but modern mass-production experts were already exploring easier methods of manufacture and 1940 seemed to be a good time to put some of their experience to good use. The

·303" SAA Ball
·303" SAA Ball (clip)

individual who finally produced the answer was Mr. H. Faulkener, chief designer for the famous Birmingham Small Arms Company, who abandoned all thought of milling and machining and the various other processes previously considered indispensible in the manufacture of firearms, particularly automatic weapons. He began to think and plan in terms of pressings, and pinnings, and spot welding and a variety of other inelegant but effective means of speeding up manufacturing processes. Two marks of gun were finally produced, the one illustrated being a Mark 2 and both bore a strong resemblance to their parent Bren. The body was made entirely of pressings, riveted and spot welded with a non-adjustable bipod fitted over a sleeve at the forward end. The barrel, although robust and well rifled, was roughly finished externally, with a handle, a simple tubular flash hider, and a foresight on a bracket. There were no locking lugs as such, the barrel being held into the body by the action of a half-round pin on the body being rotated by a lever into a groove at the breech end. The gas passed to the piston through a simple flanged gas regulator which could be turned by the point of a bullet and was held in place by a pin suspended by a link chain from the foresight block. The piston, which was severely plain, held the return spring; as the piston blew back the end of the return spring frame was held firmly by a vertical pin, the milled head of which can be seen below the breech, thus allowing the spring to be compressed. The breechblock, of simple rectangular design with top feed pieces and a floating striker moved with the piston, and when the breechblock stopped on its forward travel the piston continued a little and a ramp on it caused two rectangular studs to rise from the rear end of the block and engage in two recesses in the top of the body, thus locking it firmly at the time of firing. The backsight consisted of an L-shaped flip for three hundred and five hundred yards. The main difference between the two marks was in their method of cocking; in the Mark 1 there was a cocking handle which was attached to the piston and worked with it; in the Mark 2 a small catch at the pistol grip was depressed and the whole grip pushed forward and then drawn sharply back, which allowed the sear to engage with the piston and draw it back also. The Mark 1 also had a simple skeleton butt, but for the Mark 2 this had been filled in with wood. Both types had provision for mounting the gun on a tripod, the ends of the mounting pins being visible on the toe of the butt and under the body; and both were, of course, designed to take the standard Bren magazine. In the event some almost incredible combination of luck and fate decided that the Royal Small Arms Factory should survive the bombing unscathed to continue its production of the Bren. Thus as things turned out, the Besal, or Faulkener as we should perhaps call it, remained no more than an unused emergency precaution consisting of a few prototype models and a quantity of drawings and specifications ready to be despatched if it should be necessary. The gun, therefore, is now little known, which in many ways is a pity because in its day it was a somewhat revolutionary weapon. Even the Sten, one of Great Britain's most famous mass-productions, had not then appeared, and although later many successful sub-machine guns were produced by the same simple methods there appears to be no record of any similar automatic weapon, intended to fire a full sized rifle cartridge, being actually manufactured or even projected.

Italy
BREDA MODELLO 30

Length: 48.5" (1232mm)
Weight: 22.75lb (10.32kg)
Barrel: 20.5" (520mm)
Calibre: 6.5mm
Rifling: 4 groove r/hand
Operation: Blowback
Feed: 20-round box
Cooling: Air
Cyclic Rate: 500 rpm
Muzzle Velocity:
2063 f/s (618 m/s)
Sights: 2188 yds (2000m)

The name Breda has long been a famous one in the world of automatic weapons. The firm was converted from a factory producing railway engines when World War I made it necessary to change over to the manufacture of firearms. The first of these were Revelli machine guns made under licence and it is interesting to note the influence of these early guns on some of their own later models. After the Armistice of 1918, the Italian Government decided that its automatic weapons were out of date and required replacing. The world-wide demand for arms had slumped after the war so that the news of this decision, with its promise of lucrative

contracts at a time when they were hard to find, naturally induced the various Italian armament factories to see if they could produce acceptable models. In 1924 the Breda factory produced its first independently designed gun, which in accordance with custom was given the Model number of the last two figures of its year of initial production. This New Modello 24 was in many ways an unusual weapon, chiefly because it was in some ways close to what would now be classed as a general purpose machine gun. It had both spade grips and rifle-type butt, complete with buttstrap, and could be fired from a light adjustable tripod, either from the shoulder as a light machine gun, or by the spade grips in the medium role. Cooling was allowed for by a rapid system of barrel change and the gun had an odd feed system which will be described later. It operated by recoil and blowback but low tolerances in manufacture made it impossible to control head space; this made it necessary to lubricate the cartridge so that it would come back smoothly at the instant of discharge and settle

its base firmly against the face of the breechblock, thus avoiding the risk of a ruptured case. This gun was reasonably successful and development continued, a second and very similar model appearing in 1928. In 1930 the Breda company took over all the armament work previously carried out by the Fiat factory, and in the same year they produced their new Modello 30 which is the subject of this caption. This was strictly a light machine gun, weighing under twenty-three pounds (10.4kg) and fired from a bipod by means of a normal rifle-type butt, pistol grip, and trigger. Mechanically it was somewhat similar to the earlier Revelli gun which the Breda company had manufactured during World War I under licence from the patent holder, Fiat, since it worked on a combination of gas and recoil. When the round was fired the barrel recoiled for about 0.5" (12.7mm) and then stopped; this allowed the breech to unlock, and once this had happened the working parts were able to move further backwards, partly due to the recoil and partly due to the residual gas pressure in

the barrel. When they reached their rearward limit they struck a buffer which, together with the compressed recoil spring, thrust them forward again, allowing the bolt to strip a round from the magazine, chamber it, lock itself to the barrel, and allow the firing pin to function, after which the cycle continued as long as the trigger was pressed and rounds were available. The gun would fire automatic only. The barrel, which was connected to the barrel extension by means of robust interrupted threads, could be changed very quickly, extra barrels being carried for this purpose. The use of direct blowback without any preliminary starting of the cartridge case is always liable to lead to extraction problems—even when headspace adjustment is possible, which was not the case with the Modello 30, and this led to the continued use of an oiler to lubricate the rounds as they went into the chamber. Possibly the most unusual feature of the gun was its feed system which consisted of a box magazine on the right side but hinged to the gun at its front corner so that by releasing a catch the

whole magazine could be pivoted forwards until it was parallel with the barrel. The cartridges were prepacked in flat cardboard charger-type containers whence the gunner could force the rounds into the magazine, then swing it back on its hinge until the catch engaged. This was said to allow for more careful machining of the magazine lips than would have been the case with detachable magazines bumping about in boxes or pouches, but it made reloading rather slow. The best that can be said about the Modello 30 is that it was adequate, but no more; the slowness of reloading has already been mentioned and this, combined with the fact that any damage to the magazine, which was necessarily exposed and liable to knocks and dents, could put the gun out of action, made it to some extent unreliable. The system of barrel changing was quick and simple, but as there was no carrying handle on the barrel it was impossible to hold it when hot without an improvised glove. The barrel front bearing was also of inferior design which allowed

undue vibration and caused the individual shots from a burst to scatter badly. Worst of all probably was its fussy design which made it difficult to keep free from dust; this, in combination with the necessary use of an oiler, must have meant that in desert or similar dry climates the working parts were moving in a perpetual grinding paste which would have led to excessive wear. And with no carrying handle, the unhappy gunner must have made heavy weather of it. The Modello 30 was the standard light machine gun of the Italian Army in Abyssinia and in its campaigns in North and East Africa during World War II. When the Italian Army briefly introduced a larger round of 7·35mm calibre as a result of its experience against the Abyssinians in the 1930s, a number of Modello 30s were converted to fire it. The Breda factory also produced the standard Italian medium machine gun, the Modello 37, which is described elsewhere. The Italian Army no longer uses the Modello 30, having conformed to modern practice by adopting a general purpose machine gun, the German MG42/59.

6·5mm Modello 95
·303" SAA Ball (clip)

Length: 41·5" (1054mm)
Weight: 20lb (9·07kg)
Barrel: 21·75" (553mm)
Calibre: 6·5mm
Rifling: 4 groove r/hand
Operation: Gas
Feed: 30-round box
Cooling: Air
Cyclic Rate: 550 rpm
Muzzle Velocity:
2400 f/s (732 m/s)
Sights: 1749 yds (1600m)
(Provision for telescopic sights)

It was the Japanese who first saw and exploited the value of the machine gun as an offensive weapon. The long established armies of the other major nations of the world had been very slow to perceive the possibilities of the new weapon. Those with overseas possessions found it a useful adjunct in their more or less continuous colonial campaigns, but here the principal tactical concept, generally speaking, was to plunge deep into enemy territory and there take up a strong position and await attack. When this came, as it usually did, it consisted of little more than wild charges of swarms of horse and foot, and against these the machine gun was deadly. However, its role in modern warfare was far less clearly defined. The Japanese Army, only recently emerged from centuries of seclusion, had no pre-conceived ideas on tactics, and in their siege of Port Arthur in the war against the Russians in 1904-5, they employed their French Hotchkiss type guns in close support of their attacks, handling them boldly close behind their infantry and scoring many successes by doing so. Having seen little except naval action in World War I the Japanese had not been under the same pressure as the nations of Europe and America to develop light automatic guns and it was not until 1922 that they produced their first domestically designed and manufactured light machine gun, often referred to as the Nambu Type II machine gun after General Nambu who was at that time responsible for small arms development. Although by no means a successful weapon it had several unusual features, chief of which was the system by which, instead of the more usual magazine or belt, it fired five-round rifle chargers by means of a hopper on the left-hand side. Six chargers were placed in it and held down firmly by a spring-loaded arm, and on the backward action of the gun, which was gas operated, a sliding ratchet drew the rounds into the gun leaving the clip outside. The theory that this system enabled riflemen to feed the gun easily and quickly was by no means a bad one but had the serious disadvantage that in action the hopper collected mud and dust and ground it all through the mechanism, thus greatly increasing wear. There was also trouble with extraction which meant that the cartridges had to be oiled. This made the dirt and fouling into an even worse abrasive paste and finally led to the introduction of a less powerful round which more or less solved the problem, but only at the expense of increasing the complications of ammunition supply in the field. In spite of these various disadvantages, however, some of these guns were still in use at the end of World War II. The gun illustrated, the Type 96, was introduced in 1936 as a replacement for Type II. At this time the Japanese were engaged in more or less continuous warfare with their ancient enemies the Chinese, and as usually happens extensive practical experience led to a number of improvements being incorporated in the new gun. It was still of basic Hotchkiss design, to which the Japanese usually remained faithful, one of the principal differences from its predecessor being the abolition of the inefficient system of charger loading by hopper and the substitution of a more orthodox top-mounted box magazine. It still fired the rather unsatisfactory 6·5mm cartridge but the oil

6·5mm Meiji 30
·303" SAA Ball (clip)

pump was situated in the magazine loader and thus completely divorced from the gun itself, which was a considerable improvement. The gun also had a quick system for changing barrels which did something to help its capacity for sustained fire without overheating. It had a carrying handle and a distinctive one-piece butt and pistol grip combined, and would take the standard infantry bayonet, although this was largely to demonstrate the offensive spirit, since a twenty-pound (9·07kg) gun makes a poor basis for a thrusting weapon, particularly for the Japanese who although strong and wiry tend to be of small physique. Perhaps its oddest feature was the frequent incorporation of a low powered telescopic sight. A sight of this type is not usually considered to be of great value on an automatic weapon although in this case it may have been intended as a simple visual aid. The cartridge used was still the reduced charge pattern used

in the previous gun, which must have continued to cause complications over resupply of ammunition. Japanese experience in Manchuria had highlighted the problems of using a gun which would only function properly with lubricated cartridges and work began in 1937 to develop a new light machine gun free of this disability. The result was the Type 99 which was really no more than an improved version of its predecessor. The improvements were, however, significant ones, being a new and better round and a method of adjusting headspace which finally did away with the need to lubricate each round. It bore in fact a much closer resemblance to the Czechoslovakian ZB, from which came the Bren. It was fitted with a monopod under the butt which in theory enabled it to be laid on fixed lines, but in practice the vibration very soon shook the gun off its target. Although a considerable advance on its predecessors it came rather

too late to be of much service since Japanese industry was already too overloaded to allow it to be produced in very significant numbers. As was to be expected from a nation which had largely pioneered the effective use of the machine gun in war, the Japanese made very extensive use of light machine guns in World War II. Apart from their own weapons they never had any apparent hesitation in pressing into service a variety of captured weapons which must have increased considerably the already grave complications which must have ensued simply to make sure that the right ammunition got to the right guns in the field. Their guns were handled with great boldness, often by a gunner and a number two apparently operating almost independently, and always well forward. Perhaps fortunately for the Allies the quality of Japanese shooting was never equal to their courage and boldness, possibly due to poor sight, but also due to their habit of

firing extremely long bursts. British experience over the years has shown that the best effect is obtained from a light machine gun by firing bursts of not more than five rounds, but the Japanese tended to fire off whole magazines with the result that a large proportion of their fire went high. This was particularly noticeable when they charged firing from the hip, as they often did. When World War II ended many Japanese light machine guns were left in the territories previously occupied by them, and some, mainly Type 99, were converted by the Chinese to 7·62mm. Although Japan now technically has no army as such she has a Self-Defence Force which is very much the same thing under a different name. This currently uses a general purpose machine gun known as the Model 62, a well designed gas-operated weapon of European type, although it is believed that the Japanese are proposing to convert to 5·56mm in conformity with the United States.

Soviet Union
RPD (RUCHNOI PULEMYOT DEGTYARYEV)

Length: 40·8" (1036mm)
Weight: 15·6lb (7kg)
Barrel: 20·5" (520mm)
Calibre: 7·62mm
Rifling: 4 groove l/hand
Operation: Gas
Feed: Belt
Cooling: Air
Cyclic Rate: 700 rpm
Muzzle Velocity:
2400 f/s (732 m/s)
Sights: 1094 yds (1000m)

In World War II the Soviet Union used light and medium machine guns chambered for their normal rifle cartridge, as indeed did all the other combatant nations at that period. As the war progressed, however, the Russians became more and more impressed with the German machine carbine Model 42 which fired what

was usually referred to as an intermediate round in that it gave a performance somewhere between the pistol cartridge as used in a sub-machine gun and the then standard type of rifle round in general use. Degtyaryev, the well-known Russian designer, soon set to work on a new light machine gun to fire a similar round, and by 1944 had done much of the basic work. Huge demands were, however, being made on the Soviet economy at that period, so that as long as the war continued relatively little progress was made with either gun or cartridge. Once it was over, priorities changed and the Russians, always apprehensive at the mere thought of being left behind in any warlike developments, speeded up their efforts to put a new gun into the hands of

their soldiers as quickly as they possibly could. The new weapon appeared in due course under the title of *Ruchnoi Pulemyot Degtyaryev,* which was almost invariably abbreviated to RPD. Its chief merits were soon seen to be its lightness and simplicity of working. The new gun, like its predecessor from Degtyaryev, was gas operated, and in fact used a basically similar mechanism to the earlier weapons. The bolt continued to be locked by means of hinged lugs, which were normally retained flush with the body of the bolt, but which were forced outwards into recesses in the receiver so as to lock the breech at the instant of firing. in the older guns, however, the outward thrust had been powered by the final movement of the firing pin whereas in the new one it was

done by a wedge mounted on top of the slide. Probably the principal difference, however, was its method of feed which had changed from the characteristically large flat drum to a system of belt feed. The belt consisted of a series of open metal pockets, each designed to hold one of the new rimless rounds and linked together by short pieces of spiral spring. Belts held fifty rounds but two could if necessary be fixed together very simply by slipping the tongue of the end link of one belt into the starting link of the second and then inserting a cartridge to lock them firmly together. The gun could be loaded in two ways. If the belt had a feed tab all that was necessary was to insert it into the feed way from left to right until it was fully home and cock the gun. If the belt had

7·62mm Patrone 1943g
·303" SAA Ball (clip)

88

no feed tab it was then necessary to undo the catch at the rear of the hinged top cover, raise the cover, and put the belt in position and cock. It was, of course, essential to make sure that the belt was inserted so that the open sides of the cartridge pockets were downwards. Once firing started the belt was fed through the gun by a roller worked by the piston. When, as often happened, the gun was required to be used in a mobile role the belt could be coiled tightly into a sheet metal drum with a hinged lid. This drum had a dovetail on it which engaged with a plate positioned under the feed way, and once in place could be locked by a catch to prevent it sliding backwards off the gun whilst firing. The gun was fitted with a rotatable gas regulator and had a fixed

barrel. As it would only fire automatic, overheating could only be avoided by the gunner ensuring that he did not exceed one hundred rounds a minute, which was probably adequate for most battle situations. Over the years there were a number of modifications made to the original basic gun. The first model had a reciprocating cocking handle which worked backwards and forwards with the piston, the latter having a hollow head which fitted over the gas spigot. The second model revised the piston head arrangements and added protectors for the backsights, while the third model finally incorporated a folding, non-reciprocating handle and a much needed dust cover over the ejector opening. It was not, however, until the fourth model that any significant change was made;

the power of the gun had always been marginal as regards its capacity to move a fairly heavy belt, so the size of the piston was significantly increased in an effort to improve this. Another problem had been the vibration caused by the rapid backward and forward action of the mechanism which was particularly noticeable because of the light weight of the gun and had an adverse effect on its accuracy; this was alleviated by the addition of a buffer at the rear end of the receiver. One or two other minor changes have also been made since, including the provision of a folding cleaning rod carried in a trap in the butt. All models had the characteristically club-footed butt which looked ugly but which was designed to suit the underhand grip usually employed by the Russians,

and many others, in which the left hand is cupped under the butt with the thumb on the inside. The RPD was made in very large numbers and was the standard section or squad gun, not only in the Soviet infantry but also in the armies of Russia's satellites. It is now largely obsolete in the Warsaw Pact armies which have mainly gone over to the RPK, which is essentially a light machine gun version of the AK 47 assault rifle. It is, however, still widely used by Communist countries in South-East Asia and also appears to be popular with a variety of guerrilla forces in Africa and elsewhere. The Communist Chinese, who were originally largely re-equipped by the Russians after their revolution, still make and use their own version of the RPD, which they designate the Type 56.

Soviet Union
DEGTYARYEV PAKHOTNYI (DP)

Length: 50·3" (1290mm)
Weight: 20·5lb (9·30kg)
Barrel: 23·8" (605mm)
Calibre: 7·62mm
Rifling: 4 groove r/hand
Operation: Gas
Feed: 47-round drum
Cooling: Air
Cyclic Rate: 500 rpm
Muzzle Velocity:
2750 f/s (849 m/s)
Sights: 1641 yds (1500m)

Imperial Russia, which was largely an agricultural nation with very little industrial capacity, relied entirely on outside sources for her automatic weapons. She used a version of the Maxim in her war against Japan in 1904-5, but also equipped her cavalry with the light Madsen gun at the same time. During World War I she again relied principally upon her allies, and bought considerable quantities of Colt machine guns from the United States and even some American-made Vickers guns designed to fire the standard Russian 7.62mm round. In the years following the Revolution of 1917 such a wide variety of weapons was used that it is difficult to untangle them, but the only Russian-made automatic of the period appears to have been the Federov; this in fact seems to have been more of a light automatic rifle than a true machine gun, but it is of some interest because it was its inventor who really discovered Vasily Degtyaryev and took him on as chief assistant in his design office. Degtyaryev started work on the design of his first original light machine gun in

1921. This gun was put into limited production in 1926 and after two years of exhaustive trials was adopted for service by the Soviet Army; its full title was Ruchnoi Pulemyot Degtyaryeva Pakhotnyi which literally translated meant automatic weapon, Degtyaryev, Infantry, but is very often abbreviated to DP. The original gun was of simple but reasonably robust construction and contained only sixty-five parts altogether, having been designed for manufacture and assembly by semi-skilled labour. Not surprisingly, in view of the strained circumstances under which it was developed and made, the gun had some defects, principally in its very large bearing surfaces which caused undue friction in action, and in its susceptibility to the ingress of dirt. Over-heating was also a problem because removing the barrel was a relatively slow and tedious business, and was in any case useless because no second barrel was carried. The earliest guns had finned barrels to help dissipate the heat, but the problem was never fully overcome except by the obvious means of

restricting the rate of fire to the capacity of the barrel to disperse it. The gun was used extensively in the Spanish Civil War of 1936-39 which afforded both the Fascist and the Communist powers a very useful opportunity to test weapons and techniques under the true conditions of warfare. As a result of this experience certain improvements were made in the gun which eliminated its worst faults. The gun worked on the normal system of tapped-off gas impinging on a piston and driving it to the rear, taking with it the bolt, which was then forced forward again by the action of the compressed return spring. The arrangements for locking the bolt were relatively unusual; on each side of the bolt there was a hinged lug which normally lay in its own recess, being externally flush with the outside surface of the bolt so as not to interfere with its free movement backward and forward in the receiver. Once the bolt face was firm against the base of the round in the chamber it naturally stopped, but the piston continued briefly, taking with it a slider to which was attached the firing pin. It was

during this final short movement that the firing pin cammed out the locking lugs into recesses cut into the side walls of the receiver, thus locking the whole breech mechanism very firmly at the actual instant of firing. By the time the tapped-off gas passing through the gas port and onto the piston had begun to force it to the rear, the pressure in the bore had dropped to a level where it was safe to unlock the breech and allow the working parts to go to the rear. This was accomplished by the reverse movement of the firing pin which forced the locking lugs out of the recesses in the receiver wall and back into their own recesses in the bolt, which was then able to move backwards, extracting the fired case as it went. The feed system was reasonably efficient; rimmed cartridges usually cause some problems in light automatics, but they tend to be worse in those using box magazines because the rims occasionally get hooked behind one another when the magazine has been hastily and carelessly filled. This naturally causes stoppages. The large flat single-deck

drum of the Degtyaryev at least eliminated the problem of double feed, although its very size and thinness naturally tended to make it rather susceptible to damage. Unlike the rather similar drum on the British Lewis gun, the Degtyaryev magazine was not driven by the action of the gun, but by an integral clockwork mechanism in the magazine itself. The magazine capacity was originally forty-nine rounds but in practice, in common with others notably the Bren gun, this was found to be excessive, and it was necessary to reduce it by two to forty-seven, with which number it worked satisfactorily. All Degtyaryev magazines are stamped 47 PATRON as a guide to those filling them. The modified guns, of which the one illustrated is an example, had removable barrels, but even so a special spanner had to be used on them which made the process rather cumbersome in the heat of action. They also had their mainsprings modified. These had originally been coiled round the piston underneath the barrel, but experience had found that the heat quickly

affected the temper of the spring. In the improved version therefore, it was placed in its own sleeve below the receiver, which effectively dealt with the problem. The gun, which fired automatic only, worked on the open bolt system in which the bolt

remained back when the gun was not firing, thus allowing the air to reach and cool the chamber. It was fitted with a gas regulator with three settings. The weapon gave good service in World War II and was subsequently used in Korea and Vietnam.

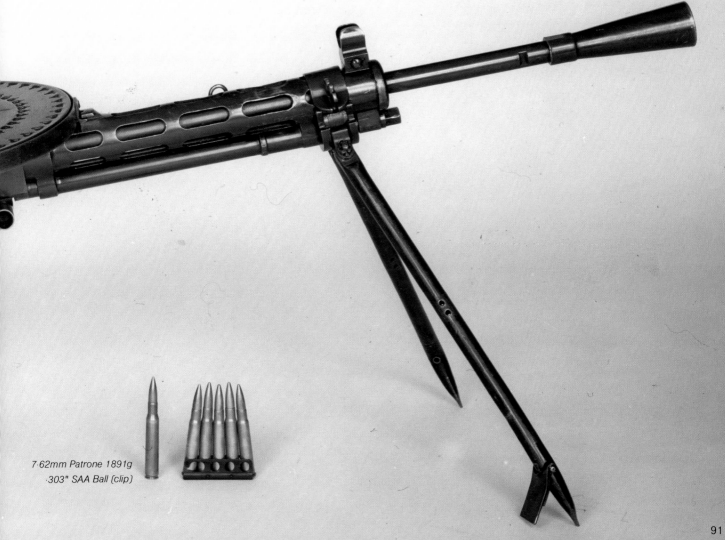

7·62mm Patrone 1891g

·303" SAA Ball (clip)

RUCHNOI PULEMYOT KALASHNIKOVA (RPK)

Length: 40·5" (1029mm)
Weight: 11lb (5kg)
Barrel: 23·3" (592mm)
Calibre: 7·62mm
Rifling: 4 groove r/hand
Operation: Gas
Feed: 30-round box or
75-round drum
Cooling: Air
Cyclic Rate: 600rpm
Muzzle Velocity: 2410 f/s
(735 m/s)
Sights: 875 yds·(800m)

The relatively recent rise in the importance of the assault rifle has led to a number of changes in the type and function of the heavier infantry automatic weapons. The original concept was a medium machine gun for support, and a lighter version at squad or section level, but after the end of World War II, this separate concept gave way to the idea of the so-called general purpose machine gun, based largely on the considerable success enjoyed by the German MG34s and 42s, perhaps particularly by the latter in the new dual role. Many countries seem recently to have come to the conclusion that the general purpose machine gun is in practice something of a mixed blessing, in that it tends to be too light for true sustained fire yet too heavy as an individual weapon. The modern tendency, therefore, seems to be to relegate the true machine

gun to a close support role at company level and replace it at squad or section level by what is in effect an improved and upgraded version of an assault rifle. Many countries, for example, use the heavy barrelled NATO rifle, converted for full automatic fire in this role, while the British are even now considering two types of a light individual weapon which can adequately fill the roles previously played by the general purpose machine gun in the light role and the current self-loading rifle.
Strangely enough the Russians did not follow the common line, in that they never really showed any great enthusiasm for the general purpose concept, but stuck fairly steadily to two separate types of gun, each tailor-made to its own particular role. These guns are dealt with elsewhere in this book so that there is no need to refer to them in detail here. One of the results

of the introduction of the automatic assault rifle had been to make the light machine gun relatively less important in-as-much as all Soviet riflemen now have an automatic capacity. This capacity is not, however, very sustained, due to the obvious problem of rifles overheating, so that a need still clearly exists for a somewhat heavier arm. Soon after the general introduction of the AK47 the Soviet Military Authorities set their experts to work to design a heavier version which could in due course replace the current infantry light machine gun, the RPD. This was a good, reliable weapon and is still in fact extensively used by various Communist countries in South-East Asia and by a variety of guerrilla groups throughout the world. But the advantages of a heavier version of the AK47 obviously outweighed all other considerations. As will be seen

from the photograph this new grade of automatic weapon is essentially similar in general appearance to the AK47 assault rifle, from which it was in fact developed by the original inventor, the prolific and highly successful designer Kalashnikov. Its principal external differences are its very characteristic club butt and its appreciably longer and heavier barrel. It is equipped with a bipod, fitted well forward and designed to be folded back and held by a clip when not required as a support. The weapon is of course gas-operated. When the first, manually loaded, round is fired part of the gases pass through a vent in the barrel and thence into the cylinder visible above it, where they strike and force back the piston. The initial rearward action of the piston causes the bolt locking lugs to rotate anti-clockwise, thus allowing the breech to open, after which the bolt continues to the rear with the piston compressing the return spring as it does so. In due course, the power of the gas having been exhausted, the return spring takes over and drives the mechanism forward, and during this phase the bolt strips a round from the magazine and forces it into the chamber. It then stops, but the piston continues sufficiently to cause the locking lugs to engage with the locking shoulders after which the striker is free to fire the round and the cycle continues. There is a change lever on the right hand side of the receiver above the trigger — it is pivoted at the rear end and is pushed up for safe, centrally for automatic and down for single rounds. The new weapon is primarily intended to take the normal thirty-round magazine of the assault rifle but is also equipped with a drum type holding seventy-five rounds. This drum magazine has an angled extension piece which fits into the magazine opening, the drum itself then being tilted forward at an angle of about 45°. This drum is heavy and slow to fill, so it is anticipated that it would only be used when the maximum volume of fire was needed as, for example, in the last stages of an assault or at some critical point when repelling an attack. The gun has no gas regulator which means that it must necessarily be set to ensure that the weapon will fire under the very worst conditions. This simplifies production, but means that there is a good deal of vibration when the gun is clean, with a gradual settling down as a degree of fouling builds up and slows down the cyclic rate. Nor is there any means of changing barrels, which means that the problem of keeping the gun reasonably cool must be left to the good training and discretion of the gunner. It is probable that its maximum rate of fire is of the order of eighty rounds a minute which seems barely adequate for a gun of this type. There is a degree of inter-changeability with the AK47 and in most cases it will accept a bolt taken at random from a rifle, although this depends to some extent on the question of head space. It does, however, mean that in the event of a breakage the RPK can be kept in action at the expense of a rifle. It appears overall to be a good and reliable arm, its lightness of design being of course largely due to the useful Soviet intermediate round. It is of interest to note that the Soviet Union is currently producing a new weapon, the PK, a true general purpose gun and the first ever produced by them. There are versions of this for firing from a tripod or armoured vehicle.

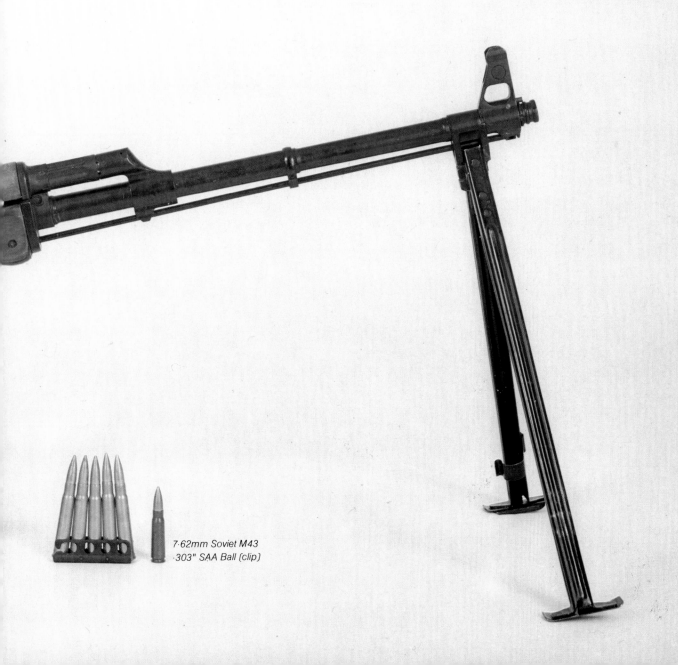

7·62mm Soviet M43
·303" SAA Ball (clip)

United States of America
BROWNING MODEL 1919A4

Length (gun): 41" (1041mm)
Weight (gun): 31lb (14kg)
Weight (tripod): 14lb (6·35kg)
Barrel: 24" (610mm)
Calibre: ·30"
Rifling: 4 groove r/hand
Operation: Recoil
Feed: Belt
Cooling: Air
Cyclic Rate: 500 rpm
Muzzle Velocity:
2800 f/s (854 m/s)
Sights: 2400 yds (2195 m)

The United States entered World War I in a very ill-prepared state and although she rapidly converted a good deal of her great industrial capacity to war production, the war was over before very much of it had reached the hands of her fighting soldiers. One of the weapons lacking in the new range coming into service, largely the brainchild of John Browning, was a light machine gun comparable to the British Lewis gun, for although the Browning automatic rifle was an excellent weapon of its type, that type was in fact a very limited one. The Americans had seen, and been impressed with, the French concept of marching fire in which attacking infantry were preceded by vast volumes of fire, not from supporting troops but from weapons in the hands of the attackers themselves. The Browning Automatic Rifle had proved excellent for this, but in view

of its light weight it naturally and inevitably lacked a very high capacity for sustained fire. A modified version of the medium Browning, mechanically very similar to the original gun but with a light pierced casing round the barrel instead of the bulky water-jacket, had been tried experimentally and with some success as a weapon for army aircraft. This was followed in 1919 by a similar model but with a heavier barrel and intended as a tank gun. The next unit to come into the picture was the United States cavalry. Since the Civil War of 1861-5 they had realized that although they might be useful as horsemen in border patrols and such like, their real function in modern war would be to act as mounted infantry. They would have to rely on their horses for mobility but fight on their feet, and once this was clear they obviously required as much portable

firepower as possible. They had been issued with Browning Automatic Rifles, but wanted something with a greater capacity for sustained fire without much increase in weight, and so there came into existence the Model 1919A2 which had a conveniently small tripod and which could easily be carried on a led packhorse together with a reasonable quantity of ammunition. This proved successful and from it there developed the Model 1919 A4, a sort of general purpose light machine gun which, with minor changes in mounts, could be used in tanks and armoured cars, as a multiple anti-aircraft gun, and in a ground role. It was, in essence, very similar to its predecessor the cavalry gun, the principal difference being that as weight was not quite such a critical factor it had a larger and somewhat more rigid tripod. The mechanism of this gun was substantially

·30" M1906
·303" SAA Ball (clip)

similar to that of the Model 1917 water-cooled Browning. It worked by the recoil power of the barrel which in a brief rearward thrust unlocked the breechblock and sent it to the rear, extracting the case as it did so. The force of the compressed return spring provided the motive power for the forward action in which a new round was stripped from the belt, chambered, and fired. It had a heavy barrel enclosed in a light perforated outer casing. In the earliest of these, the perforations were elongated, but in most versions they are circular. Feed was by means of a woven fabric belt designed to hold one hundred and fifty rounds and with brass tags at each end to facilitate loading. At normal operating temperatures it was reckoned that the gun could maintain an actual rate of fire of sixty rounds per minute for up to thirty minutes without any serious problems of

overheating. The weapon had a single pistol-type grip, very similar in shape and appearance to that of the Colt revolver, and its trigger, which had no guard, protruded almost horizontally from the rear of the receiver. When used in the ground role the gun was mounted on the standard M2 tripod. This was of light but strong construction, and its general shape and functioning can best be seen from the illustration. The two rear legs are joined by a traversing bar on which is situated the rear mounting gear which incorporates a wheel for elevation and depression. Forward mounting is by a pintle permanently attached to the gun and held in position on the tripod head by a latch. The accessories for cavalry use included a light metal fitting designed to fit the standard United States pack saddle and which would carry the gun, the tripod, a spare

barrel, a spare parts chest and three ammunition chests each carrying two belts of ammunition. The gun was simple to handle and reliable in use, the few stoppages to which it was liable being easy to deal with. The detachment consisted of two men, and although no special anti-aircraft stand was provided the Basic Field Manual of 1940 showed more elevation being obtained by the number one propping one leg of the tripod onto the knee of his number two. It may be of interest to know that this Field Manual was prepared under the direction of the Chief of Cavalry. Guns in vehicles naturally had proper mountings provided for them but the general rule was that a tripod M2 should also be carried for each gun to allow for ground firing if it should become necessary. The Browning M1919A4 was used extensively in World War II, principally as a Company

level weapon for local support, and also in a very wide variety of armoured vehicles. In the course of the war it was somewhat modified to bring it more into line with what may be described as other more orthodox light machine guns. These modifications included the provision of a rifle-type butt incorporating a pistol grip, a light adjustable bipod, a carrying handle and a flash hider, all of which made it more suitable for a mobile role. This new and improved model was known as Model 1919A6. The Browning light machine gun is now obsolete in the United States and has not been manufactured for many years, but it is still probably quite widely used by countries for whom the United States have provided military aid in the past. Perhaps surprisingly a number are still in use with the British Royal Armoured Corps.

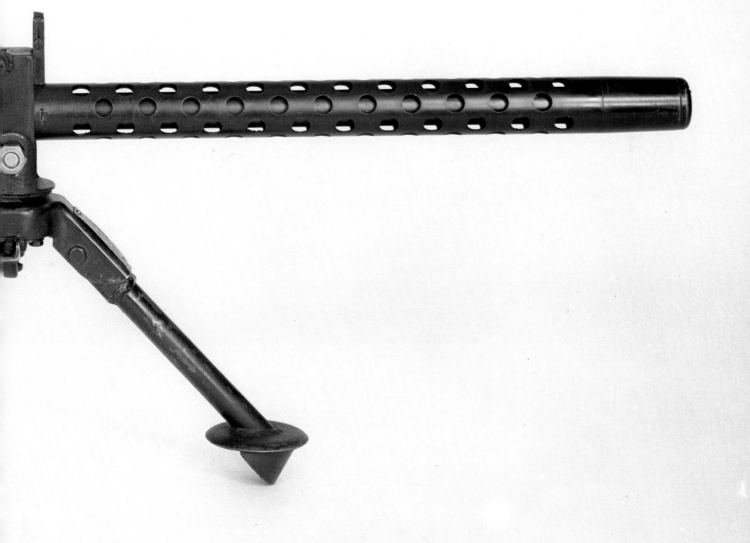

United States of America
BROWNING AUTOMATIC RIFLE 1918A2

Length: 48" (1220mm)
Weight: 19·5lb (8·85kg)
Barrel: 24" (610mm)
Calibre: ·30"
Rifling: 4 groove r/hand
Operation: Gas
Feed: 20-round box
Cooling: Air
Cyclic Rate: 350 or 600 rpm
Muzzle Velocity:
2800 f/s (855 m/s)
Sights: 1500 yds (1372m)

It is a surprising but undeniable fact that the United States, which even as early as 1917 was rapidly becoming one of the major industrial nations of the world, was almost entirely unprepared for war when she declared it in April of that year. Although the actual event was precipitated by the sinking of the *Lusitania* by a German U-boat it had been clear for some time that America would inevitably enter the war on the side of the Allies, whom she had been supplying with considerable quantities of munitions for three years. Much of her unpreparedness was due to relative neglect of her small army in the first few years of the 20th century and in particular her failure to insist on the development of modern automatic weapons which clearly would play a vital role in any further war. She was fortunate, perhaps more fortunate than she knew, in having available the services of John M. Browning, whose undoubted genius was only matched by

his patriotism. As early as 1910 he had developed and perfected an excellent water-cooled medium machine gun, but in the absence of military customers he had set this aside. In the period 1914-1917 he had also seen the need for a lighter automatic weapon and some time before America entered the war he had working prototypes available. These he demonstrated in February 1917, together with his medium machine gun, and although the latter was put back for further trials the United States adopted the light weapon, which Browning designated an automatic rifle, on the basis of its first very convincing demonstration. The new weapon weighed just under sixteen pounds (7·25kg) and was correctly described as a rifle, since its general appearance and handling qualities allowed it to be used in that particular role. Indeed, as the first models had no bipods there was no other way in which it could be used. Strictly speaking it would

probably be described in modern terminology as an assault rifle and was indeed an early forerunner of the species. The need for such a weapon had long been obvious, although the various combatants on both sides had tended to veer to one side or the other by using either light machine guns or an early form of sub-machine gun. The United States Military Authorities had a clear concept of what they described as walking fire, in which a line of infantrymen advanced steadily spraying their objective with a sufficient volume of fire to subdue its defenders. It was, of course, argued that this sort of largely unaimed fire was extremely wasteful except at close ranges but the American view was that it was better to waste ammunition than men. Certainly such an advance must have had a serious effect on enemy morale. Much of Browning's original work on the automatic rifle, which was of normal gas and piston operation, had been done at the Colt factory,

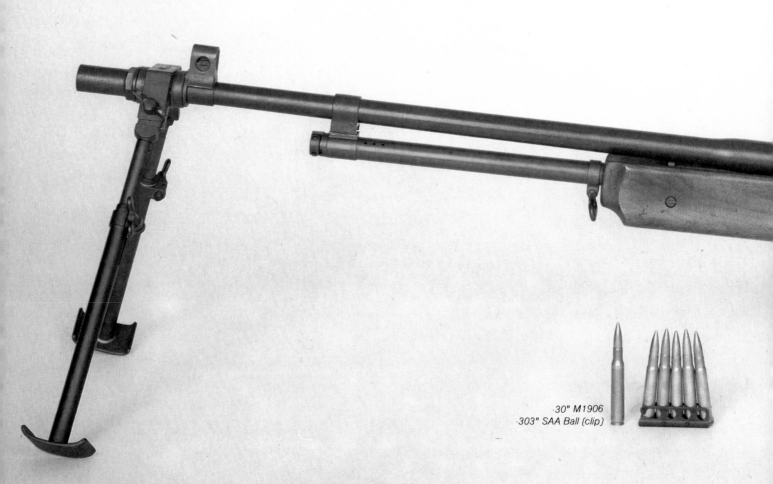

·30" M1906
·303" SAA Ball (clip)

but Winchester also gave a good deal of assistance later. Manufacture started early in 1918 and after some inevitable teething troubles, went well, and production from all sources at one time reached over seven hundred daily, the final total production being in excess of fifty thousand. Unfortunately the great bulk of these had appeared too late for use in the war, their first recorded use in action being on 13 September 1918. The United States newspapers were always full of its merits and it must have been irritating in the extreme for the bulk of the American infantry in France to read these glowing reports and then have to go into action with the French Chauchat, one of the worst light automatic weapons ever to be used in action. The Browning Automatic Rifle was received with great enthusiasm by the Allies, none of whom had a weapon of quite the same type, and they were ordered in large numbers, France alone asking for fifteen thousand. It

must have been gratifying to the inventor to know that his son, Lieutenant Valentine Browning, had actually used the automatic rifle in action against the Germans. After the outcome of World War I interest in things military in the United States largely died away, as indeed it did in the other democracies, and although the Browning remained in service there were few alterations to it. The only really new type to appear was the Model 1922 which was introduced principally as a support weapon for the United States cavalry which was then, of course, horsed. It was basically similar to the original gun but had a heavier, finned barrel, a bipod and a butt rest, and was designed to fire automatic only. Although it appears to have been well suited as a cavalry weapon it was not apparently issued in very large numbers. There was also a Model 1918A1, which like the original was able to fire bursts or single rounds as required. Unlike its parent weapon it had a bipod, the

experience of 1918 having shown this to be a desirable addition even though it increased the weight by a couple of pounds. The next change came in 1940 with the introduction of yet another variation, the Model 1918A2. This also was fitted with a light bipod which in this version was attached well forward to the tubular flash hider and like the cavalry model had a butt rest which kept the weapon roughly horizontal when raised. This model also had an additional feature known as a buttstrap, a flat piece of metal hinged to the heel of the butt in such a way that when it was turned back a firer in the prone position could keep the weapon in the shoulder while using both hands for other purposes; this attachment can be clearly seen in the photograph. One interesting variation on this model was the fact that, although it would only fire bursts, it incorporated a selector which would allow two cyclic rates, the higher being some six hundred and the lower being three

hundred and fifty rounds per minute. The actual effective service rate was about one hundred and twenty rounds per minute. The Basic Field Manual on the Model 1918A2, published in 1940, shows both the bipod and the butt rest in use, but by 1942 the new edition omitted both, and appears to have envisaged a reversion to the original 1917/18 role of assault rifle. The Maintenance Manual of the same year, however, includes the bipod, which seems to have remained in general use. This model remained in service as the standard squad automatic weapon in World War II and in Korea. In spite of its somewhat uneasy position, which made it rather heavy for a rifle and rather light for a machine gun, the Browning Automatic Rifle was used by many countries and was made in Belgium as the Herstal. A number were sold to Great Britain in 1940 and were used to arm the Home Guard, where they gave good service but caused some problems over calibre.

United States of America
M60

Length: 43.75" (1111mm)
Weight: 23lb (10.43kg)
Barrel: 25.5" (647mm)
Calibre: 7.62mm
Rifling: 4 groove r/hand
Operation: Gas
Feed: Belt
Cooling: Air
Cyclic Rate: 600 rpm
Muzzle Velocity:
2800 f/s (853 m/s)
Sights: 1100 yds (1006m)

The main rifle calibre automatic weapons used by the United States Army in World War II were the two guns invented by John Browning, his water-cooled medium gun and his even more famous Automatic Rifle, which had arrived in France too late to be used in the fighting which ended in November 1918. In spite of their good service, the Americans, like a number of other countries, had been impressed by the flexibility provided by the German general purpose machine guns and once the war was over they set about designing a version of their own. A good deal of the preliminary design work for the M60 had in fact been done in 1944 and 1945, using examples of captured German guns so that the first experimental gun which appeared, the T44, was largely based on the best features of the MG42 and the early assault rifle the FG42. This early prototype proved disappointing and a great deal more work was done on it, particularly in relation to the piston. This resulted in the T52 which was not quite right either, principally because the feed arrangements caused much trouble, but these were eventually put right and the modified gun was designated the T161. After a good deal of testing, and apparently some hesitation, the gun was pronounced satisfactory and officially adopted by the US Army. The finished gun was of modern manufacture and relied largely on stampings, rubber, and plastics, and had a somewhat fussy over-cluttered look about it. But sadly it was of faulty orthodox design. Gas from the first manually loaded round was tapped off through a hole drilled in the bore about eight inches (203mm) from the muzzle, whence it entered the gas cylinder, struck the head of the piston, and drove it back, taking with it the operating rod and the bolt. The rearward movement of the piston itself was less than three inches (76mm) but in that time it was travelling with sufficient speed and power to drive the rod and bolt on rearwards to complete that part of the cycle. The return spring then took over, forcing the bolt forward; on its travel a lug on the top of the bolt struck the rear of the cartridge and forced it from its link and into the chamber. The bolt then entered the extension to the chamber where it was rotated and locked firmly; this action also released the firing pin and fired the round, after which the cycle was repeated as long as the trigger was pressed and there were rounds in the belt. This system included a number of unusual and not necessarily beneficial features. In the first place there was no gas regulator on the gun, that is to say the supply of gas was fixed, and quite outside the control of the firer. The theory was that as the piston began to move, it automatically cut off the supply of gas, and that once it was moving with sufficient energy to achieve this it must equally have enough energy to complete the cycle. This, however, was not always true in action where dirt, dust and fouling could slow the piston after it had cut off its own supply of gas so that the gun either stopped, or less usually, ran-away. A run-away gun is the term given to the situation where the working parts go back far enough to feed, chamber and fire another round, but not far enough to be engaged by the sear so that even when the finger is removed from the trigger the gun goes on firing. This is a

disconcerting business, by no means confined to the M60, which can only be stopped by holding on to the belt, and preventing it feeding. The system of locking, although very reliable, depended on an unusually long rearward movement of the operating rod, which together with the assistance of a rather soft, energy-absorbing buffer tended to slow the cyclic rate down to appreciably less than that of the British equivalent and somewhat less than half that of the MG42. The M60 had no system under which single shots could be fired, but with its slow rate it was possible for a good gunner to fire single rounds simply by quick trigger release. Like all air-cooled guns the M60 could only fire a limited number of rounds before it overheated, and in order to allow sustained fire a second barrel was provided, but the arrangements for changing it were poor. Because of the peculiar design of the piston, a new gas cylinder and bipod were permanently attached to

the barrel. Although this of course added weight, it had the advantage that a new fairly free cylinder came with the barrel. Unfortunately no barrel handle was fitted, and as the barrel might well have reached a temperature of over 500° Centigrade, great care had to be taken. An asbestos mitten was in fact issued with each gun for that specific purpose, but that kind of item got lost easily enough in action, in which case any handy piece of rag, towel, or old socks had to be used instead, which probably led to some picturesque language from the gunner and his number 2 whose duty it was to do the job, and do it fast. The feed system, which was a modified form of that on the German MG42, was adequate and it was claimed that a clean gun could lift a belt of up to one hundred rounds vertically without faltering. One of the best features of the gun was that its barrels were not only chromium plated but had stellite liners for the first six

inches (152mm) from the chamber. Stellite is a non-ferrous metal made up of cobalt, chromium, molybdenum and tungsten and the liner made a considerable difference to the life of the barrel. It will be remembered that the original British general purpose gun was intended to have the same sort of linings but this did not come about. The most precise machining is of course necessary to achieve success in this particular operation because the alternate contraction and expansion of the barrel through sustained firing can allow highly corrosive gases to penetrate between liner and bore with serious results. The sights on the gun were adequate although the system of zeroing was not. All automatic guns shoot differently with different barrels and the ideal way of ensuring that accuracy is maintained is to zero by the foresight. The barrels on the M60 had fixed foresights and zeroing was done by

adjusting the backsight for both lateral and vertical adjustment. This was very simple to do but it meant that each time the gunner changed barrels he had to remember by how much to change his backsight. This was just possible on a range but it must have taken a remarkably cool gunner to remember it in action. A belt box was supplied when the gun was being used on the move, and a simple, robust tripod was available for the sustained fire role. The original M60, perhaps like its British counterpart, was not a complete success, possibly because both countries expected too much of a general purpose gun which inevitably tends to be too heavy for the light role and too light for the heavy. The M60 was used extensively in Vietnam and partly because of practical experience there, it was improved considerably and issued as the M60E1. It is still the standard general purpose machine gun in the US Army.

7·62mm NATO
·303" SAA Ball (clip)

99

The Sub-Machine Gun

A sub-machine gun is an automatic weapon which fires pistol cartridges and which is light enough to be used two-handed from the shoulder or hip without other support. Arms of this type first came into use in World War I where the need for close-range firepower was predominant; the first country to adopt them was Italy who introduced the Villar-Perosa as early as 1915. This was a somewhat unusual double-barrelled arm firing a 9mm rimless self-loading pistol cartridge, but in spite of its obvious utility in trench warfare it was not as widely adopted as might perhaps have been expected. The British Army tried it but rejected it, mainly because of their continuing pre-occupation with the need for accurate long-range fire which the sub-machine gun could not, and cannot, provide.

The next in the field were the Germans who found it advantageous to arm a proportion of their infantry, mainly senior non-commissioned officers, with stocked self-loading pistols of the type made popular by Luger and Mauser; these were not of course true automatic weapons, since the trigger had to be pressed for each shot, but nevertheless they provided a compact and convenient source of rapid close-range fire well suited to the needs of trench warfare. In order to reduce the amount of reloading required the Germans also developed magazines with a capacity of thirty or more rounds, and from here it was but a short step to the production of a true sub-machine gun which they called, and indeed still call, a machine pistol.

Work on this new type of weapon started in 1916, the designer being the famous Hugo Schmeisser, and by 1918 the first guns had been produced. As the work was done at the Bergmann factory the gun is usually known by that name although its official designation was the MP 18 (*maschinen-pistole* 1918). After one modification, which extended its designation to MP 18.1, it was put into full production and by the summer of 1918 some thirty-five thousand had been made. This new weapon proved useful to the German infantry, particularly in their major assault in the early spring of 1918, but by then things had gone too far; the war, as it turned out, had been irretrievably lost for Germany, and after 1918 her small army was not permitted to retain the sub-machine gun with the result that its significance was to some extent lost. The Bergmann was, however, in a very real sense the prototype of almost all weapons of similar type thereafter,

so that a brief description of its functioning will serve for all.

It had a barrel just under eight inches (20cm) long and a heavy cylindrical bolt with a cocking handle permanently attached to it, its 9mm cartridges being carried in a so-called 'snail-drum' magazine, the reason for this title being obvious from the illustration (see pages 120-121). When it was required to fire the gun, the bolt was drawn back manually against a spring and held to the rear by a sear. When the trigger was pressed the sear was freed and the bolt was forced forward by the spring, stripping a cartridge from the magazine, forcing it into the chamber, and firing it. There was no locking device, nor was one necessary. The heavy bolt was still moving forward as it fired the cartridge and by the time this impetus had been first stopped and then reversed by the rearward thrust of the cartridge case the pressure had dropped to a safe level, a process accelerated by the very short length of the barrel. The bolt was then forced forward again and the cycle repeated as long as the trigger was pressed and there were rounds remaining in the magazine. There was thus no round in the chamber and therefore no risk of a shot being fired accidentally by the residual heat of the barrel, which after prolonged firing was quite considerable. The actual cyclic rate of fire was about four hundred rounds a minute and there was no provision for single shots, although this refinement was later added to virtually all SMGs.

THE BERGMANN AND LATER DEVELOPMENTS

This original Bergmann, which was fitted with a heavy, rifle-type stock, was a formidable weapon at close quarters. It was in fact sighted to one thousand metres but this was quite unrealistic. The bullet might have been reasonably accurate up to about two hundred metres but would have had relatively little stopping power at that range, since it was, after all, fired from a low-powered pistol cartridge.

It is noticeable that the only real attempt made by the Allies to produce a weapon of similar performance was the American Pedersen Device, which was a small machine pistol which could be fitted into the breech of the standard Springfield rifle and fired a magazine

1 *A British soldier fires his 9mm L2A3 sub-machine gun.*
2 *British troops with 9mm Sten Mark 2 sub-machine guns in the streets of Arnhem in 1945.*

Israel
UZI SUB-MACHINE GUN

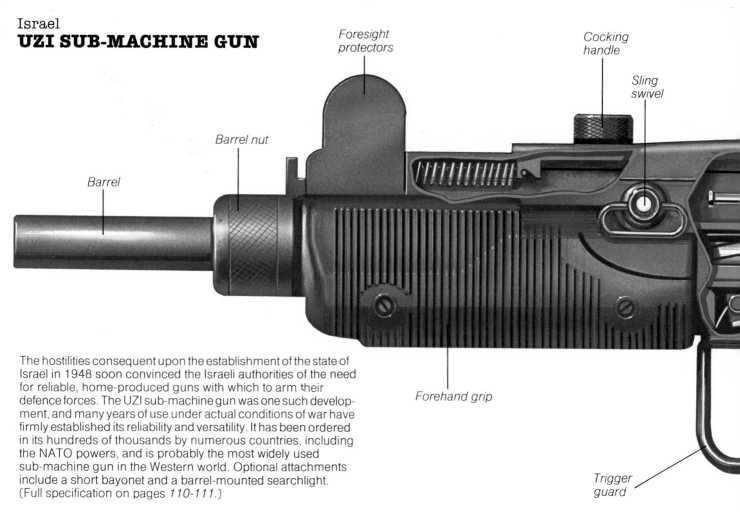

Foresight protectors

Cocking handle

Sling swivel

Barrel nut

Barrel

Forehand grip

Trigger guard

The hostilities consequent upon the establishment of the state of Israel in 1948 soon convinced the Israeli authorities of the need for reliable, home-produced guns with which to arm their defence forces. The UZI sub-machine gun was one such development, and many years of use under actual conditions of war have firmly established its reliability and versatility. It has been ordered in its hundreds of thousands by numerous countries, including the NATO powers, and is probably the most widely used sub-machine gun in the Western world. Optional attachments include a short bayonet and a barrel-mounted searchlight. (Full specification on pages *110-111*.)

Blowback (left)
When the round is fired the expanding gases force the bullet up the barrel, but they also force the cartridge case backwards. This is done with enough force to drive the bolt backwards against the resistance of the return spring.

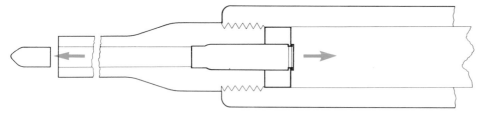

UZI with butt extended

Cartridge:
*Far left, ·303" SAA Ball
Left, 9mm Parabellum*

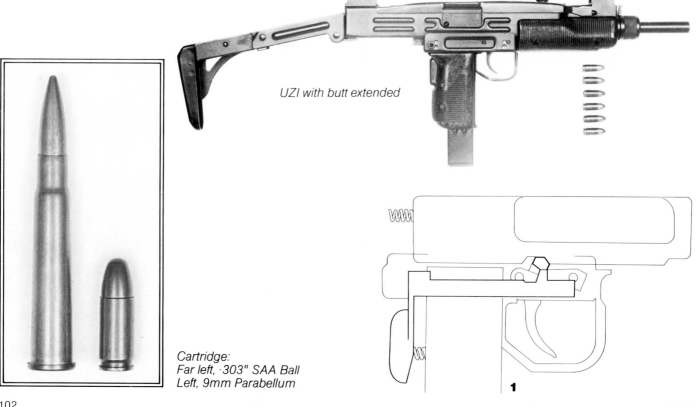

1

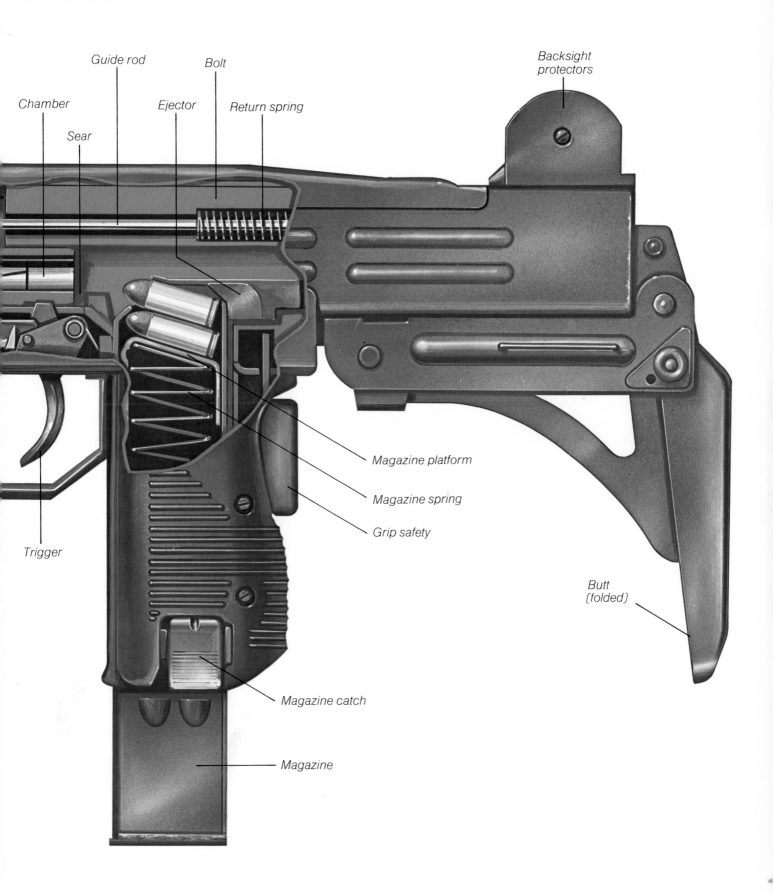

Chamber

Sear

Guide rod

Ejector

Bolt

Return spring

Backsight protectors

Trigger

Magazine platform

Magazine spring

Grip safety

Butt
(folded)

Magazine catch

Magazine

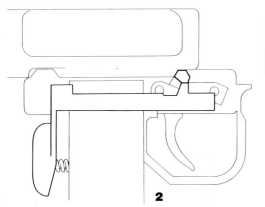

2

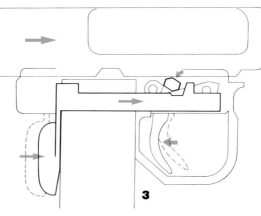

3

Grip Safety (left)
The grip safety, which is located behind the pistol grip, works whether the weapon is uncocked (**1**), or cocked (**2**). The general principle is that the safety is connected to a horizontal rod with a top lug which normally fits under the sear and prevents it from moving. When the grip safety is pushed forward against its spring the lug disengages from the sear and allows the trigger to function (**3**).

of special pistol ammunition. It was never used in action and its use was discontinued in 1923 whereupon the remaining stocks were destroyed.

During the course of World War I Colonel (later Brigadier—General) J. T. Thompson initiated experiments to produce a sub-machine gun. He had spent many years in the United States Army Ordnance department, but had retired in 1914 to work for the Remington Arms Corporation. He quickly saw the utility of this type of weapon in trench warfare, but unfortunately the first gun to bear his name only appeared in 1921. This was a bad time to sell any new type of weapon to the economy-conscious armies of the world, and very

few were sold to what may be described as legitimate buyers. A number, presumably purchased in the United States by sympathizers, were sent to Ireland where they were used extensively in the 1922-23 Civil War. They proved popular, so popular indeed that for many years the traditional picture of an Irish Republican Army man was of an individual in a trilby hat with the brim down, a grubby trench coat, and a Thompson gun, a picture only modified relatively recently by the availability of newer and vastly more effective terrorist weapons.

The other people who valued them were the gangsters who came into prominence as a result of the introduc-

1 A Finnish soldier with a 9mm Konepistooli m/31, otherwise known as 'Suomi', sub-machine gun.
2 The 0·45in M1A1 Thompson sub-machine gun, Bastogne, 1944.
3 The 0·45in M1928A1 Thompson sub-machine gun with a Cutts compensator on the muzzle.
4 The M1 Thompson was basically a much simplified M1928A1.

tion of total prohibition into the United States with the Constitutional Amendment of 1920. It is probable that relatively few of such weapons were available, but their use provided the kind of sensation beloved by the popular press, and the so-called 'Chicago

5

6

piano' became very much a symbol of criminal violence.

The final pre-war model appeared in 1928, but in spite of its reputation it never really caught on with the authorities; a few police forces and other law-enforcement agencies purchased a small number but their continued manufacture was very much in doubt until 1938 when the Thompson was finally officially adopted by the United States Army. Then the war came, and in the course of the next few years hundreds of thousands were made, a simplified model being produced for ease of wartime manufacture in 1942. Brigadier-General Thompson died in 1940 and so never saw the belated

boom in his invention. In some ways its late adoption was ironical, for there were by then a number of more modern weapons in existence. The Thompson, however, old fashioned though it had begun to appear, was available, and as no one could afford to wait, its wartime fame was assured.

During World War II the United States produced a variety of other sub-machine guns. The Reising was complex and not wholly reliable, and the M3 was a functional all-metal weapon, usually known as the 'grease-gun' from its clear resemblance to that useful tool. None achieved the fame of General Thompson's original weapon, which added a new word, 'tommy-gun', to the

5 A Vietcong surrenders with his US 0·45 M3A1 sub-machine gun.
6 US troops in Brest, 1944. The man in the centre is carrying an M1A1 Thompson sub-machine gun.

vocabularies of the world.

It is of interest that all American sub-machine guns fired the standard .45″ cartridge for the 1911 Colt self-loading pistol. This is not surprising when we take into account the fact that Thompson was closely concerned with its original introduction; although an excellent cartridge, it was in many ways too powerful and made the weapons too heavy to handle.

The period between the two World

105

Wars saw a steady increase in the use of the sub-machine gun, which was used particularly extensively in the Spanish Civil War. In spite of these clear indications, however, Great Britain took no really positive steps to develop a weapon of this type in preparation for World War II even when many people saw it to be inevitable. This was partly for reasons of economy but largely because of her continuing dedication to the high velocity cartridge, a relic perhaps of the devastation wrought by her almost legendary riflemen of 1914. She did in fact test various models, usually referred to in the proceedings of the Small Arms Committee as 'gangster guns', but when the war actually broke out in 1939 she was compelled to order a large number of Thompsons. They were reliable enough but heavy and old fashioned compared with those of her opponents, and she hastily began to design and produce sub-machine guns of her own.

The first to go into production was a copy of the German MP 28, which was itself a close development of the original Bergmann MP 18.1. This new weapon, which was known as the Lanchester after its British designer, was a robust, old-fashioned, brass-bound sort of weapon, and in the event was issued almost entirely to the Royal Navy, who retained it for many years after the war, but who probably used it very little, having bigger and better weapons available. Meanwhile research was continuing for a light, simple, easily manufactured weapon for mass-production, and early in 1941 there appeared the Sten gun. The name came from the initial letters of the two men principally responsible, Shepherd and Turpin, added to the first two letters of Enfield, and in spite of some inevitable defects the gun proved a success. It was jokingly known to the British Army as the 'tin Tommy-gun' and was produced by the million for the use of the British Army and certain allies, and for dropping to partisans in enemy-occupied territories. It went through a series of Marks, becoming more and more simple for ease of manufacture, and even ran to a silenced version for use mainly by special forces. As the bullet did not exceed the speed of sound there was no 'sonic boom' to contend with, and the silencer, though bulky, was a relatively simple device. Bursts could not be fired through it except in emergencies but on single shots it was useful for the silent elimination of sentries and similar tasks. Even German ingenuity could not improve on the Sten as a simple arm for mass-production and it was copied by them, mainly for use by their home defence force, the *Volkssturm*.

One rather unusual weapon developed by the British during World War II was the de Lisle silenced carbine. As it did not fire automatic, it was not a sub-machine gun in the proper sense of the word, but in many ways this section seems to be the best place to include it. It was based on a standard service rifle, very considerably shortened and rechambered to fire the same ·45″ Colt cartridge already being used in the Thompson guns. Its main point of interest was its silencer, which although rather bulky was extremely effective. It shot well to two hundred metres or more and was used by Special Forces. It was also resurrected for the Malay emergency where its ability to deal silently with sentries guarding bandit camps made it useful.

TREATY RESTRICTIONS

After 1918 the small remaining German army was very seriously restricted in the use of automatic weapons by the Treaty of Versailles, and the Bergmann disappeared as a military weapon although the police were permitted to retain a few for internal security purposes. Ways round the irritatingly restrictive treaty were however soon found, and by 1922 Germany was again making Steyr-Solothurn sub-machine guns in Switzerland under cover of a Swiss subsidiary company. Within a very few years she finally abandoned all serious pretence at compliance with the Treaty of Versailles, and began extensive re-

1 Covered by an L2A3 sub-machine gun, a British paratrooper clears a derelict house in Berlin.

armament. In 1938 the German Army adopted the MP38; this was commonly referred to as the Schmeisser, although it is unlikely that the famous Hugo had much to do with it, and within a few years it had established a notable reputation. It was a modern, all-metal weapon wth a folding stock, and although it underwent a number of modifications during the war it remained substantially unchanged.

The Russians do not appear to have developed or used a successful sub-machine gun until 1934. During the fighting between the Communists and the White Russians in 1919 a light automatic weapon was in fact used but it was more of an early type of assault rifle than a sub-machine gun and therefore may be disregarded. There was also an early invention of Tokarev, perhaps better known for his revolver, but this was a failure, largely because it fired rimmed revolver cartridges which caused constant jams in the magazine. The first forerunner of a long series was the PPD, the *Pistolet Pulemyot (machine pistol) Degtyaryev*, of 1934. This was a sound and reliable weapon with a seventy-one round drum which made it rather heavy, and like all later Soviet arms of this type it fired the bottle-shaped 7·62mm pistol cartridge.

The Russians were without doubt the major users of the sub-machine gun in World War II. This was not apparently due to any pre-conceived ideas as to its superiority, but rather as a matter of necessity to overcome manufacturing problems. In the course of their early extensive reverses at the hands of the Germans, a great deal of their industrial capacity was lost or destroyed. The sub-machine gun was easier to make than the more sophisticated weapons, and so it was produced by the million. It proved a successful arm in the desperate close-quarter fighting in the various besieged Soviet cities, and whole regiments were eventually armed with it. The war saw the appearance of a whole range of PPs, none differing very greatly from its predecessor. The last was the PPS 43, many of which are still in use in various countries in Asia.

There were of course a number of other successful sub-machine guns, notably perhaps a whole series of Italian Berettas, and the Australian Owen gun.

Post-war development of the sub-machine gun was to be complicated, and largely inhibited, by the rise in importance of a new type of weapon, the assault rifle. This has been dealt with in the introductory chapter on the rifle so that all that needs to be said here is that it was in essence a sub-machine gun but one firing a cartridge more akin to that of an orthodox rifle than the pistol cartridge previously used. This new arm naturally had its effect on the sub-machine gun, because it could do all that a sub-machine gun could do, and a good deal more besides. The cartridges naturally weighed more, and being more powerful increased the weight and complexity of the new weapon, but this was a small price to pay for the increased utility. The Germans had started the trend, followed soon after the war by the Russians who based their AK 47 closely on the German original, and by the Americans with their Colt Armalite range. The only new sub-machine gun of any real significance to emerge out of either country was the United States Ingram which is illustrated on pages 152-153 and which is very much more a weapon for police and other security forces than a military arm. The Colt Commando, it is true, has sub-machine gun characteristics but as it is a lightened version of the Armalite rifle, and fires the same ammunition, it is probably fairer to leave it in the assault rifle class.

Even the nations which did not adopt assault rifles immediately made relatively little progress. Great Britain, having rejected her very advanced EM 2 rifle, finally abandoned the Sten gun and adopted the L2A1, now the L2A3, perhaps better known as the Sterling. Germany, once allowed to re-arm, ex-

2 *An American soldier examines a Chinese-made copy of the Russian 7.62mm PPSh 41 sub-machine gun, designed by G. S. Shpagin for ease of manufacture.*

perimented with several more or less orthodox designs, and is now developing a weapon to fire a new type of caseless round. Israel, having gained independence in 1948, had an urgent need for arms to defend herself against her Arab neighbours and soon adopted the excellent UZI, while France developed her MAT 49.

DECLINE OF THE SMG

The old sub-machine gun was a popular weapon in the Far East and was extensively used by the Chinese in Korea and by the Vietnamese in Indo-China, but has now been largely superceded by Russian type assault rifles. This, in fact, is the general trend. The sub-machine gun is essentially a weapon of moderate capacity but cheap and easy to make, its principal limitation being its relatively weak 9mm cartridge. The only significant improvement would appear to be in using a more powerful round, but it is difficult to see how this can be done without changing its whole character. On balance it seems likely that its military significance will dwindle, but that it will remain a useful arm for security forces for the foreseeable future.

Czechoslavakia
ZK 383

Length: 35·4" (899mm)
Weight: 9·37lb (4·25kg)
Barrel: 12·8" (325mm)
Calibre: 9mm
Rifling: 6 groove r/hand
Feed: 30-round box
Cyclic Rate: 500 and 700 rpm
Muzzle Velocity: 1250 f/s (365 m/s)
Sights: 875 yds (800m)

This weapon, which was designed by the Koucky brothers at Brno, first appeared in 1933 and was still in production three years after the end of World War II. It is a most sophisticated and very well made weapon, manufactured of precision castings of excellent finish, and cannot have been cheap to produce. It is of particular interest in having a dual rate of fire; this is achieved by removing a

Czechoslavakia
VZ 61 (THE SKORPION)

Length (folded):
10 65" (271mm)
Weight: 2 9lb (1·31kg)
Barrel: 4·5" (114mm)
Calibre: 7·65mm
Rifling: 6 groove r/hand
Feed: 10/20-round box
Cyclic Rate: 700 rpm
Muzzle Velocity:
970 f/s (294 m/s)
Sights:
Flip, 82 and 164 yds
(75 and 150m)

This is a good example of the rather small number of true machine pistols, its general dimensions being comparable to those of the Mauser pistol model 1896. It is therefore of relatively limited use as a military weapon, except possibly for tank crews, motor cyclists and similar categories for whom a compact secondary weapon is more important than performance. Its small calibre also reduces its stopping power although of course the use of automatic fire helps considerably in this

respect. There is also a bigger version, made only in limited quantities, which fires a 9mm round and is in consequence a good deal heavier although similar in essence. The Skorpion works on the normal blowback system. Very light automatic weapons often have the disadvantage that their cyclic rate of fire is unacceptably high, but in this weapon the problem is largely overcome by the use of a type of buffer device in the butt. It has a light wire butt for use from the shoulder; this can be

folded forward when not required without affecting the working of the weapon. Although the size and capacity of the Skorpion reduces its military efficiency, it is an excellent weapon for police or other forms of internal security work since it is inconspicuous and easily concealed. Its low muzzle velocity also makes it relatively easy to silence, and an effective model is available which is an additional advantage in this sort of role. It has been sold to many African countries.

weight on the bolt, which increases its rate of functioning. There is also a quick release barrel, although it is not clear whether this was for changing in action or simply to facilitate cleaning. The ZK 383 will fire either single rounds or automatic as required, the change lever above the trigger being pushed back or forward as necessary. The stud behind it is the push-in safety. The pierced barrel casing carries the foresight and a well made tangent backsight. Another unusual feature is its folding bipod, which when not required for use is turned backward into a recess in the woodwork. This bipod is said to make a considerable improvement in the accuracy of the gun, but even so it is likely that the maximum setting of 800 yards is optimistic.

This was the standard sub-machine gun used by the Bulgarian Army during and after World War II. The Germans continued to manufacture it after they had over-run Czechoslovakia and it was used by their SS troops. A modified version was also produced for police use. It had no bipod and no tangent sight. It is believed that there was a variation of the standard gun with a bipod which folded forward. Some models took a bayonet.

The Skorpion with butt folded

9mm Parabellum

7·65mm Auto Pistol

·303" SAA Ball

Israel
UZI

Length: 25·2" (640mm)
Weight: 7·7lb (3·5kg)
Barrel: 10·2" (260mm)
Calibre: 9mm
Rifling: 4 groove r/hand
Feed: 25/32/40-round box
Cyclic Rate: 600 rpm
Muzzle Velocity:
1280 f/s (390 m/s)
Sights:
Flip, 110-219 yds (100/200m)

At midnight on 14 May, 1948 the British mandate over Palestine ceased, and the Jewish State of Israel was declared. On the very next day the new state was invaded by its Arab neighbours, and there followed nearly eight months of war, at the end of which Israel had not only defended her own territory successfully but had

also occupied some of that belonging to her attackers. In spite of her success however it was clear that she needed a reliable weapon which she could make from her own resources in sufficient numbers to arm the bulk of her population if necessary, and by 1950 Major Uziel Gal of the Israeli Army had designed the

Denmark
MADSEN MODEL 50

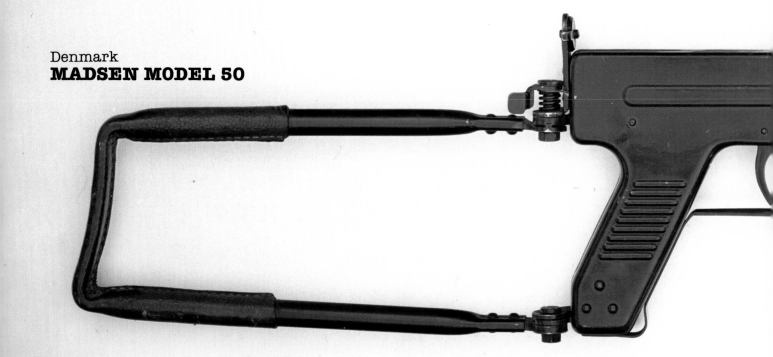

Length: 31·25" (794mm)
Weight: 6·95lb (3·15kg)
Barrel: 7·8" (199mm)
Calibre: 9mm
Rifling: 4 groove r/hand
Feed: 32-round box
Cyclic Rate: 550 rpm
Muzzle Velocity:
1250 f/s (365 m/s)
Sights: Fixed

The first sub-machine gun to be made in Denmark was a type of Finnish Suomi, made under licence by the Danish Madsen Industrial Syndicate in 1940. Production continued throughout the war, the gun being used not only by the Danes themselves but by the Germans and the Finns. The same syndicate has made all Danish sub-machine guns since. The first weapon of the present series was the Model 1946, and the Danes, profiting from wartime advances in mass production, made sure

that it was designed in such a way as to be able to take advantage of these improved techniques. The main body, including the pistol grip, is made from two side pieces, hinged together at the rear, so that the weapon can be easily opened for repair, cleaning or inspection. It does, however, have the disadvantage that springs are liable to fall out unless care is taken. The Madsen works on the normal blowback system and will fire single rounds or bursts as required. One of its unusual

weapon illustrated. Production started almost immediately and still continues to date.

The UZI works on the normal blowback principle and is made from heavy pressings in conjunction with certain heat-resistant plastics. The rear end of the barrel extends backward into the body and the front of the bolt is hollowed out so as to wrap round this rear projection. The magazine fits into the pistol grip which affords it firm support and also keeps the point of balance above it, so that the gun can if necessary be fired one-handed like a pistol. It fires single rounds or bursts as required. Most of the early UZIs had a short wooden butt 8 inches long, as illustrated, but a very few were made longer. Later models have a folding metal stock. It is made under licence in Holland and used by many other countries.

features is a grip safety behind the magazine housing which (with the magazine itself) acts as a forward hand grip. Unless this safety is in the gun will not function, which makes it impossible to fire it one-handed. The tubular metal stock is on a pivot and folds onto the right side of the weapon. The Model 50, the gun illustrated, is similar to the Model 46, the main difference being the milled knob cocking handle which replaced the flat plate of the earlier model. When the new Model was demonstrated in 1950 many countries showed great interest in it and the delegation from Great Britain was sufficiently impressed to recommend that it should be considered in the search for a new weapon to replace the Sten gun. It was tested against other arms and was recommended for adoption by non-fighting troops if the new British EM 2 rifle made a sub-machine gun unnecessary for the infantry. In the event the new rifle was not adopted and the Sterling was taken into general use. The curved magazine actually belongs to the later model.

9mm Parabellum

9mm Parabellum

·303" SAA Ball

BERGMANN MP18.I

Length: 32" (813mm)
Weight: 9·2lb (4·18kg)
Barrel: 7·88" (200mm)
Calibre: 9mm
Rifling: 6 groove r/hand
Feed: 32-round snaildrum
Cyclic Rate: 400 rpm
Muzzle Velocity:
1250 f/s (365 m/s)
Sights:
Flip, 110-219 yds (100/200m)

By the end of 1914 World War I had settled down to a static if bloody business of opposing trenches resembling a two-sided siege on a huge scale and this relatively new type of warfare brought into use a whole host of new weapons; some of these, like mortars and grenades, were simply modernized versions of long obsolete items, but some were genuinely new, and the sub-machine gun comes into this latter category. The first to appear on the actual battlefield was the Italian Villa Perosa of 1915. This was, however, rather complex and in spite of its obvious potential it does not seem to have made any great impression.

The Germans soon began to arm a proportion of their infantry with stocked pistols of the Mauser and Luger type (both of which are dealt with elsewhere in this book), and it was a short step to the introduction of a somewhat heavier version with the capacity to fire bursts. Work on a prototype weapon started in 1916 at the Bergmann factory, the designer being Hugo Schmeisser, the famous son of an almost equally famous father, and by the early months

BERGMANN MP28.II

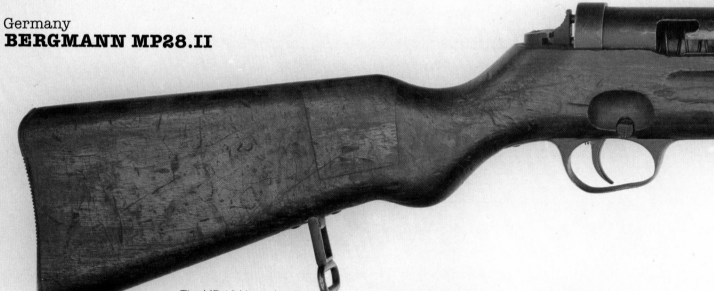

Length: 32" (812mm)
Weight: 8·8lb (4kg)
Barrel: 7·8" (199mm)
Calibre: 9mm
Rifling: 6 groove r/hand
Feed: 20/30/50-round box
Cyclic Rate: 500 rpm
Muzzle Velocity:
1250 f/s (365 m/s)
Sights: 1094 yds (1000m)

The MP 18.I issued to the German police for internal security purposes in 1919 had been slightly modified by Schmeisser in the light of practical experience in the previous year. The chief change was a new magazine housing designed to take a straight box magazine of modern type rather than the complex clockwork-operated snail drum which had given a good deal of trouble in the conditions of trench warfare. A few years later the same designer made even more improvements, and as these were sufficient to warrant a new designation the modified MP 18.I appeared in 1928 as the MP 28.II, the II denoting two minor modifications to the prototype. The new gun had some interesting features, chief of which was its ability to fire either bursts or single shots as required. This was controlled by a circular stud above the trigger, which had to be pushed in from the right for automatic, and from the left for single shots. The gun also incorporated an elaborate tangent backsight graduated by hundreds up to a thousand metres, which must have been far outside any practical service range. It was equipped with straight box magazines, but the magazine housing was so designed that it would if necessary accept the old snail drum type. These various improvements did not change

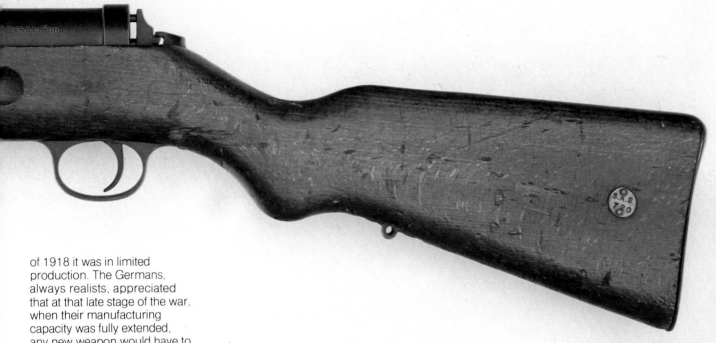

of 1918 it was in limited production. The Germans, always realists, appreciated that at that late stage of the war, when their manufacturing capacity was fully extended, any new weapon would have to be simple to make and the MP 18.I fulfilled that requirement. The techniques of mass production by the use of pressings, spot welding, and pinning were, however, hardly developed so that 'simple' is a relative term when compared with, say, the Sten gun of a quarter of a century later. The Bergmann was machined, and

although elaborate milling had necessarily been abandoned, its general finish was relatively good. Its weakest component was its magazine, which was a of a type originally developed for the Luger pistol, and which was too complex and liable to stoppage to be fully reliable. The Germans proposed to

have six guns per company; each was to have a number two to carry ammunition, and there were to be three hand carts in addition, which presupposed a type of barrage fire, but it came too late. Its main interest is therefore its influence on future design, which was very significant.

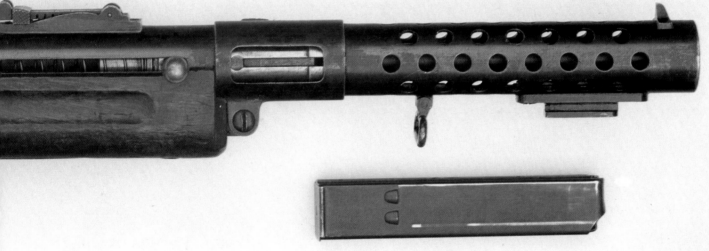

its general appearance very materially so that it still resembled the old MP 18. The Bergmann MP 28.II was produced in Germany by the Haenel Weapon Factory at Suhl, but as there were still some restrictions on domestic production of military firearms a great many more were produced under Schmeisser licence by a Belgian company in Herstal, and it was adopted by the Belgian army in small numbers in 1934. The

Bergmann soon established a reputation for reliability and was purchased in South America (where it was extensively used in a series of small wars there) and by the Portuguese who used it as a police weapon. Although it was mainly manufactured in 9mm Parabellum, it also appeared in 9mm Bergmann, 7·65mm Parabellum, 7·63mm, and even for the American ·45" cartridge. It seems probable that its main use was in the

Spanish Civil War of 1936-39, where its robust construction made it an ideal weapon for the militias by whom the war was mainly fought. It ceased to be made before World War II, but had a revival in the shape of the British Lanchester.

9mm Parabellum
9mm Parabellum

·303" SAA Ball

Germany
STEYR-SOLOTHURN S100

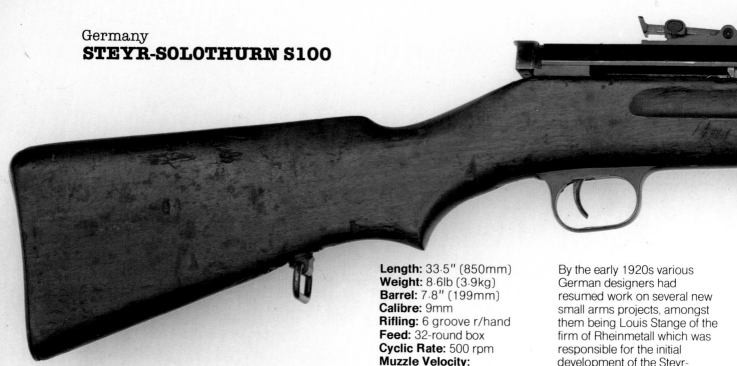

Length: 33·5" (850mm)
Weight: 8·6lb (3·9kg)
Barrel: 7·8" (199mm)
Calibre: 9mm
Rifling: 6 groove r/hand
Feed: 32-round box
Cyclic Rate: 500 rpm
Muzzle Velocity:
1375 f/s (417 m/s)
Sights:
Tangent, 547 yds (500m)

By the early 1920s various German designers had resumed work on several new small arms projects, amongst them being Louis Stange of the firm of Rheinmetall which was responsible for the initial development of the Steyr-Solothurn S100. German arms production was of course seriously restricted in the years immediately following World War I and various means were taken to evade the provisions of the Treaty of Versailles. In 1929

Germany
MASCHINENPISTOLE MP40 (SCHMEISSER)

Length: 32·8" (833mm)
Weight: 8·87lb (4·024kg)
Barrel: 9·9" (251mm)
Calibre: 9mm
Rifling: 6 groove r/hand
Feed: 32-round box
Cyclic Rate: 500 rpm
Muzzle Velocity:
1250 f/s (365 m/s)
Sights:
Flip, 110/219 yds (100/200m)

In spite of the success of the Bergmann sub-machine gun in the closing months of World War I the German Army of the 1930s, or at least a powerful faction of it, appears to have regarded the type as being primarily a police weapon, having perhaps had some place in the trenches but none in the new type of warfare for which they were planning. By 1938 however, perhaps because of the lessons of the Spanish Civil War, orders were given to the Erma factory to design and produce a reliable and easily manufactured sub-machine gun, mainly for use by armoured and airborne troops. This was quickly achieved, and in the same year the new weapon had been issued as the MP 38, the first weapon of

its type to be adopted by the German Army since 1918. This weapon, with its immediate successors, was to prove one of the most popular and best known sub-machine guns of World War II. It was the first arm of its type ever to be made entirely from metal and plastic, with no woodwork of any kind. Gone was the heavy Bergmann type butt and carefully machined body, and in their place had come a folding tubular metal stock and a receiver of steel tube, slotted to reduce weight. One unusual item was the projection below the barrel near the muzzle; this was said to have been placed there so that the weapon could be fired through the port in an armoured vehicle without the risk that a sudden jolt might

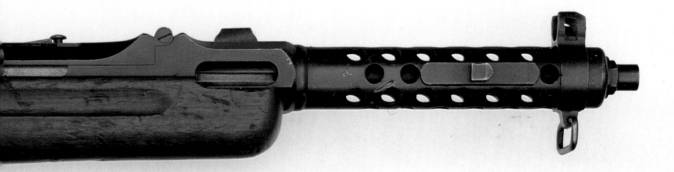

Rheinmetall acquired the Swiss firm of Solothurn so as to be able to make and sell arms legally, and it was there that the main developments took place. Once the gun was perfected, however, bulk production was sub-contracted to the Austrian firm of Steyr which started work in 1929. The origins of the weapon are thus to some extent international, but the main initiative undoubtedly came from Germany. The Steyr-Solothurn which was of orthodox mechanism, was extremely well made, the machining, milling and general finish being of an unusually high standard which must have made it expensive to produce. Most weapons have provision for a bayonet and a small number were made with longer barrels. A light tripod mount was also designed but never produced commercially. Most of the production models were also fitted with an unusual device in the shape of a built-in magazine filler. The magazine housing had a slot on top with recesses to take the Mauser pistol type clip, and a magazine locking device underneath. In 1934 two of these guns, one the normal version and one with the longer barrel, were bought and tested by the British Government who were at that time showing some interest in weapons of that type, but although it was well reported on no further action was taken regarding it. Many other countries, however, showed an even greater interest in the gun which was widely sold. At least four South American countries bought it in considerable quantities and it was used in the war fought in the primeval forest of Argentina's Gran Chaco in 1932. It was also adopted by Austria for her army and her police, the gun in this case being modified to fire the more powerful Mauser cartridge, and manufactured in Austria.

cause the gun to be pulled back, still firing, into the vehicle itself. The MP 38, although an excellent weapon, was relatively slow and expensive to produce, and as soon as the early fighting of World War II had shown the desirability of this sort of arm, steps were taken to produce a similar weapon in large quanitities. This led to the gun illustrated, the MP 40, which although of similar appearance to its predecessor made more extensive use of pressing, spot-welding, and brazing. Perhaps its most important change was the introduction of a safety device, it having been found (like the Sten) that a moderately severe jolt was sometimes enough to bounce the bolt back and fire a round. A number of the earlier 1938 models were also modified in this way as a result of active service experience. Most of the later MP 40s were made with horizontal ribs on the magazine housing. Only a few, like the one illustrated, were made without them.

A later model was fitted with a double side-by-side magazine in a sliding housing. Oddly enough the famous Hugo Schmeisser had no hand in the original design of the MP 38 (although his factory manufactured the MP 40).

Nevertheless the name stuck, and the gun became one of the most famous weapons of World War II, some even being used by Allied soldiers in preference to their own sub-machine guns. Over 1,000,000 had been produced by 1945.

9mm Parabellum

9mm Parabellum

·303" SAA Ball

Great Britain
LANCHESTER MARK I

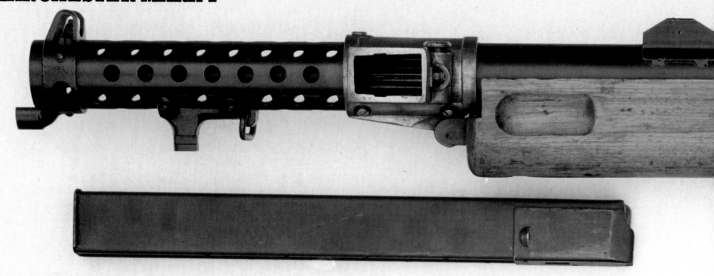

Length: 33·5" (851mm)
Weight: 9·65lb (4·38kg)
Barrel: 7·9" (200mm)
Calibre: 9mm
Rifling: 6 groove r/hand
Feed: 50-round box
Cyclic Rate: 600 rpm
Muzzle Velocity:
1200 f/s (365 m/s)
Sights:
Tangent, 600 yds (549m)

In June 1940 Great Britain was in a very serious situation. Her expeditionary force had been compelled to make a hasty evacuation, mainly through Dunkirk, leaving behind it the bulk of its heavy weapons, and there was a very real risk that the victorious German Army would invade the country. One of the weapons which

had belatedly impressed the British military authorities was the sub-machine gun, but although large numbers had been ordered from the United States there was no British model available. Arrangements were therefore hastily made to copy the German MP 28 which was known to be reliable, and a British version was designed by

Mr George Lanchester of the Sterling Armament Company, after whom the completed weapon was named.
The new weapon was at first intended for the Royal Air Force and the Royal Navy, and in the event most of them went to the latter. The Lanchester, which bore an obvious resemblance to its parent arm,

Great Britain
STEN MARK 1

Length: 35·25" (896mm)
Weight: 7·21lb (3·27kg)
Barrel: 7·8" (198mm)
Calibre: 9mm
Rifling: 6 groove r/hand
Feed: 32-round box
Cyclic Rate: 550 rpm
Muzzle Velocity:
1200 f/s (365 m/s)
Sights: Fixed

By mid-1941 large numbers of sub-machine guns were arriving from the United States. Great Britain and the Commonwealth were, however, engaged in raising and equipping new armies and in addition there were urgent demands for supplies and replacements for North and East Africa where British and Colonial troops were operating against the Italians. It was thus

clear that there was an urgent requirement for a simple, home-produced sub-machine gun, and by the middle of 1941 a weapon had not only been designed but was in limited production and undergoing user trials. This was the famous Sten, which took its name from the initial letters of the surnames of the two people most closely concerned with its development Major (later

Colonel) Shepherd who was a director of the Birmingham Small Arms Company and Mr Turpin, the principal designer, allied to the first two letters of Enfield, the location of the Royal Small Arms factory

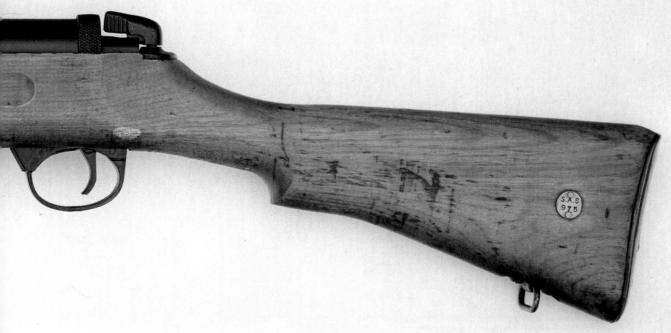

was a robust and reliable gun; British industry had not then been converted to a war footing so that the machining and finish of the weapon was of a very high quality, with a rifle type walnut stock (complete with brass buttplate), and a brass magazine housing. It was also fitted with a standard and boss to allow the ordinary Lee

Enfield bayonet to be fixed if necessary.
It had a simple blowback mechanism and could fire either single rounds or automatic as required. It functioned well with most of the standard makes of 9mm rimless cartridge with the exception of the one for the Beretta. There was also a later

Mark I which only fired automatic. The Lanchester saw little real service except with the occasional boat or landing party, but it remained in service with the Royal Navy for a long time. Many years after the war most HM ships carried racks of them, chained for security, though rarely used.

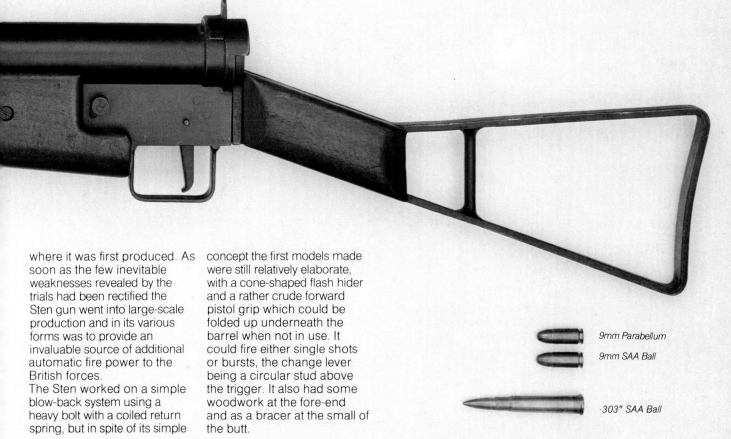

9mm Parabellum

9mm SAA Ball

·303" SAA Ball

where it was first produced. As soon as the few inevitable weaknesses revealed by the trials had been rectified the Sten gun went into large-scale production and in its various forms was to provide an invaluable source of additional automatic fire power to the British forces.
The Sten worked on a simple blow-back system using a heavy bolt with a coiled return spring, but in spite of its simple

concept the first models made were still relatively elaborate, with a cone-shaped flash hider and a rather crude forward pistol grip which could be folded up underneath the barrel when not in use. It could fire either single shots or bursts, the change lever being a circular stud above the trigger. It also had some woodwork at the fore-end and as a bracer at the small of the butt.

Great Britain
STEN GUN MARK 2

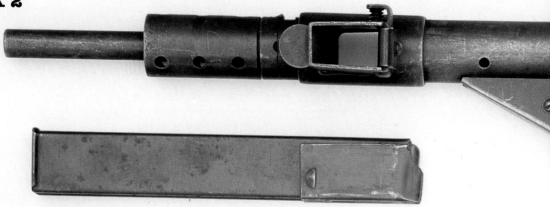

Length: 30" (762mm)
Weight: 6·65lb (3kg)
Barrel: 7·75" (197mm)
Calibre: 9mm
Rifling: 6/2 groove r/hand
Feed: 32-round box
Cyclic Rate: 550 rpm
Muzzle Velocity:
1200 f/s (365 m/s)
Sights: Fixed

Towards the end of 1941 a modified version of the Sten Mark I appeared in the form of the Mark 2, this being the first of a long series of changes in the general design of the weapon. The Mark 2 was basically a somewhat stripped-down version of the Mark I, the intention being to simplify manufacturing processes wherever possible. The British gun trade had always prided itself on the finish of its weapons almost as much as on their effectiveness, and the tradition of machined and blued metal allied with polished walnut was a strong one. Nevertheless Great Britain was by this time fighting very literally for her existence and had therefore reached the inevitable conclusion that in emergencies, appearance was not important, only effectiveness, which set a fashion particularly in world sub-machine guns, for many years afterwards. This resulted in the Sten gun Mark 2, the ugliest, nastiest weapon ever used by the British Army. It looked cheap because it was

Great Britain
STEN GUN MARK 2 (SECOND PATTERN)

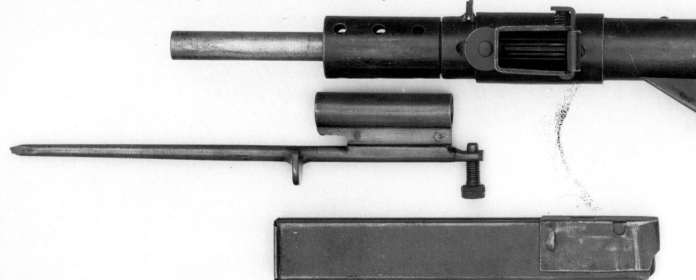

Length: 30" (762mm)
Weight: 6·65lb (3kg)
Barrel: 7·75" (197mm)
Calibre: 9mm
Rifling: 2 or 5 groove r/hand
Feed: 32-round box
Cyclic Rate: 550 rpm
Muzzle Velocity:
1200 f/s (365 m/s)
Sights: Fixed

The British and Colonial forces appeared to have an insatiable appetite for Sten guns. Over one hundred thousand of the earlier Marks had been produced by early 1942 and there was still no slackening of the demand. Apart from the inevitable loss and damage in action, more and more troops were being raised and trained, and as the prospect of an invasion of North West Europe, with the probability of extensive street fighting in towns and villages, drew closer the need for sub-machine guns continued to increase. Apart from the regular armies there was also an increasing demand for light, easily concealed automatic weapons from the various Resistance movements in occupied Europe so that production had to be increased accordingly. There was, however, an equal need for

cheap, with its great unfiled blobs of crude welding metal, its general appearance of scrap-iron, and its tendency to fall to pieces if dropped onto a hard surface. Nevertheless it worked, and not only worked but managed to incorporate one or two improvements, notably by attaching the magazine housing to a rotatable sleeve, held by a spring, so that in bad conditions it could be turned upwards through 90° thus acting as a dust cover for the ejection opening. This was a most useful refinement at a

time when the British Army was engaged in large-scale fighting in North Africa. Although the British Army, accustomed to its high quality Short Magazine Lee Enfield rifles and handsomely finished Bren light machine guns, joked about their 'tin Tommy-gun' they got good value out of it. Perhaps one of the most persistent weaknesses in the make-up of the wartime Sten gun was in the relatively poor quality of its magazine, although in the circumstances of hasty construction with poor

metal this is not altogether to be wondered at. In particular the lips were very susceptible to damage, which had a serious effect on the feed and led to endless stoppages. It was also found that the dirt and dust inseparable from the fighting in the Western desert, tended to clog the magazine, and although careful attention to cleanliness helped in this respect the problem was never really solved with this particular weapon. Despite these drawbacks, the Mark 2 was an important weapon.

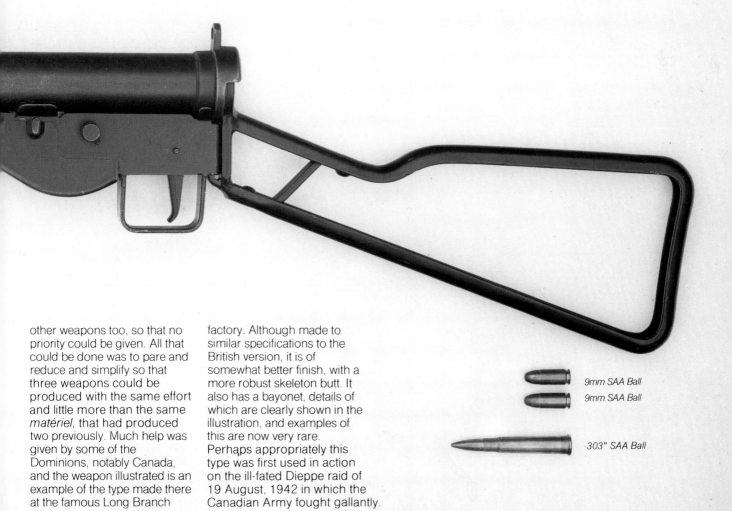

9mm SAA Ball

9mm SAA Ball

·303" SAA Ball

other weapons too, so that no priority could be given. All that could be done was to pare and reduce and simplify so that three weapons could be produced with the same effort and little more than the same *matériel,* that had produced two previously. Much help was given by some of the Dominions, notably Canada, and the weapon illustrated is an example of the type made there at the famous Long Branch

factory. Although made to similar specifications to the British version, it is of somewhat better finish, with a more robust skeleton butt. It also has a bayonet, details of which are clearly shown in the illustration, and examples of this are now very rare. Perhaps appropriately this type was first used in action on the ill-fated Dieppe raid of 19 August, 1942 in which the Canadian Army fought gallantly.

Great Britain
STEN GUN MARK 6(S)

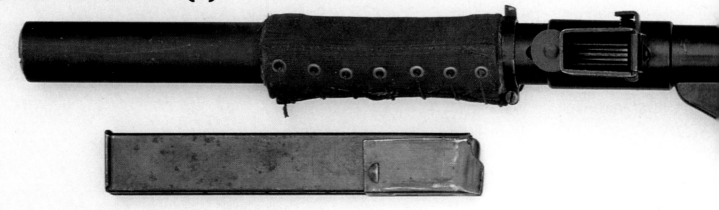

Length (silenced):
35.75" (908mm)
Weight: 9.8lb (4.45kg)
Barrel: 7.80" (198mm)
Calibre: 9mm
Rifling: 6 groove r/hand
Feed: 32-round box
Cyclic Rate: 550 rpm
Muzzle Velocity:
c1000 f/s (305 m/s)
Sights: Fixed

The Mark 2 Sten, which has already been described, probably marked the lowest point in the gun's history, and thereafter quality began to improve. Practically all components were still made in small factories and workshops with no previous connection with the manufacture of firearms, but, perhaps due to experience, the general finish was markedly better than in the early days. There was a Mark 3 (similar in appearance to the Mark 2) which was made in huge numbers and this was followed by a Mark 4, which never went into full scale production. This in turn was followed by probably the best Sten of all, the Mark 5, which was to see service from 1944 until well into the 1950s. Although very similar to its predecessors it was of more robust construction with a wooden butt (some with brass buttplates) and pistol grip, and provision was made for it to take the standard bayonet. Experiments had been conducted earlier with a silenced Mark 6 Sten which was sufficiently successful to attract the admiration of Colonel Skorzeny, the famous German who rescued Mussolini, and in 1944 it was decided that a weapon of this type was again required. The standard Mark 2 silencer was

Australia
OWEN MACHINE CARBINE

Length: 32" (813mm)
Weight: 9·35lb (4·24kg)
Barrel: 9·75" (250mm)
Calibre: 9mm
Rifling: 7 groove r/hand
Feed: 32-round box
Cyclic Rate: 700 rpm
Muzzle Velocity:
1375 f/s (420 m/s)
Sights: Fixed, offset

When Japan entered World War II on the side of the Axis powers, Australia found herself in a precarious position. Most of her small army was engaged in the Middle East and her vast and sparsely inhabited country presented a most attractive target to a warlike race seeking living room. Although there was a well established arms factory in existence at Lithgow, Australia was not then a very industrialized country, but she began to produce arms as a matter of hard necessity. One of her first efforts was an Australian Sten, known, perhaps inevitably, as the Austen, but although by no means a bad

boom' effect, but by drilling gas escape holes in the barrel the velocity was brought down to the required figure. The silencer tended to heat rapidly so a canvas hand guard was laced over it. It was not considered advisable to fire bursts through the silencer except in extreme emergencies. The Mark 6 Sten was used mainly by airborne forces and Resistance fighters in World War II and as late as 1953.

thus fitted to the Mark 5, which was then re-designated Mark 6(S). The muzzle velocity of the Mark 5 bullet was in excess of the speed of sound which posed a number of problems in connection with the 'sonic

weapon it was never popular with the Australian Army. The first locally designed sub-machine gun was the work of Lieutenant E. Owen, of the Australian Army, which was adopted in November, 1941 and put into production immediately. It was a well made weapon, if a little on the heavy side, and was an immediate success with the soldiers. It was of fairly orthodox design and its point of balance was

immediately above the pistol grip which allowed it to be fired one-handed if necessary. The magazine was vertically above the gun and although this involved offset sights the idea was popular because it helped when moving through thick cover. All Owens were camouflaged after 1943 and provision was made for a bayonet in 1944. The Owen was a thoroughly good weapon and was still in use in the 1960s.

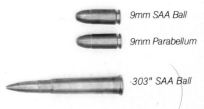

9mm SAA Ball

9mm Parabellum

·303" SAA Ball

Great Britain
De LISLE SILENT CARBINE

Length: 35" (889mm)
Weight: 7lb (3·18kg)
Barrel: 9" (228mm)
Calibre: ·45"
Rifling: 7 groove l/hand
Feed: 10-round magazine
Operation: Bolt feed
Muzzle Velocity:
c1200 f/s (366 m/s)
Sights: 600 yds (549m)

The de Lisle carbine is something of a hybrid weapon and was originally produced in small numbers in the course of World War II, when a number of small, unorthodox special forces were demanding a variety of equally unorthodox special weapons. The carbine which was made at the Royal Small Arms Factory at Enfield, was in fact a conversion of the standard Short Magazine Lee Enfield rifle, altered to fire a rimless pistol cartridge. This involved the shortening of the bolt and a corresponding

rearward extension to the chamber which can be clearly seen in the forward end of the body in the photograph. The new short barrel of ·45" calibre was then screwed into this, and a new magazine opening fitted below. The rest of the weapon consisted of a sheet metal tube fifteen inches long and one and three-quarter inches in diameter; this housed the silencer which was of course by far the most interesting aspect of the arm, and the casing of the top weapon has been cut away to show its

interior. It consisted in essence of ten metal discs which just fitted into the diameter of the outer casing. These discs each had a central hole of a little over a half an inch diameter with a smaller hole on either side, and each was cut along one radius. The pieces on either side of the cut were then pulled apart, so that when the discs were strung along two parallel rods one on either side of the barrel three-quarters of an inch apart and with stops between they formed a continuous Archimedean screw. The front end of the

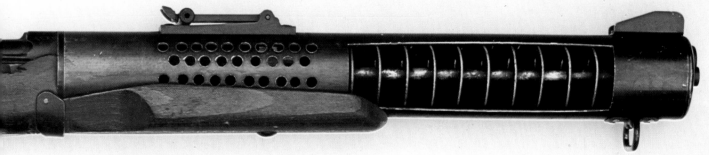

De Lisle Silent Carbine (cutaway)

De Lisle Silent Carbine (folding stock)

·45" ACP

·45" ACP

·303" SAA Ball

casing was closed by a circular plug with a hole for the bullet to leave by, and two small screw sockets to hold the front ends of the silencer rods. Bearing in mind that the bullet used never exceeded the speed of sound, and that therefore there was no 'sonic boom', this system of silencing worked remarkably well, the sound of the discharge being quite inaudible a few yards away. The series of holes through which the bullet passed had neccessarily to be as small as possible, and examination of different specimens of the carbine show that the plates have sometimes been slightly distorted, presumably by bullets yawing slightly. The carbine was equipped with a tangent backsight and shot accurately to about three hundred yards, which indicates the extra power given to a pistol cartridge by a relatively long barrel and a locked breech. There are minor variations in different specimens of the carbine, chiefly in the question of the butt. Many had the standard walnut rifle butt, but others, like the lower one in the photograph, had light folding metal stocks, combined with a wooden pistol grip. Some also had cooling holes in the casing below the backsight, others not. There is relatively little use for silent small arms in war, since there is inevitably so much other, ineradicable noise, that the results are hardly noticed. On occasion however silent arms can be useful; a silent sniping rifle might be useful for example, although silencing a high-velocity weapon produces many problems. The de Lisle carbine was principally of use in the eradication of sentries who for various reasons could not be stalked or disposed of silently in any other way, and it proved very effective for this purpose. It also had a certain amount of use in Malaya during the emergency of 1948-1960. It can be argued that strictly speaking the de Lisle should not be in this section, but although it is not an automatic weapon this seems a suitable place for a weapon that is in a category of its own.

Great Britain
BSA EXPERIMENTAL 1949

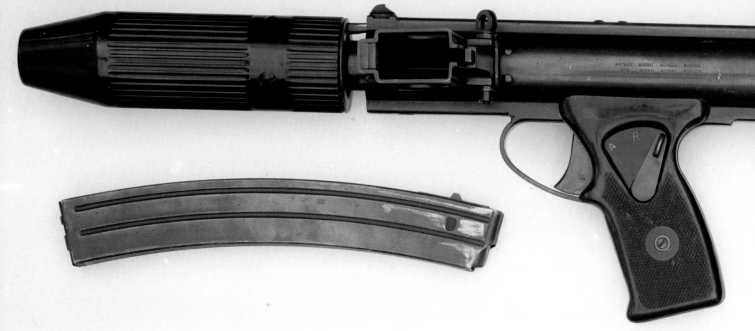

Length: 27·9" (697mm)
Weight: 6·45lb (2·9kg)
Barrel: 8" (203mm)
Calibre: 9mm
Rifling: 6 groove r/hand
Feed: 32-round box
Cyclic Rate: 600 rpm
Muzzle Velocity:
1200 f/s (365 m/s)
Sights:
100/200 yds (91·5/183m)

The main British sub-machine gun during World War II was the famous Sten, which although hastily designed and roughly finished did its job very well. It was, however, a strictly wartime expedient and even before the war was quite over a new General Staff specification had been issued for a post-war sub-machine gun. This laid down the basic requirements that it should weigh a maximum of six pounds

Great Britain
MCEM 2

Length: 23.5" (598mm)
Weight: 6lb (2.72kg)
Barrel: 8.5" (216mm)
Calibre: 9mm
Rifling: 6 groove r/hand
Feed: 18-round box
Cyclic Rate: 1000 rpm
Muzzle Velocity:
1200 f/s (365 m/s)
Sights: Fixed

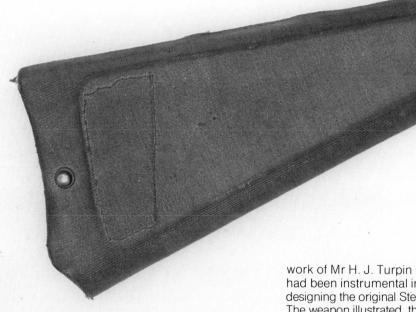

Although the Sten gun had served Great Britain well in the period 1941-45 it was not really of the quality required for the post-war army, and after the war was over tests began to find a suitable successor for it. A good deal of design work had been going on, both by native British designers and by a variety of Polish experts, so there was not likely to be any shortage of contenders. The series developed by Enfield were given the collective description of Military Carbine Experimental Models (MCEM), the various types being denoted by a serial number; as a matter of interest the first in the series was the work of Mr H. J. Turpin who had been instrumental in designing the original Sten gun. The weapon illustrated, the MCEM 2, was the work of one of the rival designers, a Polish officer named Lieutenant Podsenkowsky, and it was in many ways an unusual weapon. It was under fifteen inches long and its magazine

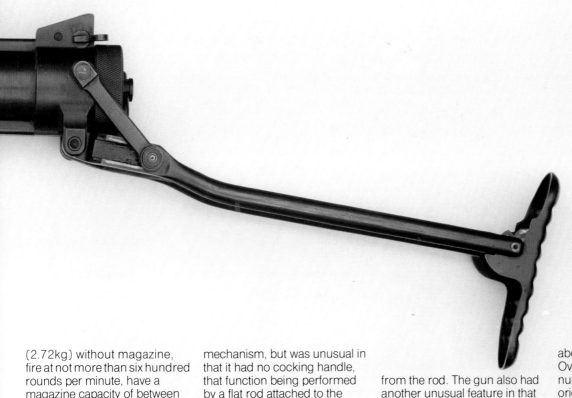

(2.72kg) without magazine, fire at not more than six hundred rounds per minute, have a magazine capacity of between thirty and sixty rounds, and take the No 5 rifle bayonet. Various tests were arranged between 1947 and 1952 for which a number of weapons were entered, among them the Birmingham Small Arms Company's weapon of the type illustrated. It was of conventional blowback mechanism, but was unusual in that it had no cocking handle, that function being performed by a flat rod attached to the plastic covered fore-end grip. When the grip was twisted and pushed forward the rod went with it and the end of it engaged the bolt which was then in the forward position. As the grip was pulled back the rod forced the bolt back also until it was caught by the sear, at which stage it disengaged from the rod. The gun also had another unusual feature in that the magazine housing could be released and swung forward on a hinge without removing the magazine, which was thought to facilitate the clearing of stoppages. It was fitted with a sturdy folding stock which did not interfere with the firing of the gun when forward, and its change lever was situated above the left-hand pistol grip. Over the years there were a number of variations in the original design; the first model took a straight magazine, later ones being curved as illustrated, and as a result of a change in specification it was modified to take a bayonet. There were also variations in the shape of the forehand grip. The gun was not finally accepted for service and specimens of it are now quite rare.

fitted into the pistol grip; it was also well balanced which meant that it could be fired one-handed like an automatic pistol. The bolt was of advanced design and consisted of a half cylinder 8½ inches (216mm) long with the striker at the rear, so that at the instant of firing almost the whole of the barrel was in fact inside it. There was a slot above the muzzle into which the firer placed his finger to draw the bolt back to cock it, and the gun had a wire-framed canvas holster which could also be used as a butt. It fired at a cyclic rate of one thousand rounds per minute which made it very hard to control and which may have led to its rejection.

9mm SAA Ball

9mm SAA Ball

·303" SAA Ball

Great Britain
STERLING L2A3

Australia
F1 SUB-MACHINE GUN

Length: 28" (800mm)
Weight: 6lb (2·75kg)
Barrel: 7·8" (198mm)
Calibre: 9mm
Rifling: 6 groove r/hand
Feed: 32-round box
Cyclic Rate: 550 rpm
Muzzle Velocity:
1200 f/s (365 m/s)
Sights: 100 and 200 yds
(91·5 and 183m)

Length: 28·1" (925mm)
Weight: 7·2lb (3·266kg)
Barrel: 8" (203mm)
Calibre: 9mm
Rifling: 6 groove r/hand
Feed: 34-round box
Cyclic Rate: 600 rpm
Muzzle Velocity:
1200 f/s (365 m/s)
Sights: Fixed

The standard sub-machine gun of the Australian Forces during World War II was the reliable and well tried Owen gun, which remained in service until 1962. In spite of its excellent reputation the Owen had certain drawbacks, principally its weight, its somewhat high cyclic rate of fire, and the fact that due to the exigencies of wartime manufacture many of its components were not interchangeable which made maintenance difficult. Before the war was over the

Australians canvassed the views of many soldiers with battle experience as to what an ideal sub-machine gun should be, so that they had ample information on which to base any specifications for a new weapon. The first gun to be based on these ideas was similar in many ways to the Owen, but much lighter and with its magazine in the pistol grip. This model was not a success and was not developed. However, in 1959 and 1960 two further models

were produced; these were known provisionally as the X1 and X2, and after minor modifications became the weapon illustrated, the F1. It was based largely on the original specification and is light

This gun was designed by a Mr George Patchett and was at first known as the Patchett sub-machine gun. It was originally patented in 1942 and by the end of the war a small number had been made by the Sterling Engineering Company, which had earlier been involved in the production of the Lanchester. A few of these early guns were used by British airborne troops towards the end of the war and their reports on them were encouraging. In the course of

the search for a replacement for the Sten this gun was tested against various others in 1947; none was accepted as a result of this first trial because all were considered to need modification. By the time of the next trial in 1951 the Patchett, as it was still then called, was clearly the best gun of those available, and in September 1953 it was finally accepted for service in the British Army. Its official title was the SMG L2A1, but from the date of its

introduction it was commonly known as the Sterling. The gun, which is well made and finished, is of normal blowback mechanism but is unusual in having a ribbed bolt which cuts away dirt and fouling as it accumulates and forces it out of the receiver. This allows the gun to function well under the

most adverse conditions. The gun underwent a good many modifications after its initial introduction, notably in the addition of foresight protectors, varying shapes of muzzle and butt, and on one light version a spring-loaded bayonet. Some of the earlier models also took a straight magazine. The current version is the L2A3, and the standard Canadian SMG is closely based on it. Several other countries also use it.

in weight and with a much lower cyclic rate than its predecessor. It retains the top magazine of the Owen which was universally popular, although it requires offset sights. The backsight is a shaped metal flap which folds forward over the receiver when not required. The height of this sight is made necessary because the butt is a prolongation of the barrel, which makes for accurate shooting but which requires the sight line to be high. The

cocking handle, which is on the left of the body, has a cover attached to it to keep dirt out of the cocking slot. Although the cocking handle is normally non-reciprocating, the F1 incorporates a device by which it can be made to engage the bolt. This means that if the mechanism becomes jammed with dirt the bolt can be worked backwards and forwards by means of the handle in order to loosen it. The pistol grip is a standard rifle component.

9mm SAA Ball

9mm Parabellum

·303" SAA Ball

Length: 34·25" (870mm)
Weight: 10·34lb (4·69kg)
Barrel: 12·5" (317mm)
Calibre: 9mm
Rifling: 6 groove r/hand
Feed: (See text)
Cyclic Rate: 900 rpm
Muzzle Velocity:
1312 f/s (400 m/s)
Sights:
110-547 yds (100-500m)

Suomi is the native word for Finland, and the first of the series bearing the name was developed from 1922 onwards which makes it one of the earliest sub-machine guns to appear. It was designed by the well-known Finnish designer Johannes Lahti, and the first finished models appeared in 1926. They were effective but very complex weapons, designed to fire the 7·62mm Parabellum cartridge from a magazine with such a

Italy
TZ 45

Length: 33·5" (851mm)
Weight: 7·20lb (3·26kg)
Barrel: 9" (229mm)
Calibre: 9mm
Rifling: 6 groove r/hand
Feed: 20/40-round box
Cyclic Rate: 550 rpm
Muzzle Velocity:
1250 f/s (365 m/s)
Sights: Fixed

So many Italian sub-machine guns have been produced by the famous Brescian firm of Beretta that it sometimes comes as something of a surprise to people to find an Italian weapon of this type produced by some other firm. World War II, however, saw the appearance of a considerable variety of other weapons, the TZ 45 being amongst them. It was designed by the Giandoso brothers as a wartime expedient and first went into limited production in 1945. This new gun, which worked on the

normal blowback system, was very crudely made and finished, partly of roughly machined parts and partly of stampings. This is not surprising in view of its date of manufacture, by which time the quality of most other countries' products had dropped correspondingly. One of the interesting features of this gun is that it incorporates a grip safety; this consists of an L-shaped lever just behind the magazine housing (which also acts as a forward hand grip). Firm pressure on the vertical

pronounced curve that three of them placed end to end formed a complete circle. This gun was only produced in very small numbers and is thus chiefly of interest because it was the first of a series. The model illustrated was also designed by Lahti, but although it retained some of the features of the Model 26, so many changes were made that it was virtually a new weapon. Although patents were not finally granted until 1932 the gun was in use by the Finnish

Army in the previous year, hence its final designation of Model 31. It worked by normal blowback system and had no less than four different magazines, a single 20-round box, a double 50-round box, and two drums, one of 40-round capacity and one of 71. Like most sub-machine guns of its vintage it was very well made of good steel, heavily machined and milled and unusually well finished. The end product was therefore an exceptionally

reliable and robust weapon and although it was very heavy by modern standards (with the bigger drum magazine it weighed over fifteen pounds) this at least had the merit of reducing recoil and vibration and thus increasing its accuracy, for which it was very well known.

It was made under licence in Sweden, Denmark, and Switzerland, and apart from Finland was also used by Sweden, Switzerland and

Norway and to a lesser extent Poland. It is still used in many units of the Finnish Army, although all surviving weapons have been modified to take a modern 36-round box magazine of improved pattern. At the end of 1939 the Russians, having failed to persuade the Finns to make some territorial adjustments to enhance Soviet security, invaded Finland. The Finns fought bravely and made good use of the Suomi.

part of the lever (which is clearly visible in the photograph) causes the horizontal arm to be depressed sufficiently to withdraw an upper stud from the bolt way, thus allowing the working parts to function. This device which was similar to the one employed on some models of the Danish Madsen sub-machine gun, was a useful one, but it did of course prevent the weapon being used single-handed. The TZ 45 had a retractable stock, made of light tubing; when pushed in the

front ends engaged in holes in a plate below the barrel about six inches (153mm) from the muzzle. Although probably not specifically intended for the purpose it presumably also acted as a stop to prevent the weapon being pulled back from a port in an armoured vehicle by some sudden jolt, rather like the attachment on the German 'Schmeisser'. There are two parallel slots cut into the top of the barrel at the muzzle end which act as a crude but moderately effective compensator. Although it was

an adequate weapon the TZ 45 came too late in the war to be of much use and only about six thousand were made. These were chiefly used by Italian troops on internal security duties including the rounding up of the armed deserters of half-a-dozen nationalities who

had happily taken to banditry in the last months of the war. After the war the gun was offered commercially on the world market, but only the Burmese showed interest, a number being locally made there in the early 1950s. These guns were manufactured under the title BA 52.

9mm Parabellum

9mm Parabellum

.303" SAA Ball

Italy
BERETTA MODELLO 38A

Length: 37·25″ (946mm)
Weight: 9·25lb (4·97kg)
Barrel: 12·4″ (315mm)
Calibre: 9mm
Rifling: 6 groove r/hand
Feed: 10/20/40-round box
Cyclic Rate: 600 rpm
Muzzle Velocity:
1378 f/s (420 m/s)
Sights: 547 yds (500m)

The Northern Italian firm of Beretta had a deservedly high reputation for its sub-machine guns, most of which have been designed by their most talented engineer, Tullio Marengoni, who worked for them for many years. Among the weapons he produced was the Modello 38A which probably has good claims to be regarded as his most successful sub-machine gun. It had its origins in a self-loading carbine which was first

Italy
BERETTA MODELLO 38/42

Length: 31·5″ (800mm)
Weight: 7·20lb (3·26kg)
Barrel: 8·4″ (216mm)
Calibre: 9mm
Rifling: 6 groove r/hand
Feed: 20/40-round box
Cyclic Rate: 550 rpm
Muzzle Velocity:
1250 f/s (381 m/s)
Sights: 219 yds (200m)

After a year or so of war the Italians, like all other combatants, soon realized that they would have to accept modern mass-production methods if their supplies of war *matériel* were to keep pace with demand. As far as sub-machine guns were concerned, this realization resulted in the Beretta Modello 38/42, which like most of its predecessors was invented by Marengoni, and which came into full production in 1942. It was for all practical purposes a utility version of the earlier

Modello 38, although it also incorporated a number of features from another sub-machine gun, the Modello 1, which had been designed, needless to say by Marengoni, in 1941 as a weapon for airborne forces on the lines of the German MP 40, but which had never gone into production due to its complicated construction. The whole weapon had also of course been considerably simplified to conform to modern mass-production methods, but in spite of this it was an efficient

and popular gun. As far as external appearances were concerned there were a number of differences. The rifle-type stock, although similar, was cut short at the magazine housing, and the adjustable rearsight disappeared, as did the perforated jacket which had been such a notable feature of many Beretta guns. The barrel had deep parallel fluting along its whole length, this being intended to assist the dissipation of heat in the absence of the jacket, while the compensator was reduced to

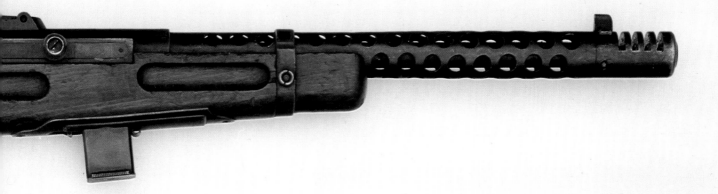

produced in small numbers for police use in 1935, but which by 1938 had been improved to the point where it could be manufactured as a true sub-machine gun. It came of course far too early for the mass-production techniques developed a few years later and was made to the high pre-war standards customary among gun makers. It was therefore well machined and finished which made it expensive to

produce, but which resulted in a most reliable and accurate arm. It functioned by normal blowback and had a separate firing pin, again a somewhat unusual refinement. Its forward trigger was for single shots, the other for bursts. The first model can be distinguished by the elongated slots in its jacket, by its compensator, which consisted of a single large hole in the top of the muzzle with a bar across it, and by the fact

that it was fitted with a folding, knife-type bayonet. Not many of these were produced before the elongated cooling slots were replaced by round holes, which thereafter remained standard. The third version, which is the one illustrated, was mainly distinguished by the absence of a bayonet and by its new compensator consisting of four separate cuts across the muzzle. This version remained as the production model for the

remainder of the war, although there are some minor concessions to the principles of mass-production, notably in the use of a pressed and welded jacket. This version was used extensively by both the Italian and the German armies, and captured specimens were popular with Allied soldiers. The Beretta Modello 38A was also used by a number of countries, notably Romania and Argentina.

two cuts only instead of the previous four. The bolt was somewhat simplified with a fixed firing pin integral with it instead of the separate mechanism previously used. The main return spring worked on a rod, the end of which extended appreciably beyond the rear of the receiver, and as before the gun had two triggers, the forward one for single rounds, the rear one for bursts. The cocking handle, which does not move with the bolt, had a dust cover attached to it to keep the internal

mechanism as clear as possible. The general appearance of the gun was utilitarian as compared with its predecessors, stampings and welding having been used wherever possible, although the finish was surprisingly good and the whole weapon strong and serviceable. Later productions had plain barrels instead of the distinctive fluted ones and were sometimes referred to as the Modello 38/44. There was a later variation still, in which the weight and dimensions of the

bolt were reduced; this led in turn to a somewhat shorter return spring and rod, which did not protrude beyond the rear of the receiver as in the earlier models. The date that this model went into production is not very clear, but most of them seem to have come off

the assembly lines after the end of the war so that its designation 38/44 is somewhat in doubt. The Beretta 38/42 was widely used by the Italians and Germans and after the war a number of the 38/44 Model were sold to various countries including Syria and Pakistan.

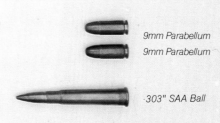

9mm Parabellum

9mm Parabellum

·303" SAA Ball

People's Republic of China
TYPE 50

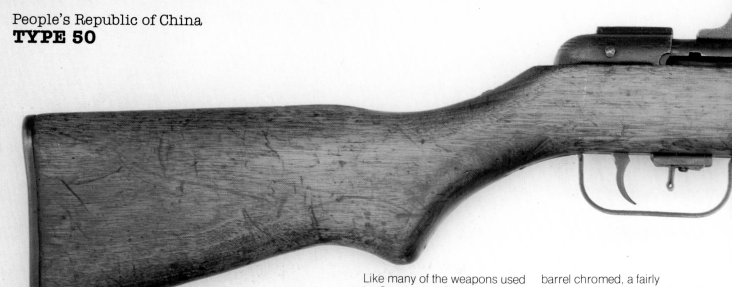

Length: 33·75″ (858mm)
Weight: 8lb (3·63kg)
Barrel: 10·75″ (273mm)
Calibre: 7·62mm
Rifling: 4 groove r/hand
Feed: 35-round box
Cyclic Rate: 900 rpm
Muzzle Velocity:
1400 f/s (472 m/s)
Sights:
110-219 yds (100/200m)

Like many of the weapons used by Communist China, their sub-machine gun Type 50 had its origins in a weapon first produced by the Soviet Union, in this case the PPSh 41. As with most other combatant nations the Russians soon saw the need for mass production and the new gun was largely made of heavy gauge stampings, welded, pinned and brazed as necessary. The gun was of normal blowback mechanism and had the interior of the barrel chromed, a fairly common Soviet device. One of its distinctive features is that the front end of the perforated barrel casing slopes steeply backward from top to bottom, thus acting as a compensator to keep the muzzle down. In spite of its high cyclic rate of fire the gun was reasonably accurate and could be fired in single rounds if required. The earliest versions had a tangent backsight but this was soon replaced by a simpler flip sight. The Chinese Communists

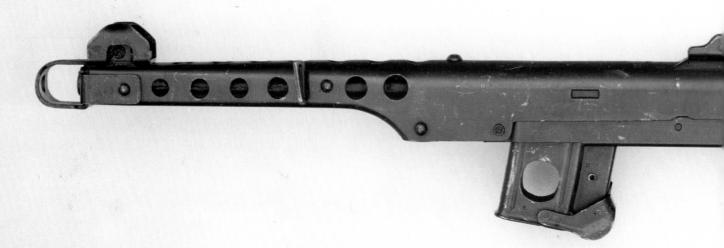

People's Republic of China
TYPE 54

Length: 32·25″ (819mm)
Weight: 10″ (254mm)
Barrel: 10″ (254mm)
Calibre: 7·62mm
Rifling: 4 groove r/hand
Feed: 35-round box
Cyclic Rate: 700 rpm
Muzzle Velocity:
1600 f/s (488 m/s)
Sights:
Flip, 110-219 yds (100/200m)

The origins of this particular weapon are unusual, since it was designed by A. Sudarev at Leningrad in 1942 when the city was under actual blockade by the Germans. Arms were in short supply and as none could be brought in it became necessary to improvise from local resources. The new gun originally known as the Russian PPS 42, was therefore made in the city itself, so that weapons coming off the production line were liable to be used in action in a matter of hours. As was to be expected the gun was made of stampings, using any suitable grade of metal, and was held together by riveting, welding, and pinning. Nevertheless it was not only cheap but it turned out to be effective. It worked on the usual simple blowback system and would only fire automatic; perhaps its oddest feature was its semi-circular compensator, which helped to keep the muzzle down but increased blast considerably. This was followed by the PPS 43, modified and improved by the same engineer who had been responsible for the earlier model. Its most unusual feature was that it had no separate ejector in the normal sense of the word. The bolt moved backwards and

received many of these guns in and after 1949 and started their own large scale manufacture of them in 1949 or 1950. Their version was essentially similar to its Russian counterpart, but had a somewhat lighter stock. It is also designed to take a curved box magazine though it will also fire the 71-round drum which was the standard magazine on the original Russian model. All Chinese versions have the two-range flip sight. The first locally-made weapons were crude in the extreme and gave the impression of having been made by apprentice blacksmiths (as perhaps they were). Nevertheless they worked, which was the first and only requirement of the Chinese. The Type 50 was used extensively by the Chinese in the Korean war where it earned the inelegant but expressive nickname 'burp-gun' from its high rate of fire. Many were also used against the French in Indo-China in the 1950s.

forwards along a guide rod which was of such a length that as the bolt came back with the empty case, the end of the rod caught it a sharp blow and knocked it clear.

After the Chinese revolution of 1949, the Soviet Union naturally supplied its new ally with a considerable quantity of arms including large numbers of the PPS 43, and by 1953 the Chinese had begun large-scale manufacture of these weapons, virtually unchanged in appearance from the Russian prototypes. The only way in which it can be distinguished is by the fact that the plastic pistol grips often bear a large letter K in a central design. This, however, is by no means universal and other designs, including a diamond, may be found. The gun is still often found in South East Asia.

7·62mm M1930g

7·62mm M1930g

·303" SAA Ball

Soviet Union
PPD 34/38

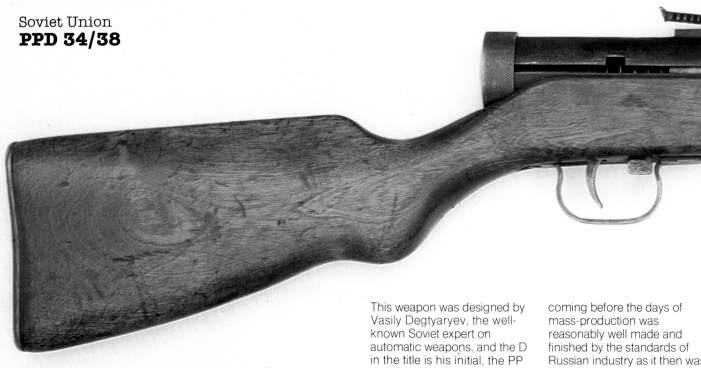

Length: 30·6" (779mm)
Weight: 8·25lb (3·74kg)
Barrel: 10·75" (272mm)
Calibre: 7·62mm
Rifling: 4 groove r/hand
Feed: 71-round drum
Cyclic Rate: 800 rpm
Muzzle Velocity:
1600 f/s (489 m/s)
Sights: 547 yds (500m)

This weapon was designed by Vasily Degtyaryev, the well-known Soviet expert on automatic weapons, and the D in the title is his initial, the PP standing for Pistolet-Pulemyot, the usual Russian term for what we know as a sub-machine gun. It initially appeared in 1934 and may be regarded as the first really successful weapon of its type to be used in the Soviet Army.
It was based fairly closely on the German MP28.II, and coming before the days of mass-production was reasonably well made and finished by the standards of Russian industry as it then was. The PPD worked by normal blowback on the open bolt principle single rounds or bursts being obtained by the use of a selector in front of the trigger. Both bore and chamber were chromed to prevent undue wear. The cartridges were fed from a near-vertical drum with an

Soviet Union
PPSh 41

Length: 33·1" (841mm)
Weight: 8·0lb (3·63kg)
Barrel: 10·6" (269mm)
Calibre: 7·62mm
Rifling: 4 groove r/hand
Feed:
71-round drum/35-round box
Cyclic Rate: 900 rpm
Muzzle Velocity:
1600 f/s (489 m/s)
Sights: 547 yds (500m)

At the outbreak of World War II in 1939, the Soviet Army was armed with the PPD 34/38, but by the beginning of 1940 this was gradually being replaced by a modified version of the PPD 40 which was similar in appearance but took a different type of drum. Almost immediately the gun illustrated was put into limited production, and after stringent testing by the Russian Army was finally approved early in 1942, after which production was on a vast scale. It was designed by Georgii Shpagin, another well-known Russian expert, and this fact is denoted by the inclusion of his initial in the official designation of the new gun. The PPSh was an early and successful example of the application of mass-production techniques to the manufacture of firearms, a change made essential by the Soviet Union's huge military commitments at that time. As far as possible it was made from sheet metal stampings, welding and riveting being used wherever feasible, and although it retained the rather old-fashioned looking

134

unusual extension piece which fitted into the bottom of the receiver; this drum, which was worked by clockwork, was very similar mechanically to that of the Finnish Suomi, and held seventy-one rounds. This gave the soldier using it a good reserve of fire without having to reload, but made the gun heavy. As drum magazines are susceptible to dirt, there were probably also problems over stoppages; there was in fact also a curved box magazine but this was very rarely used. One or two minor variations to the original model were made, the most obvious being the reduction in the number of jacket slots from rows of eight small ones to three larger ones. Although the gun was technically replaced by the PPD 40 in 1940 it was used in the Finnish campaigns and probably also saw later service elsewhere.

wooden butt it was a sturdy and reliable arm. It worked on the usual blowback system with a buffer at the rear end of the receiver to reduce vibration and had a selector lever in front of the trigger to give single rounds or burst as required. As its cyclic rate of fire was high and would have tended to make the muzzle rise when firing bursts, the front of the barrel jacket was sloped backwards so as to act as a compensator, a simple and reasonably successful expedient. Feed for the PPSh was either by a seventy-one round drum, basically similar to that of the earlier PPD series but not interchangeable with them, or by a thirty-five round box. In order to reduce wear and help cleaning, the bore and chamber of these guns were all chromed. There appear to have been only two basic models of this gun; the first model, the one illustrated, had a somewhat complicated tangent backsight, while the second one made do with a perfectly adequate two aperture flip sight. The Soviet armies greatly favoured the sub-machine gun and on occasions whole battalions were armed with it, so it is not surprising that the total numbers manufactured should have exceeded five million. It was also widely copied by other Communist countries, and although long obsolete in the Soviet Union itself it is probably still extensively used elsewhere. The Chinese in particular copied it as their Type 50 and must themselves have produced it in vast numbers.

7·62mm M1930g

7·62mm M1930g

·303" SAA Ball

Sweden
CARL GUSTAV MODEL 45

Length: 31·8" (808mm)
Weight: 7·62lb (3·45kg)
Barrel: 8·0" (203mm)
Calibre: 9mm
Rifling: 6 groove r/hand

Feed: 36/50-round box
Cyclic Rate: 600 rpm
Muzzle Velocity:
1210 f/s (369 m/s)
Sights: 328 yds (300m)

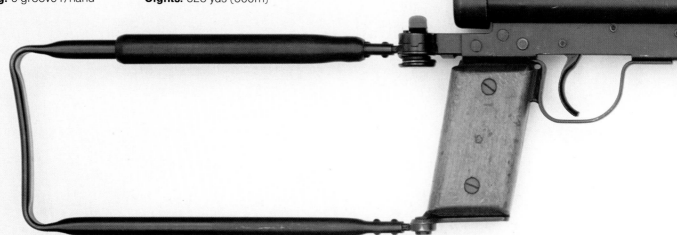

Sweden did not adopt a sub-machine gun until 1937, when she began to manufacture a slightly modified form of the Finnish Suomi, which was made under licence by the Carl Gustav factory. This was replaced soon afterwards by a second version of the same gun, which had a shorter barrel, a very large trigger guard, which could accommodate gloved fingers in winter, and a much straighter stock than the original Finnish gun; this gun was made by the firm of Husqvarna. In the course of World War II Sweden, although neutral, increased her army considerably to defend herself if necessary and this led to the realization that she had no simple sub-machine gun for mass-production. She set out to rectify this but the result, the Model 1945, was not in fact put into production until after the war. The Model 1945 was made of stampings from heavy gauge steel, riveted or welded as necessary, and within the limits imposed by these methods was a sound and reliable weapon.

Mechanically it bore a strong resemblance to the British Sten gun, but had a rectangular stock of tubular metal which could be folded forward on the right of the gun without in any way interfering with its working. Although it was designed for firing on automatic only, single rounds could be fired by anyone with a reasonably sensitive trigger finger. It fired a special high velocity cartridge, and the original model used the old Suomi fifty-round magazine. Later versions fired a new thirty-six round type but as large stocks of the older magazine, which was not interchangeable, remained, the new gun had an easily detached magazine housing which could be replaced by one of the older type if required. This was a temporary provision only until adequate supplies of the new magazine became available, and the latest models have riveted magazine housings.

Switzerland
REXIM-FAVOR

Length: 32·0" (813mm)
Weight: 7·0lb (3·18kg)
Barrel: 10·75" (273mm)
Calibre: 9mm
Rifling: 5 groove r/hand
Feed: 20-round box
Cyclic Rate: 600 rpm
Muzzle Velocity:
1300 f/s (396m/s)
Sights: Flip, 100/200 yds
(91·5/183m)

The history of this weapon is somewhat obscure. It was presented by the Turkish Army, attractively cased with a variety of accessories, to a senior British service officer attending an international rifle meeting in 1968. The Turks are not known to make sub-machine guns and there is no reason to suppose that it was locally made. The various inscriptions on the change lever and elsewhere are in the Turkish language but there is little doubt that it is one of the many varieties of the Swiss Rexim sub-machine gun which appeared from 1953 onwards, under the auspices of the Rexim Small Arms Company located in Geneva. It was at one time known as the Favor sub-machine gun, and is believed to have been made under contract by the Spanish Arsenal at Corunna. Extensive attempts were made in the mid-1950s to sell the Rexim in the Middle East, but there seems to be no record of any substantial deals being made, principally because the gun was considered to be too complicated, never a good recommendation for a sub-machine gun in which simplicity is almost the most important factor. The chief interest of the Rexim was that it fired from a closed bolt, that is, the round was fed into the chamber by the action of the cocking handle and remained there until pressure on the trigger allowed the firing pin to go forward. Motive power was

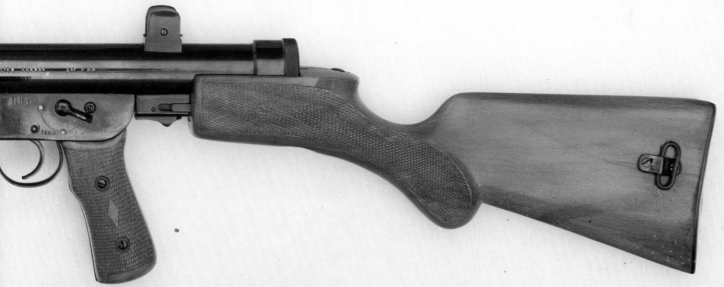

provided by two coiled springs, one working inside the other with an intermediate hollow hammer, and looking exactly like an old-fashioned three-draw telescope. When the trigger was pressed the depression of the sear released the hammer which went forward under the force of the large outer spring, struck the firing pin, and fired the round. Normal blowback then

followed and the cycle continued. The gun was well made, chiefly of pressings, but with a superior finish. It had a quick release barrel, in which the withdrawal of the small catch under the milled nut allowed the nut to be unscrewed and the barrel pulled out forward. In the model illustrated the butt had a separate pistol grip, presumably designed as a rear

hand grip when using the short spring bayonet permanently attached to the muzzle. It took a magazine identical with that of the

German MP40 gun. The gun illustrated is probably one of a small number purchased at some time by Turkey but never adopted for service.

9mm M/39B

9mm Parabellum

·303" SAA Ball

137

United States of America
THOMPSON M1928A1

Length: 33.75" (857mm)
Weight: 10.75lb (4.88kg)
Barrel: 10.5" (267mm)
Calibre: ·45"
Rifling: 6 groove r/hand
Feed:
50-round drum/20-round box
Cyclic Rate: 800 rpm
Muzzle Velocity:
920 f/s (281 m/s)
Sights: 600 yds (549m)

Some mention has already been made of the Thompson sub-machine gun in the introduction to this section, since it was in many ways the most famous of all weapons of its type. It was developed in the course of World War I by Colonel (later Brigadier-General) J. T. Thompson but came too late to be used in action. Very few people wanted sub-machine guns after the war had ended so that the Auto-Ordnance Corporation which made them found it very difficult to keep going, particularly in the depression of the 1930s. Good advertising and publicity helped, however, and there was a small but steady sale to law enforcement

United States of America
REISING MODEL 50

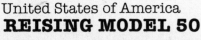

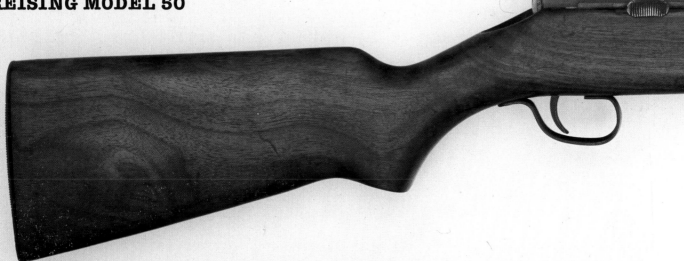

Length: 35.75" (908mm)
Weight: 6.75" (3.06kg)
Barrel: 11.0" (279mm)
Calibre; ·45"
Rifling: 6 groove r/hand
Feed: 12- or 20-round box
Cyclic Rate: 550 rpm
Muzzle Velocity:
920 f/s (280 m/s)
Sights: 300 yds (274m)

The success of the sub-machine gun in the Spanish Civil War caused a good many arms designers to turn their attention to weapons of this type. One of those who did so was Eugene Reising who produced the weapon named after him in 1938; after incorporating some improvements he patented it in 1940 and the well-known United States arms firm of Harrington and Richardson began the manufacture of it at the end of the next year. After several tests had led to minor improvements in the gun, it was accepted for service by the United States Marine Corps and was first used in action on Guadalcanal where it proved to be a complete failure, jamming so frequently that the

Wesson were advised to convert it to a full automatic weapon in the larger calibre and re-submit it, but there is no record that they did so. It is said that a few of the original prototypes were made to fire automatic, which marginally justifies its inclusion as a sub-machine gun, but if so they were never tested, probably because Smith and Wesson had enough war work on their hands at the time. A slightly modified version of the type illustrated was in fact re-issued in 1940, when Great Britain, desperate for arms, bought the whole batch of two thousand for the Royal Navy, all the tools and gauges being forwarded with the order. The main thing that strikes one about this weapon is its quality; the bolt and barrel were made of chrome nickel steel, the remainder of the metalwork being of manganese steel, and the machining, blueing and general finishing are fully up to the peacetime standards expected of such a famous firm. It worked on the usual blowback system and fired from the open bolt position. One of its unusual features was that the back of the very wide magazine housing contained an ejector tube down which the empty cases passed after firing. In view of the small numbers made, specimens of this gun are very rare and much sought after. Official records of it are scarce and its history obscure.

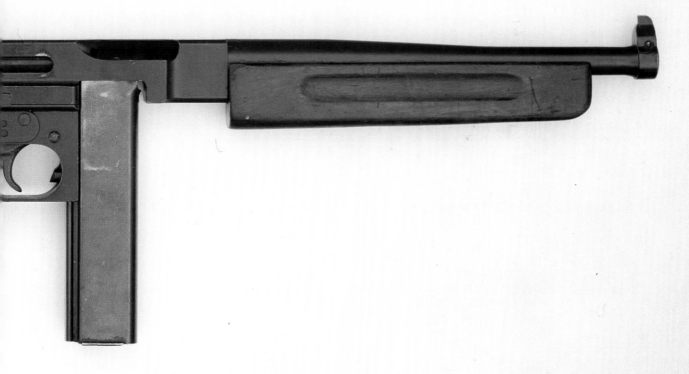

compensator on the muzzle, the substitution of a straight forehand for the forward pistol grip (although this had been optional on the Model 28), the removal of the rather complex backsight, and its replacement by a simple flip. One main difference in functioning was that the new gun would not take the fifty-round drum, but as this had never been very reliable in dirty conditions it was no loss. A new thirty-round box magazine was introduced at the same time, and the earlier twenty-round magazine would also fit the new model. There was yet another simplification, the incorporation of a fixed firing pin on the face of the bolt; this resulted in the M1A1 which is the weapon illustrated. Although almost a quarter of a century old by then, the Thompson gave excellent service in 1939-45, for even if it was heavy to carry it was reliable, and its bullets had very considerable stopping power.

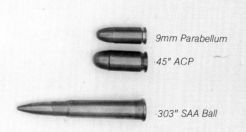

9mm Parabellum

·45" ACP

·303" SAA Ball

United States of America
UNITED DEFENSE MODEL 42

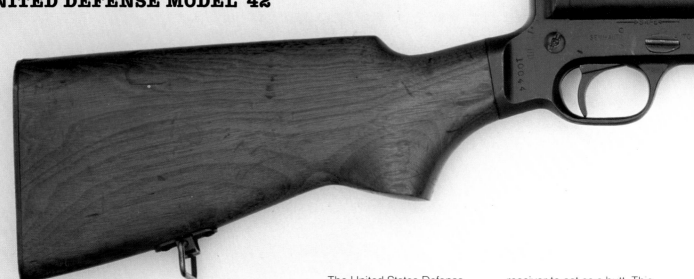

Length: 32·3" (820mm)
Weight: 9·12lb (4·14kg)
Barrel: 11·0" (279mm)
Calibre: 9mm/·45"
Rifling: 6 groove r/hand
Feed: 20-round box
Cyclic Rate: 700 rpm
Muzzle Velocity:
1312 f/s (400 m/s)
Sights: Fixed

The United States Defense Supply Corporation was a United States Government corporation which was formed in 1941 to supply weapons to the various Allied nations involved in World War II. The first weapon it submitted for trial was a rather odd one with interchangeable barrels, one of 9mm and the other of ·45", the barrel not actually being used for its proper function being screwed to the back of the receiver to act as a butt. This gun was a failure and never went into production. The UDM42, the sub-machine gun illustrated, was actually designed in about 1938 by a Carl Swebilius and was manufactured by the well-known Marlin Firearms Company. The Model 42 was of normal blowback operation with a separate firing pin inside the bolt, and after one or two modifications it performed

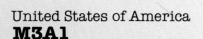

United States of America
M3A1

Length: 29·8" (757mm)
Weight: 8·15lb (3·70kg)
Barrel: 8·0" (203mm)
Calibre: ·45"
Rifling: 4 groove r/hand
Feed: 30-round box
Cyclic Rate: 400 rpm
Muzzle Velocity:
920 f/s (280 m/s)
Sights: Fixed

In 1941 the Small Arms Development Branch of the United States Army Ordnance Corps set out to develop a sub-machine gun in accordance with certain guidelines proposed by the various combat arms. The intention was to produce a weapon which could be mass-produced by modern methods, and once the basic design had been established by George Hyde, a well-known expert in the field of sub-machine guns, the production side was put into the hands of Frederick Sampson, an expert of equal standing in his own field. A very detailed study of the methods used to manufacture the successful British Sten gun was

also made, and the work went ahead so quickly that prototypes had been successfully tested well before the end of 1942, and the new weapon accepted as standard under the designation of M3. The new gun was a very utilitarian looking arm, made as far as possible from stampings and with practically no machining except for the barrel and bolt. It worked by blowback and had no provision for firing single rounds, but as its cyclic rate was low this was acceptable. Its stock was of retractable wire and the calibre was ·45" although conversion to 9mm was not difficult. It bore a strong resemblance to a grease gun,

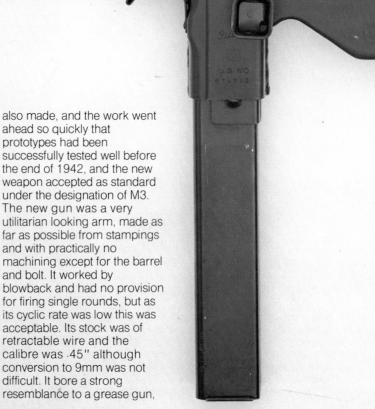

particularly well, being accurate, easy to handle, and almost impervious to dirt. The original models were of .45" calibre and took a twenty-round box magazine, but the production models were all of 9mm and were fitted with double back-to-back magazines, with a total capacity of forty rounds.

The gun was probably one of the best to have been produced in the United States at that period. It was of the pre-war style of manufacture, made of machined steel and very well finished, but its main problem was that it came at a time when the United States already seemed to be well-equipped with sub-machine guns, as simplified wartime versions of the Thompson were available in production quantities. Perhaps even more important was the fact that the mass-produced M3 gun was in an advanced state of preparation and once that became available guns of pre-war quality and finish largely disappeared from the scene. It was a sad end for an excellent gun.

from which it derived its famous nickname. Large-scale use revealed some defects in the gun, and further successful attempts to simplify it were initiated; these resulted in the M3A1 which is the weapon here illustrated. Like its predecessor the new gun was made by modern methods and was generally reliable. It worked, as before, by blowback but had no cocking handle, this process being achieved by the insertion of a finger into a slot cut in the receiver, by which the bolt could be withdrawn. The bolt, which had an integral firing pin, worked on guide rods which saved complicated finishing of the inside of the receiver and which gave smooth functioning with little interruption from dirt. An oil container was built into the pistol grip and a small bracket added to the rear of the retractable butt acted as a magazine filler. It used a box magazine which was not altogether reliable in dirty or dusty conditions until the addition of an easily removed plastic cover eliminated this defect. By the end of 1944 the new gun had been adopted and three months later it had officially replaced the Thompson as the standard sub-machine gun of the United States Army. Early in 1945 a simple flash hider, held in place by a wing nut, was added, and some were fitted with silencers.

9mm Parabellum

.45" ACP

.303" SAA Ball

Length: 10·5″ (267mm)
Weight: 6·4lb (2·84kg)
Barrel: 5·75″ (146mm)
Calibre: ·45″
Rifling: 5 groove r/hand
Feed: 30-round box
Cyclic Rate: 1100 rpm
Muzzle Velocity:
900 f/s (275 m/s)
Sights: Fixed

This weapon was named after its inventor, Gordon Ingram. Having fought in World War II he was a practical man with clear views of what a good sub-machine gun should be, and all his weapons were simple, reliable, and relatively cheap to make. In 1946 he produced his first prototype weapon; as United States sub-machine guns had already reached Model 3 he left the next designation clear and called his first version the M5. It was, however, a bad time to try and sell a new sub-machine gun because the world was full of war surplus weapons, so the

M5 never got beyond a single model, the whereabouts of which is unfortunately not known. Ingram was not discouraged, but worked on a new model for two years. Then in 1949 he set up a firm known as the Police Ordnance Company in partnership with some fellow veterans and soon afterwards produced his Model 6. It came in two types, one in ·38″ calibre, which looked superficially like a Thompson, and another in ·45″ calibre, and both sold reasonably well, partly to Police Departments and partly to South American countries. Although the

company soon broke up, Ingram persevered and by 1959 had produced Models 7, 8 and 9, all of which were sufficiently successful to encourage him to go on with the series. In 1969 he went to work for a firm specializing in supressors and during the next year this firm produced a subsidiary, the Military Armament Corporation, for whom Ingram then went to work. Once established he began to design weapons entirely different from his earlier ones and the two Models, Numbers 10 and 11, soon appeared. These were virtually

identical except for size, the Number 10 being designed for a ·45″ cartridge and the smaller Number 11 being designed for a ·38″ cartridge. The general appearance of these new weapons was similar in a general way to the early Webley automatic pistols; they worked on blowback but had wrap-around bolts which made it possible to keep the weapon short, and improved control at full automatic fire. The cocking handle, which was on the top, was equally convenient for right- or left-handed firers; it had a slot cut in the centre of it so as not to interfere with the line of sight. The magazine fitted into the pistol grip and the gun had a simple retractable butt. The whole thing was made of stampings with the exception of the barrel, even the bolt being made of sheet metal and filled with lead. The Models 10 and 11 were both fitted with suppressors which reduced the sound very considerably. The future of weapons of this rather specialized type is not yet very clear. The almost universal adoption of assault rifles of one kind or another has made it possible for virtually every soldier to be armed with one, which must make the future of the sub-machine gun uncertain, if only because its disappearance would eliminate one type of cartridge. It may be that certain types of soldiers would be better armed with these specialist weapons, the kinds which come immediately to mind being wireless operators, drivers and mortarmen. On balance however, they may become accepted as weapons for plain clothes police or other security men, being light to carry and not very difficult to conceal, because of their compact shape.

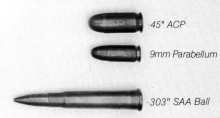

·45″ ACP

9mm Parabellum

·303″ SAA Ball

The Rifle and Carbine

A rifled firearm is one in which the projectile is made to spin on its way up the bore. This gives it a considerable degree of stability in flight, so that its path can be predicted with great accuracy and the projectile directed onto a target by means of sights. The principal method of achieving this spin is by cutting slow spiral parallel grooves into the bore, and contrary to widely held beliefs the system is a very old one. Hand guns in reasonably recognizable modern form did not come into use much before the middle of the fifteenth century, yet by 1520 or thereabouts rifled weapons were in existence.

It is sometimes said that the grooves were originally no more than straight gutters for collecting the heavy fouling from the crude black powder then in use, and that they were only eventually made spiral in order to increase their length and capacity. This however is mere conjecture and is at best doubtful, for there is good reason to believe that the concept of spinning arrows or crossbow bolts was well known, which at least suggests that the discovery of rifling was intentional rather than accidental.

There were two serious disadvantages to early rifled weapons. The first was

that they were slow and expensive to make, and the second, and more important, was that they were very slow to load. The spherical lead ball, then the almost universal small-arms projectile, had to be a tight fit to be spun by the rifling, and in the absence of any effective system of breechloading the ball had to be forced down the full length of the barrel from the muzzle end. This was a lengthy business, particularly when fouling had built up from previous discharges, so that for many years the rifle remained a weapon for the sportsman for whom one or two slow but well placed shots were very

146

much more important than sheer volume of fire. In Great Britain the only game for a rifleman was deer, and as these were usually only shot by rich landowners, expense was not important and a few fine early rifles were made. Some were even loaded at the breech end by means of screw-plug devices, although as these were both complicated and susceptible to fouling they probably made little improvement in terms of loading time. It is possible that a few of these rifles, or 'screwed guns' as they were then usually called, were used as sniper-type weapons in the defence of various Royalist fortified manor houses

besieged by the Parliamentary forces, but if so their numbers were few.

The rifle was a somewhat more common sporting arm on the mainland of Europe where the great forests were full of boar and deer. During the religious wars of the seventeenth century many German gun-makers emigrated to North America where their rifled weapons were eagerly sought after by the frontiersmen, who relied on deer not only for their food but for much of their clothing as well. The earliest German rifles tended to be of short barrel and large calibre, but there soon evolved a fairly characteristic

1 The British 4·85mm experimental Individual Weapon has a x4 SUSAT sight and is intended to replace the L2 sub-machine gun and L1 rifle.
2 Russians with 7·62mm Mosin-Nagant rifles during World War I.

North American model with a barrel length of up to four feet (1.22m) and a calibre of not much over 0.5in (12mm). Speed of reloading was improved by wrapping the ball in a circular patch of oiled leather or linen, an idea probably also originally imported from Europe.

It was in this theatre that the British Army first encountered the rifle in the

147

hands of the frontiersmen, who had found by experience that although initially a sporting arm it was equally useful in forest fighting. The main opponents were the Red Indians who were not much given to wild charges; instead they slipped forward from cover to cover with great skill and it needed accurate shooting to stop them.

In the Seven Years War of 1756-63 the main opponents were the French, so that the British colonists fought on the side of the British Army and gave excellent services as flankers and skirmishers, but during the War of Independence they became formidable enemies. It is, as a matter of fact, probable that the rifle did not play quite such a vital role in that war as later romantic literature may have led us to believe, for the bulk of the American colonists were armed with smoothbore muskets not markedly different from the Tower muskets in the hands of the King's soldiers. The riflemen, as before, acted on the flanks but although very useful they were probably not the deciding factor in the struggle. The shaggy backwoodsman, clad in greasy leather and armed with a long rifle, has taken his place in United States folklore and tradition, but he was probably no more than an auxiliary, although an extremely useful one. There were of course a few riflemen on the British side too, partly drawn from the large loyalist element and partly regulars armed with the ingenious breech-loading rifle invented by Captain Patrick Ferguson.

RIFLE REGIMENT RAISED

The value of the rifle as a specialist arm was not lost on many of the British officers who had served in America in the period 1776-1783, and when the French Revolutionary Wars started ten years later their novel system of preceding their attacks with swarms of active skirmishers made it necessary to oppose them with at least a protective screen of similar troops. Most of the British light companies retained the smoothbore musket, but in 1800 a Rifle Regiment was also raised. It was armed with a flintlock rifle invented by Ezekiel Baker, a noted gunsmith of Whitechapel, and this was a light and handy weapon which shot reasonably well to 300 yards (274·2m), use being made of the greased patch to facilitate loading. Some battalions of the 60th Regiment were also armed with this rifle, which proved sufficiently effective during the Napoleonic Wars, particularly in the Peninsula and at Waterloo, to be retained afterwards as a specialist weapon by the Rifle Regiment (which had by then become the Rifle Brigade) and by the 60th. It was finally replaced by the percussion Brunswick in 1838.

The mid-19th century was a time of great technical advances in many fields

including that of firearms. The French, who were engaged in extensive colonial wars in North Africa, were particularly active in this sphere, having found that the long guns of their mounted opponents were often more effective than those of their own soldiers. In spite of patches and other expedients the real problem was how to load a tight bullet easily, and various methods were tried to expand a lead bullet into the rifling *after* it had been rammed down. At first these involved hammering the bullet onto either a central spike or a circumferential ledge in the breech of the rifle by means of a heavy ramrod, a rough and ready method which certainly expanded the bullet but also distorted it to the stage where it was ballistically unstable. Eventually it was discovered that an elongated projectile with a hollow base achieved the same end, and when this became clear the British adopted a rifle of this type which had been developed by a French rifleman, Captain Minié. The adoption of a French invention was not wholly popular in Britain, particularly since two Englishmen, Norton and Green, both had claims to prior development of similar bullets, but the rifle was a success. It was approved in 1851 and issues began soon afterwards, not only to Rifle Regiments but as a general weapon. It gave good service in the Crimean War of 1854-6 but its actual life was short since replacement of it by a new and improved Enfield rifle had begun before the war was over. This new weapon, which fired a simplified bullet of smaller calibre than its predecessor, was a great success and by about 1858 had become the universal British military arm. Although still slow to load, two rounds per minute being a good average rate, it shot well to half-a-mile and was a great advance on anything previously known, although the relatively high trajectory made a careful estimate of distance essential at anything but point-blank range. In the same period most of the modern armies of the world had been re-armed with rifles of similar type and capacity, the only exception being that of Prussia, whose special arrangements will be discussed later in this chapter (see page 150).

The first great test of these new and improved percussion rifles came in the American Civil War of 1861-65. Both sides used rifles of Enfield type (and indeed many of actual Enfield manufacture) and their effect on tactics was profound. In the old smoothbore days the effective fire zone of infantry in defence was little more than 100 yards (91.4m), a distance which a strong and resolute body of attackers might cross in a single bold rush without suffering excessive casualties, but now those days had gone. In terms of collective

1 *The French 8mm Model 1916 infantry rifle had a five-round magazine in place of the Model 1907/15's three-round magazine.*
2 *Germany's standard carbine, the 98K.*

fire the new rifles shot well enough to 800-900 yards (731-822·5m) and no-one could expect to sustain a charge over this distance. A tired, heavily laden infantryman could hardly expect to cover half-a-mile (800m) cross-country in less than twenty minutes during which time each defending rifleman, well ensconced behind cover, could fire thirty or more careful shots.

Battles thus became more open and started at greater ranges. Everyone dug as a matter of survival and the spade became as important as the rifle. Artillery could no longer gallop close to formed bodies of infantry and scourge them with grape, because at grape ranges teams and detachments would all be shot before they could halt and

unlimber. No-one tried frontal attacks any more if they could possibly find a way to outflank, although it took some horrifying casualties (particularly on the Union side) before the lesson was finally learnt. Cavalry charges against infantry became rare and desperate affairs, to be risked only for some tactical gain which was so vital that losses did not matter. War, in fact, suddenly became modern.

Most of the military powers of Europe, confident in their technical superiority, tended to ignore military events in North America on the ground that the war there was an amateur and confused series of brawls between mere armed mobs, but in this they were foolish and short sighted. Some of the earlier engagements may have been of this type, but both sides soon became highly professional in all but name and by the end of the war would have given a remarkable good account of themselves against any army in the world.

In spite of the various improvements to the muzzle-loaded percussion rifle the real need was clearly for an effective breech-loader. The first nation to make a decisive move in this direction was Prussia, then very much the rising star of Europe, who as early as 1849 had begun the adoption of their famous needle-gun. This was a single-shot, bolt action weapon firing a non-metallic consumable cartridge. The cap was situated at the base of the bullet and the striker thus had to penetrate the paper case and pass through the powder charge to reach it, hence its distinctive needle-like shape which gave the weapon its name. It was in many ways a poor rifle, lacking range and power, and leaking gas so badly from the breech that the soldiers armed with it were reluctant to use it from the shoulder after a few rounds and simply blazed away from the hip.

The British Government obtained a specimen of the needle-gun soon after

3 *New Zealand infantryman with a 7·62mm L1A1 self-loading rifle.*
4 *US firing squad with 0·3in Model 1903A3 magazine rifles.*
5 *The man on the left carries a 0·303in Rifle No 1, SMLE Mk III*, and the one in the lead a Thompson.*

its introduction and in 1850 made a small number of replicas for test purposes, but decided against any change. It is to be presumed that most of the other major countries of Europe came to the same conclusion, for none followed the Prussian example. The need for a reliable breech-loader was still accepted, particularly perhaps for the cavalry. In the face of the increasing effectiveness of the infantry rifle, the mounted arm (although of course they were reluctant to admit it) were being driven more and more to use firearms, and in the nature of things it was clearly very difficult for a mounted man to reload a muzzle-loader.

1

Although self-contained cartridges existed, the British at least professed to distrust them on the grounds that if a soldier's pouch was hit the whole thing would explode. They therefore continued to experiment with capping breech-loaders in which a cartridge of powder and ball in some easily consumable case was fired by a separate cap.

Then the blow fell, for in 1864 the Prussians defeated the Danes in a lightning campaign which surprised Europe. There were of course a variety of reasons for their success, but to soldiers at least the most obvious one appeared to be the needle-gun, which proved conclusively that even a poor breech-loader was a good deal more effective than the finest muzzle-loader. The great advantage of the needle-gun appeared to be the speed at which it could be reloaded. It was not because the Prussians needed to fire much faster on the average but because they could never be caught unprepared while going through the long ritual of cartridge, ramrod, and cap, inseparable from the muzzle-loader. The new arm could moreover be reloaded in the prone position; this allowed the Prussian infantry to fire lying down which not only increased the steadiness of their aim but also reduced the size of the target they presented.

As was understandable the European nations reacted quickly. The British for example assembled a committee to consider the problem, a committee which moreover succeeded in producing a highly serviceable breech-loader in something less than two years. The British answer, partly for economy but largely for speed, was to convert their existing excellent Enfield by the addition of a hinged-block type breech invented by a Dutchman called Snider. The long-standing and largely irrational fear of the self-contained cartridge (which American experience had shown to be perfectly safe and reliable) was at last overcome, with the result that a modern brass and cardboard centre-fire round, not dissimilar to the present shotgun cartridge, was adopted. The Snider, reliable though it was, was in fact no more than a stop gap and even before it was in full issue its replacement, a single-shot, falling-block breech rifle, the Martini-Henry, was in production. This weapon, which was in general issue by about 1874, fired a cartridge the body of which was at first made of coiled brass foil but within ten years this had been replaced by a more reliable one with a solid-drawn case.

In 1866 the Prussians defeated the Austrians, who were still armed with muzzle-loaders, and four years later came the inevitable clash with the French. By then the French army had been re-equipped with the Chassepot, a weapon not dissimilar in principle to the needle-gun but greatly superior to it in terms of range, accuracy, and reliability. This, however, did not save them, and they were soundly defeated by an army immeasurably superior in organization, discipline, staff work and general efficiency. As was to be expected, this first major war between armies both armed with breech-loaders was an extremely bloody one. The Prussians, who were usually on the offensive, based their tactics on the lessons of earlier wars and attacked in thick skirmish lines supported by formed bodies of reserves and a numerous and efficient artillery. Once the attack came under effective fire almost all order was lost above company level. Everyone pushed on boldly, suffering heavy casualties, so that even when an attack was successful the confusion was so great that it was difficult to exploit success. This loss of control, which was greater than anyone anticipated, might well have been at least partially avoided if more heed had been given to the lessons of the American Civil War. After the war both contest-

ants adopted new rifles, both single-shot, bolt-action arms firing solid drawn cartridges.

The next real changes came in the 1880s with the so-called small bore rifles of a calibre of about 0·3in (8·5mm). These were originally developed mainly by the Swiss and their elongated jacketed bullets gave better range and trajectory. They were bolt-action weapons and in order to increase the rate of fire they were equipped mainly with box magazines, although the Swiss Vetterli and the French Lebel favoured tubular magazines below the barrel. Then came smokeless powder, first adopted by the French in their Lebel, and with its arrival the rifle may be said to have reached its peak performance.

BOER WAR TACTICS

In 1899 Britain went to war with the Boer colonists, her first major war for almost half a century. She soon found that her tactical system, principally designed for use against savage enemies in colonial wars, was not adequate against a brave and enterprising European foe, well mounted, well armed with the latest Mauser rifles, and operating in a vast empty country where the few inhabitants were their friends. The first phase of the war was in fact won fairly quickly, but the second guerrilla phase took up a great deal of men, time, and trouble.

Great Britain was not then very popular in Europe and there was a good deal of barely concealed joy at her discomfiture. The German official account of the first phase, fair if sharply critical, rather implied that Britain's failures were due to her lack of determination to press her attacks in the face of casualties on the European scale, for which her colonial experience had not prepared her. However, the causes were deeper than that, and once the war was won Great Britain set out to modernize her Army. One of the corner-stones of her tactical system was to be a tremendously effective fire power and many efforts were made to increase her scale of machine guns. In spite of the later lessons of the Russo-Japanese war of 1904, in which the fearsome efficiency of automatic weapons was well demonstrated, no increases were authorized, so some alternative had to be found, and this turned out to be a vast improvement in rifle shooting. One of the leading lights in this was Lieutenant-Colonel N. R. McMahon DSO of the Royal Fusiliers who was at the time Chief Instructor at the School of Musketry at Hythe. Despairing of an increase in machine guns he turned his attention to rapid rifle fire and with the whole-hearted

2 *Men of the 1st Parachute Logistics Regiment with 7·62mm L1A1 self-loading rifles.*
3 *British infantry with 0·303in Rifles No. 1 SMLE Mk III or III**
4 *An American mortarman is preceded by infantry with 0·3in M1 rifles and an M1 carbine—St. Malo, 1944.*
5 *Soviet infantry fire their 7·62mm AKM assault rifles.*

support of his superiors he transformed the British system of musketry.

By this time the British Army had adopted the new short-magazine Lee-Enfield, an excellent weapon, and the results it achieved are too well known to need much repetition. On the outbreak of World War I in 1914 the most gallantly pressed German attacks were halted time after time by rifle fire of a speed, accuracy and intensity never before seen on a battlefield. It is given to few soldiers of relatively low rank to make such an important contribution to his country's military standards as the one made by McMahon. He went to France in 1914 in command of a battalion of his regiment and it must have been with a certain sober satisfaction that he looked at the fearful heaps of enemy dead in front of the British battalions and saw that his efforts had not been wasted. He was promoted to Brigadier-General and was killed in action on 11 November, 1914.

Although the powers of the modern magazine rifle were demonstrated at their peak by the British Expeditionary Force of 1914, its descent thereafter was rapid. The expert riflemen of the early battles were mostly dead or dispersed, and there was no time to train the vast new armies who succeeded them to anything like the same high standards. Trench warfare, moreover, had given rise to the need for a variety of other weapons, all of which tended to overshadow the rifle, and although it remained the standard arm of the infantry it never even remotely regained its former supremacy.

The post World War I years saw at least a partial return to the high standards of musketry prevalent in 1914, but even so the rifle remained in second place to the various automatic weapons whose fire traditionally dominated the battlefield. Experiments began in Great Britain on a new rifle to replace the fine but complex short-magazine Lee-Enfield and resulted in the Number 4, a simplified version of its famous predecessor which could be more easily mass-produced in the event of another war. This of course came, and the new rifle was produced by the million, although many thousands of the earlier model remained in service. Towards the end of the war yet another rifle appeared. This was the Number 5, a shorter, lighter version of the Number 4 and specifically designed for jungle warfare in the Far East.

Most other countries entered World War II with rifles of similar type and capacity. The Germans mainly used the KAR 98K, a shortened version of their reliable 1898 model, while the French had their MAS 1936 and the Russians their M1891/30. Only the Americans were fully equipped with a self-loading rifle, the ·300 M1(Garand) together with a carbine of similar calibre but firing a much lighter cartridge. The Germans did in fact experiment with self-loaders in 1941–43 but without great success, and weapons of this type did not become general until after the end of the war.

World War II also saw the rise in importance of the sub-machine gun, a light automatic carbine firing pistol ammunition, and the general form in the infantry was to intersperse a number of these among the rifles. The experiences of the first few years made it clear that with the vast number of supporting weapons the need for the old-fashioned long-range rifle had been greatly reduced. Once this had become apparent efforts were made to produce an intermediate weapon, which can best be described as a hotted-up sub-machine gun, which would fulfil both roles. Arms of this type were later to be known as assault rifles, and the first in this field were the Germans with their

FG42, an excellent weapon firing the standard rifle cartridge; this was followed after some intermediate experiment by the MG 44, another excellent weapon designed to fire a round intermediate between the 9mm pistol and the rifle cartridge. Russia followed this lead after the war with their AK47, closely based on the German rifle, as did the United States with their Colt Armalite range of weapons, and many other countries. Great Britain, after some experiment with a successful prototype, the EM2, did not adopt it after all. At the time of writing she is experimenting with a new small-bore assault weapon of broadly similar type, which has a heavy barrelled version capable of acting as the section automatic weapon.

New arms of this type have many advantages including lightness and portability, particularly in the close confines of the various armoured personnel carriers in which the infantry now spend much of their time, and it seems probably that in the future they may largely replace both the sub-machine gun and the more orthodox rifle. The only exception is likely to be the retention of the older bolt-action rifle fitted with a telescopic sight in the role of a sniping rifle, a function which it performed well in both World Wars and various later operations.

EFFECTIVE RANGES

It may be useful to include in this introduction a brief note on the ranges of rifles, since the maximum backsight settings are liable to be misleading on their own. The original late-19th Century small-bore bolt-action magazine rifles were usually sighted to about 2000 yards (1829m) and some had auxiliary long-range sights to 2800 yards (2560m). Under ideal conditions (ie well trained soldiers and a clear atmosphere), fire could be directed to these extreme ranges in the sense that twenty or thirty men firing together could bring collective fire to bear onto an area target. The steep angle of descent of the bullets at these ranges made accurate judgement of distance essential, good observation by telescope or binoculars also being necessary to verify the actual fall of the bullets, and even in the best conditions a high proportion of shots were wasted. Nevertheless tests against canvas screens indicated that this fire could be described as marginally effective, if only to disturb the enemy and make them keep their heads down.

All things being equal, fire effect increased as the range shortened, so that at 800 yards (731·5m) or so well controlled collective fire could be deadly. At the battle of Omdurman in the Sudan campaign of 1898 the Dervish charges across open desert, al-

though pressed with the greatest gallantry, rarely succeeded in approaching closer to the British firing line than about 400 yards (366m) and then only at terrible cost. In South Africa, a very different sort of war, the Boers shot well to 1000 yards (914m) or so, and being adept at taking cover were not usually much worried by the British return fire. It was found that long-range collective volley fire was sometimes effective, but again, to pin the Boers down rather than actually inflict many casualties. South Africa was, however, in many ways an aberration and the Russo-Japanese war probably showed much more clearly the way that modern warfare was likely to develop. Thus by 1914 the British at least had decided that the real answer was rapid fire at ranges which would really cause casualties, which having regard to the very high standard of British musketry really meant up to

1 *US troops in South Vietnam, armed with 5·56mm M16A1 rifles, distinguishable from the M16 by the plunger on the right of the body to push the bolt home when necessary.*
2 *Firepower demonstration by M1 rifle and M1918A2 BAR.*

500 yards (475m), and in the event it proved deadly. Thereafter automatic weapons largely took over the task of delivering greater volumes of fire, and the effective range of the rifle was reduced accordingly. Most modern rifles are still sighted to about 800 yards (731·5m), but they are rarely used at much over 300 yards (274m), which may therefore be considered the maximum truly effective range by modern standards. Much the same standards apply in practice to light machine guns, although their capacity to fire bursts often makes it permissible to use them at longer ranges.

SHORT MAGAZINE LEE-ENFIELD MI

The British Army first adopted the magazine Lee-Metford in 1888. This fired a cartridge loaded with compressed black powder until 1895 when the introduction of cordite led to the need for a new barrel with deeper rifling. The short rifle was introduced at the end of the South African war which had shown that all services needed a proper long-range rifle. The particular construction of the breech mechanism made the rifle very suitable for rapid fire and from 1909 onwards the British Army, anticipating a war with Germany in which it would be greatly outnumbered, concentrated on this form of shooting with deadly results. The rifle illustrated, the Mark III*, was a World War I product but although it had been simplified in some respects it was essentially similar to its predecessor. (Full specification on pages *170-171*.)

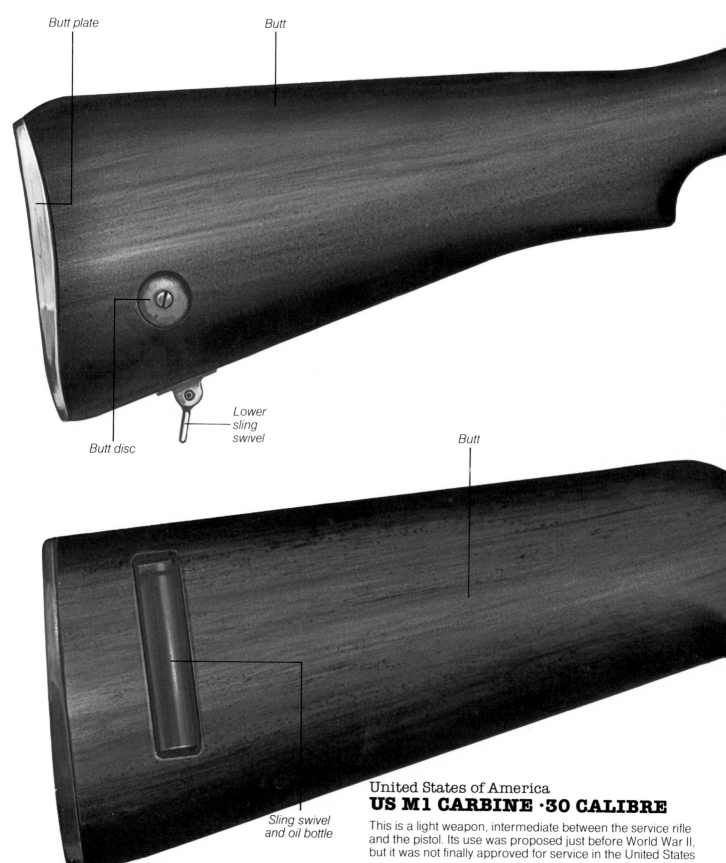

Butt plate

Butt

Butt disc

Lower sling swivel

Butt

Sling swivel and oil bottle

United States of America
US M1 CARBINE ·30 CALIBRE

This is a light weapon, intermediate between the service rifle and the pistol. Its use was proposed just before World War II, but it was not finally approved for service in the United States

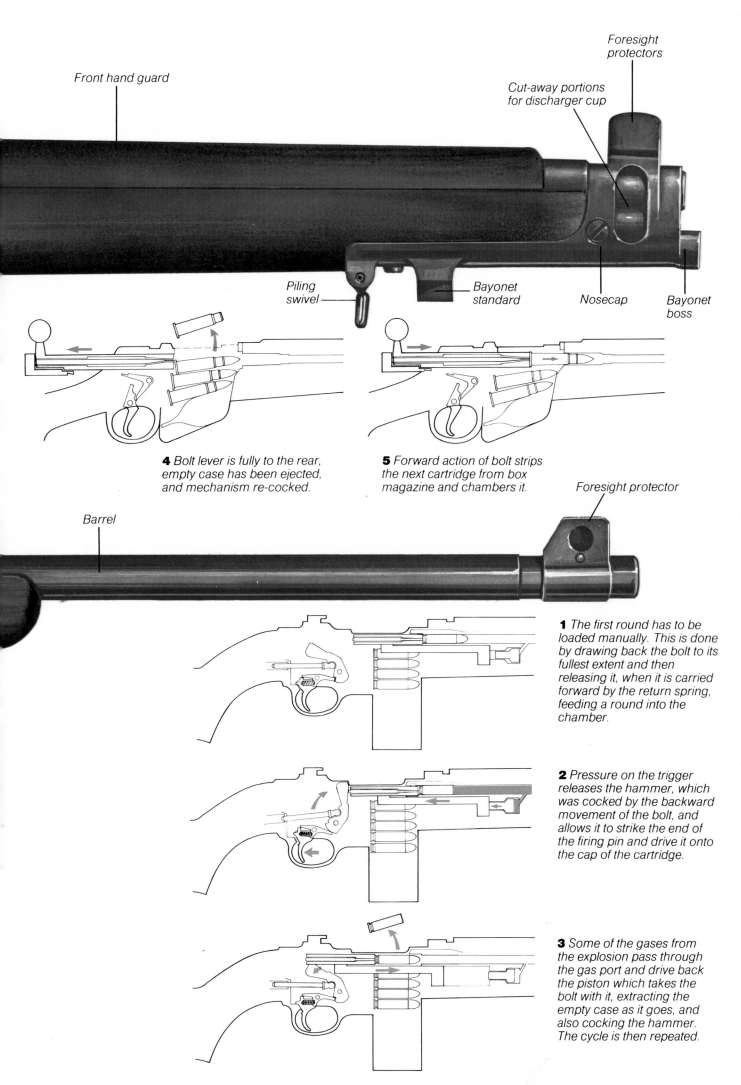

Front hand guard

Foresight
protectors

Cut-away portions
for discharger cup

Piling
swivel

Bayonet
standard

Nosecap

Bayonet
boss

4 Bolt lever is fully to the rear,
empty case has been ejected,
and mechanism re-cocked.

5 Forward action of bolt strips
the next cartridge from box
magazine and chambers it.

Foresight protector

Barrel

1 The first round has to be
loaded manually. This is done
by drawing back the bolt to its
fullest extent and then
releasing it, when it is carried
forward by the return spring,
feeding a round into the
chamber.

2 Pressure on the trigger
releases the hammer, which
was cocked by the backward
movement of the bolt, and
allows it to strike the end of
the firing pin and drive it onto
the cap of the cartridge.

3 Some of the gases from
the explosion pass through
the gas port and drive back
the piston which takes the
bolt with it, extracting the
empty case as it goes, and
also cocking the hammer.
The cycle is then repeated.

157

Soviet Union
AK 47 (KALASHNIKOV)

The Russians learnt the value of firepower in World War II and as soon as it was over they set out to produce a basic infantry arm capable of automatic fire but with a greater degree of range and accuracy than the various sub-machine guns on which they had relied in the war. They were, in particular, impressed with the German MP44 and it is likely that they were helped by captured German designers. The final result of their efforts was the weapon shown (the designer responsible being Michael Kalashnikov), which was introduced into the Soviet Army from 1951 onwards. It was also extensively made in various Warsaw Pact countries and the Chinese assault rifle is closely based on it. Although obsolescent in Russia there must be thousands of them in the hands of various subversive and terrorist organisations.

(Full specification on pages *184-185*.)

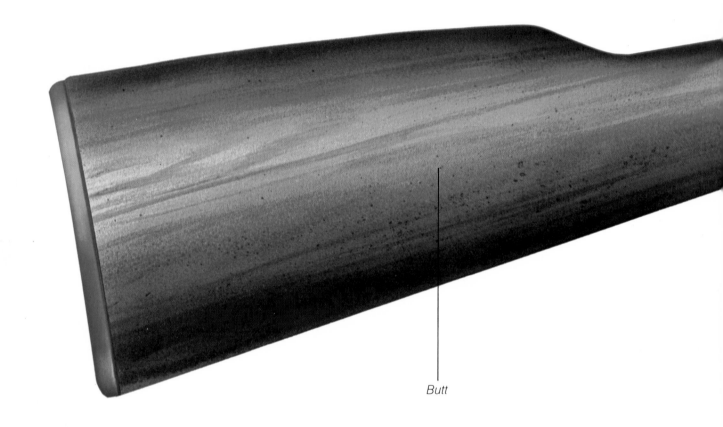

Butt

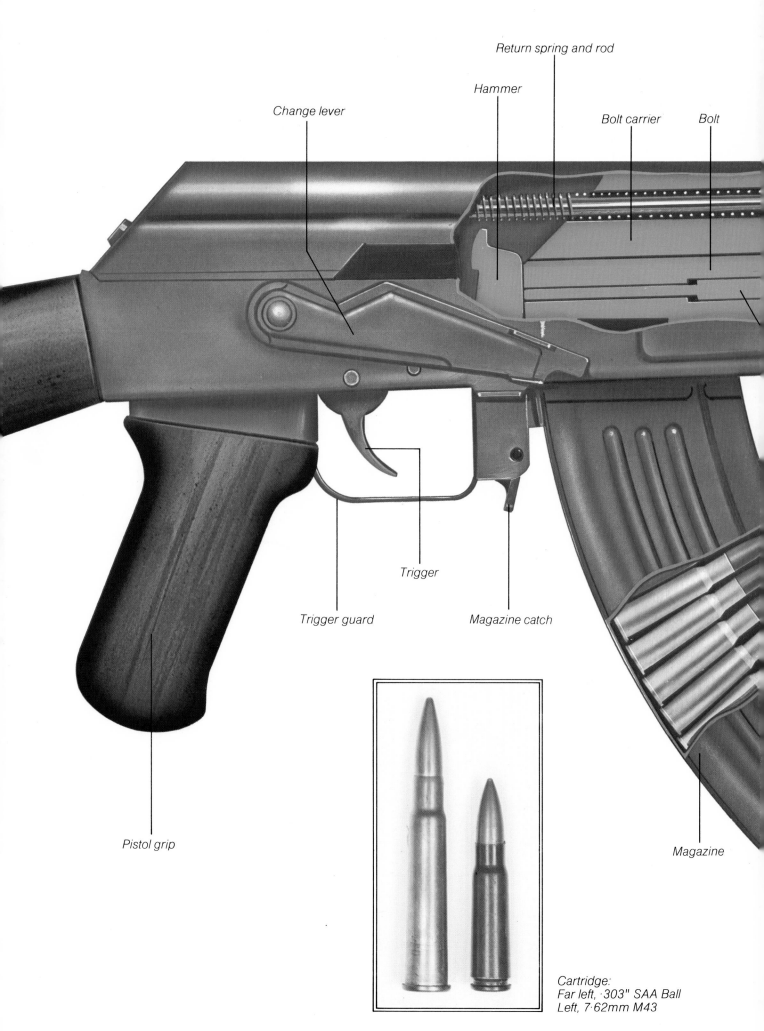

Return spring and rod

Hammer

Change lever

Bolt carrier

Bolt

Trigger

Trigger guard

Magazine catch

Pistol grip

Magazine

Cartridge:
Far left, ·303" SAA Ball
Left, 7·62mm M43

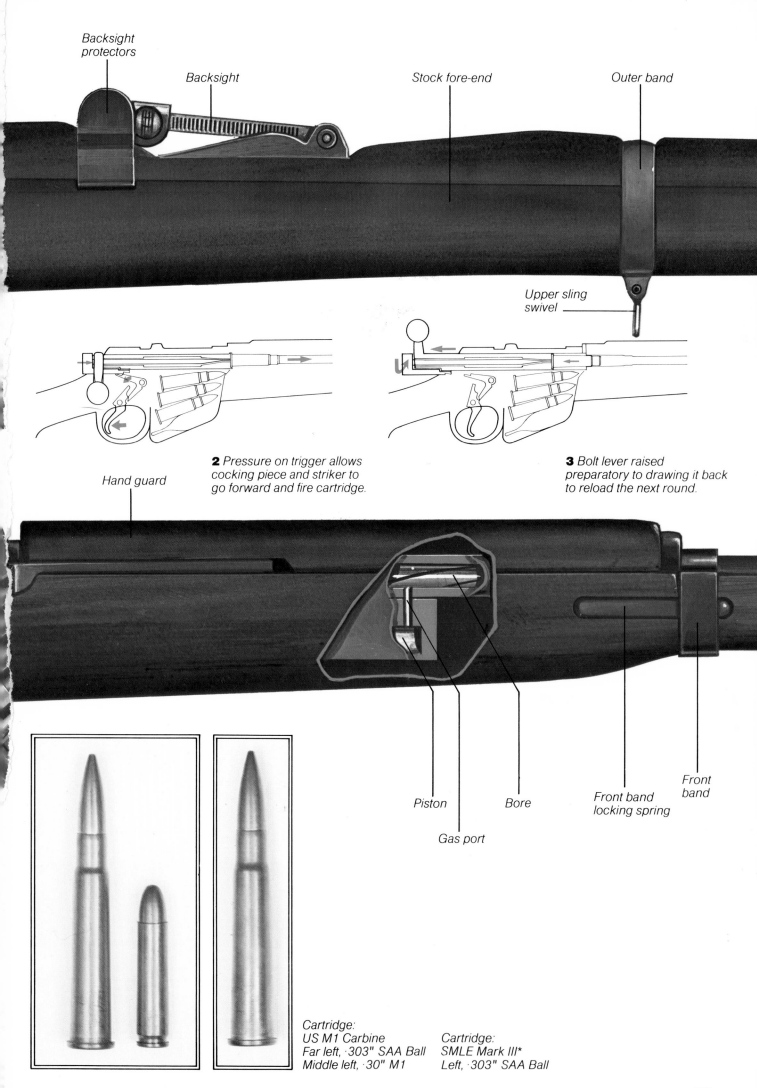

Backsight
protectors

Backsight

Stock fore-end

Outer band

Upper sling
swivel

Hand guard

2 *Pressure on trigger allows
cocking piece and striker to
go forward and fire cartridge.*

3 *Bolt lever raised
preparatory to drawing it back
to reload the next round.*

Piston

Bore

Gas port

Front band
locking spring

Front
band

Cartridge:
US M1 Carbine
Far left, ·303" SAA Ball
Middle left, ·30" M1

Cartridge:
SMLE Mark III*
Left, ·303" SAA Ball

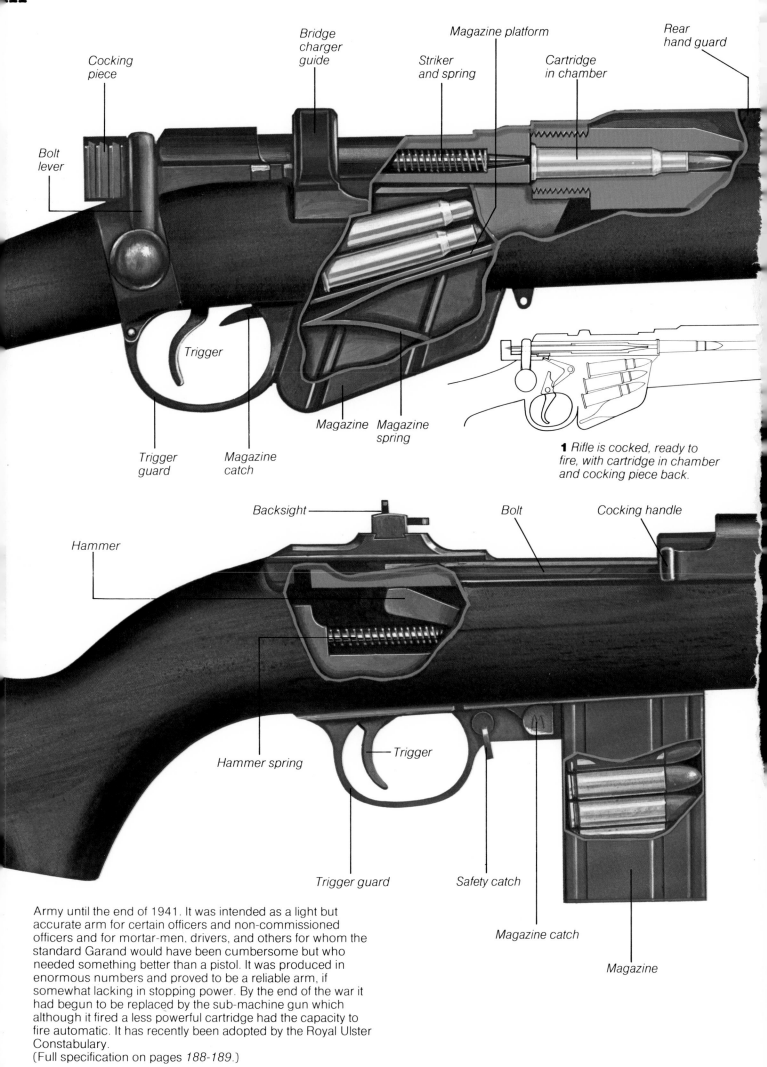

Cocking
piece

Bridge
charger
guide

Magazine platform

Striker
and spring

Cartridge
in chamber

Rear
hand guard

Bolt
lever

Striker
and spring

Trigger

Magazine   Magazine
spring

Trigger
guard

Magazine
catch

1 Rifle is cocked, ready to
fire, with cartridge in chamber
and cocking piece back.

Backsight

Bolt

Cocking handle

Hammer

Hammer spring

Trigger

Trigger guard

Safety catch

Magazine catch

Magazine

Army until the end of 1941. It was intended as a light but
accurate arm for certain officers and non-commissioned
officers and for mortar-men, drivers, and others for whom the
standard Garand would have been cumbersome but who
needed something better than a pistol. It was produced in
enormous numbers and proved to be a reliable arm, if
somewhat lacking in stopping power. By the end of the war it
had begun to be replaced by the sub-machine gun which
although it fired a less powerful cartridge had the capacity to
fire automatic. It has recently been adopted by the Royal Ulster
Constabulary.
(Full specification on pages 188-189.)

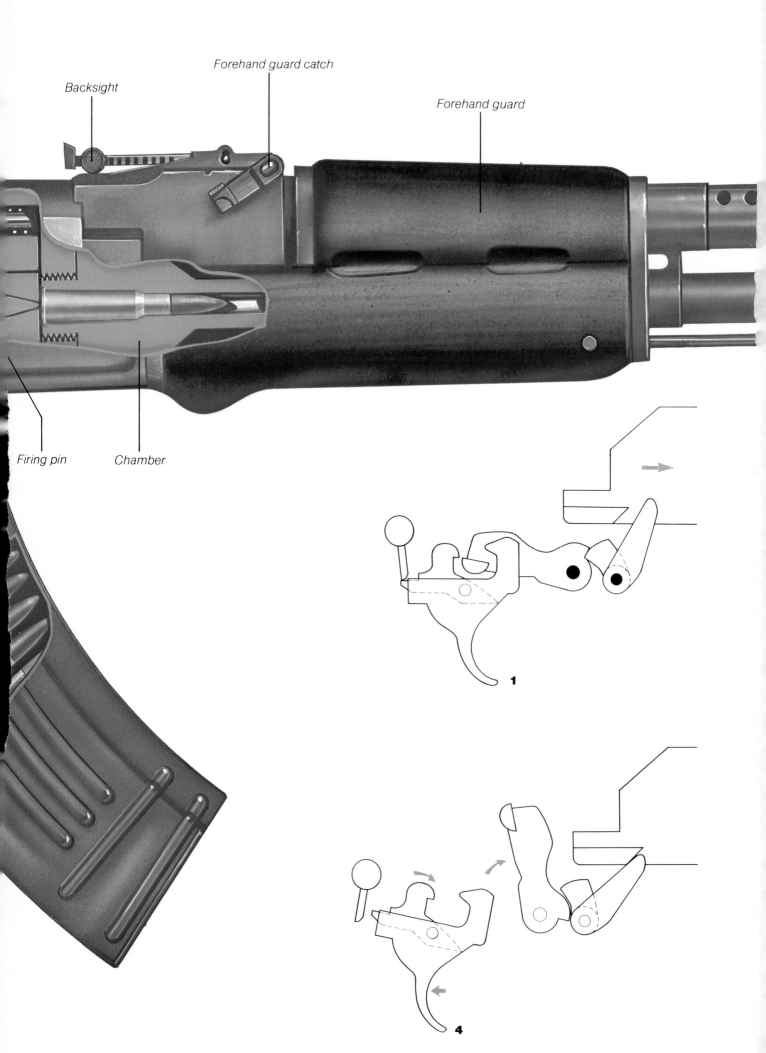

Backsight

Forehand guard catch

Forehand guard

Firing pin

Chamber

1

4

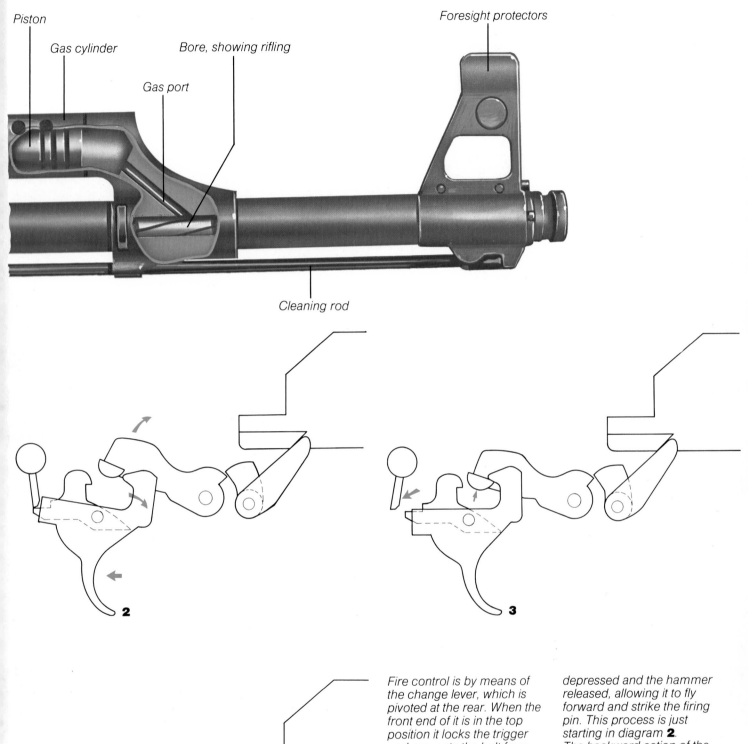

Piston

Gas cylinder

Gas port

Bore, showing rifling

Foresight protectors

Cleaning rod

2

3

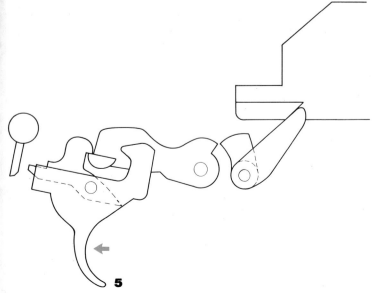

5

Fire control is by means of the change lever, which is pivoted at the rear. When the front end of it is in the top position it locks the trigger and prevents the bolt from being opened sufficiently far to chamber a round; when central it allows for automatic fire, and when fully depressed it gives single shot. Diagram **1** shows the weapon cocked and set for automatic, the hammer being held back by the sear. When the bolt is forward and locked and the trigger pressed, the sear is depressed and the hammer released, allowing it to fly forward and strike the firing pin. This process is just starting in diagram **2**. The backward action of the bolt carrier forces the hammer back and it is held briefly (**3**) until the next round is chambered, when the process is repeated. At single rounds the hammer, having been forced back in the normal way, is held by an auxiliary sear and cannot be released until the trigger has again been pressed (**4** and **5**).

Belgium
SELF-LOADING EXPERIMENTAL MODEL

Length: 44" (1117mm)
Weight: 9.5lb (4.31kg)
Barrel: 23.25" (591mm)
Calibre: 7.92mm
Rifling: 4 groove r/hand
Operation: Gas
Feed: 10-round box
Muzzle Velocity:
2400 f/s (730 m/s)
Sights: 1094 yds (1000m)

This weapon was originally designed in Belgium in the 1930s by a M. Saive, who envisaged it as a replacement for the existing bolt-action rifles of Mauser type then in use in the Belgian Army. In May 1940, however, soon after the outbreak of World War II the Germans invaded Belgium and all work on the new rifle

Belgium
FN FAL RIFLE

Length: 41.5" (1054mm)
Weight: 9.5lb (4.31kg)
Barrel: 21" (533mm)
Calibre; 7.62mm
Rifling: 4 groove r/hand
Operation: Gas
Feed: 20-round box
Muzzle Velocity:
2800 f/s (853 m/s)
Sights: 656 yds (600m)

The Belgians, who have long been well known as arms makers, had made considerable progress in developing a self-loading rifle before the war. The designer escaped to Britain with the plans for this weapon which was later made in England and which subsequently formed the basis of all future Belgian development. Full details of this early weapon are given at the top of this page. The FAL (Fusil Automatique Légère) first appeared in 1950; it was originally intended to fire the German intermediate round, but was subsequently altered to fire the standard NATO cartridge, after which it very soon became popular. It was gas-operated, could fire automatic or single shots as required, and was generally a robust and effective arm well suited to military needs, and sold to a great many countries. Although it had the capacity to fire bursts this led to problems

of accuracy due to the inevitable tendency of the muzzle to rise, and most countries therefore had their rifles permanently set at semi-automatic which still allowed twenty or thirty well-aimed shots to be fired in one minute. There was also a heavy barrelled version with a light bipod which some countries adopted as a section automatic. There have been many modifications in design to suit the particular needs of different purchasers, but most of these are relatively minor ones. When Great Britain abandoned her EM 2 she decided, like many other countries, to adopt a version of the Belgian self-loader and purchased one thousand of them for trials, the lower weapon illustrated being one of these originals. As usual some modifications were incorporated and the weapon was fairly extensively tested under operational conditions in Kenya, Malaya, and elsewhere before being taken into use, after which it was made in England. The upper of the two rifles illustrated is a very early version of the Fusil Automatique Légère rifle made to fire the .280" round originally designed for the British EM2 rifle. The object of this is not known, but presumably if the British rifle had been accepted some countries might have preferred a more orthodox looking weapon but in the same calibre as the British EM 2.

naturally stopped. The designer managed to escape from Belgium with the plans for his new weapon which he took with him to Britain.

Saive, like other refugees, continued to work for Great Britain on various wartime projects but nothing was done about his own rifle until the end of the war when a number were made at the Royal Small Arms Factory at Enfield, being generally known as the Self-Loading Experimental Model,

often abbreviated to SLEM. They were gas operated with a gas cylinder above the barrel, and had a bolt very similar to that of the Russian Tokarev rifle. They were in general well made and full-stocked in walnut which made them very expensive weapons to produce. These prototypes, which were all made to fire the full size German 7·92mm Mauser round, were extensively tested, but although they proved to be most successful the British

were then also carrying out tests on their own EM 2, and so they took no further action on the Belgian rifle. When M. Saive returned to Belgium, however, he continued his work there and soon perfected an improved model known usually as the Model 49, after the date of its appearance. This was a time when a good many countries were looking for cheap and reliable self-loaders with which to re-arm their infantry, and the Model 49 was an

immediate success, being sold to a considerable number of countries including Columbia, Venezuela, Egypt and Luxemburg. The Belgians, understandably anxious for business, were more than ready to produce what their customers wanted and the Model 49 was manufactured in a variety of calibres. The Belgian Army also adopted it and it saw service in Korea. It subsequently developed into the highly successful FAL.

FAL ·280" (Experimental)

FAL 7·62mm (Trials model)

7·92mm Patrone 98

·280" Experimental

7·62mm NATO

·303" SAA Ball

Czechoslovakia
MODEL VZ 52

Length: 40" (1016mm)
Weight: 9lb (4·08kg)
Barrel: 20·5" (521mm)
Calibre: 7·62mm
Rifling: 4 groove r/hand

Operation: Gas
Feed: 10-round box
Muzzle Velocity:
2440 f/s (740 m/s)
Sights: 984 yds (900m)

This self-loading rifle was designed and developed in Czechoslovakia towards the end of World War II, some time before the country was swept into the Communist bloc. It incorporates a considerable variety of ideas borrowed from earlier arms of similar type. It was originally designed to fire an inter-mediate-type cartridge of purely Czech design and not interchangeable with any other, and was gas-operated. The method actually adopted however was somewhat unusual in that the weapon had no gas cylinder or piston of the usual type, power being transmitted by a sleeve round the barrel which was forced

France
MODELE 1886 (LEBEL)

Length: 51" (1295mm)
Weight: 9·3lb (4·22kg)
Barrel: 31·5" (800mm)
Calibre: 8mm
Rifling: 4 groove l/hand

Operation: Bolt
Feed: 8-round tubular
Muzzle Velocity:
2350 f/s (716 m/s)
Sights: 2187 yds (2000m)

The first breechloading rifle adopted by France was the Modèle 1866 or Chassepot, a bolt action needle-fire weapon firing a consumable paper cartridge. It was similar to the Prussian needle-gun, although of superior performance, and was used by the French in the war of 1870-71. It was converted to fire a modern metallic cartridge in 1873 and replaced by the Gras, a very similar weapon, in 1874. Four years later the French Marine Infantry was rearmed with the

France
FUSIL MAS 36

Length: 40·15" (1020mm)
Weight: 8·31lb (3·76kg)
Barrel: 22·6" (574mm)
Calibre: 7·5mm
Rifling: 4 groove l/hand
Operation: Bolt
Feed: 5-round box
Muzzle Velocity:
2700 f/s (823 m/s)
Sights: 1312 yds (1200m)

By the end of World War I it was clear to the French that they required a new rifle cartridge. The original Lebel smokeless round of 1886 had been revolutionary in its day but inevitably more modern rounds had been developed since. Its real disadvantage was its shape, since its very wide base and sharp taper made it a very difficult cartridge to use in automatic weapons. As by 1918 these dominated the battlefield a change was necessary. In 1924 therefore, a new rimless cartridge was developed, based fairly closely on the German 7·92mm round. The first priority was to develop suitable automatic weapons which are described elsewhere in this book, but once

sharply to the rear by the pressure of the gas tapped off from the bore and taking the bolt with it. The bolt was rather unusual in that it worked on the tilting principle under which the front end of the bolt dropped into a recess cut into the bottom of the body which had the effect of locking it firmly at the instant of firing.

The rifle performed well with the original cartridge for which it was designed, but the Russians later compelled the Czechs to abandon that round in favour of their own less powerful version which adversely affected its performance even though it helped standardization. The new modified rifle was generally known as the Model

52/57. The original VZ 52 was relatively heavy which reduced recoil but added to the soldier's load. It lacked any simple system of gas regulation, so that any change involved the removal of the foregrip before the gas stop could be adjusted, and then only on a trial and error basis which would have made it inconvenient in

service. It was often stocked in poor quality wood of a dirty yellow colour and had a generally cheap and clumsy look about it. It was fitted with a permanently attached blade bayonet which folded back along the right-hand side of the body when not in use. Both the VZ 52 and the VZ 52/57 are now deemed to be obsolete.

Austrian Kropatschek rifle, and it was on this weapon that the new Modèle 1886 was based. The Modèle 1886 was probably much better known as the Lebel, the name being in honour of Lieutenant-Colonel Nicholas Lebel, a member of the French Small Arms Committee at the time and the officer chiefly responsible for its introduction. It was a bolt-action rifle which incorporated the somewhat unusual feature of a tubular magazine, concealed in the woodwork

below the barrel, in place of the more general box. This type of magazine, which had been largely developed by the United States, had also been a feature of the earlier French Marine rifle. It incorporated a powerful coil spring at its front end, the rear end of the spring being fitted with a close fitting plug, and the rifle was loaded by pushing the rounds nose first into the magazine opening below the chamber until the full capacity of eight had been reached. The contents of the

magazine could if necessary be kept in reserve by a cut-off device, allowing the rifle to be used as a single-loader until a more rapid burst of fire was required. The most important feature of the Lebel was undoubtedly the fact that its cartridges were loaded with a recently developed smokeless propellant instead of the old black powder, the French being the first to make this important change. Smokeless powder had two obvious advantages, in that the firing

line could be easily concealed while the target was never obscured by smoke as had often been the case with black powder. In order to get the maximum power from the cartridge, it was made bottle shaped instead of cylindrical so as to get as much propellant in as possible. Smokeless powder cartridges soon came into general use, but in view of the greater pressures which developed, older pattern rifles could not always be adapted and new arms were vital.

this was complete a new rifle was also put into production. MAS 36 was a bolt action rifle of modified Mauser type, but with the bolt designed to lock into the top of the body behind the magazine. This made it necessary to angle the bolt lever forward so as to be in reach of the firer's hand, the general effect being rather ugly. The magazine was of standard integral box type with a capacity of five rounds

and there was no manual safety catch. The rifle had a cruciform bayonet carried in a tube beneath the barrel. It was fixed by withdrawing it and plugging its cylindrical handle into the mouth of the tube where it was held in place by a spring. Small numbers of a modified MAS 36 were later made for airborne troops; they had shorter barrels and folding butts and were designated the MAS 36 CR39.

7·62mm Soviet M43

8mm Mle 86

7·5 Mle 29

·303" SAA Ball

Germany
GEWEHR 98

Length: 49.25" (1250mm)
Weight: 9lb (4.1kg)
Barrel: 29.25" (740mm)
Calibre: 7.92mm
Rifling: 4 groove r/hand
Operation: Bolt
Feed: 5-round box
Muzzle Velocity: 2850 f/s (870 m/s)
Sights: 2188 yds (2000m)

Germany
GEWEHR 41(W)

Length: 44.5" (1130mm)
Weight: 11lb (4.98kg)
Barrel: 21.5" (546mm)
Calibre: 7.92mm
Rifling: 4 groove r/hand
Operation: Gas
Feed: 10-round box
Muzzle Velocity:
2550 f/s (776 m/s)
Sights: 1313 yds (1200m)

Germany
FALLSCHIRMJÄGERGEWEHR 42

Length: 37" (940mm)
Weight: 9.95lb (4.5kg)
Barrel: 20" (508mm)
Calibre: 7.92mm Patrone 98
Rifling: 4 groove r/hand
Operation: Gas
Feed: 20-round box
Cyclic Rate: 750 rpm
Muzzle Velocity:
2500 f/s (762 m/s)
Sights: 1313 yds (1200m)

This was one of the earliest assault rifles, being introduced in 1942. Its main disadvantage was that although the Germans had gained some success with intermediate cartridges, this particular arm fired the full-sized rifle round which was really too powerful for it. In spite of this it proved to be a remarkably good weapon to the limited number of troops armed with it, most of whom were parachutists. It was capable of single rounds or bursts. When bursts were employed the FG 42 fired from an open bolt, that is, there was no round in the chamber until the bolt drove one in and fired it in the same movement; the reason for this was that the chamber tended to get sufficiently hot to fire a cartridge

The Gewehr 98 with the 20-round experimental box magazine.

The Germans were the first nation to adopt a bolt action rifle which they did as early as 1848 when their needle-gun officially came into service. Thereafter, unlike the British who went off at a tangent with hinged and falling block rifles, the Germans remained constant to this original system which they developed progressively. The first rifle to fire a smokeless round was introduced in 1888 and was of 7·92mm calibre; this was followed in 1898 by the model illustrated which was made by the well-known firm of Mauser. It was a strong and reliable arm with the forward locking lugs made famous by the makers, and a five-round magazine the bottom of which was flush with the stock, and although its straight bolt lever was clumsy and not well adapted to fast fire, this was a minor disadvantage which did nothing to detract from its popularity. In one form or another it was sold to a great number of different countries and there can have been few rifles produced in such large quantities. A considerable number of the earliest ones were bought by the Boers who used them with tremendous effect in their war with the British which broke out a year later, and it served the German Army well in World War I. In 1918 the Germans experimented with a twenty-round magazine to prevent the constant entry of mud from the continuous reloading inseparable from the five-round magazine, but this was not a success chiefly because a spring powerful enough to lift such a column of cartridges made manual operation difficult.

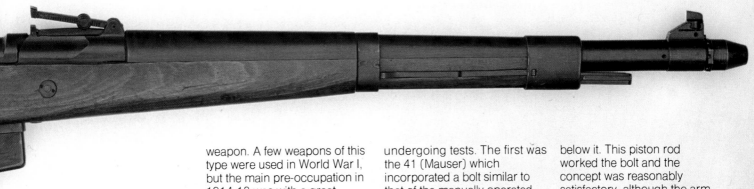

The Germans were among the pioneers of self-loading rifles and had a complete regiment armed with weapons of this type as early as 1901. This experiment was not followed up, principally because although valuable information was obtained the rifle then used was too heavy for an individual weapon. A few weapons of this type were used in World War I, but the main pre-occupation in 1914-18 was with a great volume of fire from somewhat heavier automatic weapons so again no progress was made. It was not therefore until the appearance of the Russian Tokarev self-loader just before World War II that any real attention was paid to the subject and by 1941 two separate models were undergoing tests. The first was the 41 (Mauser) which incorporated a bolt similar to that of the manually operated rifle; it was never a success and was soon abandoned. The second was the 41 (Walther) and this was a good deal more successful. It incorporated a muzzle cap which deflected part of the gases back onto an annular piston that worked a rod placed above the barrel, its return spring however being below it. This piston rod worked the bolt and the concept was reasonably satisfactory, although the arm had certain defects notably its weight and balance, together with a serious tendency to foul very badly round the muzzle cap. It was manufactured in some quantity and issued chiefly to units on the Russian front. It was eventually replaced by the MP 43/44, a much superior weapon.

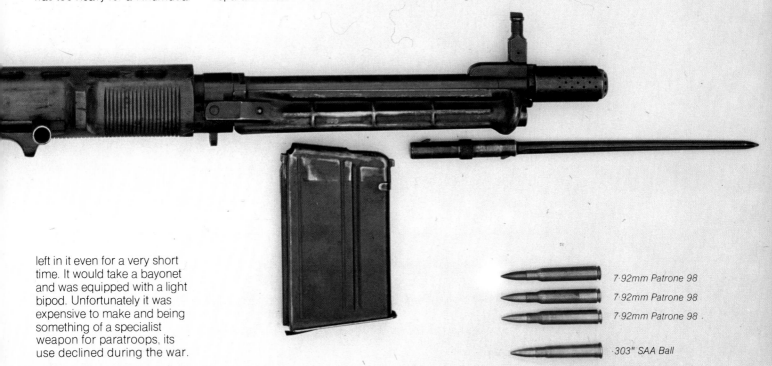

left in it even for a very short time. It would take a bayonet and was equipped with a light bipod. Unfortunately it was expensive to make and being something of a specialist weapon for paratroops, its use declined during the war.

7·92mm Patrone 98

7·92mm Patrone 98

7·92mm Patrone 98

·303" SAA Ball

Germany
MASCHINENPISTOLE MP44

Length: 37" (940mm)
Weight: 11·25lb (5·1kg)
Barrel; 16·5" (420mm)
Calibre: 7·92mm
Rifling: 4 groove r/hand
Operation: Gas
Feed: 30-round box
Muzzle Velocity:
2125 f/s (647 m/s)
Cyclic Rate: 500 rpm
Sights: 875 yds (800m)

The experience of World War I led the Germans to the opinion that in the future the infantryman should have a lighter weapon than the standard rifle. Work on this project started before the war and by 1941 they had produced an efficient intermediate round suitable for a weapon of the kind proposed. Perhaps surprisingly this round does not seem to have been considered for the FG 42, which was being developed at

that time but which fired the standard rifle round. Instead a number of weapons were developed for it, and by 1942 these had been whittled down to two, one by Haenel, the other by Walther, both being described as machine carbines. The Haenel version was modified by Schmeisser in 1943 in the light of actual combat experience, after which it became the MP 43, the Walther alternative being dropped at the same time.

Germany
HECKLER & KOCK HK 33

Length: 37" (940mm)
Weight: 7·7lb (3·5kg)
Barrel: 15" (382mm)
Calibre: 5·56mm
Rifling: 6 groove r/hand
Operation: Blowback
Feed: 20-, 30-, 40-round box
Muzzle Velocity:
3145 f/s (960 m/s)
Cyclic Rate: 600 rpm
Sights: 437·5 yds (400m)

This weapon has a long and somewhat involved history. It had its origins in a German rifle designed in the course of World War II. After the war this rifle was largely redesigned by a number of German designers and engineers who were working in Spain, the resulting weapon being the Spanish CETME. When the German

Army was reformed in the 1950s the German firm of Heckler-Koch, which had been involved with the CETME, developed the design somewhat further and produced a rifle known as the Gewehr 3. This soon became the weapon of the German Army and is, or has been, extensively used by a

considerable number of other countries, some of whom bought them from Heckler-Koch while others made them themselves under licence. The G3 was of somewhat unusual design in that it worked not on gas (by far the most common method) but on delayed blowback. The breech was never fully locked in the strict

The new weapon, which was gas operated through a piston working in a gas cylinder above the barrel, was an immediate success and by the end of 1943 the German Army had received fourteen thousand of them. The long-term idea seems to have been to make the MP 43 a universal weapon at squad or section level, so doing away with rifles, sub-machine guns and light machine guns in favour of the new arm. Perhaps fortunately, production declined very rapidly after the first few months of 1944 and so the new concept was never realized. There were some variations to the standard type, notably an MP 43 (1) which had a fixture allowing it to fire grenades, but no really significant changes. In 1944 the designation was changed to MP 44, apparently to mark the change in year since no other reason was ever offered, and by the end of the same year the weapon had been given the additional title of Sturm-Gewehr, or Assault Rifle. It is said that the expression was coined by Hitler himself; whether this is true or not it was a very apt description and one which has been used ever since. The MP 44 had a profound effect on the development of infantry firearms; the Russians in particular were quick to see the advantages of this new type of arm, and very soon developed their own version in the shape of the AK 47.

sense of the word; it was equipped with rollers which the forward movement of the firing pin forced outwards into recesses in the receiver. The shape of these recesses and their relationship to the rollers was such that the breech was held closed until the pressure dropped to a safe level when the rollers were forced out of the recesses. The residual gas pressure in the chamber blew the empty case backwards, taking the bolt with it and compressing the return spring which caused the cycle to be repeated. This method proved to be successful although the use of a full-sized rifle cartridge does often cause problems in a breech of this nature. The main difficulty is that the bolt comes back fairly fast, with no preliminary turning motion to start the case, and this can cause problems of extraction; this was basically the problem of the American Pedersen rifle which is dealt with elsewhere in this section. In the G3 the problem was dealt with by fluting the chamber and by ensuring that the quality of brass used in the case was sufficient to withstand the initial jerk without having its base torn off. The HK 33 was simply a logical development of this earlier weapon, to which it bears a strong resemblance both externally and mechanically. The chief, and important difference is that the HK 33 was designed to fire an intermediate round which offered some advantages. It gave good performance at reasonable ranges and allowed for much more accurate automatic fire than was ever the case with the more powerful 7·62mm cartridge.
The HK 33 is no longer made but there are several derivations from it, including some with telescopic butts, a sniper model, and a shortened version.

7·92mm Kurz

5·56mm x 45mm

·303" SAA Ball

SHORT MAGAZINE LEE-ENFIELD MARKS III AND V

Length: 44·5" (1130mm)
Weight: 8·2lb (3·71kg)
Barrel: 25" (635mm)
Calibre: ·303"
Rifling: 5 groove l/hand
Operation: Bolt
Feed: 10-round box
Muzzle Velocity:
2440 f/s (738 m/s)
Sights: 2000 yds (1829m)

British experience in the South African war of 1899-1902 showed the need for a short rifle for universal use and even before the end of the war a new weapon had been produced and a thousand made for trials. It was also tested operationally in the fighting against the Mad Mullah in Somaliland, and after

some modification emerged as the Short Magazine Lee-Enfield Mark II in 1907. It was an excellent weapon and although slightly less accurate than its predecessor it had certain compensating advantages, notably its easy breech mechanism which allowed a fast rate of

Great Britain

PATTERN 1913 RIFLE

Length: 46·3" (1176mm)
Weight: 8·7lb (3·94kg)
Barrel: 26" (661mm)
Calibre: ·276"
Rifling: 5 groove l/hand
Operation: Bolt
Feed: 5-round box
Muzzle Velocity:
2785 f/s (843 m/s)
Sights: 1900 yds (1738m)

Although the Lee-Enfield series of rifle had proved remarkably successful there was still some residual prejudice against its bolt in favour of the forward locking Mauser sytem, and this seems to have been the main reason for the development of this new rifle. Work started on it in 1910 and by 1912 it was in

limited production for troop trials which began the next year, hence the designation of the arm. Although of unmistakeable Enfield parentage it differed from the earlier range in that it had a Mauser-type bolt and fired a rimless cartridge from an integral five-round magazine. It also had an

aperture backsight protected by a somewhat bulky extension on the body above the bolt way. It is perhaps not unfair to describe the Pattern 1913 as a near disaster, for although it was very accurate there was little else to say for it. It was slow and clumsy to manipulate, particularly for men

SMLE Mark III

SMLE Mark V

manipulation. The British Army had concentrated on rapid rifle fire to the stage where every soldier could fire at least fifteen well-aimed shots in a minute, and the devastating effects of this were clearly seen in the first few months of World War I when the gallant German infantry suffered heavily. The Mark III was a complex weapon to make, and in 1916 various simplifications were introduced, notably the abolition of the magazine cut-off and the disappearance of the special long-range collective fire sight which was clearly unnecessary in the age of the machine gun. These changed its designation to the Mark III*, perhaps the most famous rifle in British military history. It remained an excellent weapon with an eighteen inch sword bayonet for close quarter work and the ability to project grenades, either rodded or from a screw-on cup. Soon after the end of the war the British began to consider a new rifle, similar to its predecessor but easier to make by modern mass-production methods. The first step in this direction resulted in a new Mark V rifle which appeared in small numbers as early as 1923. Apart from an extra barrel band near the muzzle its main difference was that it had an aperture backsight rather than the open U-type of the earlier rifles, experience having shown that this type of sight was easier to teach, while the increased distance between backsight and foresight reduced the margin of error and made for more accurate shooting. In the end, however, it was decided that the conversion of the large existing stocks of rifles would be too expensive and although the development of a new rifle was maintained the British Army continued to rely on its well-tried Lee-Enfield until well after the outbreak of war in 1939. No separate data is given for the Mark V because apart from the fact that it was only sighted to 1400 yards it differed little from its predecessor.

accustomed to the Lee-Enfield; it was subject to excessive metallic fouling in the bore; it had a tremendous flash and a correspondingly loud report; worst of all, the breech heated so fast that after fifteen rounds or so there was a distinct risk of the round firing as it went into the chamber, which was not conducive to good morale. Although extensive modifications were at once put in hand the project was finally shelved as far as the British Army was concerned by the outbreak of World War I which in view of the major role played by the British rifle in 1914 was probably just as well. Soon after the war started the rifle was converted to fire the standard British service round, but as there were no suitable facilities for making it in the United Kingdom arrangements were made to have it manufactured in the United States by the Winchester, Eddystone, and Remington factories. This new rifle was then designated the Pattern 1914 and in view of its accuracy it was eventually used as a sniping rifle with the addition of a telescope sight. Apart from its different calibre its main external difference from its predecessor was in the absence of the inclined finger slots cut in the stock at the point of balance. The Pattern 1914 was also modified for use by the United States Army, by whom it was designated the Enfield 1917; large numbers of these were bought by Great Britain in 1940, mainly for the use of her Home Guard and the fact that they were of ·30" calibre led to some confusion.

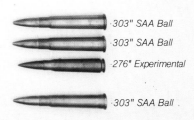

·303" SAA Ball

·303" SAA Ball

·276" Experimental

·303" SAA Ball

Great Britain
ROSS RIFLE MARK III

Length: 50.5" (1283mm)
Weight: 9.87lb (4.48kg)
Barrel: 30.15" (765mm)
Calibre: .303"
Rifling: 4 groove l/hand

Operation: Straight Pull
Feed: 5-round box
Muzzle Velocity:
2600 f/s (794 m/s)
Sights: 1200 yds (1098m)

This rifle was designed by a Canadian, Sir Charles Ross, towards the end of the 19th Century, first issues being made in 1905 to the Royal Canadian Mounted Police. The rifle was unusual in being of the 'straight-pull' type in which the bolt handle was drawn straight

Great Britain
FARQUHAR-HILL RIFLE

Length: 41" (1042mm)
Weight: 14.5lb (6.58kg)
Barrel: 27" (686mm)
Calibre: .303"
Rifling: 5 groove l/hand
Operation: Long recoil

Feed: 20-round drum
Cyclic Rate: 6/700 rpm
Muzzle Velocity:
2400 f/s (732 m/s)
Sights: 1500 yds
(1372m)

Great Britain/USA
PEDERSEN T2E1 RIFLE

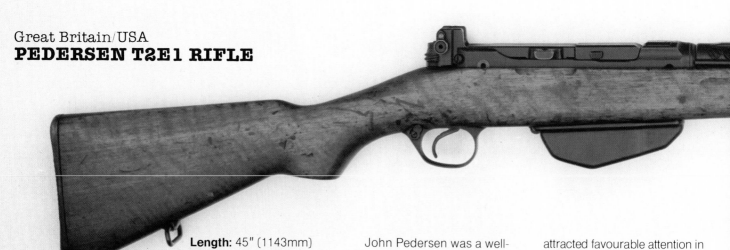

Length: 45" (1143mm)
Weight: 9lb (4.1kg)
Barrel: 24" (610mm)
Calibre: .276"
Rifling: 6 groove r/hand
Operation: Blowback
Feed: 10-round box
Muzzle Velocity:
2500 f/s (762 m/s)
Sights: 1200 yds (1098m)

John Pedersen was a well-known designer of firearms in the United States, one of his best known inventions being a device to convert the standard Springfield rifle into a sub-machine gun in 1918. Between the wars he designed a self-loading rifle, together with a special cartridge for it, which attracted favourable attention in America. This new weapon also came to the notice of Messrs Vickers who manufactured a number under licence in England. The Pedersen was unusual in that its breech was not positively locked at the moment of discharge. Instead it made use

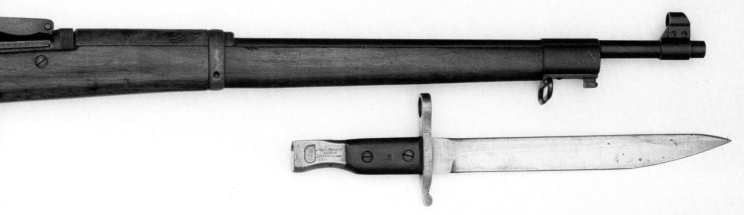

back, the breech being unlocked by the rotation of the locking lugs by means of cams. It had a magazine capacity of five rounds which in the early models had to be loaded singly, and it proved to be an excellent target rifle. There were, however, fundamental defects in its design which rendered it unsuitable as a service rifle and although a whole series of modifications were hastily made there was no significant improvement. The British School of Musketry reported unfavourably on it but in spite of this the Canadian Army went to war with it in 1914, their particular weapon being the Mark III which could be loaded by charger. Its main fault, that the bolt stop bore on one of the locking lugs causing it to burr, led to disastrous consequences, particularly in the mud of the trenches when Canadian soldiers were seen angrily kicking their rifle bolts to open them during German attacks. It was quickly replaced by the Lee-Enfield and little more was heard of it although a few were resurrected for the British Home Guard in the early years of World War II.

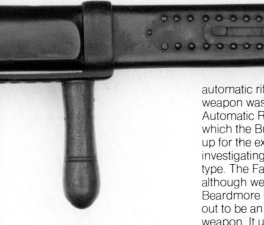

In 1908 a Major M. G. Farquhar produced an automatic rifle which he had invented in conjunction with Mr. Hill. There was at that time some military interest in automatic rifles and the weapon was tested by the Automatic Rifle Committee which the British Army had set up for the express purpose of investigating weapons of this type. The Farquhar-Hill, although well made by the Beardmore Company, turned out to be an extremely complex weapon. It utilized the system of long recoil, but faulty design kept the barrel and breech locked together long after the bullet had left the muzzle; this and other complications led to problems of feed and the gun was rejected. Nothing more was heard of it until 1917 when a second version appeared; this was described, very accurately, as a light machine gun with some potential as an aircraft gun, but was in fact an improved version of the earlier gun; its main difference was in its unusual magazine which was in the shape of a truncated cone, motive power being provided by a clockwork spring. This version was also tested and rejected, being very liable to fouling and prone to a variety of complex stoppages. It was in any case somewhat late, since it appeared at a time when the Lewis gun was giving good service. The inventors were extremely persistent and as late as 1924 they submitted the weapon illustrated. This had a similar but much smaller magazine with a capacity of ten rounds (as compared with up to sixty-five in the earlier versions) but again it was unsatisfactory (still mainly because of its defective magazine) and was not therefore adopted. Thus it passed into history.

of a hesitation-type lock, similar in principle to that of the Luger pistol but so designed that its various bearing surfaces held it closed until the chamber pressure had dropped to a safe level. The rifle was tested by the British Government in 1932 and it was described as being the most promising arm of its type that the Small Arms Committee had then seen. In spite of a magazine capacity of only ten rounds it was reported to have fired 140 rounds in three minutes, a remarkable performance. Unfortunately however the breech, although safe, began to open when the chamber pressure was still quite high. This led to difficulties of extraction and in order to overcome this Pedersen had his cartridges dry waxed. This, reasonably enough, was not acceptable in a military cartridge which would have to be stored world-wide in a variety of conditions and climates, so the Pedersen was not finally accepted after all. This was a pity because it was a neat, handy weapon which shot well and its cartridge was of exceptionally good performance. It is possible that it might have performed well with a fluted breech, which was later designed for this type of contingency, but by that time better self-loading rifles were available. It could fairly be argued that this weapon should be listed under the United States. As however the model illustrated was made in England for test by the British Government for possible use by the British Army it seems reasonable to include it under British weapons.

·303" SAA Ball

·303" SAA Ball

·276" Pedersen

·303" SAA Ball

Great Britain
NUMBER 4 AND NUMBER 5 RIFLES

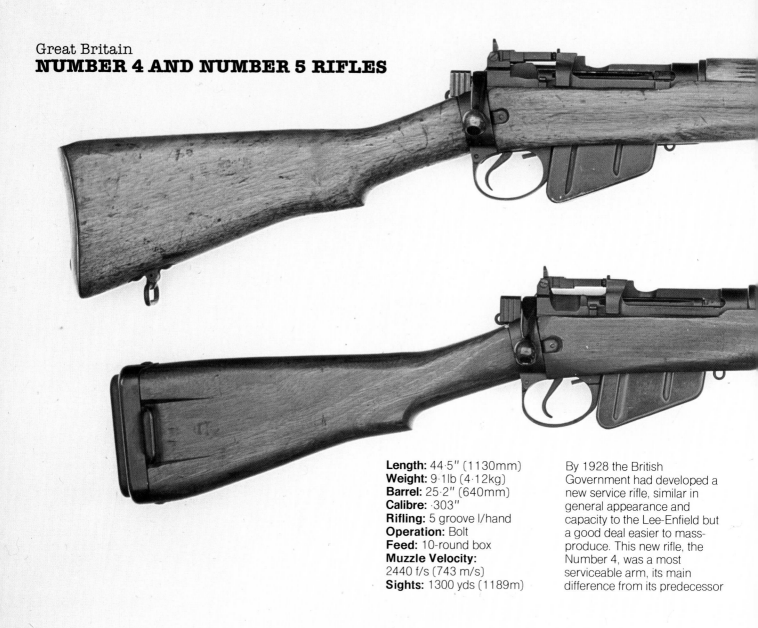

Length: 44·5" (1130mm)
Weight: 9·1lb (4·12kg)
Barrel: 25·2" (640mm)
Calibre: ·303"
Rifling: 5 groove l/hand
Operation: Bolt
Feed: 10-round box
Muzzle Velocity:
2440 f/s (743 m/s)
Sights: 1300 yds (1189m)

By 1928 the British Government had developed a new service rifle, similar in general appearance and capacity to the Lee-Enfield but a good deal easier to mass-produce. This new rifle, the Number 4, was a most serviceable arm, its main difference from its predecessor

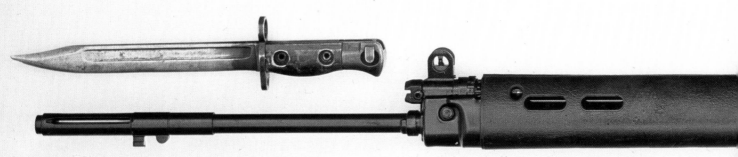

Great Britain
L1A1 RIFLE

Length: 44·5" (1130mm)
Weight: 9·5lb (4·31kg)
Barrel: 31" (533mm)
Calibre: 7·62mm
Rifling: 4 groove r/hand
Operation: Gas
Feed: 20-round box
Muzzle Velocity:
2800 f/s (854 m/s)
Sights: 600 yds (549m)

Once the EM 2 rifle had been rejected, the British Army decided to adopt a new self-loading rifle firing the standard NATO cartridge. After extensive tests it was decided to adopt the Belgian FN rifle, which was already in use by many other contries and this, with a number of modifications, became the L1A1. The British version is a self-loader only and will not fire bursts; nor did the British Army adopt the heavy barrelled version which

some countries use as their squad or section light machine gun.

The early rifle has been modified in some respects, particularly as regards the use of glass fibre instead of wood, but still remains unchanged in principle. It is gas-operated, and capable of thirty or forty well-aimed shots a minute and is generally a sound and reliable weapon. Its principal disadvantage is its length; when it was adopted the British had

commitments world-wide and needed a rifle for all purposes but now that her role is largely confined to North-West Europe, she is likely to change to a shorter assault rifle, which would be a good deal more manageable when operating from armoured fighting vehicles and would also be capable of automatic fire in street fighting or other close-quarter work. The specimen illustrated is fitted with a night sight. There are a variety of

Number 4 Rifle

Number 5 Rifle

being its aperture sight. It was produced from 1941 onwards, mainly in Canada and the United States, although some were made in England. It underwent some modifications, mainly in the substitution of a simple two-range flip back sight for the earlier and more complex one, and some were made with two-groove rifling, but otherwise remained substantially unchanged, the main feature being perhaps the variety of bayonets made to fit it. Selected specimens were fitted with No 32 telescopic sights and detachable cheek-rests and were successfully used as sniper rifles. It remained in service in the British regular army until 1957, and some are still used by cadets. It was popular as a target rifle and the current British sniper rifle is based on it. Experience in the Far East showed the need for a shorter weapon for jungle fighting and by 1944 a new Number 5 rifle had been developed. It was closely based on the Number 4 but was five inches shorter and 1·6lb lighter. Its shorter barrel made a flash hider necessary and reduced its muzzle velocity slightly. It was sighted to 800 yards and fitted with a recoil pad to counteract the extra recoil resulting from its reduced weight.

these, varying from the simple foresight with a self-powered light source to the Trilux sight shown, which can be quickly and easily mounted. It is self-energizing and easily adjusted for intensity and is useful not only for night work but against indistinct targets by day. It has been in service since 1974, its official designation being the Sight Unit Infantry Trilux.

·303" SAA Ball

·303" SAA Ball

7·62mm NATO

·303" SAA Ball

Great Britain
SNIPER RIFLE L4A1

Great Britain
EM 2 RIFLE

Length: 35" (889mm)
Weight: 7·55lb (3·42kg)
Barrel: 24·5" (623mm)
Calibre: ·280"
Rifling: 4 groove r/hand
Operation: Gas
Feed: 20-round box
Muzzle Velocity: 2530 f/s (772 m/s)
Cyclic Rate: 450 rpm
Sights: 600 yds (549m) or optical

Soon after the end of World War II work began at the Royal Small Arms Factory, Enfield, on a new assault rifle to replace the existing bolt action Number 4, one of its principal designers being Mr Stefan Janson. The new arm was of somewhat unconventional design with the working parts and magazine housed behind the trigger in a rearward extension of the body, which also had the buttplate attached to it. As the buttplate was in line with the axis of the barrel it was necessary to elevate the line of sight and this was done by incorporating an optical sight as part of the carrying handle. Although the sight was non-magnifying it did away with the need to focus and align front and rear sights and target. All that was

necessary was to align the pointer on the target image which made it very quick to handle. It did very well on trials, its only minor disadvantage being that owing to the situation of the ejection opening on the right side above the magazine the rifle could not be fired from the left shoulder. In spite of its effectiveness NATO, and in particular the United States who then comprised the backbone of the organization, rejected it, mainly because of understandable American reluctance to change calibre at a time when they had huge stocks of the current cartridge and the almost unlimited capacity to produce more. A few EM 2s were rebarrelled experimentally to take the existing round, but the rifle

really needed a major re-design to do this and as time was pressing Great Britain reluctantly abandoned it in favour of a Belgian type of self-loader.

Great Britain
4·85mm INDIVIDUAL WEAPON

Length: 30·3" (770mm)
Weight: 8·5lb (3·86kg)
Barrel: 20·4" (518mm)
Calibre: 4·84mm
Rifling: 4 groove r/hand
Operation: Gas
Feed: 20-round box
Muzzle Velocity: 2952 f/s (900 m/s)
Sights: Optical

After NATO's rejection of the EM 2 Britain relied for many years on her self-loading rifle. By the early 1970s however it was finally clear than an assault rifle was necessary, partly for reasons of morale but also because the existing rifle was too long and bulky for modern armoured warfare. The weapon

Length: 42·15" (1071mm)
Weight: 9·75lb (4·42kg)
Barrel: 27·5" (699mm)
Calibre: 7·62mm
Rifling: 4 groove r/hand
Operation: Bolt
Feed: 10-round box
Muzzle Velocity:
2750 f/s (838 m/s)
Sights: Telescopic

Sniping first came into large scale use in World War I and World War II soon proved that there was still a need for it. After 1945 the British Army neglected sniping until their long experience in internal security duties round the world made them think differently. Modern self-loading rifles are not well suited to a telescopic sight, so it therefore became necessary to look back rather than forward for a suitable weapon and it so happened

that a commercial conversion of the Number 4 rifle, the Enfield Envoy, was available. It had been developed for target use, principally by being rebarrelled to fire the standard NATO rifle cartridge and by cutting it down to half stock. The Royal Small Arms Factory at Enfield then converted a number of specially selected Number 4s in similar fashion and fitted them with sights which are a modified version of the original No 32 telescopic sight.

about 80% of the components are common to both weapons. A thirty-round magazine is available for this type, although each will take both kinds of magazine. The gun fires from a closed bolt, i.e. the round is pre-positioned in the chamber ready to fire. This can in theory lead to premature discharge, when the chamber is very hot.

so the weapon has now been successfully modified to fire bursts from an open bolt. NATO trials with this and other weapons are still in progress. As the main object of these is to produce a standard cartridge, it would be possible to convert the new rifle to some other calibre if the 4·85mm round is unacceptable.

finally developed bears a strong outward resemblance to the EM 2 but is small and lighter and mechanically more advanced. It works by the normal method of gas and piston with a rotating bolt, and extensive trials have proved it to be highly effective. It has an optical sight and will fire either single rounds

or bursts as required. Its magazine holds twenty of its new rounds which are just under half the weight of the current NATO cartridge, and it can be adopted to fire grenades. There is also a heavy-barrelled version of it which is identical in operation. This has a light tripod and

7·62mm NATO

·280" Experimental

4·85mm Experimental

·303" SAA Ball

Italy
CEI-RIGOTTI AUTOMATIC RIFLE

Length: 39·4" (1000mm)
Weight: 9·55lb (4·3kg)
Barrel: 19" (483mm)
Calibre: 6·5mm
Rifling: 4 groove r/hand
Operation: Gas
Feed: 25-round box
Muzzle Velocity:
2400 f/s (730 m/s)
Cyclic Rate: up to 900 rpm
Sights: 1531 yds (1400m)

Italy
MANNLICHER-CARCANO CARBINE M1891

Length: 36·2" (920mm)
Weight: 6·6lb (3kg)
Barrel: 17·1" (444mm)
Calibre: 6·5mm
Rifling: 4 groove r/hand
Operation: Bolt
Feed: 6-round magazine
Muzzle Velocity:
2300f/s (701 m/s)
Sights: 1640 yds (1500m)

The Model 91 weapons were
the first of a series developed
for the Italian Army towards
the end of the 19th Century.
In spite of the inclusion of the
word Mannlicher in its
official title, it was primarily of
Mauser design, the only
remaining feature of
Mannlicher origin being the

Italy
MANNLICHER-CARCANO CARBINE MODEL 1938

Length: 40·2" (1022mm)
Weight: 7·6lb (3·45kg)
Barrel: 21" (533mm)
Calibre: 6·5mm
Rifling: 4 groove r/hand
Operation: Bolt
Feed: 6-round magazine
Muzzle Velocity: 2300 f/s
(701 m/s)
Sights: Fixed 328 yds (300m)

In the course of their
Abyssinian campaign of
1936-38 the Italians were
somewhat disconcerted to
find that their 6·5mm
cartridge lacked stopping
power. In 1938 therefore
they provisionally introduced
a 7·35mm round and
developed a modified version

Captain Cei-Rigotti, an officer in the Italian Army, appears to have started experiments with gas-operated automatic rifles as early as 1895 when he demonstrated one to his Divisional Commander, the Prince of Naples. Some years were spent in further development thereafter and it was not until 1900 that his efforts were made public in a Roman newspaper, which published a long and laudatory account of his achievements. This included a reference to the use of Mounted Infantry in the war in South Africa, and it was probably this which first drew British attention to the new weapon. Specimens were obtained and a series of tests carried out both by the Small Arms Committee and their Royal Navy counterparts. The rifle worked by a short-stroke piston from the barrel to a rod connected to the bolt, this rod and the cocking handle at its rear end being clearly visible in the photograph, and was designed to fire both single shots and bursts. Although some success was achieved the tests were generally unfavourable, both authorities commenting on the difficulties of ejection and the high rate of misfires, although these may possibly have been due to the fact that the ammunition used had been exposed to seawater on the voyage from Italy. It was also reported that the bolt came so far to the rear in operation that accurate fire was impossible, and some adverse comment was made on the general quality of the workmanship, which was perhaps unfair. It is clear, nearly eighty years later, that the rifle had great potential and many of its features have been copied.

six-round clip with which the weapons were loaded and which remained in the magazine until the last round had been fired. They were developed at Turin by S. Carcano, a designer at the Italian Government Arsenal there, and the name of General Parravicino, President of the Italian Small Arms Committee, is often associated with them. The first of the series was a full-length infantry rifle, but this was closely followed by the weapon illustrated, the Model 91 cavalry carbine which actually went into service in 1893. In those days of course, the cavalry still rode horses and therefore needed a short, handy weapon which could be carried either slung across their backs or in a scabbard or bucket on the saddle. The cavalry of most nations at that time were still inclined to delude themselves as to the superiority of the sword and professed to regard fire-arms as of little importance but the pretence was wearing thin. One feature of the Model 91 carbine is its folding bayonet which indicates that even then the Italian cavalry understood that it might have to act as Mounted Infantry and fight on foot. One interesting feature of these early models, which were otherwise undistinguished, was that their rifling was of the type known as progressive twist, i.e. the degree of twist increased progressively towards the muzzle. This was a system originally experimented with by the English inventor, Metford, but soon abandoned as being not worth the increased difficulties of manufacture. The Model 91s were succeeded by a whole series of others, all of similar principle and differing only in detail. These included a model 1938 carbine almost identical with the one illustrated except that it had a fixed backsight. It is illustrated immediately below this entry.

of their earlier Model 91 to fire it. This new project was however short-lived because when the Italians entered the war in 1940 they were naturally reluctant to embark at the same time on a major change of calibre, so they reverted to their 6·5mm round. There are thus two versions of the Model 1938 carbine, which except for calibre are virtually indistinguishable, the one illustrated being an example of the later reversion to the small calibre. One of its unusual features was the abandonment of the tangent backsight in favour of a fixed one, set at 300 metres. This model 1938 carbine is of considerable interest as being of the type used to assassinate President Kennedy in November, 1963. The particular weapon was an item of Italian war surplus, fitted with a cheap Japanese telescope and purchased by mail order for a few dollars, and it seems to have been an odd choice. The Carcano has no great reputation for accuracy and although its bolt works smoothly enough, the rate of fire must have been slowed down by the telescope. It is notoriously difficult to shoot rapidly through this type of sight, particularly on a carbine with a good deal of recoil, and there has been speculation as to whether the three shots known to have been fired could have come from a single weapon of this type.

6·5mm Modello 1891	
6·5mm Modello 1891	
6·5mm Modello 1895	
·303" SAA Ball	

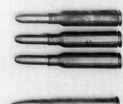

Japan
MEIJI CARBINE 38th YEAR TYPE

Length: 34·2" (868mm)
Weight: 7·3lb (3·3kg)
Barrel: 19·2" (487mm)
Calibre: 6·5mm
Rifling: 4 groove r/hand
Operation: Bolt
Feed: 5-round magazine
Muzzle Velocity:
2400 f/s (732 m/s)
Sights: 2188 yds (2000m)

Japan
RIFLE TYPE 99

Length: 44" (1117mm)
Weight: 8·6lb (3·90kg)
Barrel: 25·75" (655mm)
Calibre: 7·7mm
Rifling: 4 groove r/hand
Operation: Bolt
Feed: 5-round box
Muzzle Velocity:
2350 f/s (715 m/s)
Sights: 2625 yds (2400m)

People's Republic of China
CHINESE TYPE 56

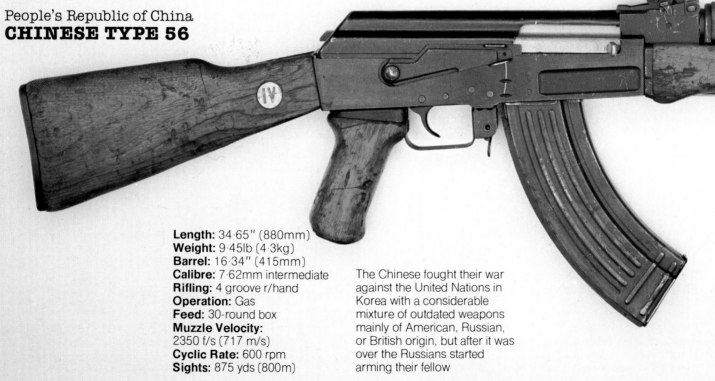

Length: 34·65" (880mm)
Weight: 9·45lb (4·3kg)
Barrel: 16·34" (415mm)
Calibre: 7·62mm intermediate
Rifling: 4 groove r/hand
Operation: Gas
Feed: 30-round box
Muzzle Velocity:
2350 f/s (717 m/s)
Cyclic Rate: 600 rpm
Sights: 875 yds (800m)

The Chinese fought their war
against the United Nations in
Korea with a considerable
mixture of outdated weapons
mainly of American, Russian,
or British origin, but after it was
over the Russians started
arming their fellow

Japan made a remarkable change from a medieval to a modern state in the second half of the 19th Century. Her first rifle was a single shot bolt action model of 11mm calibre which appeared in 1887 but which was replaced almost immediately by a rifle of smaller 8mm calibre with a tube magazine. Her war with China in 1894 showed some defects in her armament and a

commission headed by Colonel Arisaka was appointed to investigate the whole matter and make recommendations for improvement. The result was a series of Mauser type rifles, first adopted in 1897 and often known as Arisaka rifles. Their alternative title was the Meiji 30th year type, having been made in the 30th year of the rule of Emperor Meiji. Rifles of this type were used in the

war against Russia in 1904-5 and a number were purchased by the British in 1914 to train their new Armies. The 38th year type came into use in 1905 and was an improved version of the earlier model. It had a long life, being used in World War II. The 38th year carbine was simply a shortened version of the rifle for use by arms other than infantry, and would take the standard

bayonet. It had a metal dust cover over its bolt, similar to the one on the British Lee-Metford, but it proved very noisy in close-quarter jungle fighting. In many ways it would have been a better service weapon for the infantry than the long rifle, being much handier. Like most carbines however it suffered from fairly heavy recoil. There was a 1944 version with folding bayonet.

Japanese experience in China in the 1930s (like that of the Italians in the same period) showed the need for a more powerful cartridge than the 6·5mm they then used, and after a good deal of experiment they settled in 1939 for a rifle built to fire a rimless version of their 7·7mm round already used in their 1932 model medium machine gun. The original intention of the Japanese had been to use a

carbine, which would have been a good deal handier type of weapon in view of the small size of most of their soldiers. Carbines however, particularly when firing powerful rounds, inevitably have increased recoil, which would adversely affect any lightweight soldiers, however tough and hardy they might be. As a compromise the new rifle, which was designated the Type 99, was made in two lengths, a 'short' rifle in line with

modern European custom, and a 'normal' version some six inches longer, the one illustrated being of the shorter type. This new rifle had a rather odd attachment in the shape of a folding wire monopod which was designed to support the rifle when fired from the prone position, but although of some theoretical advantage it can

have been of little practical value due to its lack of rigidity. The backsight was also fitted with two graduated horizontal extensions to right and left, intended to be used to give a degree of lead when firing at crossing aircraft; nothing is known regarding their effectiveness. The Type 99 was not widely used in World War II.

Communists with a variety of more up to date Russian arms notably the SKS carbine, the AK 47 assault rifle, and the RPD light machine gun, all of which fired the same 7·62mm intermediate cartridge. The demand however was enormous and as soon as they were able to do so the Chinese set up their own factories to manufacture military weapons. As there was considerable urgency over the matter, the Chinese wasted no time in trying to produce new or original designs, but simply stuck as closely to the originals as their own somewhat less

sophisticated manufacturing techniques allowed them. The weapon which they originally concentrated on was a locally developed version of the SKS, but this now seems to have been relegated to a training role in favour of their Type 56 assault rifle. Mechanically this is a very close copy of the original AK 47, the principal difference being a permanently attached folding bayonet of cruciform section. Although this is a very old idea, the Chinese are by now the only country still using it, all others having opted for a detachable knife-type bayonet which the

soldier can use as a general purpose implement, which is what most modern bayonets are now used for. Chinese-made Type 56 rifles were extensively used in Vietnam by the Viet Cong who found them to be ideal weapons for soldiers who were

mostly small and slight by Western standards; the specimen illustrated is one of the many captured there by the American Army. They are also found in considerable numbers in the Yemen and other Middle East countries and as insurgent weapons in African nations.

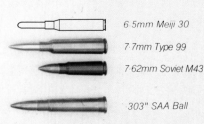

6·5mm Meiji 30

7·7mm Type 99

7·62mm Soviet M43

303" SAA Ball

Soviet Union
MOSIN-NAGANT CARBINE MODEL 1944

Length: 40" (1016mm)
Weight: 8·9lb (4kg)
Barrel: 20·4" (518mm)
Calibre: 7·62mm
Rifling: 4 groove r/hand
Operation: Bolt
Feed: 5-round magazine
Muzzle Velocity:
2700 f/s (823 m/s)
Sights: 1093 yds (1000m)

The first Mosin-Nagant arms were developed by Colonel Sergei Mosin of the Russian Artillery, and a Belgian designer named Nagant. The 1891 model was the first of the modern small-bore bolt-action magazine rifles to be used by Russia and virtually all her later rifles of

Soviet Union
7·62mm SKS CARBINE (SIMONOV)

Length: 40·2" (1022mm)
Weight: 8·5lb (3·86kg)
Barrel: 20·5" (521mm)
Calibre: 7·62mm
Rifling: 4 groove r/hand
Operation: Gas
Feed: 10-round box
Muzzle Velocity:
2410 f/s (735 m/s)
Sights: 1093 yds (1000m)

Soviet Union
AK 47 (Folding Butt) (Avtomat-Kalashnikova)

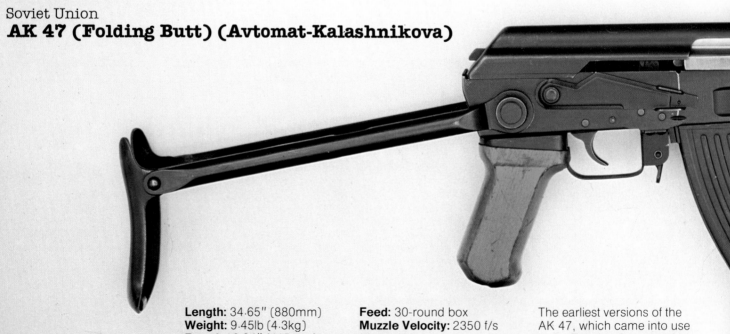

Length: 34·65" (880mm)
Weight: 9·45lb (4·3kg)
Barrel: 16·34" (415mm)
Calibre: 7·62mm
Rifling: 4 groove r/hand
Operation: Gas
Feed: 30-round box
Muzzle Velocity: 2350 f/s
(717 m/s)
Cyclic Rate: 600 rpm
Sights: 875 yds (800m)

The earliest versions of the AK 47, which came into use in the Russian Army in 1951, had wooden butts. These, like many other early Soviet arms, were of poor quality timber

the type are based on it. The basic rifle was of fairly orthodox design and took a somewhat outmoded socket bayonet. There were several variations, chiefly in the length of the barrel. The calibre was originally measured in an old Russian unit known as a line and equivalent to 1/10". As a result they were often known as 'three-line' rifles

until the metric system was introduced after the Revolution. Their sights were also calibrated in arshins, another ancient measurement based on the human pace. Many of these earlier rifles were made in other European countries, and during World War I the United States manufactured one and a half million of them

for Russia. The next major change came in 1930, although even this was little more than a general modernization of the early type. It did however lead to the production of a sniper version with a telescopic sight. The weapon illustrated was introduced towards the end of World War II and was the very last of the Mosin-

Nagant series to be made. It was still very similar to its predecessors, but incorporated a permanently attached bayonet which folded back along the right side of the rifle when not in use. It had an unpleasant chisel point which can be seen just behind the backsight in the illustration of the carbine above.

This was an early type of self-loader, developed and produced by Russia in the course of World War II. It was a gas operated weapon of orthodox appearance, and was designed to fire an 'intermediate' round of the type originally developed by the German Army for their MP 43/44. It had a magazine capacity of ten rounds which could be loaded either

separately or by clips, and was equipped with a folding bayonet of bladed type, which turned back under the barrel when not required. The woodwork was of laminated beech, heavily varnished. The SKS was an efficient weapon, if somewhat heavy, and the cartridge gave adequate power at the sort of ranges envisaged in modern war, which by Russian techniques

were of the order of three or four hundred metres. This was probably a perfectly practical maximum for an Army well equipped with machine guns of one kind or another. The SKS was used and manufactured by many Communist bloc countries, and a number of non-communist states, among them Egypt, were equipped with it. At one period it

became very much a standard guerrilla arm, being widely used in Aden, the Yemen, Oman and elsewhere in the Middle East, but by now it has been largely superseded by the ubiquitous AK 47 in its various forms, and survives mainly as an arm for watchmen, village home guards, and other relatively humble organizations which do not require advanced firearms.

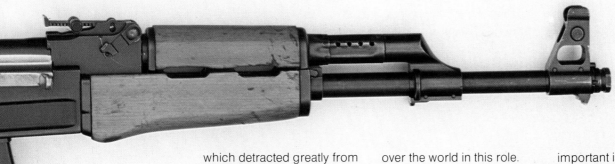

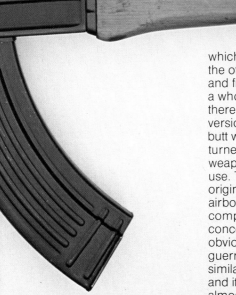

which detracted greatly from the otherwise excellent quality and finish of the new arms as a whole. Soon afterwards there appeared an alternative version with a folding metal butt which could if required be turned forward under the weapon without affecting its use. This type was probably originally intended for use by airborne troops, but its compactness made it easily concealed and therefore an obvious weapon for guerrillas, terrorists, and similar irregular organizations and it now appears to be almost universally used all

over the world in this role. Apart from its compactness the AK 47 has certain other obvious advantages in this respect; it is strongly made and shoots as well as an orthodox rifle to four hundred metres with the additional advantage of automatic fire if needed. Perhaps even more

important is its general simplicity; the sort of organizations using it rarely have the time or facilities for extensive training of recruits so that something which can be taught quickly to an individual with no previous experience of firearms is useful.

7·62mm 1891g

7·62mm Soviet M43

7·62mm Soviet M43

·303" SAA Ball

Soviet Union
AK 47

Length: 34·65" (880mm)
Weight: 9·45lb (4 3kg)
Barrel: 16·34" (415mm)
Calibre: 7·62mm intermediate
Rifling: 4 groove r/hand
Operation: Gas
Feed: 30-round box
Muzzle Velocity:
2350 f/s (717 m/s)
Cyclic Rate: 600 rpm
Sights: 875 yds (800m)

The Russians understood the value of sheer volume of fire, particularly if it could be produced from simple weapons by not very highly trained troops, and in World War II they had armed whole battalions with sub-machine guns. These, however, although effective in their way, suffered from serious limitations in range, but the Russians quickly saw that this disadvantage could be offset by the use of an assault rifle instead. They had seen, and been impressed with, the German MP 44 and as soon as the war was over they set out to produce a similar weapon of their own. In this project they were almost certainly helped by

Finland
M62 ASSAULT RIFLE (THE VALMET)

Length: 36" (914mm)
Weight: 8lb (3·6kg)
Barrel: 16·5" (419mm)
Calibre: 7·62mm
Rifling: 4 groove r/hand
Operation: Gas
Feed: 30-round box
Muzzle Velocity:
2350 f/s (718 m/s)
Cyclic Rate: 650 rpm
Sights: 875 yds (800m)

Finland has such a long common frontier with the USSR that it is inevitable that she has always been closely connected (by no means always amicably) with her very much larger neighbour. The two countries fought a short but bloody war in 1939-40, provoked largely by Russia's demands for bases which the Finns were not at all prepared to concede, and Finland was eventually beaten though she fought well. Later she joined forces with the Germans in an attempt to regain the parts of the country she had lost but this ambition was not of course realized and after the defeat of Germany in 1945 she was compelled to assent to a peace treaty under which she lost some 12% of her territory to Russia. In view of the long association, Finland has always employed Soviet type weapons, locally made in her own factories and often better made and finished than the originals. This reliance on her neighbour stood her in good stead in 1939 when she was able to

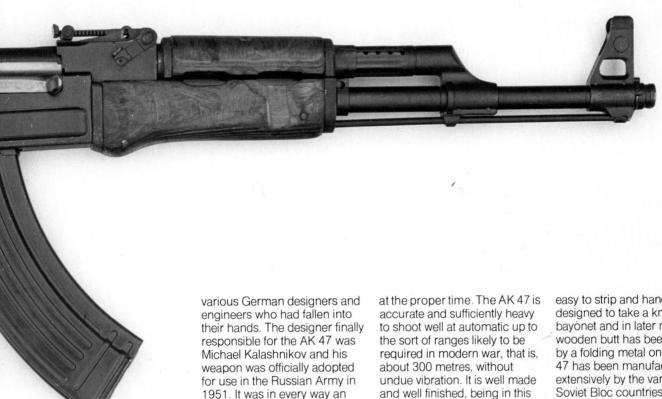

various German designers and engineers who had fallen into their hands. The designer finally responsible for the AK 47 was Michael Kalashnikov and his weapon was officially adopted for use in the Russian Army in 1951. It was in every way an exceptionally fine assault rifle. It worked by gas, tapped off from the barrel and impinging on a piston working in a cylinder above the barrel. This piston took with it the rotating bolt, the whole being thrust forward again by the coiled return spring at the proper time. The AK 47 is accurate and sufficiently heavy to shoot well at automatic up to the sort of ranges likely to be required in modern war, that is, about 300 metres, without undue vibration. It is well made and well finished, being in this respect considerably in advance of most earlier Soviet weapons. It fires an intermediate cartridge which contrary to mistakenly held beliefs is not inter-changeable with the NATO round. The bore is chromed and the weapon is easy to strip and handle. It is designed to take a knife-type bayonet and in later models the wooden butt has been replaced by a folding metal one. The AK 47 has been manufactured extensively by the various Soviet Bloc countries and must have good claim to be considered as just about the most common military firearm in the world today. It is being replaced by an improved version, the AKM, but is still an almost universal arm for subversive and terrorist groups.

make use of large quantities of captured arms and ammunition. The first Soviet type assault rifle made by the Finns was developed in the late 1950s and appeared as the Model 1960. Mechanically it was virtually identical to the Russian AK 47 but there were many external differences. The M60, which was made at Valmet, hence its name, had no woodwork on it, everything being made of metal and much of it plastic covered. It had a plastic forehand grip ventilated with a series of holes and a rather ugly tubular butt with a shoulder piece welded onto the end of it. This early model was also unusual, perhaps unique, in that it had no trigger guard in the accepted sense of the term, but only a vertical bar in front of the trigger. The object of this of course was to allow the weapon to be fired by a soldier wearing heavy gloves which are essential in the fierce Finnish winter, but it must have increased the risk of accidental discharge, particularly while operating in forest or scrub. The Model 62, the one illustrated, is essentially similar but of more modern manufacture, making increased use of pressings and riveting. It has the same curved magazine and a tangent backsight mounted on the receiver cover. The three-pronged flash hider incorporates below it a bayonet bar by which the knife-like bayonet can be fixed. It fires the Russian-type intermediate cartridge. Although out of sequence it is included here for comparision with the AK 47.

7·62mm Soviet M43

7·62mm M60

·303" SAA Ball

United States of America
KRAG-JORGENSEN CARBINE MODEL 1896

Length: 41·5" (1054mm)
Weight: 7·75lb (3·51kg)
Barrel: 22" (559mm)
Calibre: 30/40"
Rifling: 4 groove r/hand
Operation: Bolt
Feed: 5-round magazine
Muzzle Velocity:
2000 f/s (610 m/s)
Sights: 2000 yds (1829m)

United States of America
RIFLE MODEL 1895 (US NAVY)

Length: 47" (1194mm)
Weight: 8lb (3·63kg)
Barrel: 27·25" (692mm)
Calibre: ·236"
Rifling: 5 groove l/hand
Operation: Straight-pull
Feed: 5-round magazine
Muzzle Velocity:
2400 f/s (732 m/s)
Sights: 2000 yds (1828m)

United States of America
US RIFLE MODEL 1903 (SPRINGFIELD)

Length: 43·2" (1097mm)
Weight: 8·7lb (3·94kg)
Barrel: 24" (610mm)
Calibre: ·30"
Rifling: 4 groove l/hand
Operation: Bolt
Feed: 5-round box
Muzzle Velocity:
2800 f/s (813 m/s)
Sights: 2700 yds (2469m)

Soon after the introduction of
the Krag-Jorgensen rifle into
the United States Army in
1894 the authorities began to
examine the idea of yet
another rifle, this time on the
Mauser principle, and five
thousand infantry models with
thirty-inch barrels were
ordered in 1901. Before they
were made however the
United States Army decided
that the time had come for a
short universal rifle, and had
the barrels reduced to twenty-

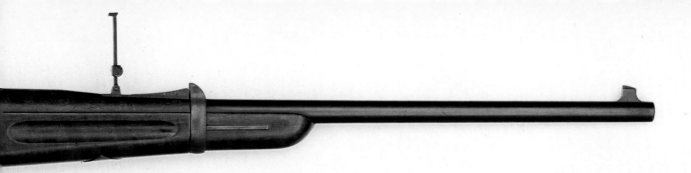

This was the first bolt-action magazine rifle to be used by the United States Army. It was officially adopted in 1892 to replace the old single-shot Springfield but did not come into general issue until 1894. It was closely based on a weapon invented by Captain Ole Krag of the Danish Army and an engineer named Eric Jorgensen, and the United States paid these inventors

one dollar for every one made in America. It was of normal bolt action, its most unusual feature being a five-round box magazine on the right hand side which had to be loaded, one cartridge at a time, through a loading gate which incorporated the magazine spring. The raised thumbpiece by which it was opened is clearly visible in the photograph. There were a

number of variations, none of them very important. It was used by the regular Army in Cuba in 1898 although the Militia still had the single-shot Springfield. Soon after the introduction of the Krag-Jorgensen, the United States decided to adopt a new rifle based on the Mauser system and the Krag then disappeared from the military scene. It was an excellent rifle

and many converted examples are still in use as sporting rifles in the United States. The specimen illustrated is of interest because it is one of the last carbines used by the United States before the adoption of a standard rifle for general issue regardless of arm or service, which occurred with the introduction of the 1903 Springfield.

This rifle is probably better known as the Lee straight-pull which indicates both its inventor and its mechanism. James Lee, a Scot by birth but educated in Canada, eventually became a citizen of the United States where all his experimental work was done. He is probably best known for his box magazine for bolt action rifles; it was widely adopted and his name appears on a long series of

British service rifles. Towards the end of the 19th Century he invented a rifle which in 1895 was adopted by the United States Navy who placed an order for ten thousand of them. The rifle was unusual in that it incorporated a 'straight-pull' breech in which direct backward pressure on the lever caused the breech to rise slightly, opening as it did so. No manual turning was

required, locking worked by an arrangement of cams on the bolt. It was of unusually small calibre and had a magazine capacity of five rounds; it was also the first United States service rifle ever to be loaded by means of a charger. Unfortunately straight pull rifles have no real advantage over the more orthodox turn bolt types, but they do have several disadvantages, chief of which

are their complex structure and the fact that their operation, perhaps surprisingly, is more tiring than that of normal types. The United States Navy disliked it very much and it soon disappeared from the service. A sporting version was also made but this also proved unpopular and the model was soon withdrawn, some 18,300 of the 20,000 produced never seeing daylight.

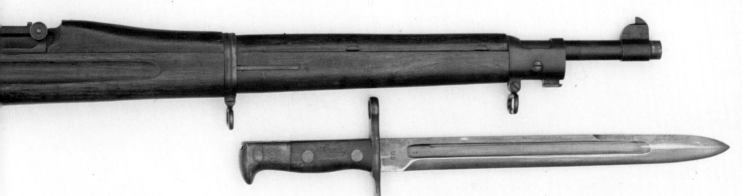

four inches. In this they were probably influenced by their experience in Cuba and also by the lessons of the Anglo-Boer War which caused the British Army to reach a similar conclusion. The new rifle, commonly known as the Springfield after its place of manufacture, had a Mauser type bolt and a five-round magazine with a cut-off, and after some basic modifications, notably the introduction of a lighter,

pointed bullet, in place of the earlier round-nosed variety, it was brought into general issue by 1906. It proved to be a very popular rifle, its chief disadvantage, a minor one, being its small magazine capacity, and remained in use for many years. In this time it underwent various modifications, notably one to allow it to be converted to an automatic weapon by the addition of the Pedersen device of 1918 and another

which added a pistol grip to the stock in 1929. There was also a target variety, equipped with a Weaver telescopic sight, which was used

successfully as a sniping rifle in World War II, together with a variety of other sporting variations, many of which are still in use.

·30" Model 1898
·236" Model 1895
·30" '06 Springfield
·303" SAA Ball

United States of America
RIFLE ·30 CAL M1 (GARAND)

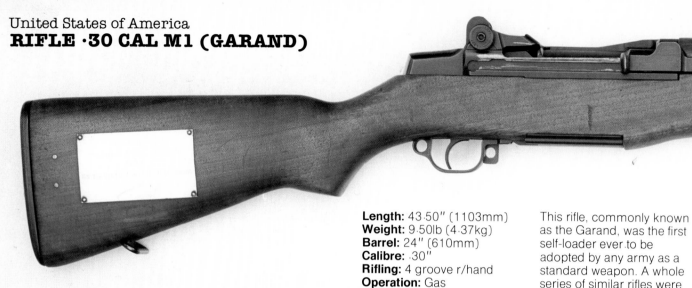

Length: 43·50" (1103mm)
Weight: 9·50lb (4·37kg)
Barrel: 24" (610mm)
Calibre: ·30"
Rifling: 4 groove r/hand
Operation: Gas
Feed: 8-round internal box
Muzzle Velocity:
2800 f/s (853 m/s)
Sight: 1200 yds (1097m)

This rifle, commonly known as the Garand, was the first self-loader ever to be adopted by any army as a standard weapon. A whole series of similar rifles were exhaustively tested before it was finally selected in 1936. It was a good weapon, very robust (and therefore heavy)

United States of America
7·62mm M14 RIFLE

Length: 44" (1117mm)
Weight: 8·55lb (3·88kg)
Barrel: 22" (558mm)
Calibre: 7·62mm
Rifling: 4 grooves r/hand
Operation: Gas
Feed: 20-round box
Muzzle Velocity: 2800 f/s (853 m/s)
Cyclic Rate: 750 rpm
Sights: 1000yds (915m)

United States of America
US CARBINE ·30 CALIBRE M1

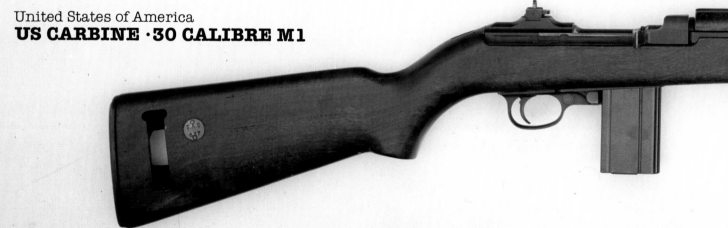

Length: 35·65" (905mm)
Weight: 5·45lb (2·48kg)
Barrel: 18" (458mm)
Calibre: ·30"
Rifling: 4 groove r/hand
Operation: Gas
Feed: 15/30-round box
Muzzle Velocity:
1950 f/s (585 m/s)
Sights: Fixed, 300 yds (275m)

The term carbine, like many military words, has meant different things at different periods. By the end of the 19th Century it was generally used to denote a short version of the standard infantry weapon for use by mounted troops, but in the next few years the universal

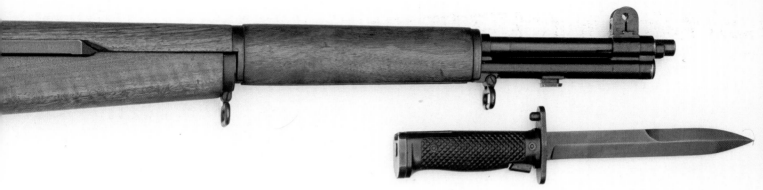

but simple and reliable. It was operated by gas and piston. The magazine had a capacity of eight rounds and had to be loaded by a special charger holding that number of cartridges in two staggered rows of four each. When the last round had been fired the empty clip was automatically ejected and the bolt remained open as an indication to the firer that reloading was necessary. The Garand was the standard rifle of the United States Army in World War II, and was the only self-loader generally used. They were made mainly by the Springfield Armoury and the Winchester Repeating Arms Company, although smaller numbers were also produced by other American arms companies and after the war a quantity were made by the Italian firm of Beretta. When manufacture finally ceased in the middle 1950s an astonishing total of some five and a half million had been produced. There were inevitably a number of variations to the Garand in its long history, including a National Match model and no less than three sniper rifles, but none of them differed from the prototype.

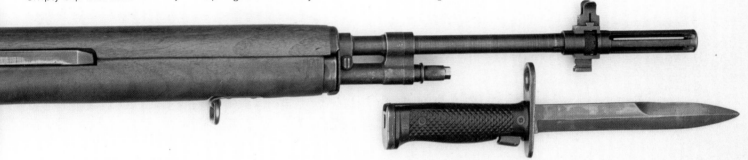

Before the end of World War II the American Military authorities were working on the concept of a selective fire weapon of assault rifle type. By 1953, NATO having settled on a common cartridge, good progress had been made, and although most European countries opted for Belgian type weapons the United States settled for the M14. This was a logical development of the Garand. Based on war experience a number of important improvements had been made, notably the abolition of the awkward eight-round clip and the substitution of a pre-filled detachable box magazine holding twenty rounds. The new rifle was capable of firing single shots or bursts, and although most were issued permanently set for semi-automatic fire only, a number were fitted with light bipods with a view to being used as squad or section light automatics. They were however only marginally suitable for this role because sustained fire caused them to overheat and there was no provision for changing barrels. A heavy barrelled version was at one time contemplated but never produced, and there was also an excellent sniper version. The M14 saw quite extensive use in the Vietnam war. Some 1,500,000 were made in all, but it is no longer manufactured and although United States NATO forces still use it, it is no longer the standard American rifle. As soon as the NATO countries finally settle on a new cartridge it will become obsolete.

rifle became common in most armies and the term tended to lapse. Just before World War II the United States Army decided that it needed a new light weapon, intermediate between the pistol and the rifle, as a convenient arm for officers and non-commissioned officers at rifle company level and as a secondary weapon for mortarmen, drivers and similar categories for whom the service rifle would have been awkward. The request, originally made when peacetime financial measures were in force, was at first refused but once war seemed inevitable it was granted and by the end of 1941 the Army had settled for the M1 carbine and it had gone into large scale production. The M1 was a short, light, self-loading rifle, and although its calibre was the same as that of the service rifle it fired a straight pistol-type cartridge, so that there was no question of inter-changeability between the two. The M1 carbine was an odd, indeed an almost unique, weapon to have been produced so late, since in a very real sense it looked back towards the arms of the stocked Luger or Mauser pistol-type, rather than forward to the sub-machine gun, which at the time of the introduction of the new carbine had amply demonstrated that it had an important part to play in modern warfare. At that period the United States sub-machine gun was however still the Thompson, heavy and expensive to produce, and these considerations probably justified the introduction of a new category of arm.

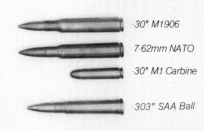

·30" M1906

7·62mm NATO

·30" M1 Carbine

·303" SAA Ball

United States of America
US CARBINE ·30 CALIBRE M1A1

Length: 36·65" (931mm)
Weight: 5·45lb (2·48kg)
Barrel: 18" (458mm)
Calibre: ·30"

Rifling: 4 groove r/hand
Operation: Gas
Feed: 15/30-round box
Muzzle Velocity:
1950 f/s (595 m/s)
Sights:
Fixed, 300 yds (275m)

United States of America
ARMALITE AR15 (M16)

Length: 39" (991mm)
Weight: 6·35lb (2·88kg)
Barrel: 20" (508mm)
Calibre: ·233" (5·56mm)
Rifling: 4 groove r/hand
Operation: Gas
Feed: 30-round magazine
Cyclic Rate: 800 rpm
Muzzle Velocity:
3250 f/s (991 m/s)
Sights: 500 yds (458m)

The prototype for this weapon was the AR-10 which first went into production in 1955. It was a very advanced arm employing plastic and aluminium wherever possible but it proved too light to fire the powerful NATO 7·62mm cartridge for which it was designed and manufacture ceased in 1962. It was soon followed by the small calibre high velocity AR-15, designed by Eugene Stoner and made under licence by the Colt company from July, 1959 onwards. This new weapon soon became popular. It was a good jungle rifle and being light and easy to handle by small men it soon found favour in various countries in the Far East. It was quickly adopted by the United States after their intervention in Vietnam and, as the M16, is now their standard rifle (except in NATO). It has no piston, the gases simply passing through a tube and striking directly onto the bolt, which is efficient but means that the weapon needs careful and regular cleaning. It was used by the British Army in small numbers in Borneo.

United States of America
COLT COMMANDO

Length: 28" (711mm)
Butt extended: 31" (787mm)
Weight: 6·55lb (2,97kg)
Barrel: 10" (254mm)
Calibre: ·223" (5·56mm)
Rifling: 4 groove r/hand
Operation: Gas
Feed: 20/30-round magazine
Cyclic Rate: 750 rpm
Muzzle Velocity:
3000 f/s (915 m/s)
Sights: 500 yds (458m)

The Colt Commando is essentially a handier version of the AR-15 and was developed for use in Vietnam. Mechanically it is identical with the AR-15, but with a ten-inch barrel instead of the twenty-inch one of the rifle. This reduced the muzzle velocity slightly and had a rather serious effect on accuracy at longer ranges; it also caused a very considerable muzzle flash which made it necessary to incorporate a four-inch flash hider which can be unscrewed if necessary. The Colt Commando has a telescopic butt which can be pulled out when it is required to fire from the shoulder, and in spite of the limitations of accuracy imposed by the shorter barrel it proved useful in Vietnam where it was used by the United States Special Forces. It is also believed to be in limited use by the British Special Air Service. The reduced accuracy of the weapon puts it into the sub-machine gun class, but in view of its similarity to the AR-15, plus the fact that it fires the same cartridge, it has been left in the rifle section.

The general details regarding the history and introduction of the ·30 calibre have already been described in the caption for the original weapon of the series. There were however a number of variations, notably the M1A1, which although the same basic weapon as the M1 was equipped with a folding stock, the central bracing plate of which carried an oil bottle. This skeleton stock was pivoted on a pistol grip so that the carbine could be fired if necessary with the stock folded, which made it a convenient weapon for parachute and airborne forces. The true gun enthusiast may feel that this spoils the general lines of the weapon as compared with its prototype and this is to some extent true. The modification however was made at a time when practical considerations were important. The M1 carbine in its various forms was the commonest weapon produced by the United States, the total production reaching the astonishing figure of just over seven million. They were light, handy weapons which in spite of some lack of stopping power fulfilled an obvious need. At one stage a selective fire version was produced which in effect converted the carbine into a sub-machine gun and there was also a version designed to take various types of night sight, no conventional sights being fitted. The two versions were known respectively as the M2 and M3.

·30" M1 [ ]ine

5·56mm x 45mm

5·56mm x 45mm

·303" SAA Ball

The Revolver and Pistol

A pistol is a light firearm designed to be fired by one hand without support. The origin of the word is uncertain, although it may derive from Pistoia, the Tuscan town where it is said to have been invented. The principal role of the pistol has always been for close-range self-defence so that it had to be carried either on the man, or on his saddle-bow if mounted, ready for instant use. In view of this it was obviously not a practical proposition in the days of the matchlock, so that the first weapons of this type had wheel-locks and probably dated from about 1530. Having said this it may also be necessary to remark that matchlock pistols *are* occasionally found, but they are almost invariably of Indian or Far Eastern origin and of relatively late manufacture.

Although wheel-lock pistols were imported into Britain it is probable that few, if any, were ever made there; with the possible exception of the clock, a wheel-lock was then the most complex mechanism known, and there were probably few craftsmen in Britain at that time capable of undertaking such difficult work. This being so it is likely that the first pistols produced here were flintlocks, dating from about 1630. A number of these were made with rifled screw-off barrels which allowed them to be loaded from the breech end, and one of the earliest recorded feats of pistol shooting was performed with a pair of weapons of this type by Prince Rupert, the famous Royalist cavalry leader in the British Civil War of 1642-5. Presumably as the result of a wager, he fired at the weathercock on a church steeple in Stafford, hitting it through the tail, and when his uncle and Commander-in-Chief, King Charles I, jokingly suggested that it was a fluke, he promptly repeated the feat with the second pistol of his pair. Years later the same dead-shot Prince was attacked by three assassins in Paris. They all fired at him from behind but all missed, whereupon their intended victim spun on his heel, drawing a pair of pistols as he did so, and knocked two of them over with a fast right and left. Considering the nature of the pieces, this was the sort of shooting which would still have earned a good deal of respect in the American West of the late 19th Century.

The Restoration of 1660 led to closer ties between Britain and France; a good many skilled continental gunmakers, some of them refugees from various religious wars, settled in England, and their example was so well followed by the native gunmakers that by 1700 or soon afterwards they were

themselves turning out very fine firearms. Pistols in particular, being largely regarded as gentlemen's weapons, were often of excellent quality, and examples are still greatly sought after. Until almost the end of the 18th Century men of quality carried swords as a matter of course, and a good many affairs of honour were settled with them. After about 1800, however, the custom disappeared, and the pistol then became, par excellence, the arm for duelling. Any man about to stake his life on his pistol shooting obviously wanted the best and this gave great impetus to pistol manufacture.

TECHNICAL ADVANCES

Soon after 1820 the percussion cap was in fairly general use, at least in civilian weapons, and the relatively clumsy flintlock then virtually disappeared. This made it possible to lighten and streamline the pistol, which led to multi-barrelled weapons of the so-called pepperbox type in which a cluster of up to six barrels revolved around a central spindle.

The next type to appear was the true revolver, with a single fixed barrel and a mechanically revolved cylinder carrying the charges. Primitive flintlock weapons of this type had in fact been produced in small numbers in Europe in the mid-17th Century and a more refined version, the Collier, had appeared in 1819. The great disadvantage of these had always been the problem of priming, and it was not until the introduction of the percussion system that the difficulty was satisfactorily overcome, the first and probably the most famous individual in the field being Colonel Samuel Colt.

Colt was born in Hartford, Connecticut, in 1814, and like a number of other American inventors of the 19th Century had little formal education. It so happened, however, that he combined mechanical and inventive genius with an almost equal flair for publicity and salesmanship, and by 1836 he had taken out both American and British patents for a revolver. He had mixed success with his new weapon until about 1848, after which he and his arms became famous and his name a household word. He was copied by many people on both sides of the Atlantic, his greatest British rival being Adams, whose fine arms eventually went far towards securing the British market.

1 *The* Freikorps *man on the left has a Mauser M1896 pistol.*
2 *The 0·45in Colt Model 1911A1 semi-automatic pistol was adopted for US service in 1926.*

Berliner Konzerthaus

Bunter Abend

Italy
BERETTA MODELLO 84

The well-known Italian firm of Beretta has been making good quality self-loading pistols since 1915 and the particular model illustrated may be taken as a reasonably typical example of a simple blow-back mechanism without any positive locking device, but relying entirely on the weight of the slide and the power of the spring. As a normal 9mm cartridge would probably be somewhat too powerful for this basic mechanism a special short cartridge is used. This works well but is rather under-powered for normal military use. This pistol has an external hammer; others have internal ones, but the principle on which they work is very much the same.

(Full specification of the Beretta Modello 1934 on page *203*.)

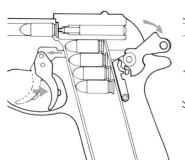 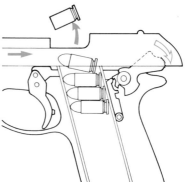 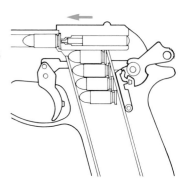

1 *The first round is loaded manually by pulling back the slide to its fullest extent and then allowing the spring to carry it forward. This cocks the hammer and feeds the top round into the chamber.*

2 *Pressure on the trigger releases the hammer which springs forward to strike the rear end of the firing pin, thus driving it onto the cap of the cartridge in the chamber and firing it.*

3 *The gases drive the bullet forward and also force the empty case back, the pressure being sufficient to operate the slide as already described. This action also ejects the empty case.*

4 *The forward action is then repeated. The next round in the magazine, having been forced upwards by the magazine spring, is fed into the chamber and the pistol is ready for the next shot.*

Great Britain
WEBLEY AND SCOTT MARK VI

The British Army retained the revolver as its service arm for many years, and from 1892 until 1927 practically all weapons of this type were provided by the famous Birmingham firm of Webley and Scott. In the period they manufactured many thousands of revolvers in a variety of models, but almost certainly the most common and best known was the Mark VI. It was first introduced in 1915 and remained in service until well into the 1930s, and apart from the British Army it was also extensively used by various Commonwealth forces and occasionally by the police.

(Full specification on page *207*.)

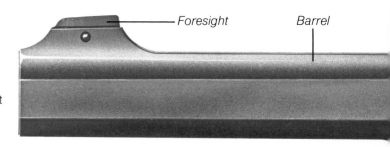

— Foresight   Barrel

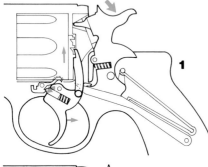 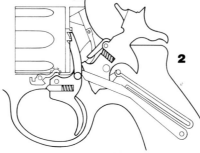

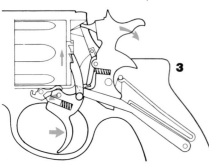 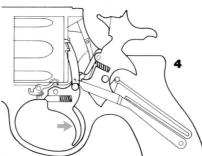

1 *Pressure on the trigger depresses the cylinder stop and allows the cylinder to rotate and bring the next chamber in line.*
3 *Steady pressure on the trigger causes the hammer to fall so that its nose strikes the cap of the cartridge. At this stage the cylinder is prevented from rotating by the stop.*

2 *The hammer may also be first drawn back manually to the cocked position, which decreases the amount of pressure required and so helps accurate shooting.*
4 *The sequence is now repeated either at double or single action until the rounds are all fired. The empty cases are then ejected.*

Cartridge:
Beretta Modello 84
Left, ·303" SAA Ball
Right, 9mm Short

Cartridge:
Webley and Scott Mark VI
Left, ·303" SAA Ball
Right, ·455" SAA Ball

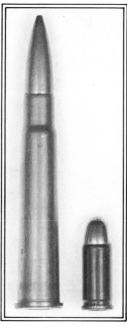 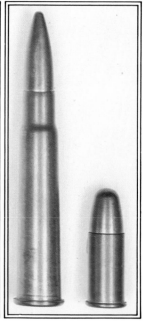

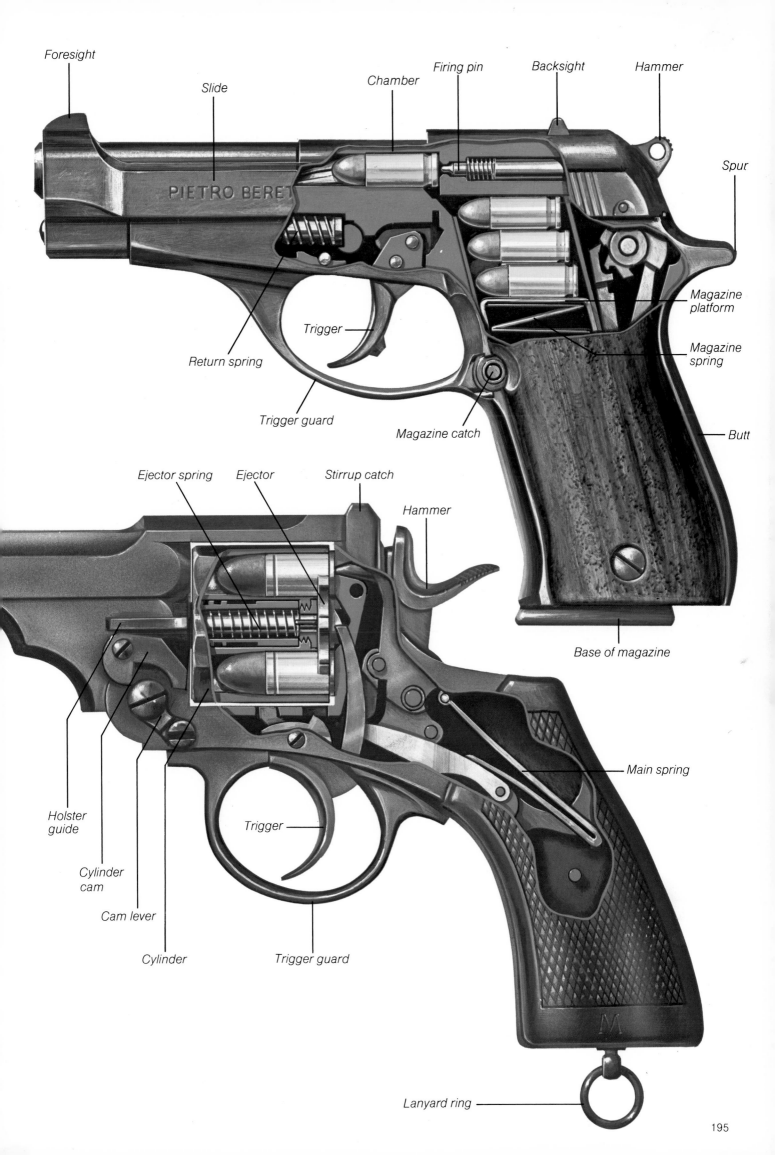

Foresight

Slide

Chamber

Firing pin

Backsight

Hammer

Spur

PIETRO BERET

Return spring

Trigger

Trigger guard

Magazine catch

Magazine platform

Magazine spring

Butt

Ejector spring

Ejector

Stirrup catch

Hammer

Base of magazine

Main spring

Holster guide

Cylinder cam

Cam lever

Cylinder

Trigger

Trigger guard

Lanyard ring

195

1 The young German escort is armed with a 9mm Walther P38 semi-automatic pistol.
2 A British sergeant with a 0·45 in Colt Browning Model 1911 semi-automatic pistol, which differs only in details for the later Model 1911A1.
3 The Enfield 0·38in Pistol No 2 Mark 1 was adopted for British service in 1932.
4 The British paratrooper on the left is holding a 0·45in Colt Browning M1911A1 pistol.
5 The Soviet 7·62mm Tokarev TT.

All these early revolvers had to have powder and a ball loaded into the front end of each chamber and a separate cap placed on each nipple. Although their performance, once loaded, was comparable to modern revolvers, they were a great deal slower to recharge and the thoughts therefore of many gunmakers soon began to turn to systems of breechloading, using self-contained cartridges. Some makers, particularly in France, Belgium and Germany, produced pin-fire revolvers but these only had a limited success. The next great advance came in 1856 when the expiration of Colt's various patents opened the field to a variety of other manufacturers. The first in this field being Smith and Wesson who were quick to patent their own bored-through cylinder to take a cartridge of modern type. This innovation, although revolutionary in its way, did not necessitate any really fundamental changes in design; all that was required was some form of loading gate so that the rounds could be loaded into the chambers, and some means of pushing out the empty cases after they had been fired.

By this time two distinct types of lock mechanism had emerged. The Americans in general preferred single-action weapons in which the hammer had to be pulled back for each shot, while the British preferred double-action arms which could either be fired in similar manner, or simply by steady pressure on the trigger. This difference in taste was probably caused by difference in use. The average American Westerner was not a gunfighter. He carried a revolver for self-defence and for use against vermin, and perhaps even small game; thus he wanted an arm for accurate shooting, often at quite long range, and this the single-action gave him, because manual cocking made the trigger action very much lighter. British users on the other hand were often officers, and for them long-range accuracy was less important because their soldiers already had rifles; what the officer needed was a pistol with which he could, if necessary, shoot his way out of a swarm of yelling savages and so in his case the paramount need was for speed. Although the single-action revolver still holds its place in the affections of many Americans, the double-action has for many years been almost universally used.

The next advance came with improved methods of loading and ejection. At first the most common device was to hinge the barrel and cylinder to the front of the frame and hold it in place by a catch in front of the hammer. When this catch was released, and the barrel pressed downwards, a star-shaped ejector automatically threw the empty cases out. The pioneers of this system were Smith and Wesson in the United States and Webley in the United Kingdom, and both firms had produced reliable systems by the 1870s. Soon, however, there came another divergence of opinion, because the British stuck to their break-down system whereas the Americans, who had always regarded it as fundamentally weak, abandoned it. Instead they mounted the cylinder on a separate hinged frame which could be swung sideways from the main revolver, the empty cases then being ejected together by simple manual pressure on a rod. Soon after 1900 this method had become very general in the United States and the break-down model had largely disappeared there, except in small, low-powered pocket arms.

The modern revolver had for all practical purposes reached the peak of its development by the beginning of the 20th Century, and although it is still a very widely used arm, no fundamental improvements in design have been made since then. This perfection of the revolver coincided very closely with the introduction of a new type of pistol, the self-loader, which is now almost universally (if

5

incorrectly) referred to as an 'automatic'.

THE SELF-LOADER

Hiram Maxim had by 1884, already made use of the recoil of one cartridge to load and fire the next one in his highly successful machine gun, so it is not surprising that the same principle was soon to be applied to pistols. The first to appear was the invention of an Austrian, Schonberg, but it achieved little success and few were made. Next in the field was Hugo Borchardt, a German by birth although he had spent most of his life in the United States. In 1891 he returned to his native country where his first self-loading pistol was put into production in 1893, but although an ingenious weapon it was not a success. It was large and clumsy, and although it shot well enough with a butt on it, it did not meet the current need for pocket arms. Another German of genius, George Luger, then simplified and improved the design, after which the Luger pistol, in a variety of shapes and calibres, became one of the best known weapons in the world.

Other European self-loaders quickly followed, chief among them being the Austrian Mannlicher, the German Bergmann, its cheaper Belgian copy the Simplex, and the Mauser, yet another German pistol which was to become almost a household word. In 1897 the American, John Browning, one of the all-time great names in the world of firearms, also began to design successful self-loaders. A few years later the British firm of Webley and Scott followed suit, first with their unsuccessful Mars but later with a series of reliable, if not particularly distinguished, arms of the same type. It is clear, however, that the self-loader, initially at any rate, had more appeal to the mainland nations of Europe than to Great Britain and the United States, and by 1914 almost every other country in the world had adopted one type or the other as its service pistol.

It may be as well here to explain simply the two principal methods by which self-loading pistols work. The simplest of them is to allow the rearward energy of the cartridge case to force back a reasonably heavy breechblock against a spring, which at the proper time thrusts it forward again, loading the next round on its way. This method is not, however, suitable for weapons firing powerful cartridges, because if the case comes back too soon, when the pressure is still high, it may burst without the support of the chamber. In this case the barrel and breechblock are locked together at the moment of firing and recoil together for a short distance. When the pressure has dropped to a safe level the barrel and breechblock unlock, and the breechblock continues backwards against a spring as in the first method. In most modern weapons the whole upper part of the pistol, variously known as the jacket or slide, moves backwards and forwards in this manner. The first shot has of course to be loaded manually.

It is probably fair to say that the pistol, unlike the other weapons dealt with in this book, has never been a really significant military weapon. By the second half of the 16th Century infantry firepower was beginning to become such an important factor on the battlefield that the cavalry had lost some of its importance. The first effort to counter this was for the mounted arm to equip itself with pistols and ride forward rank by rank to discharge them at the infantry, in the hopes of making a gap. This method never achieved much success because the fire of relatively weak pistols from restive horses could rarely equal that of infantry muskets. It was this hard fact which compelled the cavalry to discard their pistols and their armour.

By the mid-19th Century it had finally become clear that even the best cavalry could rarely achieve much success against steady infantry, for whereas neither horse nor sword had changed much over the years there had been vast and continuing improvements in firearms. Unless therefore the cavalry had some unusual advantage of ground, or bad visibility, it had to rely more and more on its firearms and less and less on the *arme blanche*. The Americans, always realists, soon saw this in their Civil War of 1861-65, and although the cavalry on both sides continued to give good service on raids, reconnaissance, and against each other, their role in any major battle became that of mounted infantry, where the rifle was predominant. Even in mounted actions, most preferred a brace of good percussion revolvers, which gave them a dozen certain shots before they had to consider re-loading, rather than rely on the sabre.

It was perhaps the American Civil War, and the period of reconstruction which followed it, which gave the revolver the secure niche it now occupies in United States' history and legend. Once the fighting was over the thoughts of numerous people, many of them restless ex-soldiers, began to turn to the idea of expansion into the vast, empty territories to the South and West, and a great migration started almost immediately. The open grassland offered excellent facilities for raising cattle with which to feed the huge industrial centres back East, the problem of transport being solved by the rapid advance of a number of railroads.

The thousands of men working on the railways needed supplies of all kinds, together with recreation, which drew after them a host of storekeepers, gamblers and saloon owners. They also needed meat which was provided by professional hunters who ruthlessly slaughtered the buffalo by the thousand; this in its turn led to trouble with the Indians whose whole economy was based on the buffalo, and thus the United States Army was drawn in also.

This vigorous, predominantly male society was inevitably a violent and brawling one. There was little law, except a degree of rough justice imposed by public opinion, and even trivial disputes arising from drink, gambling, or women, often ended in shooting. When larger organizations clashed, as for example rival ranchers quarrelling over boundaries or water, the disputes often assumed the proportions of small private wars. In this atmosphere every man carried a revolver or a pair of revolvers as a matter of course, and indeed as a matter of hard necessity. It was the era of the revolver, the 1873 Colt 'Peacemaker', the Smith and Wesson, the Remington and the British Adams, an era which had barely passed by the

turn of the century and whose spirit is not dead yet.

The cavalry of the various armies of Europe was reluctant to accept the lessons of the American Civil War, which they chose to regard as something of an aberration, and continued to consider the sword and lance as their principal weapons, carbines being carried but disdained. In the infantry the revolver became a usual part of an officer's equipment for it was soon found, particularly in colonial-type campaigns, that a sword was no answer to the more robust weapons wielded by charging Zulus, Dervishes, and the like. Their answer was a pistol, and the heavier the calibre the better. The revolver, some up to ·577″ calibre, was the most usual arm, but powerful double and even four-barrelled pistols were frequently used.

The division between revolver and self-loader was seen very clearly in World War I, for of all the original combatants the British were practically the only ones to rely on their well-tried revolvers. The Americans, when they came in, were more divided, for though many carried the reliable 1911 Colt, many more stuck to the revolver which had by then become a traditional weapon in their country. This being so, it may be as well to summarize briefly the advantages and disadvantages of the two types.

REVOLVER OR SELF-LOADER

The self-loader generally speaking, holds eight or more rounds, is slightly more accurate, and easier to conceal if necessary. It is however more complex, more susceptible to stoppage through dirt, and perhaps slower to get into action because in many models it is not very safe to carry a round in the chamber. The revolver usually holds six rounds, may be a little more difficult to fire accurately and is harder to conceal. It is, however, less susceptible to dirt and may be carried safely fully loaded and ready to draw without any need to manipulate any safety catch or other item except the trigger. The advocates of both types will continue to argue the merits of their chosen weapon, so that all that need be said here is that while almost every army now uses a self-loader, many police forces retain, and indeed on occasion revert to, the well-tried revolver.

Before leaving the subject we must mention compromise weapons, best known of which is the Webley-Fosbery, the so-called automatic revolver which was introduced in 1901. In this weapon the barrel and cylinder were mounted on a separate frame which recoiled along ribs on the top of the butt. Once the weapon was cocked and fired the recoil drove the barrel group back, turning the cylinder and cocking hammer as it did so, in readiness for the

2

next shot. Although ingenious, this type of revolver was not widely adopted, due partly to its susceptibility to dirt and partly to the fact that unless it was fired with a reasonably rigid arm the recoil was not always enough to work the mechanism. They nevertheless achieved some popularity.

Finally one should mention one or two single-shot pistols which have seen military service. Perhaps the best known is the cheap, but basically adequate, Liberator, which the United States dropped to partisans in Japanese-occupied territories in the Far East, and the silenced British Welrod, used in World War II by Special Forces for silent killing when necessary. There is also the home-made zip-gun, a basic weapon with the advantage (or perhaps disadvantage) that it can be relatively easily made by amateurs.

The whole future of the pistol as a military arm (except for persons working on undercover tasks) must be open

1

1 Men of the US 82nd Airborne Division on the range with Colt Browning Model 1911A1 pistols.
2 The 0·22in Smith & Wesson Model 41, a heavy barrel version of which is seen here, is used in military competition firing.
3 Revolver-armed US groundcrew pass 7·62mm ammunition belts up into an AC-47 Dragonship armed with three Minigun rotary weapons.
4 A US military policeman test fires a 0·38in Smith & Wesson civilian revolver into a bullet recovery tube filled with cotton.

3

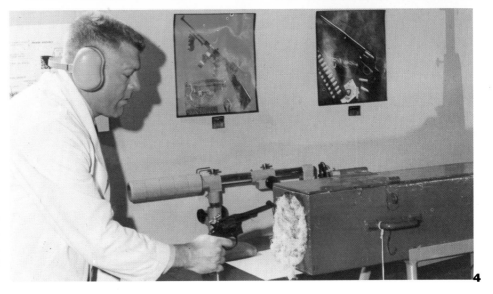

4

to doubt, since more and more reliance is bound to be placed on either the sub-machine gun or the assault rifle as a personal weapon by officers, at least in combat arms. Its role as a police weapon is, however, likely to continue and even, in the United Kingdom, increase as it becomes more and more necessary to go over to a fully armed constabulary. Unless the strictness of police and Home Office controls in Britain makes it impossible, it is also likely that the sport of pistol shooting will continue to flourish. It gives a good deal of harmless enjoyment to a considerable number of people and it would be a pity to see it go. One new and apparently flourishing aspect of the sport is the rise in recent years of long-range pistol shooting. Some of the free-style arms used bear a good deal more resemblance to rifles than pistols, but some good shooting is produced by standard models at ranges which would have seemed incredible a few years ago.

Austria-Hungary
ROTH-STEYR M07

Length: 9" (229mm)
Weight: 36oz (1·02kg)
Barrel: 5" (127mm)
Calibre: 8mm
Rifling: 4 groove r/hand
Capacity; Ten
Muzzle Velocity: 1090 f/s
(332 m/s)
Sights: Fixed

The Roth-Steyr was first patented in 1899 and after long trials was adopted as the standard pistol of the Austro-Hungarian cavalry in 1907 This was the first occasion on which any major power abandoned the revolver in favour of the self-loader. It was somewhat unusual in that it fired from a locked breech. When the round was fired the barrel, which was located in a tubular receiver, recoiled 0·5 inch (12·7mm), during which time it turned through 90° and unlocked itself from the breechblock which then continued its rearward movement. The magazine, which was in the butt, was loaded from the top by means of a ten-round clip. This pistol was later issued to the Flying Corps.

Austria-Hungary
MANNLICHER MODELL 1903

Length: 11" (279mm)
Weight: 35oz (·99kg)
Barrel: 4·5" (114mm)
Calibre: 7·65mm
Rifling: 5 groove r/hand
Capacity: Six
Muzzle Velocity:
1090 f/s (332 m/s)
Sights: Fixed

The 1903 model Mannlicher was very similar in general appearance and performance to the German Mauser which had achieved a good deal of popularity by the end of the 19th Century. Although modelled on it, it was in no sense a copy having a number of mechanical differences. It had a box magazine, which although detachable was usually loaded by a charger containing six rounds, and fired a special Mannlicher cartridge slightly less powerful than the Mauser, since this could strain the lock. It was a well made and particularly well-balanced arm, but it never remotely achieved the popularity of the Mauser. No army ever adopted it although some were carried privately in World War I by officers of the German and Austrian Armies.

8mm Roth M07

7·65mm Mannlicher

·303" SAA Ball

Austria-Hungary
MANNLICHER MODELL 1901

Length: 10" (254mm)
Weight: 33oz (·94kg)
Barrel: 6·5" (165mm)
Calibre: 7·63mm
Rifling: 4 groove r/hand
Capacity: Eight
Muzzle Velocity: 1025 f/s (312 m/s)
Sights: Fixed

Although Frederich von Mannlicher is probably best known for his service rifles, he also produced a number of automatic and semi-automatic weapons of various kinds. His first pistol appeared in 1900, followed by the one illustrated, a modified version of it, a year later. It was of simple mechanism, working on the blow-back system but with a decelerating system to keep the rearward movement of the breechblock within safe limits. Loading was by means of a clip into a magazine in the butt. This model was sold widely as a commercial arm but never officially adopted.

Belgium
GALAND TYPE REVOLVER

Length: 13" (330mm)
Weight: 46oz (1·3kg)
Barrel: 4·8" (122mm)
Calibre: 11mm
Rifling: 10 groove r/hand
Capacity: Six
Muzzle Velocity: 700 f/s (213 m/s)
Sights: Fixed

This is a heavy, service-type weapon, dating from about 1870. At that time the Belgians were well known for their large-scale manufacture of cheap pistols of all kinds, and this one, like many others, bears no maker's name. It is interesting in that it has an extractor device of the type patented by Galand. When the lever, part of which forms the trigger guard, is pulled down, the barrel and cylinder are thrust forward, leaving the empty cases in a separate ring extractor. It also has a folding skeleton stock, which is too short and too flimsy to be of much use.

7·63mm Mannlicher

11mm Galand

·303" SAA Ball

France
REVOLVER MODÈLE 1892 (LEBEL)

Length: 10" (254mm)
Weight: 28oz (·79kg)
Barrel: 4·5" (115mm)
Calibre: 8mm
Rifling: 4 groove r/hand
Capacity: Six
Muzzle Velocity: 700 f/s (213 m/s)
Sights: Fixed

This was introduced in 1892 and remained in service until World War II. It is sometimes known as the Lebel after the Colonel of that name who was deeply involved with military arms at that time. It was a solid frame pistol with a cylinder which swung out to the right on a separate frame.

When closed the cylinder was held in place by a hinged lever·on the right hand side of the frame. This can be seen in the illustration, where it has been drawn back to allow the cylinder to move. The revolver was reliable but its cartridge was somewhat under-powered.

France
MAB MODÈLE D

Length: 7" (178mm)
Weight: 27oz (·76kg)
Barrel: 4·25" (108mm)
Calibre: 7·65mm
Rifling: 4 groove r/hand
Capacity: 8 round
Muzzle Velocity: 700 f/s (213 m/s)
Sights: Fixed

The initials stand for Manufacture d'Armes de Bayonne, a French factory which has been making self-loading pistols since 1921. The basic weapons were of blowback type, very similar in principle and appearance to the pistols made by Browning and Colt, and were chiefly made commercially. They were reliable and well-made arms and had a ready sale as pocket pistols in the United States and elsewhere. When

the Germans overran and occupied France in 1940, the manufacture of these pistols continued on a limited scale and examples may be found with German markings. The Modèle D illustrated is a somewhat modernised version. It too was made for the Germans, but after liberation the French Army was also equipped with it. There was also a larger calibre version which was made in 9mm.

8mm Mle 92

7·65mm ACP

·303" SAA Ball

Hungary
FROMMER STOP PISZTOLY 19M

Length: 7·5" (190mm)
Weight: 21oz (·59kg)
Barrel: 4·25" (119mm)
Calibre: 7·65mm

Rifling: 5 groove r/hand
Muzzle Velocity: 1200 f/s (366m/s)
Sights: Fixed

In the Austro-Hungarian Empire, which was broken up after 1918, the various elements of the Army tended to be armed in different ways; as far as the Hungarian element was concerned its standard pistol was the Frommer, made at the Royal Hungarian Arsenal Fegyvergyar and often known by that name. It was of somewhat unusual type, since it worked on the principle of long recoil in which barrel and breechblock remained locked for the whole of the rearward phase. This involved the use of two return springs, one to draw the barrel forward and a second to make the breechblock follow it, chambering a fresh cartridge on its way. It fired a special round and would not accept any other.

Italy
BERETTA MODELLO 1934

Length: 6" (152mm)
Weight: 23oz (·65kg)
Barrel: 3·75" (96mm)
Calibre: 9mm
Rifling: 4 groove r/hand
Capacity: Seven
Muzzle Velocity: 825 f/s (251 m/s)
Sights: Fixed

The name Beretta is a well-known one in the field of automatic and self-loading weapons, and the earliest version of this pistol was produced in 1915. It then went through a number of modifications until 1934 when it appeared in the form illustrated. As was to be expected, it was a well-designed and well-made arm of excellent quality. It worked by simple blowback, which was only made possible in a gun of its calibre by the use of a short cartridge. This made it somewhat underpowered for military use. A number of Allied officers acquired them in the course of World War II and were then disappointed to find that they would not accept the standard Parabellum round. The magazine was easily recognizable by its spur extension which increased the gripping surface of the butt. Models were also produced in 7·65mm calibre, firing an automatic pistol cartridge, but these are relatively rare.

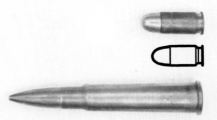

7·65mm automatic pistol

9mm Short

·303" SAA Ball

Bergmann No 5
(Data below for this model)

Bergmann No 3

Germany
BERGMANN Nos 3 and 5

Length: 9·5" (241mm)
Weight: 40oz (1·13kg)
Barrel: 4" (102mm)
Calibre: 7·63mm
Rifling: 4 groove r/hand
Capacity: Five
Muzzle Velocity:
1250 f/s (381 m/s)
Sights: 766 yds (700m)

Theodore Bergmann began making self-loading pistols in 1894. His first models were pocket pistols firing low charge cartridges and working by blowback. They were simple, well-made weapons, all basically similar in design, and they soon became popular on the Continent. They fired a tapered cartridge, some of the earliest of which had no extractor groove, being simply blown clear of the pistol by the backward thrust of the discharge gases. They were loaded in somewhat unusual fashion. The magazine in the lower pistol, which is the Model Number 3, was immediately in front of the trigger, and access to it was by a hinged cover on the right-hand side. The cartridges, which were in clips of five, were placed in the magazine and the lid closed, the clip being removed or left in as required. It was also theoretically possible to place the rounds in the magazine singly, but in practice this was not very satisfactory and was not recommended. In 1897 Bergmann produced the first of his military pistols, the Number 5, which is the upper one of the two illustrated. This was of course designed to fire a good deal more powerful cartridge than his earlier pocket arms and he therefore abandoned his simple blowback mechanism in favour of a closed breech system to cope with this new round. The barrel and bolt recoiled locked together for a short distance when the bolt was disengaged by the front end of it being displaced laterally. The barrel then stopped, allowing the bolt to continue its backward action, until the return spring started the forward cycle. The chief improvement, however, was the abandonment of the unsatisfactory magazine system for a detachable box. The Bergmann No 5 was well made and finished, with a rather slim revolver-type butt with wooden sideplates, and it is believed that a detachable stock was available since the pistol is sighted to 700 metres (766 yds). No country ever adopted it as a military arm and it is in consequence very rare. The data are for the 1897 model.

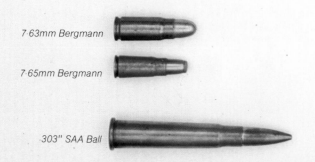

7·63mm Bergmann

7·65mm Bergmann

·303" SAA Ball

Germany
LUGER PARABELLUM P08

Length: 8·75" (222mm)
Weight: 30oz (·85kg)
Barrel: 4" (102mm)
Calibre: 9mm
Rifling: 6 grooves r/hand
Capacity: Eight
Muzzle Velocity: 1150 f/s (351 m/s)
Sights: Fixed

This was really an improved version of the Borchardt, and was developed by Georg Luger in 1900. After a rather slow start it suddenly became popular, the first army to adopt it being that of Switzerland. A large calibred version was tested by the United States in 1907 but was rejected in favour of the Colt.

Then in 1908 the German Army adopted it, and after this its future was assured and it was produced in very considerable numbers until 1942 when manufacture was finally stopped. It was a reliable and well-made weapon which for some reason established a much greater reputation than it warranted, since there were better arms of its type available at the time it was adopted. The 9mm Parabellum cartridge had been specially developed which gave it a very high muzzle velocity, but it had a fixed backsight and few claims were made regarding its accuracy beyond normal pistol ranges.

Germany
WALTHER P38

Length: 8·4" 9215mm)
Weight: 34oz (·96kg)
Barrel: 5·0" (127mm)
Calibre: 9mm
Rifling: 6 groove r/hand
Capacity: Eight
Muzzle Velocity: 1150 f/s (351 m/s)
Sights: Fixed

Carl Walther began making self-loading pocket pistols in 1906 and continued with considerable success until the early 1930s when he set out to design a military model, which by 1938 had been developed to the stage where the German Army adopted it as its standard pistol under the designation of P38. In spite of this, very large numbers of Luger pistols were still in service in 1945. The P38 was an excellent weapon, its chief advantage being that it incorporated a reliable double-action device which meant that it could safely be carried with a round in the chamber. The original Walther factory and machinery were dismantled and removed after capture by the Russians in 1945. It has been adopted for service by the Bundeswehr under the designation P1 and is also produced commercially.

9mm Parabellum

9mm Parabellum

·303" SAA Ball

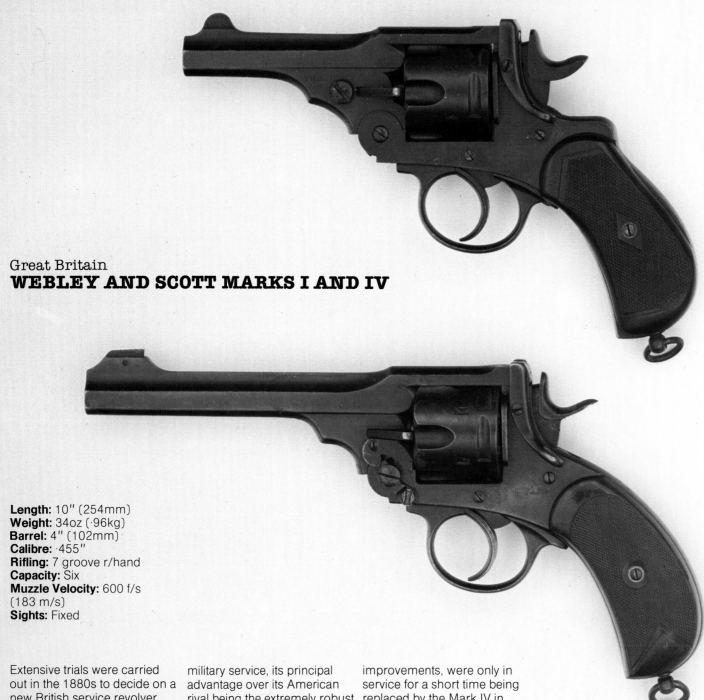

Great Britain
WEBLEY AND SCOTT MARKS I AND IV

Length: 10″ (254mm)
Weight: 34oz (·96kg)
Barrel: 4″ (102mm)
Calibre: ·455″
Rifling: 7 groove r/hand
Capacity: Six
Muzzle Velocity: 600 f/s
(183 m/s)
Sights: Fixed

Extensive trials were carried out in the 1880s to decide on a new British service revolver and after they were completed there were two weapons left in the field, an American Smith and Wesson and a British Webley, both of excellent quality. After a final test the British weapon was chosen, a decision which really marked the beginning of a virtual Webley monopoly of British military pistols. The weapon, which was officially adopted in 1887 was given the description of Mark I. It was a strong and reliable arm, well suited to

military service, its principal advantage over its American rival being the extremely robust stirrup catch holding it closed. This was so designed that unless it was fully locked it impeded the fall of the hammer and thus made accidents from this cause impossible. It was of double action mechanism with a short hexagonal barrel and a so-called bird-beak butt with a lanyard ring. The round it fired was a relatively short one and relied more on the shock effect of the heavy bullet than on high velocity. Marks II and III, which incorporated various

improvements, were only in service for a short time being replaced by the Mark IV in 1899. This date coincided with the outbreak of the South African War in which the Mark IV was so extensively used that it was often referred to as the Boer War model. It was carried by all officers, by non-commissioned officers and trumpeters of cavalry regiments, and by certain categories of artillery driver. Like its predecessors it was a good revolver, its principal point of interest being that it was made in four barrel lengths, 3, 4, 5 and 6 inches

(76, 102, 127 and 152mm). These were comparable in performance but the longer barrels naturally tended to give greater accuracy than the shorter ones, due to the greater length of the sight base. The data refers to the Mark I.

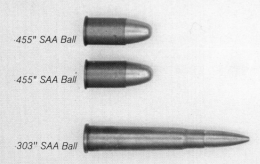

·455″ SAA Ball

·455″ SAA Ball

·303″ SAA Ball

Webley Mark VI

Webley Mark VI ·22"

Great Britain
WEBLEY AND SCOTT MARK VI

Length: 11·25" (286mm)
Weight: 38oz (1·08kg)
Barrel: 6" (152mm)
Calibre: ·455"
Rifling: 7 groove r/hand
Capacity: Six
Muzzle Velocity:
650 f/s (198 m/s)
Sights: Fixed

The Boer War version of the Webley and Scott was replaced in 1913 by a Mark V; this was very similar to its successor and had a short life, being replaced in its turn in 1915. The new weapon was the Mark VI, probably the best known of all British service revolvers. It was not greatly different from its predecessors with the exception of its butt, which was of the more usual squared-off variety instead of the bird-beak pattern. The Mark VI was made in huge numbers, and many are still coming to light as survivors of World War I disappear from the scene. In the course of the war a short bayonet was devized for close quarter fighting in trench raids and similar operations. It was never an official issue but a good many officers bought them privately. A detachable butt was also available, an interesting parallel with the stocked Mauser and Luger pistols commonly used by the Germans in the same period. The Mark VI was the last of the ·455" calibre British service revolvers and remained in service until well into the 1930s. In order to economise on ammunition and allow practice on miniature ranges, Webley and Scott produced a small calibre version of their Mark VI. It was designed to resemble the original as closely as possible, the main points of difference being the ·22" round barrel and the rebated cylinder. There was another version with a shorter cylinder and a corresponding rearward extension of the barrel. Although useful for preliminary practice, weapons of this type are not of great instructional value because of the absence of recoil which throws the muzzle violently upwards and which is the main problem to master when firing full-sized ammunition. The data are for the full-bore revolver. The Webley is still widely used by police throughout the world.

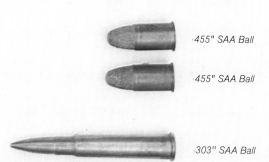

·455" SAA Ball

·455" SAA Ball

·303" SAA Ball

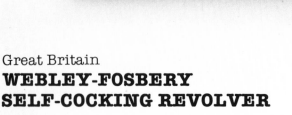

Great Britain
WEBLEY-FOSBERY
SELF-COCKING REVOLVER

Length: 11" (280mm)
Weight: 44oz (1·25kg)
Barrel: 6" (152mm)
Calibre: ·455"
Rifling: 7 groove r/hand
Capacity: Six
Muzzle Velocity:
650 f/s (199 m/s)
Sights: Fixed

In 1901 Colonel G. V. Fosbery VC invented the revolver which was named after him. Apart from being a distinguished fighting soldier he was also a weapons expert who, having watched the development of the self-loading pistol, had had the idea of making similar use of recoil to operate a revolver. His revolver, which was made by Webley, was loaded and handled like the standard pattern, with the important difference that the recoil from the first shot caused the barrel and cylinder group to recoil along guide ribs, turning the cylinder by means of a spring stud working in the zig-zag grooves cut on its surface as it did so, and also cocking the hammer in readiness for the next shot. This elimination of recoil, perhaps the main stumbling block to good revolver shooting, made a marked increase in pure target accuracy but in spite of this the Webley-Fosbery never really became popular. This was largely due to dirt and grit which are rarely absent from any battelfield and partly because the firer's arm had to be held absolutely rigidly at the moment of firing to ensure that the recoil did its job. Nevertheless some people liked it and a few veterans of World War I were still carrying them when World War II started. Apart from the standard model designed to fire the ·455" service round, a very small number were made with eight chambers to fire the smaller ·38" round. All Webley-Fosberys are rare, but particularly those in ·38" calibre, which are scarcely ever seen outside large collections.

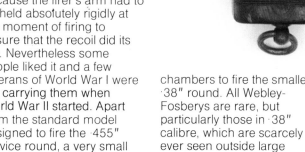

Great Britain
ENFIELD No 2 MARK I

Length: 10·25" (260mm)
Weight: 27oz (·766kg)
Barrel: 5" (127mm)
Calibre: ·38"
Rifling: 7 groove r/hand
Capacity: Six
Muzzle Velocity:
650 f/s (198 m/s)
Sights: Fixed

After the end of World War I the British Army decided that its existing revolver, the Webley and Scott Mark VI, was of too large a calibre. It had been designed principally to stop charging tribesmen and there were doubts that its soft lead bullets were acceptable in civilized warfare, if such a thing exists. The Royal Small Arms Factory at Enfield therefore set out to design a new revolver in ·38" calibre, which was generally agreed to be the minimum size with sufficient stopping power. The result was the Number 2, similar to, but of course smaller than, its predecessor. Before the outbreak of World War II it was decided to convert it to double-action only, that is it could not be cocked but had to be fired by trigger pressure only, which was considered acceptable for combat use where fast shooting was the rule. This resulted in the abolition of the comb of the hammer, which tank crews had complained about on the basis that it got caught in things in the confined space of a tank.

·455" SAA Ball

·38" SAA Ball

·303" SAA Ball

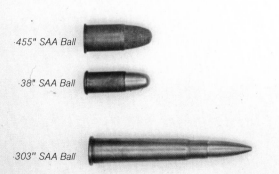

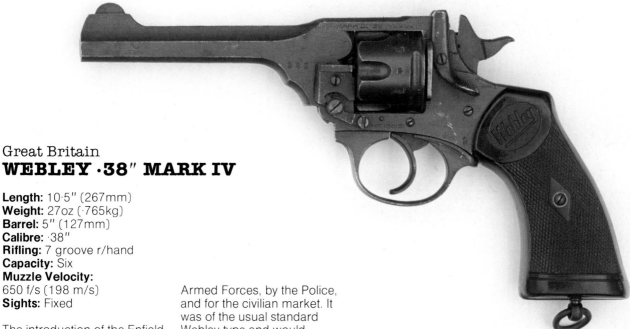

Great Britain
WEBLEY ·38″ MARK IV

Length: 10·5″ (267mm)
Weight: 27oz (·765kg)
Barrel: 5″ (127mm)
Calibre: ·38″
Rifling: 7 groove r/hand
Capacity: Six
Muzzle Velocity:
650 f/s (198 m/s)
Sights: Fixed

The introduction of the Enfield revolver in 1927 saw the end of the very long association of Webley and Scott with the British Army, for whom the firm had been sole suppliers of revolvers since 1887. There was however still a very large demand for revolvers and in 1923 Webleys produced their Mark IV revolver for use by other Armed Forces, by the Police, and for the civilian market. It was of the usual standard Webley type and would handle the standard Webley cartridge with 200 grain bullet, the ·38″ Smith and Wesson, and the ·38″ Colt Police Positive cartridge. In the course of World War II the supply of Government revolvers was not sufficient to meet demands and in 1945 the Ministry of Supply placed a considerable order for Webley and Scott Mark IV revolvers. This was promptly met, and although the components were not interchangeable the new pistols were so similar to the Enfield that no handling difficulties arose. Although a well-made and thoroughly reliable weapon it was of strictly wartime finish and inevitably lacked the usual quality appearance of Webley's normal products.

Great Britain
WELROD PISTOL

Length: 12″ (305mm)
Weight: 32oz (·91kg)
Barrel: 5″ (127mm)
Calibre: ·32″
Rifling: 4 groove r/hand
Capacity: Single shot
Muzzle Velocity:
700 f/s (213 m/s)
Sights: Fixed

The need for silent weapons in war is limited, because there is so much unavoidable noise that the effect of silencing small arms would be minimal. Individuals involved in special operations did, however, sometimes need a silenced pistol and it was for their use that the Welrod was produced. Although there is a magazine in the butt the pistol is not a self-loader, and has to be operated manually for each shot. The silencer consists of a series of self-sealing oiled leather washers, which close up after the passage of the bullet, thus trapping the sound. They wear out in a very short time.

·38″ SAA Ball

·32″ ACP

·303″ SAA Ball

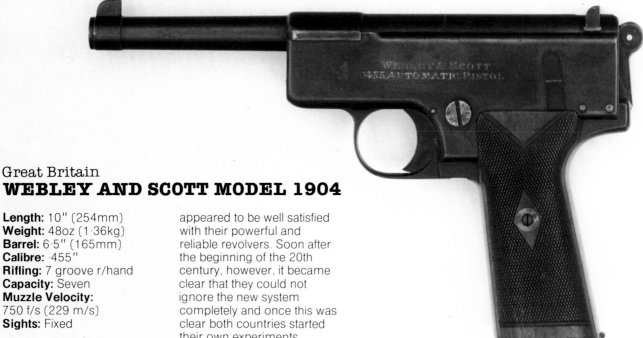

Great Britain
WEBLEY-MARS

Length: 12·25" (311mm)
Weight: 48oz (1·36kg)
Barrel: 9·5" (241mm)
Calibre: ·38"
Rifling: 7 groove r/hand
Capacity: Seven
Muzzle Velocity:
1750 f/s (533 m/s)
Sights: Fixed

In 1906 a British inventor named Gabbett-Fairfax produced a self-loading pistol on which he had worked for ten years. It was a huge, clumsy weapon which fired extremely powerful bottle-necked cartridges in either ·45" or ·38", the weapon illustrated being of ·38" calibre. The pistol, although necessarily very robust and beautifully made, was very complex mechanically, particularly since in view of the strength of the round it fired from a locked breech. At the moment of firing the bolt was locked to the barrel by four lugs which engaged in recesses behind the chamber, and when the shot was fired barrel and bolt recoiled together. The bolt then turned and unlocked itself, allowing the barrel to go forward. The bolt then followed, picked up a round from a tilting carrier and loaded and fired it.

Great Britain
WEBLEY AND SCOTT MODEL 1904

Length: 10" (254mm)
Weight: 48oz (1·36kg)
Barrel: 6·5" (165mm)
Calibre: ·455"
Rifling: 7 groove r/hand
Capacity: Seven
Muzzle Velocity:
750 f/s (229 m/s)
Sights: Fixed

The self-loading pistol was invented and largely developed in Western Europe and initially neither British nor American gunmakers showed very much interest in it since their customers appeared to be well satisfied with their powerful and reliable revolvers. Soon after the beginning of the 20th century, however, it became clear that they could not ignore the new system completely and once this was clear both countries started their own experiments. Webley and Scott produced their first successful model, the one illustrated, in 1904. It was a very large, square, well-made arm which was to set the pattern for future Webley products and was sufficiently powerful to require a locked breech. Perhaps its most unusual feature, which was also to be seen in its successors, was its recoil spring, which was of V shape and located under the right-hand grip. It was a successful, reliable pistol but its weight and cost of manufacture was too high to make it a commercial proposition.

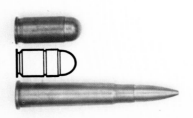

·455" SAA Ball

·38" Mars Special

·303" SAA Ball

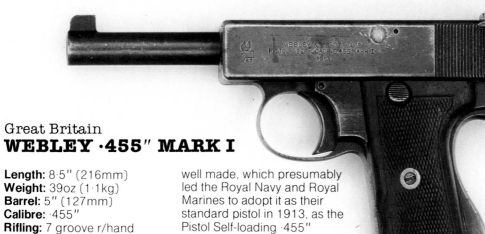

Great Britain
WEBLEY ·455″ MARK I

Length: 8·5″ (216mm)
Weight: 39oz (1·1kg)
Barrel: 5″ (127mm)
Calibre: ·455″
Rifling: 7 groove r/hand
Capacity: Seven
Muzzle Velocity: 750 f/s
(229 m/s)
Sights: Fixed

This was a modified version of the 1904 model, and of basically similar appearance and mechanism. Like its predecessor it was robust and

well made, which presumably led the Royal Navy and Royal Marines to adopt it as their standard pistol in 1913, as the Pistol Self-loading ·455″ calibre Mark I. It fired a heavy, round-nosed bullet and had excellent stopping power, but was found not to be completely reliable under service conditions. This, paradoxically, was because it was too precisely made and machined, with the result that the slightest speck of dirt tended to put it out of action.

Great Britain
WEBLEY ·25″

Length: 4·5″ (114mm)
Weight: 12oz (·34kg)
Barrel: 2″ (51mm)
Calibre: ·25″
Rifling: 7 groove r/hand
Capacity: Six
Muzzle Velocity:
750 f/s (229 m/s)
Sights: None

This was in no sense a service arm but is included to show how Webley simply scaled down to provide smaller calibre pistols. It was strictly for close quarters and was not equipped with sights of any kind.

Great Britain
WEBLEY ·32″

Length: 6·25″ 9159mm)
Weight: 20oz (·57kg)
Barrel: 3·5″ (89mm)
Calibre: ·32″
Rifling: 7 groove r/hand
Capacity: Eight
Muzzle Velocity:
900 f/s (275 m/s)
Sights: Fixed

This model was first introduced in 1906 and remained in production for nearly thirty years. It was of standard Webley type and although not of service calibre a good many British officers carried them as second

pistols in the two World Wars. They were also adopted as the standard pistol for the Metropolitan Police in 1911 on the relatively rare occasions when they were required to carry arms and many other forces adopted them at the same time. Although excellent pocket pistols they lacked stopping power and have long since been abandoned in favour of more powerful weapons. The American firm of Harrington and Richardson also made a number of pistols of this type, but their versions do not have external hammers.

·455″ SAA Ball

·32″ ACP

·25″ automatic pistol

·303″ SAA Ball

Japan
TAISHO 14

Length: 9" (229mm)
Weight: 34oz (·96kg)
Barrel: 4·75" (121mm)
Calibre: 8mm
Rifling: 6 groove r/hand
Capacity: Eight
Muzzle Velocity: 950 f/s (290 m/s)
Sights: Fixed

The original Nambu pistol appeared in about 1909 and may have been based on the Italian Glisenti which it resembled externally. It was never the standard Japanese pistol although many officers carried it. It was modified somewhat and re-issued in 1925 as the 14 Year model. This was a reasonably well-designed and well-made weapon, which worked on the closed breech principle by short recoil, the breechblock being locked during firing by a special locking piece below it. This piece was carried down after firing, allowing the block to make its rearward journey, compressing the return spring which provided the energy for the forward action. The magazine was of standard type with a guide stud working in a slot on the right hand side to help compress the spring for the last few rounds. The trigger guard was sometimes made sufficiently large to allow the pistol to be used in a gloved hand. It was the standard Japanese pistol of World War II and was reliable but lacked stopping power.

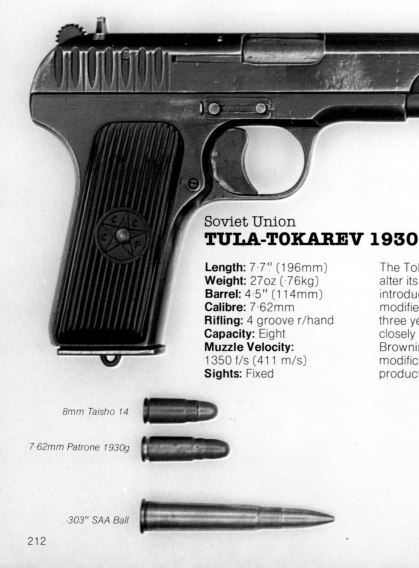

Soviet Union
TULA-TOKAREV 1930

Length: 7·7" (196mm)
Weight: 27oz (·76kg)
Barrel: 4·5" (114mm)
Calibre: 7·62mm
Rifling: 4 groove r/hand
Capacity: Eight
Muzzle Velocity: 1350 f/s (411 m/s)
Sights: Fixed

The Tokarev pistol, named after its designer, was first introduced in 1930, a modified version appearing three years later. It was closely based on the Colt and Browning pistols, with some modification to simplify production and one or two improvements. These included the incorporation of cartridge guides into the pistol itself, which reduced the dependence on the usual thin, folded metal lips of the magazine and so improved feed, and a system of removing the lock complete for cleaning. The pistol was an effective weapon, its main disadvantage being that its high-powered cartridge tended to have an adverse effect on accuracy. The Tokarev is still in service with security forces and with only minor variations is also manufactured by certain other Warsaw Pact countries.

8mm Taisho 14

7·62mm Patrone 1930g

·303" SAA Ball

Spain
EIBAR REVOLVER

Length: 11″ (279mm)
Weight: 36oz (1kg)
Barrel: 5″ (127mm)
Calibre: 11mm
Rifling: 7 groove r/hand
Capacity: Six
Muzzle Velocity:
700 f/s (213 m/s)
Sights: Fixed

In the 19th Century the Spaniards, like the Belgians, were producing large quantities of hand firearms, most of which were not better than medium quality. They were, however, cheap and therefore popular, particularly in many South American countries which provided obvious markets for Spanish arms of all kinds. In spite of the extent of their manufacture, it is probable that most Spanish service weapons were imported at that time, and it is equally clear that many of these were later copied. The weapon shown, which was made by Aranzabal, is a breakdown self-ejector. It is a heavy and apparently robust weapon, (although the lockwork is relatively poor), and bears a general resemblance to the products of Smith and Wesson.

Spain
ASTRA MODELO 400

Length: 9·25″ (235mm)
Weight: 38oz (1·08kg)
Barrel: 5·5″ (140mm)
Calibre: 9mm
Rifling: 6 groove r/hand
Capacity: Eight
Muzzle Velocity: 1450 f/s (442 m/s)
Sights: Fixed

Although the Astra Modelo 400 fires a powerful 9mm cartridge it works on simple blowback, this being achieved by the use of heavy recoiling parts and a very powerful spring. The lack of a locking system simplifies manufacture but the massive mechanism makes cocking rather difficult. The pistol first appeared commercially in 1921 and was subsequently adopted by the Spanish Army in 1922. It was made with wide tolerances in the breech and extractor which allowed it to use a variety of types of 9mm cartridge.

11mm Eibar

9mm Largo

·303″ SAA Ball

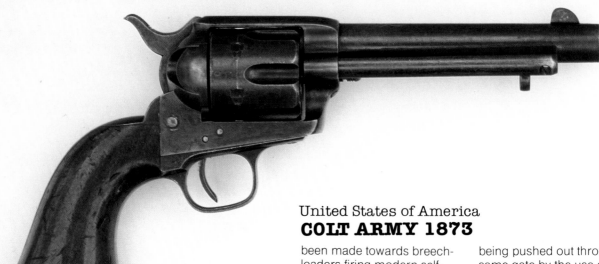

United States of America
COLT ARMY 1873

Length: 11" (279mm)
Weight: 38oz (1·98kg)
Barrel: 5·5" (140mm)
Calibre: ·45"
Rifling: 6 groove l/hand
Capacity: Six
Muzzle Velocity: 870 f/s (265 m/s)
Sights: Fixed
Cartridge: Various

The first really practical revolvers were those made by Samuel Colt from 1835 onwards. These were percussion arms in which powder and ball had to be loaded into the front of the chamber and a cap placed on the nipple. By the middle of the 19th century considerable progress had been made towards breech-loaders firing modern self-contained cartridges, and, although Colt was not quite the first in the field with a pistol of this type, his Army Model of 1873 can at least claim to have been the best known. The Colt Army, which was also known as the Frontier model or the Peacemaker, was a single-action gun and had to be loaded one round at a time through a hinged loading gate at the rear of the cylinder, the empty cases being pushed out through the same gate by the use of a spring rod in a sleeve below the barrel. The original revolver was made for .45" cartridges but has been made in other calibres since. There were a variety of barrel lengths up to 7½" inches (191mm). The revolver came at a time just after the Civil War when the West was being opened up and almost every man carried some sort of a gun as a matter of course.

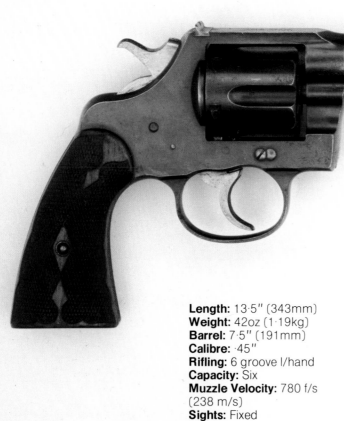

United States of America
COLT NEW SERVICE

Length: 13·5" (343mm)
Weight: 42oz (1·19kg)
Barrel: 7·5" (191mm)
Calibre: ·45"
Rifling: 6 groove l/hand
Capacity: Six
Muzzle Velocity: 780 f/s (238 m/s)
Sights: Fixed

This weapon may be said to be a typical example of the modern good quality American holster revolver. Although first introduced in 1897 the revolver had by then reached its full development so that the term modern can reasonably be used. It continued to be made with virtually no change until 1943. It was a very sound, well-finished, robust weapon and thus very suitable for military and police use. It had a rebounding hammer which meant that it could be carried safely with all six chambers loaded, and a side-swing cylinder with an ejector pin. It was made in a variety of barrel lengths up to 7·5" (191mm) and in several calibres, all sufficiently large for service use. It was extensively used by the United States Army in World War I and a great many were also sold to Great Britain. In those days British officers had to provide their own revolvers, and any make was acceptable provided it would fire the British Eley ·455" cartridge. The revolvers made for export to Britain were therefore chambered to take this cartridge. There was also a more refined version, the Shooting Master, intended principally for target work. These were made with 6" (152mm) or 7·5" (191mm) barrels.

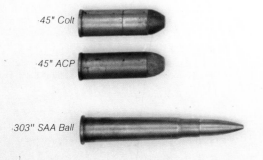

·45" Colt

·45" ACP

·303" SAA Ball

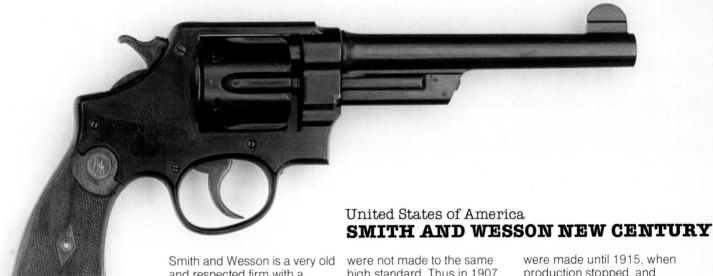

United States of America
SMITH AND WESSON NEW CENTURY

Length: 12·5" (317mm)
Weight: 32oz (·91kg)
Barrel: 6·5" (165mm)
Calibre: ·44"
Rifling: 5 groove r/hand
Capacity: Six
Muzzle Velocity:
770 f/s (235 m/s)
Sights: Fixed

Smith and Wesson is a very old and respected firm with a world-wide reputation for high quality weapons. It pioneered the bored-through cylinder to take a breech-loaded self-contained cartridge, its first revolvers of this type being of the hinged frame type with a top latch. Although their revolvers were robust and reliable, the Americans as a whole distrusted this type, probably because many cheap, mass-produced arms were not made to the same high standard. Thus in 1907 the company bowed to the inevitable and produced its New Century revolver, which may be said to have been its answer to Colt's New Service revolver which had appeared a few years before. This was a solid frame revolver with swing-out cylinder and the very smooth trigger mechanism which is characteristic of the firm's products. Only about 20,000 were made until 1915, when production stopped, and about a quarter of these were converted from their more usual ·44" calibre to take the British ·455" cartridge. There was then a second model, which was produced until 1937, and a third, which continued until 1950. The company medallion inset above the butt plate on these models was of gold colour and the type was often referred to as the Gold Seal

United States of America
SMITH AND WESSON No 3

Length: 12·5" (317mm)
Weight: 40oz (1·13kg)
Barrel: 6" (152mm)
Calibre: ·44"
Rifling: 5 groove r/hand
Capacity: Six
Muzzle Velocity:
700 f/s (213 m/s)
Sights: Fixed

The firm of Smith and Wesson were the pioneers of the hinged frame revolver which they were making by 1870. The Russians were so impressed with these revolvers that they gave the company such a huge order that their entire manufacturing capacity was taken up for five years. This made them neglect their home markets and they lost ground to Colt. In 1878, having completed their Russian order, Smith and Wesson produced a new version of their Russian model for general sale. This was their Model No 3, which at the time of its appearance was probably the best balanced and most accurate revolver available. It was of hinged frame pattern with an automatic ejector and was of single action mechanism, that is to say the hammer had to be manually cocked for each shot. It was designed, like its predecessor, to fire the ·44" calibre cartridge made specially for Russia, but was later made in several calibres, none smaller than ·38". The standard barrel length was 6" which gave almost perfect balance, but shorter models were also made. Manufacture had ended by about 1910, due probably to the inherent American distrust of large-calibre hinged frame revolvers.

·44" Smith and Wesson Special

·44" Smith and Wesson Russian

·303" SAA Ball

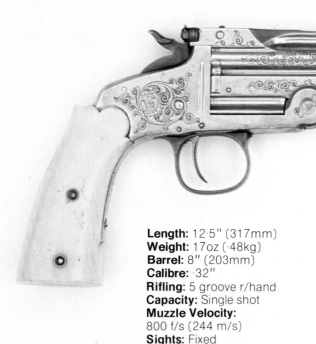

United States of America
SMITH AND WESSON
SINGLE-SHOT MODEL 1891

Length: 12·5" (317mm)
Weight: 17oz (·48kg)
Barrel: 8" (203mm)
Calibre: ·32"
Rifling: 5 groove r/hand
Capacity: Single shot
Muzzle Velocity:
800 f/s (244 m/s)
Sights: Fixed

This weapon was first produced by Smith and Wesson in 1891, its object being to provide a really accurate target pistol with the general characteristics of a long-barrelled revolver. The First Model, which remained in production until 1905, was made in three barrel lengths: 6, 8 or 10 inches (152, 203 and 254mm) and in three calibres, ·22", ·32" and ·38". It was also supplied with an interchangeable revolver barrel and cylinder assembly in a variety of barrel lengths but in ·38" calibre only, which could be quickly mounted on the existing frame to convert it into a normal revolver. This and two later models were used by the United States Olympic teams before World War I. Although they were usually blued the one illustrated is nickel-plated with ivory grips and is in ·32" calibre. Manufacture ceased in 1910.

United States of America
SMITH AND WESSON MODEL
·38" CALIBRE SAFETY

Length: 8" (203mm)
Weight: 18oz (·51kg)
Barrel: 3·25" (83mm)
Calibre: ·38"
Rifling: 5 groove r/hand
Capacity: Five
Muzzle Velocity:
745 f/s (227 m/s)
Sights: Fixed

Although there is a tendency to think of 19th Century American revolvers in terms of long, heavy calibred weapons carried openly in holsters on the belt, it must not be forgotten that at that time firearms were also habitually carried by a great many townsmen. These were carried strictly for self-defence in what was still basically a lawless environment, and the individuals concerned had no desire to advertise the fact that they were armed by carrying revolvers openly. This led to a demand for an acceptably small, compact pocket revolver in which reliability and reasonable stopping power were more important than long range accuracy; weapons of this type were turned out by a wide variety of manufacturers.

In 1887 Smith and Wesson produced the hammerless model illustrated, which quickly became popular, being safe to carry and having no hammer to catch in the lining of the pocket. At a pinch it could also be fired through a pocket without any risk of jamming. Unless the grip safety at the back was squeezed home it was not possible to fire the gun. It was made in ·38", soon followed by a ·32" version, and with minor variatións continued to be made until 1940.

·32" Smith and Wesson

·38" Smith and Wesson

·303" SAA Ball

United States of America
HARRINGTON
AND
RICHARDSON ·32″

Length: 6·5″ (165mm)
Weight: 20oz (·57kg)
Barrel: 3·5″ (89mm)
Calibre: ·32″
Rifling: 5 groove l/hand
Capacity: Eight
Muzzle Velocity:
980 f/s (299 m/s)
Sights: Fixed

This was a simple, reliable pistol of blowback design and was mainly of interest because it was closely based on the ·32″ calibre weapon made by the British firm of Webley and Scott which is illustrated elsewhere. It was, however, a hammerless version with an internal striker and spring, and it also incorporated a grip safety at the back of the butt which can be seen in the illustration.

United States of America
LIBERATOR M1942

Length: 5·5″ 9140mm)
Weight: 16oz (·454kg)
Barrel: 3·5″ (89mm)
Calibre: ·45″
Rifling: Nil
Capacity: Single shot
Muzzle Velocity: 800 f/s
(244 m/s)
Sights: Fixed
Cartridge: ·45″ M1911

This was a crude and simple single-shot weapon designed to be dropped into enemy-occupied territories in the course of World War II. It was of all-metal construction with a smoothbore barrel made from seamless steel tubing, the rest being sheet metal stampings. It was chambered for the ·45″ cartridge usually fired from the Model 1911 Colt and a few spare rounds were packed in the hollow butt. The kit also included a piece of dowel rod with which to knock out the empty case and a sheet of instructions done in strip cartoon fashion without words. Although over one million were produced, their true effectiveness has never really been assessed to the full.

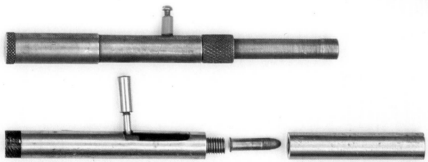

United States of America
ZIP GUN

Length: 6″ (152mm)
Weight: 4oz (·113 kg)
Barrel: 2·5″ (63·5mm)
Calibre: ·22″
Rifling: Nil
Capacity: Single shot
Muzzle Velocity:
600 f/s (183 m/s)
Sights: Nil

Once cartridges can be obtained it is not difficult for someone with access to metal-working tools to improvise a weapon from which to fire them. It is of course an extremely dangerous pastime, because locally procured materials are rarely designed to stand internal strains of several tons to the square inch and fatal accidents are common. These weapons are listed under United States because they probably originated in the black ghettoes, but they are now found in so many places that they can safely be classed as universal. The specimens shown came recently from Northern Ireland. The data is applicable to those illustrated, but naturally varies rather widely according to the place of origin.

·32″ Short

·45″ ACP

·22″ Rifle

·303″ SAA Ball

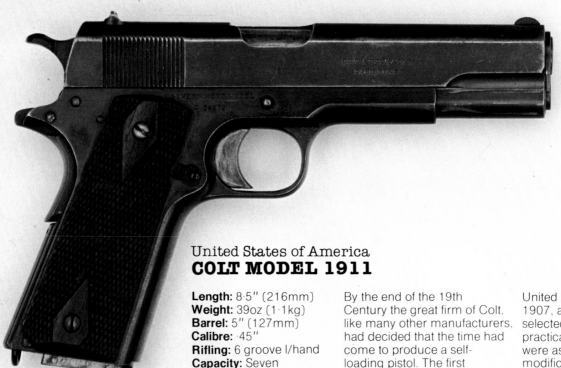

United States of America
COLT MODEL 1911

Length: 8.5" (216mm)
Weight: 39oz (1.1kg)
Barrel: 5" (127mm)
Calibre: .45"
Rifling: 6 groove l/hand
Capacity: Seven
Muzzle Velocity:
860 f/s (262 m/s)
Sights: Fixed

By the end of the 19th Century the great firm of Colt, like many other manufacturers, had decided that the time had come to produce a self-loading pistol. The first sporting model in .38" calibre appeared in 1900, and was followed two years later by a military model in the same calibre, and in 1905 by a military (Old Model) in .45" calibre. This was one of the various pistols tested by the

United States authorities in 1907, and was provisionally selected for service. After practical troop trials, Colt were asked to make certain modifications which resulted in the famous 1911 Model, perhaps the most reliable self-loading pistol ever made. It was extensively used by the United States Army in World War I, and in 1915 some were made in .455" calibre for the Canadian Army.

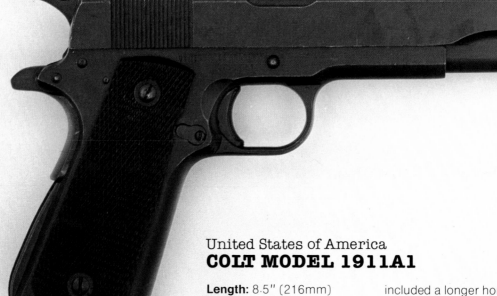

United States of America
COLT MODEL 1911A1

Length: 8.5" (216mm)
Weight: 39oz (1.1kg)
Barrel: 5" (127mm)
Calibre: .45"
Rifling: 6 groove l/hand
Capacity: Seven
Muzzle Velocity:
860 f/s (262 m/s)
Sights: Fixed

The original Model 1911 pistol remained in production virtually unchanged for ten years which included the period of World War I, but in 1921 certain modifications were made to it. These

included a longer horn on the grip safety, a slightly shorter hammer, and cutaway portions behind the trigger to accommodate the trigger finger. These resulted in the Model 1911A1 which is still in production and used by many of the world's armed forces. It remained in service with the US Army through World War II, Korea and Vietnam. The weapon illustrated is of interest because it was in fact made under contract by Remington Rand in the course of WW II.

.45" ACP

.45" ACP

.303" SAA Ball

Browning High Power
(made in Canada during World War II)

Browning High Power
(made in Belgium during the German occupation)

United States of America/Belgium
BROWNING 1935 HIGH POWER (FN GP35)

Length: 7·75" (197mm)
Weight: 32oz (·9kg)
Barrel: 4·75" (121mm)
Calibre: 9mm
Rifling: 6 groove r/hand (4?)
Capacity: Thirteen
Muzzle Velocity: 1150 f/s (341 m/s)
Sights: Fixed

The name of John Browning, probably the most famous of United States firearm designers, appears so often in this book that it is hardly necessary to list his achievements in a working life of some thirty-five years. He patented his first self-loading pistol in 1894, and the model shown here was his last before his death in 1926, although it was not formally introduced until 1935. Most of his earlier pistols had been relatively small-calibre pocket models, worked by simple blowback

and relying on the inertia of a heavy slide and spring to control the backward action, but in his last version he decided on a locked breech system more appropriate to the relatively heavy round it was designed to fire. When the first, manually loaded round was fired, the barrel and slide recoiled briefly together until a shaped cam unlocked them. The barrel then stopped but the slide continued to the rear before the compressed spring forced it forward, stripping a

round from the magazine in the butt and chambering it in readiness for the next shot. The pistol, which originally had a tangent backsight and a detachable rifle-type stock, was made by Fabrique Nationale but, just before the Germans overran Belgium in 1940, the plans were removed and sent to Canada. Here the firm of John Inglis continued to manufacture them, although with a fixed instead of a tangent sight and without the detachable stock. The Germans also

kept the Belgian factory going for its own use but it is generally believed that so many were deliberately sabotaged by the Belgian workmen that those bearing German markings are not to be trusted. After the war normal production was soon resumed at the Belgian factory and the pistol is now standard issue for many countries. Even the British, who for a long time remained faithful to their well-tried revolver, have now adopted it, as have Canada, Belgium, Denmark and Holland.

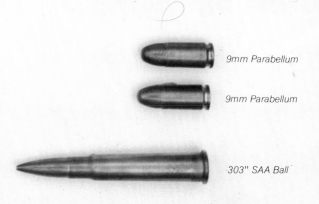

9mm Parabellum

9mm Parabellum

·303" SAA Ball

219

Germany
MAUSER MODELL 1912

Length: 12·25" (311mm)
Weight: 44oz (1·25kg)
Barrel: 5·5" (140mm)
Rifling: 6 groove r/hand
Calibre: 7·63mm
Capacity: Ten
Muzzle Velocity: 1400 f/s (427 m/s)
Sights: 1094 yds (1000m)

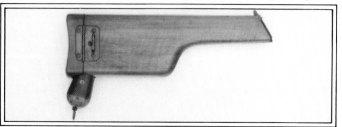

Peter Paul Mauser is probably best known for his work with rifles, since at one time an appreciable proportion of the armies of the world were armed with his products. He first became really interested in pistols in the 1870s and in 1878 he produced an ingenious revolver which was not, however, adopted by the German Army as he had hoped. He then turned to self-loading pistols, and after various experiments produced his Modèle 1896, followed by possibly the best known of all, the Modèle 98, which chiefly excited interest because it introduced the concept of a wooden holster which could also be attached to the pistol as a butt to convert it into a carbine. It was a pistol of this type that Winston Churchill carried in the Omdurman campaign when a shoulder injury prevented him from using a sword. There were several other models before the appearance in 1912 of the weapon illustrated. Like its predecessors it was a reliable and well finished weapon, as was to be expected from a factory with the reputation of Mauser. It was made in large numbers right up to 1918 and is probably the commonest

Germany
BORCHARDT-SELBSTLADEPISTOLE

Length: 14" (356mm)
Weight: 46oz (1·3kg)
Barrel: 6·5" (165mm)
Calibre: 7·65mm
Rifling: 4 groove r/hand
Capacity: Eight
Muzzle Velocity: 1100 f/s (335 m/s)
Sights: Fixed

Hugo Borchardt was a German by birth, but a naturalized American. In the late 1880s he went back to Germany to work on a new self-loading pistol. The weapon appeared in 1894 and was probably the first to have any claims to be a commercial success. It is said to have sold well on the British market which is perhaps peculiar when one considers the considerable British bias in favour of the revolver. It had a locked breech of the toggle-joint variety, later made famous by its successor the Luger, which worked roughly on the same principal as the human knee. When the joint was locked it positively could not open, but as soon as it was forced upwards it opened easily. When the pistol was fired the barrel and bolt recoiled together until lugs on the receiver broke the joint. The barrel then stopped, allowing the action to go back sufficiently far to strip the next

type to be found today. It was operated on the short recoil principle, in which barrel and bolt recoiled together briefly before the barrel stopped and the bolt unlocked to continue its rearward motion. The locking system was not absolutely positive but was perfectly reliable for the powerful bottle-shaped cartridge fired. The magazine was charged with a ten-round clip and the weapon cocked by pulling back the milled ears visible in front of the hammer. The weapon was used extensively in World War I, principally with its stock attached as a forerunner of the sub-machine gun. In 1916 large numbers were converted to fire the 9mm Parabellum round, these weapons being marked with a large figure 9 carved into the stock and filled with red paint. It is often believed that a full-automatic version was used in the period 1914-18 but this is not so, although a weapon of this kind was put into limited production in 1932. It was not a great success because it overheated.

SYSTEM BORCHARDT. PATENT.

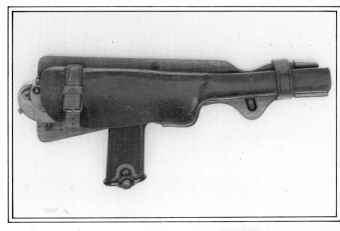

round from the magazine before chambering and firing it. This principle was not absolutely new since Maxim used a very similar device in his machine gun. It was, however, the first time it had been used in a pistol. It called for good material and fine workmanship since the whole success of the action depended on the fit and quality of the steel pins on which the joints worked. Although well made the Borchardt was an extremely bulky and clumsy weapon and must have been almost impossible to fire successfully with one hand. It was equipped with a robust, well fitting stock (which incorporated a leather holster) and it is probable that most people regarded it more as a folding carbine than a pistol. It fired a special bottle-shaped cartridge of 7·65mm, and with the stock on it shot very well since the round was a powerful one and the sightbase sufficiently long.

7·63mm Mauser

7·65mm Borchardt

·303" SAA Ball

Germany
LUGER PARABELLUM ARTILLERY MODELL 08

Length: 12·5" (317mm)
Weight: 35oz (·99kg)
Barrel: 7·5" (190·5mm)
Calibre: 9mm
Rifling: 6 groove r/hand
Capacity: 32-round drum or 8-round box
Muzzle Velocity: 1150 f/s (351 m/s)
Sights: 875 yds (800m)

The Luger Parabellum was developed by Georg Luger from the original Borchardt pistol, and was adopted as the standard pistol of the German Army in 1908. This ensured its success, and its subsequent record in World War I made it almost a household word. Like its parent it worked on a principle of short recoil, in which the barrel and toggle recoiled briefly together. The barrel then stopped, and curved ramps on the receiver broke the toggle joint and allowed it to fold upwards like an inverted V. When the breechblock had reached its rearmost position, the return spring straightened out the toggle, which in its turn forced forward the breechblock, which stripped a round from the magazine and chambered it, after which it could be fired by normal pressure on the trigger. When the last round had been fired the action remained in the rear position, that is with the toggle broken, and could not be closed except either by drawing the empty magazine down a trifle, or by replacing it with a full one. The experience of trench warfare led to the realization that light, mobile firepower was essential and by 1917 the Germans had produced a new model Luger which supplied this. It was virtually identical with the existing type except that it had been fitted with a 7·5 inch (190·5mm) barrel equipped with a

United States of America
SMITH AND WESSON REVOLVING RIFLE

Length: 35" (889mm)
Weight: 5lb (2·27kg)
Barrel: 18" (457mm)
Calibre: ·320"
Rifling: 6 groove r/hand
Capacity: Six
Muzzle Velocity: 820 f/s (250 m/s)
Sights: See text

This weapon, which is sometimes known as the repeating rifle, is almost certainly one of the rarest of modern firearms since only nine hundred and seventy-seven were made and very few of these are known to be still in existence. The model first appeared in 1879 and by the end of 1880 all but six had been made, the remainder being produced in 1886 and 1887, presumably as special orders. The weapon was built on the action and frame of the Smith and Wesson No 3, which is illustrated elsewhere in this section, with only minor mechanical differences to the mechanism, and has the same rack and gear ejector system. The barrel was made in two pieces and screwed together about 2 inches (51mm) in front of the breech, and a very faint mark is visible through the plating on the right-hand side of the arm illustrated. There were three barrel lengths, 16 inches (406mm) (of which 239 were made), 18 inches (457mm) (of which 514 were made) and 20 inches (508mm) (of which 224 were made). The one illustrated is No 222 and has an 18 inch (457mm) barrel. The foresight of the revolving rifle was blued and mounted on a dove-tailed block which fitted over the top rib of the barrel. The backsight, similarly blued, had an L-shaped two-position backsight, not graduated but possibly intended for 100 and 200 yards (91·4m-183m). There was also an optional extra sight. This consisted of an aperture, adjustable for elevation and windage, mounted on a pillar attached to the metal clamp which held the rifle butt onto the pistol. The grips and fore-end were of hard red-mottled rubber, and it is very noticeable that the pistol grips, which bear the Smith and Wesson monogram in medallions, were very much darker in colour than the fore-end, due presumably to much greater handling. The butt, which was clamped and unclamped by means of the milled screw visible immediately below the back-sight pillar, is made of good quality Circassian walnut, and has a dark brown rubber buttplate which also bears the Company monogram. In spite of the fact that it is fundamentally a revolver, the description of it as a rifle is probably an accurate one since although it can be used single-handed without its butt it is somewhat clumsy in this role, whereas it handles quite well as a long-

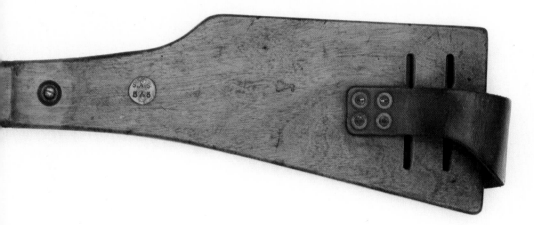

tangent backsight, and a flat wooden detachable butt, which in effect converted it into a carbine. This was not truly a new departure since commercial models on similar lines had been produced in 1903 and 1904, the latter having been adopted by the German Navy, but it was by far the best known. It should be noted that as it was a conversion many bore dates earlier than 1917. This model was initially issued to machine gun detachments, artillery observers, and similar troops requiring local protection, but it was eventually also given to forward infantry units, being in a sense the forerunner of the sub-machine gun. Its firepower was later increased by the introduction of the so-called snail drum magazine holding thirty-two rounds. This was useful but needed a special tool to load it; even so it tended to jam until the pointed bullet was replaced by a round-nosed one.

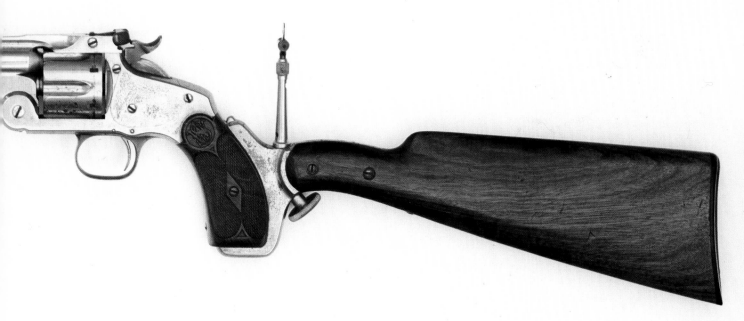

arm. The chief advantage of an arm of this type was its portability and ease of concealment, since like most combination weapons it was almost certainly not as effective in either role as the original arms would have been. The weapon illustrated was part of a consignment of guns intercepted on its way into Southern Ireland at the time of the Easter rebellion of 1916, and would in those circumstances probably have proved a very useful guerrilla weapon. Its origins are not known but as the bulk of these weapons were sold in the United States it was probably one of those. It certainly bears no foreign proof marks. It should be noted that in this particular case the data include the length and weight of the rifle butt.

9mm Parabellum

.32" Smith and Wesson

.303" SAA Ball

The Platoon Anti-Tank Weapon

The appearance of the tank in the course of World War I is almost certainly the most significant contribution made to land warfare in the 20th Century. The earliest specimens were naturally very primitive vehicles, slow and mechanically unreliable. Visibility was bad and the heat, noise and vibration inside them was intense, which put a very serious strain on their crews. Nevertheless their initial impact was considerable; as we have already seen, almost all infantry mobility had been severely inhibited by the machine gun, which was well protected and scientifically sited to cover well planned wire obstacles. Although it is perhaps too dramatic to say that this lost mobility was restored at a stroke, the tank certainly did much to redress the balance.

Initially the role of the tank was to be a mobile pill-box, trundling impartially over trench systems, barbed wire entanglements, and hostile machine gun posts, and its effect, both moral and material, was very great. The tired German infantry saw these new weapons as unstoppable, indestructible monsters, and it is not surprising that, brave though they were, they shrank from contact with them. Inevitably, the first British tanks were not available in sufficiently large numbers to force an immediate decision, and the Germans very soon recovered and began to make determined efforts to stop them with the wide variety of weapons available to them. Although tanks were reasonably proof against small arms fire, the Germans had available limited supplies of a better, high velocity cartridge, the bullet of which would often penetrate their relatively weak armour, and these were issued to selected riflemen and to machine-gunners. Light trench mortars, of which there was no lack, were also used with some success, since no tank was proof against their high explosive projectiles.

By far the best initial opponent of the tank was the fieldgun, which was extremely accurate over open sights at ranges up to half a mile or so, and which fired a highly lethal shell. There were, and indeed still are, many stories told of tank after tank being knocked out by one gun, and if some of these are apocryphal they nevertheless indicate very clearly the respect with which the fieldgun was regarded by tank crews. Inevitably, however, there were limitations to their use. Fieldguns in their more orthodox role were always dug-in some distance behind the trenches and were thus rarely well placed against tanks, at least not until they had breached the front line. The Germans did quickly develop a system of keeping specially nominated batteries in constant readiness for anti-tank defence, but bearing in mind that in 1914-18 all field artillery was horse-drawn, its speed and mobility across the shell-torn, muddy areas behind the line was greatly restricted. Nor could too many guns be withdrawn for this special role without giving the Allies superiority in artillery fire, remembering that at that late stage of the war the German economy was in no real state to produce any large number of extra guns to fill these gaps.

After this very general survey of early anti-tank measures we must revert to the main subject, which is the variety of platoon weapons sufficiently light and mobile to be carried and operated by the most forward infantry. The first arm of this type to appear was a Mauser anti-tank rifle. This was a monster, single-shot version of the standard service rifle, equipped with a light bipod and it proved reasonably satisfactory against tanks. It fired a particularly effective 13mm cartridge, a close copy of which was subsequently produced by the United States Ordnance for use in their new Browning ·50″ calibre heavy machine gun. By 1918, however, tank design and strength had improved significantly and the rifle became correspondingly less effective. This was the start of the perpetual struggle for superiority between armoured vehicles and anti-tank weapons which is still such an important military feature.

ALLIED DEVELOPMENTS

The problem of anti-tank defence in World War I was of course largely faced by the Germans, who never had more than a couple of dozen tanks available. Perhaps the most interesting development on the Allied side was the British No. 44 grenade, the first anti-tank grenade ever produced. It was equipped with a short rod which fitted the bore of a ·303″ rifle, whence it was fired by means of a special blank cartridge. As far as is known it was never used in action.

Little was done to develop anti-tank weapons immediately following the end of World War I and it was not until Germany began re-arming in the 1930s

1 Men of the Queen's Division prepare to fire a Carl Gustaf M2 84mm anti-tank recoilless gun.
2 A British infantryman with his PIAT (Projector, Infantry, Anti-Tank).

1 An Italian anti-tank crew man their Breda 20mm gun.
2 A Vietcong soldier prepares to fire his Chinese-made RPG-2 portable anti-tank rocket-launcher.
3 US infantry range-fire their 3·5in M20 anti-tank rocket-launcher, or 'bazooka'.

that any serious consideration was given to that aspect of land warfare. Even so the main direction of development was in the field of light artillery rather than portable platoon weapons, the chief exception being a reasonably successful Polish anti-tank rifle, the Maroschek, which appeared in 1935.

The British, who had both invented the tank and developed much of the tactical doctrine concerning its use, did practically nothing to develop any counter to the new weapon they had produced, little more than lip service being paid to the idea of anti-tank defence. On the rare occasions when some elderly tank appeared on manoeuvres the nearest platoon (which probably in any case consisted of a sergeant, a private soldier, and a large yellow flag) simply unfurled a smaller green flag with a diagonal cross (which indicated their possession of an unspecified anti-tank weapon) and left it to some passing umpire to decide who had come off best in the encounter. The actual appearance of the Boys anti-tank rifle, largely inspired by the Polish example, came as a pleasant surprise to the British infantry.

Tanks were used extensively in the Spanish Civil War, in which both Fascist and Communist dictatorships seized the opportunity to try out new theories involving tanks and aircraft, but there again the emphasis as far as anti-tank weapons was concerned was on artillery rather than smaller weapons. There was also, of course, a good deal of improvisation varying from

iron rails jammed in the tracks to high explosive or incendiary charges, but although these offered bright ideas to the Home Guard in 1940, they made no really significant contribution.

WORLD WAR II DEVELOPMENTS

The outbreak of World War II found all the major participants lacking really light, effective anti-tank weapons. As was to be expected there was a great rush to develop these, but naturally enough there were also great and progressive improvements in the quality of tank design, so that both tanks and anti-tank weapons continued their struggle for superiority. One thing which rapidly became clear was the almost total ineffectiveness of the anti-tank rifle against all but the most lightly armoured vehicles. When we consider that by about 1941 the two pound (·91kg) solid shot of the battalion anti-tank guns had almost ceased to penetrate the new German tanks, it is not at all surprising that the two-ounce (60gm) bullet of the Boys also failed.

Both sides naturally turned to high explosive missiles as the only alternative. Velocity was not very important in this instance, so the appropriate weapons could be reasonably light and portable. The British adopted the Projector-Infantry-Anti-Tank (PIAT) in 1942 while at about the same time the Americans produced a tube launcher, almost universally referred to as the Bazooka, which fired a rocket projectile. The Germans captured a number of these from the Russians,

and seeing their potential they soon produced their own version of them, the Raketen Panzerbuchse. This they soon followed with a lighter version, the Panzerfaust, an effective weapon but highly unpopular with the rank and file because of its terrifying tendency to premature detonation. The Russians, perhaps basing their philosophy on the lessons of Spain, relied mainly on light artillery and high explosive grenades, although they did develop two types of anti-tank rifle, the PTRD and PTRS.

The final supercession of the anti-tank rifle marked the end of the true 'small arms' period of anti-tank defence and should therefore (in theory at least) also mark the end of this introduction. It seems, however, a little odd to cut it off so abruptly, so I shall continue with a brief survey of more modern weapons, even though they are by definition outside my strict range.

The end of World War II found the Allies reasonably well equipped with light anti-tank weapons, so that it came as something of a surprise to find that the United States Bazooka did not perform well against North Korean tanks. As these were not of the latest pattern it is probable that the fault lay

either in poor ammunition or in the relatively poor standard of training in the post-war Army, but whichever was the case, the effect on morale was serious. Fortunately the United States authorities had available a well-tested prototype 3·5″ rocket launcher which was quickly put into large-scale production. It proved to be highly successful and in one form or another it remained as something of a standard weapon in many Western Armies. It was followed in 1952 by the M72, a 'modern' type weapon in which the carrying case also acted as launcher tube, being thrown away after the rocket had been fired.

In 1952 the Russians produced their PGR2, a simple but effective launcher. Only the tail of the rocket, which had folding fins and was of relatively small diameter, went into the tube, leaving the body of the bomb outside, a system which helped to reduce the size and weight of the weapon itself. The RPG2 was also widely adopted by the various states within the Communist bloc.

THE RECOILLESS PRINCIPLE

A fresh concept in light anti-tank weapons appeared with the adoption of the recoilless principle, which was a remarkably simple one. When a firearm with a closed breech is fired the backward thrust of the gases is known as recoil. With heavy guns this can be taken up by springs, buffers and similar devices, but all that can be done with light hand-held weapons is to ensure that the weight ratio between bullet and weapon is sufficiently high to

ensure that the worst of the recoil is absorbed. The rest has to be taken up by the firer, so that the limits of human endurance have to be taken into consideration when designing this sort of arm. Before World War I an American named Davis produced a barrel open at both ends, placed a charge centrally in it with an identical projectile on either side, and fired it. The result was that the two projectiles departed in diametrically opposite directions without any recoil, and so the new principle was discovered. It clearly needed further development because it was not wholly practical in war to have one projectile firing towards the enemy while its fellow ploughed back into one's own side. This problem was soon overcome; the first answer was to use a disintegrating rear projectile, e.g. a bag of buckshot or sand, but it was eventually found that by using a much larger charge and choking the path of the gases, the same effect could be obtained.

No further progress was really made until the 1930s when the German firm of Krupps conducted some experiments along similar lines, and it was not until about 1950 that the principle was successfully applied to a gun. This was the British battalion anti-tank gun, the BAT, which was 120mm calibre and weighed about one ton (1.016 tonnes). The shell was of the so-called squash-head type in which the charge of plastic explosive spread itself on the outside surface of the tank before being detonated. This caused such violent concussion that large pieces of metal

4 *An American soldier lines up his 66mm HEAT rocket-launcher, or Light Anti-tank Weapon (LAW).*
5 *The World War II 0.55in Boys Mark 1 anti-tank rifle.*
6 *8·8cm Raketen Panzerbuchse 54.*

were torn off the inside of the vehicle with disastrous effects on the crew. Once this concept of a recoilless gun was found to be really practicable it was widely adopted even in light shoulder-controlled weapons, as for example the widely used Swedish Carl Gustav. The current Soviet equivalent is the RPG7, which also fires its projectile by a recoilless charge but which employs small auxiliary rockets on the projectile itself to allow it to maintain its velocity after launching.

Many weapons of recoilless type are in current use, although the heavier ones are tending to be replaced by guided missiles. These, however, go far beyond any definition of small arms and it is not therefore proposed to discuss them further. It is perhaps inevitable that the missile will eventually win the day. The tank has obvious practical limits to size and weight, if only because of the limited capacity of roads and bridges to support it. Failing the discovery of some new metal of vastly improved resistance it can thus be argued that the tank is near the limits of its development while the missile is still relatively in its infancy. It may, however, take quite a time for the outcome to become clear and in the meantime the struggle continues.

Germany
MAUSER TANK-GEWEHR MODELL 1918

Length: 66" (1676mm)
Weight: 39lb (17·7kg)
Barrel: 38·7" (983mm)
Calibre: 13mm
Rifling: 4 groove r/hand
Capacity: Single shot
Muzzle Velocity:
3000 f/s (913 m/s)
Sights: 500 metres

The invention of the tank was an unusually well-kept secret which came as a complete surprise to the Germans when first used in battle in 1916, and its initial effect was as much on morale as physical. The German infantry, although first class

13mm Mauser A/Tk
·303" SAA Ball (clip)

Great Britain
BOYS ANTI-TANK RIFLE

Length: 63·5" (1613mm)
Weight: 36lb (16·33kg)
Barrel: 36" (914mm)
Calibre: ·55"
Rifling: 7 groove r/hand
Capacity: 5 round box
Muzzle Velocity:
3250 f/s (990 m/s)
Sights: See text

The tank had not been a menace to the Allies in World War I because the Germans had not been able to produce them in sufficient quantities to have any serious effect on the

soldiers, had no experience to guide them, and apparently no weapons with which to stop this new invention and being essentially practical men they either surrendered or ran. Fortunately for them the early tanks were only deployed in small numbers,

and after mechanical defects had taken their toll the totals actually available were small. It also came about that for various reasons they were not used again until the spring of 1917 by which date there had been time to develop counter-measures. The Germans soon found that even high-velocity rifle bullets would often penetrate a tank and from here it was only a matter of time and ingenuity to produce an even more formidable answer in the shape of an anti-tank rifle. This was basically a large-scale version of the standard service rifle, designed to fire a special 13mm calibre round, which had itself to be invented since nothing of that size existed in the German armoury. Although of normal bolt action it was a single-shot weapon, half-stocked and

with a simple bipod and an unusually long barrel, and as it was impossible to grasp it with the right hand in the normal way a pistol-grip was added. As was to be expected, this rifle had a fearsome recoil and was not universally popular with the Germans. Nevertheless there were always some hardy souls to fire it, and when grouped in well defended anti-tank localities its effect was considerable. However, it came far too late to have any seriously adverse effect on the bigger and better tanks then in production. It was the forerunner of several similar weapons and was also of particular interest in that its cartridge was closely copied by the Americans in order to provide a suitable round for the ·50″ Browning, which was just coming into production.

course of the operations. Once the war was over Germany was disarmed and occupied, and as everything seemed to be set for a peaceful future no one was

prepared to spend more than a minimum of money on armaments. It was not, therefore, until the 1930s that the western world saw with some surprise that Germany was re-arming as fast as she possibly could, and began to make some very belated attempts to counter this new threat from an old quarter. As far as the British Army was concerned one of its requirements was for a reasonably light anti-tank weapon and in October 1934 instructions were given to prepare designs for a weapon of this type. The officer directly concerned was a Captain Boys and for security reasons the new project was

given the code-name 'Stanchion'. Good progress was made and tests proved encouraging, with penetration of 25mm being obtained in armour plate, so the new weapon was put into production and named after its designer who had unfortunately died just as his project reached completion. The Boys rifle was essentially a large-scale version of a service rifle firing as large a

bullet with as big a charge as a reasonable man might be expected to hold, given the help of a spring absorber, a muzzle brake, and a front support. In the original weapon the muzzle brake was circular, and the front support was a monopod like an inverted T. In the second version, the one illustrated, the muzzle brake was flat with holes on either side and the monopod had been replaced by a bipod. Both models were bolt-action weapons with detachable top-mounted box magazines holding five rounds, but while the first model had a double sight for 300 and 500 yards (274 and 457m) the second had a fixed

sight only. The first few were in the hands of the infantry by 1937 but unfortunately tank design had advanced, and soon after the outbreak of war it was clear that the weapon was of limited use. It was also uncomfortable to fire due to its enormous recoil and by 1943 it had largely been replaced by the PIAT. A shortened version was briefly re-introduced for airborne troops but in the absence of a muzzle brake this recoiled even more severely than its predecessor and was soon abandoned. It was finally clear that the rifle bullet, however fast, was not the answer, and thereafter all light anti-tank weapons used HE projectiles.

·55″ SAA Boys
·303″ SAA Ball (clip)

PROJECTOR INFANTRY ANTI-TANK

Length: 39" (990·6mm)
Weight: 34·5lb (15·65kg)
Range: 115yds (105m) (Anti-tank)
Range: 350yds (320m) (Housebreaking)
Bomb: 2·5lb (1·13kg)
Muzzle Velocity: 450 f/s (137 m/s)

The earliest tanks were relatively poorly protected against anything larger than the standard rifle bullet so the first answer seemed to be to increase the size, weight, hardness and velocity of the projectile to the stage where it would penetrate. The first weapon of this type was the German Mauser, which was extensively copied as time went by. The tank, however, being new, had probably greater capacity for development than the bullet, so that the anti-tank rifle began to lose ground in favour of larger weapons, which naturally led to even greater improvements in tank armour. This meant, for example, that whereas at the outbreak of World War II the two-pounder was considered

adequate, before the end of it the standard weapon had become a seventeen-pounder. These were artillery pieces and, although in fact manned by the infantrymen and forming an integral part of the infantry battalion, they were very immobile by infantry standards. The only weapon available at company and platoon level in 1939 was the Boys, but this soon proved to be largely ineffective against anything but light armoured cars. It was very clear that the proper answer was to abandon the concept of a high-velocity solid projectile at that level and concentrate instead on achieving penetration and destruction of tanks by means of high explosive missiles. In 1942, therefore, there appeared the weapon illustrated. It was a combination of two broadly similar weapons produced quite independently by designers named Wallis and Jeffries, and its long and cumbersome title was soon reduced to its initials PIAT. It is under this abbreviated title that most people remember it and it must have strong

claims to be the central subject of more Allied World War II stories than all other infantry weapons put together. The general appearance of this new and unorthodox arm can be seen from the photograph. It consisted of a cylindrical sheet-metal body, two feet (610mm) long and just under three inches (76mm) in diameter, with a basic T-shaped canvas covered butt at the rear end and a ten inch (254mm) long semi-circular trough at the front. The sights, both of which folded back into simple metal protectors when not in use, were mounted on the left hand side of the body, which also carried the trigger with a basic pistol grip and a very large trigger guard. Just behind the trough a monopod was clamped to the body. This had a flat base which could quickly be dug in if necessary so as to lower the profile of the weapon. The whole thing, although robust enough, was roughly finished, being stamped, welded and riveted from low grade materials. The body of the gun was chiefly taken up

with a huge coil spring, which had down its centre a steel sleeve with a spigot on its front end, and inside this spigot there was a cocking rod and striker. When the spring was not compressed, that is when the weapon was not cocked, about 7½ inches (190·5mm) of the spigot projected into the trough. The first requirement was to cock the weapon which was very easy to do in theory but extremely difficult in practice. The easiest way (relatively speaking) was to hold the weapon vertically between the knees, trough upwards, place both feet on the butt, grasp the body by the trigger guard or any other convenient projection, twist it anti-clockwise and at the same time pull it upwards until the spring was fully compressed and held by the sear. The spring, however, was enormously powerful and needed a pull equivalent to 200 pounds (90·7kg) to cock it, so it was easier to describe the method than to carry it out. It called for a combination of knack and physical strength, plus an operator of sufficient height to

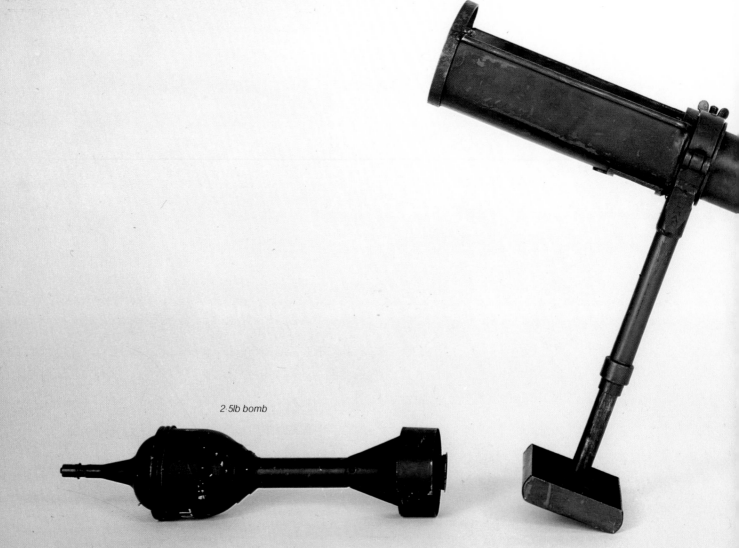

2·5lb bomb

straighten up for the necessary distance, and there were many ominous stories told of ruptures and strained backs, by no means all of them exaggerated. This was of course the easiest method, but there were times in action when for obvious reasons no one wanted to stand upright for a moment longer than necessary and in these circumstances some genius developed a method of cocking the PIAT lying down, an uncomfortable business with a strong resemblance to a bout of all-in wrestling. Once the weapon was cocked the spigot was completely withdrawn into the body, leaving the trough ready to receive the bomb. The general appearance of the bomb can also be seen from the photograph. It was 15 inches (381mm) long with a diameter of 3·5 inches (89mm) and worked on the hollow charge principle. The explosive was shaped round a hollow cone with its base towards the front, which caused the main force of the explosion to be concentrated forward into a narrow space.

This phenomenon, although well known as the Munro effect, has never been fully explained but it was certainly highly effective against armour. The bomb had a hollow tubular tail with four fins and a circular fin ring and came with its propellant cartridge in position at the front end of the tail tube. The fuze was packed in a container which clipped onto the fin ring, and when it was required to prime the bomb all that was necessary was to remove the thimble-like cap from the front of the nose, take out the transit plug, insert the fuze, and replace the cap. The bomb was then placed into the trough where it was held lightly in position by the ring at the front end in readiness for firing. When this dread moment came the gunner came into the aim, left hand on the canvas sleeve near the breech end of the body, right hand on the pistol grip with all four fingers on the trigger, braced himself and pulled the trigger, an operation requiring the full strength of his right hand. The first thing that happened was that the coil spring drove the

spigot forward with great force so that it entered the tail tube and fired the cartridge, upon which the bomb departed with sufficient recoil to drive the spigot back and recock the weapon ready for the next bomb to be loaded. There was an art in holding the PIAT because it lurched forward when first fired under the influence of the spring and then recoiled violently under the influence of the bomb. If the firer was ready and resolute all was well but if he let the shock push him backwards it often happened that the residual recoil was not enough to recock the weapon which then had to be done manually. It is of course always desirable to be behind as much cover as possible when engaging tanks, but this was particularly true of the PIAT for the excellent reason that when the bomb burst against a vertical surface the tail tube acted as a gun barrel in its own right, the projectile being the brass case which blew backwards along its original trajectory with considerable accuracy and a good deal of velocity. Nevertheless, in spite of its

disadvantages, the PIAT was the first light weapon to put the infantryman on even terms with the tank and a great many of the latter were destroyed by it. The maximum range was 115 yards (105 metres) but twenty-five or thirty were a good deal better, if more dangerous. The PIAT could also be used as a housebreaking weapon. This was achieved by turning the butt sideways to give more elevation and laying it along a white line on the top of the body. The rearsight incorporated a simple elevation gauge with a spirit level, and quite good shooting could be obtained to 350 yards (320 metres). The weapon was frequently used in this way in built-up areas in North-West Europe. The PIAT was also equipped with a simple cast-iron practice shot which could be re-loaded. It was smaller than the real bomb and an auxiliary trough had to be fitted to the weapon to use it. In spite of its crudeness the PIAT remained in service until 1951 when it was replaced by a rocket launcher.

Germany
RAKETEN PANZERBUCHSE 54 (PANZERSCHRECK)

Length: 64·5" (1638mm)
Weight: 20·5lb (9·3kg)
Calibre: 88mm
Range: 164 yds (150m)
Weight of
Projectile: 7lb (3·18kg)
Penetration: 3·95" (100mm)

There is an old saying that the best defence against a tank is another tank, and this may have been in the minds of the German High Command when it was planning its new model army in the 1930s. It is clear that the German infantry anti-tank weapons were somewhat out of date, no better in fact than those of their opponents. They

consisted in the main of anti-tank rifles, issued on a similar scale to the British Boys rifle, together with an anti-tank company of 37mm guns at regimental level, but although weapons of this type had proved adequate in the Spanish Civil War, that great practical testing ground for the Axis weapons, and even in the brief Polish campaign, they failed badly against the relatively heavily armoured British tanks in 1940. Thus, as in an earlier war, resort had to be made to field guns to deal with them. After the brief *blitzkrieg* campaign of 1940 was over efforts were made by the Germans to improve their anti-tank capacity, but these almost all tended to

favour the relatively larger gun, to the neglect of smaller and more portable infantry weapons. As things turned out this did not greatly matter in North Africa where much of the fighting was tank versus tank, and it was not really until the German infantry found itself against the newest Russian tanks that their lack of anti-tank protection became apparent. As had happened in 1916

they had to improvise, and being essentially good soldiers they did so with some success, using pole-charges, bunches of grenades, and similar suicidal expedients in their attemtps to destroy the Russian armour. Then the Germans had a real stroke of luck, for in 1942 the United States had despatched a shipload of their Bazookas to the Russians, and some of these fell into German hands,

United States of America
2·36" ROCKET LAUNCHER (BAZOOKA)

Length: 61" (1549mm)
Weight: 13·25lb (6kg)
Calibre: 2·36" (60mm)
Range (max):
234yds (214m)
Weight of Projectile:
3·4lb (1·54kg)
Penetration: 3·95" (100mm)

When the United States entered the war on the side of the Allies in 1941, she was remarkably ill-prepared for it, having for many years set her face firmly against the concept of intervention in a global conflict if it could

possibly be avoided. It is true that since 1939 she had been increasing her armed forces as a precautionary measure but with relatively little sense of urgency until the Japanese attack was actually launched. In fairness, however, it must also be said that much of her industrial capacity had been placed at the disposal of the Allies. In 1941 she relied almost entirely for anti-tank defence on 37mm guns and the ·50" calibre Browning machine gun, together with a few hastily improvised self-propelled guns, her infantry having no truly portable anti-tank weapons of any kind. In

1940 the American Army had been impressed with a hollow charge grenade produced by a Swiss (who had already had it rejected by the British) and a large quantity were hastily put into production before anyone had seriously considered how best to project them, since they were far too heavy to be fired from a rifle. It was at this stage, as sometimes happens in war, that the American Army had an unexpected stroke of luck. One of their Colonels named Skinner had been interested in rockets since boyhood and had been rather labelled as a crank because of it. In 1942

he had the bright idea of firing the new grenade, officially designated the M10, from a launcher of his own invention, which he quickly modified, the system of ignition being hastily improvised from torch batteries. This worked well and Colonel Skinner then went off to a Government proving ground where he found a demonstration of some other anti-tank devices in progress. He and his assistant joined in unofficially and after the tank target had been hit by the only nine rockets available, the weapon,

232

together with a quantity of ammunition. They at once saw the potential of this new approach to anti-tank warfare and in a matter of months had developed an improved version and issued it to their troops in Russia. Although similar in principle to the American prototype, this new weapon was of larger calibre and fired a bomb twice the size and with a good deal better penetration. It proved

to be highly effective against even the most powerful Russian tanks, and was also useful against houses and similar strongpoints. It was light enough to be carried and operated by one man although the normal team was two, the second acting as loader and carrying the containers of bombs. Its chief disadvantage was that the rocket motor continued to burn for the first seven or

eight feet (2·13-2·44m) of its flight, and the flame and gases generated were liable to be very dangerous to the firer. A large square shield (missing from the one illustrated), was therefore attached to the weapon and protective clothing worn. In spite of this disadvantage the German infantry thought highly of it and it remained in service in very large numbers and in all the various theatres

of war in which the German Army was engaged until the war finally ended in 1945. At one stage a much larger calibre version of it, 100 milllimetres as opposed to 88 (3·9/3·46in), was tried but the additional weight of thirty-odd pounds (13·6kg) to the launcher was not matched by the same increase in range or effect so that it was soon quietly dropped and the original concept adhered to.

universally known as the Bazooka after a comic wind instrument played by a well-known American entertainer, was not only promptly accepted for service but put into production so quickly that the first five thousand were completed in a month. It soon proved itself to be effective and gave good service throughout the war, although by 1945 it was beginning to lose ground

against the improved German tank armour. This had been foreseen, and a larger model developed, but for various reasons this version did not go into production until the Korean War finally showed that the original weapon had finally had its day.
There were of course some modifications and improvements made to it in the course of its life, including the use of a small generator

instead of batteries, and a two-piece version to facilitate carriage. All versions had a light mesh face shield to protect the firer from the rocket's gases. Although the Bazooka gave good service to the Allied cause it is perhaps ironical to consider that it was also largely responsible for the rapid development of a German weapon of a similar type. Some early specimens of the

American launcher were captured from the Russians and from these the Germans quickly developed a larger and, in some ways, a better version of their own, the Raketenpanzerbuchse which is described above. Oddly enough this enemy version was of 88mm calibre, which was almost exactly the 3.5" calibre of the United States version rejected by the War Department in 1945.

Soviet Union
RPG2 AND RPG7

Launcher (RPG2)

Length: 39·4" (1000mm)
Weight: 15lb (6·8kg)
Calibre: 1·58" (40mm)
Range: 547 yds (500m)

Bomb

Weight: 3·75lb (1·7kg)
Type: High Explosive
Hollow Charge
Calibre: 3·94" (100mm)

Launcher (RPG7)

Length: 37·5" (953mm)
Weight: 15·4lb (7kg)
Calibre: 1·56" (40mm)
Range: to 990 yds (900m)
Self Destruction

Bomb

Weight: 4·96lb (2·25kg)
Penetration: 12·6" (320mm)

The Russian infantry fought World War II with somewhat out-moded anti-tank weapons, since they relied on a combination of high-powered grenades, which at best were suicidal weapons, and anti-tank rifles, the latter being extremely long and heavy weapons and therefore relatively immobile. Very surprisingly they made no apparent effort to copy the German or American bazooka-type weapons. Possibly this was because their industry was very seriously overloaded and unable to undertake new commitments, however important they might seem. It was not until some years after the war that the Soviet Union produced its first shoulder-controlled rocket launcher, the RPG2. It was a simple device, based fairly closely on the German Panzerfaust of World War II and was a reasonably effective weapon, its main disadvantage being its high trajectory which

Sweden
84mm RCL CARL-GUSTAF

Length: 51" (1295mm)
Weight: 36lb (16·33kg)
Calibre: 3·3" (84mm)
Effective Range:
350yds (320m)
Penetration:
15·75" (400mm)
Weight of A/Tk Round:
5·7lb (2·6kg)

After the end of the Korean War the British Army adopted the United States 3·5" (89mm) rocket launcher, a weapon which had been developed, although never put into production, during World War II. Although a good weapon in its time, it could not eventually cope with the progressive improvements in tank armour and design, and by 1964 the British Government decided that the time had come for a change. There was some hesitation as to an alternative, and for some time the excellent Canadian Heller was the favourite but eventually it was decided to adopt the weapon illustrated, the Carl Gustaf, which the British Army calls the 84mm Infantry Anti-Tank Gun. It was invented as early as 1941 by a Swedish designer named Abramson and after some improvement was adopted for service. The calibre was increased to its present size in 1946 and after that it was extensively adopted by a considerable number of countries, particularly those of NATO. It is a very well-made weapon and works on the recoilless principle which is described earlier in the introduction to this section. The breech is the truncated cone at the rear, which swivels to the left to allow the

limited its range to one hundred metres (109yds) and made it hard to aim off for movement. Its penetrative power was said to be in the region of 7″ (178mm) of armour. This was adequate when it appeared, but when used later by the Viet Cong against modern United States tanks its short-comings were obvious. This weapon was later replaced by the launcher illustrated, the RPG7, which is in every way a much superior weapon. It still consisted of a basic tube, open at both ends, and continued to fire a projectile of which only the tail

unit and its folding fins went into the launcher, the body remaining outside. The general appearance can be seen from the illustration. It has a conical blast shield and much of it is covered in wood which acts as a heat-shield. It has a fixed battlesight and a telescopic sight as well, and is effective up to 500 metres (547yds). Unlike its predecessors its rocket has a double means of impetus, being launched by the normal propellant and then boosted by its own motors which gives it better velocity and consequently a lower

trajectory. Its penetration is said to be up to 12·6″ (320mm) of armour plate which makes it a highly effective weapon. The bomb has an electric fuse and destroys itself automatically at 900 metres (984yds) from the muzzle, and the sight can be illuminated for night use. The RPG7V is still in service in the Soviet Union and its satellite countries, many of whom make their own version of it. There is also a light version of it (RPG7D) which can be divided in two for ease of transportation. This version is used mainly by

airborne troops in the Warsaw Pact countries. Like many other Soviet weapons the RPG7 is widely distributed to a variety of guerrilla and subversive organizations and it is hardly possible to see a photograph or newsreel of one of these bodies without being able to pick them out, slung casually from the bearer's shoulder with the body of a rocket protruding menacingly from the top. A few have appeared in Ulster in the hands of the Provisional IRA, but do not seem to have been used with any great success.

84mm HEAT projectile

round to be loaded. It is fired by a normal trigger and striker acting on a cap at its base, and its backblast is very considerable up to thirty yards (27·4m). It has three kinds of sight, open, telescopic, and infra-red and will fire a variety of types of round including anti-tank, high-explosive, smoke and illuminating. It also has a sub-calibre practice device consisting of a round-shaped

body incorporating a 6·5mm rifle barrel. The whole can be loaded and fired exactly like the standard round but on shorter ranges and without any backblast. Although still a good weapon it is steadily losing its effectiveness in relation to the improved protection being built into tanks, and is likely to have to be replaced in the foreseeable future. It is also rather heavy for a one-man weapon.

·303″ SAA Ball (clip)

Bibliography

Title	Author/Editor	Place and year of publication
1. Weapons general		
Jane's Infantry Weapons	Archer (Ed)	London 1977
Military Small Arms of the 20th Century	Hogg and Weeks	London 1977
Brasseys Infantry Weapons of the World	Owen (Ed)	London 1975
Small Arms of the World	Smith	London 1973
Illustrated Arsenal of the Third Reich	Normount	Wichenburg Arizona 1973
Arms and Armament	ffoulkes	London 1945
The Soldier's Trade	Myatt	London 1974
British and American Infantry Weapons of World War II	Barker	London 1969
German Infantry Weapons of World War II	Barker	London 1969
Pistols, Rifles and Machine Guns	Allen	London 1953
Superiority of Fire	Pridham	London 1945
Small Arms Operation and Identification of Small Arms	Johnson (US Army Publication)	USA 1971
NATO Infantry and its Weapons	Owen (Ed)	London 1976
Warsaw Pact Infantry and its Weapons	Owen (Ed)	London 1976
Text-book for Small Arms	HMSO	London 1919
Text-book for Small Arms	HMSO	London 1929
Text-book of Ammunition	HMSO	London 1926

Note: Much use has been made of a variety of British and Foreign Military textbooks and pamphlets held in the Museum Reference Library.

Title	Author/Editor	Place and year of publication
2. Pistols		
Automatic Pistols	Pollard	London 1920
Textbook of Automatic Pistols	Wilson/Hogg	London 1975
German Pistols and Revolvers	Hogg	London 1971
The Book of the Pistol	Pollard	London 1917
English Pistols and Revolvers	George	London 1961
The Revolver 1818-1865	Taylerson, Frith, Andrews	London 1968
The Revolver 1865-1888	Taylerson	London 1966
The Revolver 1888-1914	Taylerson	London 1970
The Art of Revolver Shooting	Winans	New York 1901
The Webley Story	Dowell	Leeds 1962
Pistols and Revolvers	Smith/Bellah	Harrisburgh Pa 1962
Shooting to Live	Fanbairn/Sykes	Edinburgh 1942
3. Machine Guns		
The Book of the Machine Gun	Longstaffe/Atteridge	London 1917
Pictorial History of the Machine Gun	Hobart	London 1971
Machine Guns: Their History and Tactical Employment	Hutchison	London 1928
Machine Gun Tactics	Applin	London 1910
My Life	Maxim	London 1915
The Machine Gun	Chinn	Washington 1951
Machine Guns	Canadian Mil HQ (official use only)	London 1945
4. Sub-machine Guns		
The World's Sub-machine Guns	Nelson/Lockoven	London 1977
Pictorial History of the Sub-machine Gun	Hobart	London 1973
5. Rifles		
The Book of the Rifle	Fremantle	London 1901
The Englishman and the Rifle	Cottesloe	London 1945
The Book of Rifles	Smith	Harrisburgh Pa 1965
The Lee-Enfield Rifle	Reynolds	London 1960
Remarks on the Rifle (11th Ed)	Baker	London 1935
English Guns and Rifles	George	London 1947
6. Anti-tank Weapons		
Men Against Tanks	Weeks	London 1975
Field Rocket Equipment of The German Army	Gander	London 1972

Below: A series of six spark shadowgraphs showing the penetration of a 7·62mm L2A2 Ball cartridge through a polypropylene plate at a velocity of c. 840 m/s.

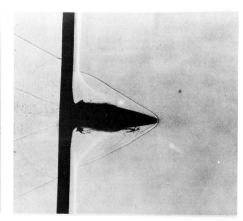

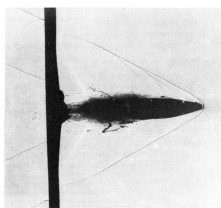
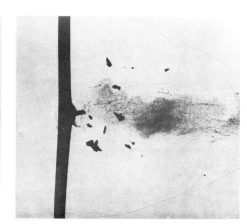

Index

All figures in bold type
refer to illustrations

Picture Credits

Unless otherwise credited, all pictures in this book were taken by Bruce Scott in the Weapons Museum, British School of Infantry, Warminster, Wiltshire.

The publisher wishes to thank the following organisations and individuals who have supplied photographs for this book. Photographs have been credited by page number; where more than one photograph appears on a page, references are made in the order of the columns across the page and then from top to bottom.

10-11: Fabrique Nationale Herstal; 11: Vickers Ltd; 12: IWM (Imperial War Museum, London); 13: IWM/US Signal Corps; 14: IWM; 14-15: US Army; 16: US Army; 17: US Army/Soviet Studies Centre, Sandhurst; 100-101: Central Office of Information, London; 101: IWM; 104: Sipho SA (Will Fowler Collection)/IWM/ IWM/Photo S. A (Will Fowler Collection); 105: United Press International (Will Fowler Collection)/IWM; 106: Central Office of Information, London; 107: US Signal Corps; 146-147: MoD, London (Peter Stevenson); 147: Novosti Press Agency; 148: Photo CNET (Will Fowler Collection)/Kriegsberichter Kirsche (Will Fowler Collection); 149: US Army (Chris Foss Collection)/IWM/IWM; 150: US Signal Corps; 151: Central Office of Information, London/IWM/US Army/E and TV Films, London; 152-153: US Army; 153: US Army; 192-193: IWM/IWM (Will Fowler Collection); 197: E and TV Films, London; 198: US Army; 199: US Air Force/US Army; 224-225: Central Office of Information, London; 225: Chris Foss Collection; 226: IWM/US Defense Department (Marine Corps); 227: US Army/IWM/Süddeutscher Verlag; 236: Royal Military College of Science, Shrivenham.

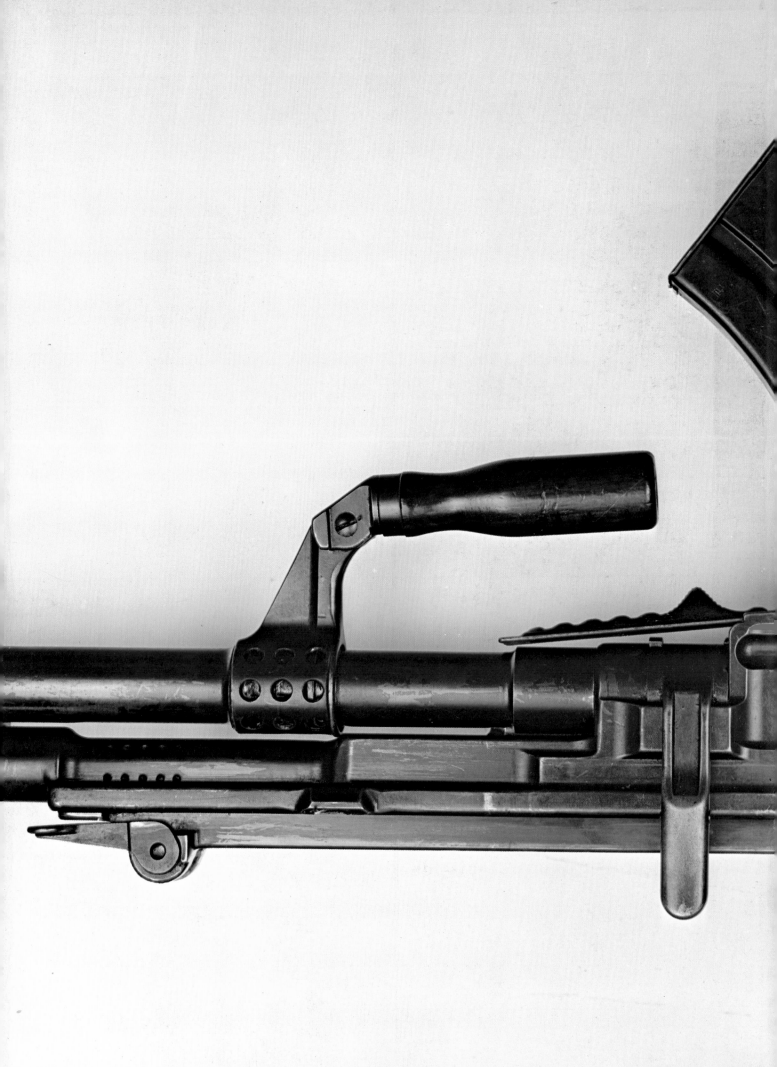